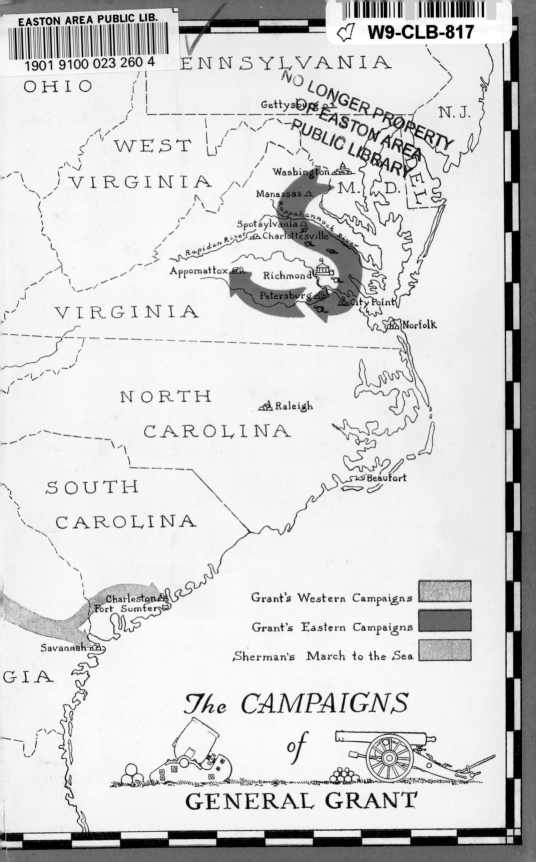

W9-CLB-817

OHIO

PENNSYLVANIA

N. J.

Gettysburg

WEST

VIRGINIA

Washington

Manassas

M. D.

DEL.

Rappahannock River

Spotsylvania

Rapidan River

Charlottesville

Appomattox

Richmond

Petersburg

City Point

Norfolk

VIRGINIA

NORTH

Raleigh

CAROLINA

SOUTH

CAROLINA

Beaufort

Charleston
Fort Sumter

Savannah

GIA

Grant's Western Campaigns

Grant's Eastern Campaigns

Sherman's March to the Sea

The CAMPAIGNS

of

GENERAL GRANT

THIS new type of biography is the first non-fiction book to receive a Literary Fellowship Award. It is a book primarily concerned not with a man who made history, but with how history made a man. Ulysses S. Grant was the focus of some of the most dramatic events our nation has endured. It was Grant to whom Lee surrendered; Grant who came to Washington shaken by horror at Lincoln's assassination, and in a few years was maneuvred into being the bitterest enemy of President Johnson, who was trying to carry out Lincoln's policies. It was Grant who undertook the Presidency because the people wanted a man above politics, and whose administrations have become a synonym for corruption.

Yet this story of a man's sudden success, followed by long, bewildering failure, rose to a final triumph based on sheer courage.

'A Man Named Grant' uses many devices of the novel in its presentation. All the characters, and all the significant incidents, however, are facts of history. This is a view of Grant the man, a simple citizen who became involved in the headlong career of a young country. Above all, it is a biographical reconstruction that puts the readers into Grant's heart and mind and makes them party to the inmost thoughts and emotions of a General and a President.

GRANT

Houghton Mifflin Fellowship Books

A MAN NAMED
GRANT

By

HELEN TODD

Illustrated by John O'Hara Cosgrove

HOUGHTON MIFFLIN COMPANY · BOSTON

The Riverside Press Cambridge

1940

The Riverside Press
CAMBRIDGE · MASSACHUSETTS
PRINTED IN THE U.S.A.

TO
A. J.

ALL the characters and all the significant incidents in this book are historic fact. The motives and states of mind I have attributed to these characters are facts so far as they can be determined: beyond that point I have followed what seemed to me the probabilities.

The sources I have most frequently consulted are the *Personal Memoirs of U. S. Grant*; Porter's *Campaigning with Grant*; Badeau's *Grant in Peace*; Hesseltine's *Ulysses S. Grant, Politician*; and Nevins's *Hamilton Fish: The Inner History of the Grant Administration*. I wish to thank Mr. J. Walter Goldstein of St. Louis for the use of his collection of Civil War material.

H. T.

ST. LOUIS,
March, 1940

CONTENTS

Confederate Flag
1863

PART ONE

Colonel's Sword and Stripes

The Country Wakes to War

I. EDUCATION OF A COMMANDER

CHAPTER ONE

T HE General is still busy.' The young aide spoke kindly
enough, but it seemed to Ulyss that an edge of impatience was
appearing in his tone.

'I'll wait,' said Ulyss. It was easy enough to say, and he had
had much practice in these fruitless two days, but it was becom-

ing not so easy to do. He sat down again, crossed his legs, and slouched a little. The anteroom was crowded with people who had an air of urgent business to be settled at once for the sake of the country. Contractors by the dozen, half drunk with the necessity of unending streams of supplies for a tottering nation. Ulyss looked at them coldly. He had known them when he had been a quartermaster in Mexico, and again in California, and he did not like them. Politicians, some from this town of Cincinnati, tempering the winds of military authority; some from Kentucky across the river, full of the larger concerns of that state's precarious neutrality. These Ulyss gazed at with uneasy respect. He distrusted them here in McClellan's anteroom, but in their own sphere they were the nation, the representatives of the people, by elective alchemy the authority beyond generals, the will of America. Officers: some regulars; more volunteers, moving with the exaggerated precision of newly learned drill, their words abrupt with new authority, their eyes filled with grave excitement. Ulyss looked at them again and again, tried to watch the others but returned helplessly to the men in uniform, the men who took and gave orders, the men who had a place. When they came in they did not have long to wait. The contractors and the politicians and the miscellaneous crowd waiting for the General stood aside, just as the nation was standing aside to let the armies move.

The aide nodded to a man standing nearby, and for a moment Ulyss thought the signal was intended for him. He half rose, but the aide's eyes slid over him and returned to the papers on the desk. Ulyss trusted that his face had shown neither his hope nor his disappointment, and he sat down with eyes lowered and mouth set.

Two months ago, when the shot fired in Charleston harbor had broken the pattern of the country's life, he had thought that now surely he would find his place again. He had been out of the army for seven years, and the manner of his going, as those in the army knew, was not to his credit. (The drink unsteady in his legs, the drink thick on his tongue, but never enough drink in his mind to burn away the loneliness and the monotony.) In those seven years he had failed at farming, failed in business, failed to get a post as teacher of mathematics, failed in everything to which he put his hand. ('Sorry, Captain Grant, not now. Some other time . . .' Glances at him, sometimes impatient, sometimes pitying. The awkwardness of receiving the refusal as though it were not important; the blankness of considering what to do next.)

But it had not been his fault. He knew it in all honesty, and Julia knew it. She had stood with him: never once had she wavered from the losing struggle of the life he gave her back to the comfort and protection she could have had from her father. He had never seen anything but trust and love in her eyes. When Fort Sumter fell and the President called for men, she may have been afraid, but she had said nothing, and he had gone from her warm with the knowledge that at last he could bring her something other than the tale of failure. True, the Galena company had not elected him captain, but there would be another place for him. He had been trained at West Point, he had known war in Mexico. He would be needed now at last. If he were lucky, he might even be given command of a regiment. He thought he could manage one. It was a great responsibility, but the Governor was being prodigal with commissions to prominent citizens whose closest contact with war had been setting off cannon in Fourth of July celebrations. Ulyss would say nothing, it was bad luck to use pressure to get what you wanted, but the Governor would certainly give him something.

He was given a place in the adjutant general's office, ruling forms. There were not enough of the printed forms yet, and Ulyss ruled them by hand, and taught young clerks how to fill them out. That was not all he did. Young civilians suddenly become captains, colonels, came to him to ask about army ways.

Sometimes he mustered in the regiments that were springing out of the Illinois earth. War, which had been an impossible theory of gloomy men a year ago, had become the center of life, and the two halves of the nation rose to meet it. From California, an island of America across the empty plains, to the thriving cities of the eastern states, the young men became dots in the long lines facing south. The ponderous engine began to move, and Ulyss saw that it was leaving him behind. He had thought that the footling work in the adjutant general's office would lead to something, a man and a patriot did his best wherever he was put, but now even that was slipping from him. The printed forms had come, the clerks knew the routine of their work, all the regiments were mustered in. Soon there would be nothing left for him to do that could not be better done by a trained clerk.

The leather store in Galena where he worked for his younger brothers rose again in his mind, a trap waiting to recapture him. He could feel the stiff, stinking hides; hear the townspeople's offhand, 'Morning, Cap'; sense the knowledge in their eyes and in his heart that he had been given work there because a decent family looks after its own, even those who have bitterly disappointed it. There was a sickness in him at the thought of going back, yet he would have no choice if he could not find another place.

He asked for leave of absence to see his father in Covington. He did not want to see his father. There had been no pleasure in their meetings since Ulyss had resigned from the army, at his superior's suggestion, and thereby one of Jesse's boasts had become one of the neighborhood's snickers. But across the river from Covington was Cincinnati, and in Cincinnati were the headquarters of General McClellan, head of the Department of the Ohio. Ulyss had been friendly to McClellan the plebe at West Point, and had known him in California. He would ask nothing, but surely McClellan, who must need men for his staff in his new department, would be reminded by a call.

Two days. Hour after hour of waiting, trying to remain hopeful, fighting against the slow bitterness of humiliation. Now, in the second day, a memory was forcing itself upon Ulyss, recognized at first unwillingly and with disbelief, but as the hours went by and other callers disappeared through the inner door, acquiring the uncompromising cruelty of the single explanation. He sat now remembering, over and over, McClellan's visit to him in Fort Vancouver, and how they had drunk together to the memory of old days and to the hope of some vague, glorious future. Drunk only a little, but as usual that little thickened Ulyss's words, and made his hands unsteady when he searched in his pockets for Julia's letters, and the traced handprint of the baby son he had never seen. He had looked up, and found McClellan's eyes on him filled with sad surprise. McClellan was his friend, but not intimate; bound to him chiefly by memories now almost twenty years old. McClellan was also a friend of Colonel Buchanan, that superior who had suggested that Ulyss write out his resignation, and had inexorably dated and accepted it when he appeared reeling to pay off his men.

Certainly Ulyss was ashamed of his drinking, but it was not a thing to blight a man's life. Many an officer drank himself into a coma at night, yet appeared stiff and impeccable on the parade ground next morning, and was accounted a fine soldier. Ulyss was never impeccable. His clothes always looked accidental on him, and he suspected that this was part of Buchanan's reason for asking for his resignation, just as his own loneliness for Julia and the children was part of his reason for giving it. He had supposed that McClellan understood all this. It was perhaps not a very creditable story, but it was surely not a mark black enough to stand against a man in these days of desperate need. Yet as he sat and watched the door that never opened to him he had to find some explanation, and this was the only one he could invent. He sat quietly, his face unmoved, as he thought it over carefully; then he rose and advanced on the aide. 'When will the General be free?' he demanded.

'It's hard to say,' the young man answered. 'He's mighty busy these days.' He looked at the bearded face above him and added with some compunction, 'Perhaps tomorrow ——'

'No,' said Ulyss. 'I can't wait any longer. I'm busy too.'

He walked out quickly, the more hurried as he realized that there was nothing to do. It made no difference to anyone but himself and Julia where he went or what he did, or whether his pride was still strong enough to make a gesture. Once his father would have been concerned. Long ago a phrenologist had prophesied that the boy Ulyss would be President of the United States, and Jesse had kept the forecast alive in tavern talk for years. He had contrived to get this son with a brilliant destiny into West Point, and had seen the first fruits of the prophecy in Ulyss's quite ordinary record in the Mexican War. Another man might have lost the vitality of his faith during the drab years of army routine, but Jesse had the tenacity of a fanatic, and found confirmation even in such things as Ulyss's commission as a captain and assignment to Fort Vancouver. 'You'll see — he's started up, and holy hell won't stop him. You take it from me, that fellow knew what he was talking about. Feels the boy's head like this and he says ——' The neighbors were weary of the tale, but not one of them had ever found a way to stop him.

When the news came that Ulyss had resigned from the army Jesse was shaken, and when he proved unable to support himself in civil life the old man was filled with the agonized bitterness of the believer in miracles who finds he has been tricked. 'Shiftless, a son of mine!' The edge on his voice was jagged as well as sharp.

'But times aren't very good right now ——'

'Argh!' All the contempt and disappointment of which a grasping man is capable were crammed into the single syllable. 'Don't talk to me — ye're lazy and ye're stupid, and ye don't give a damn that I humbled myself to give ye the chance I thought ye'd use . . .' And more, and more, until Ulyss would leave the room. Anger writhed in his heart, fanged with despair since there was no possible rejoinder he could make. He himself might feel that he was not lazy nor stupid, but he could not prove it, and those who believed in him without proof seemed condemned to inevitable disappointment.

There were only a few who had ever believed: his father, who would talk of nothing else to him; Julia, who never mentioned it even in the silent ways that women have; himself. His own figure was shadowy to him, he had no very clear notions as to what he was or how he was related to his life, but he had had his dreams. They had not been clear either, but they had involved gaining respect and admiration from others, and assurance in himself, and happiness for Julia. There was no point in dreaming any more — a man of thirty-nine had better be occupied in thinking how he was to feed his family.

In the office of Governor Yates of Illinois a committee from the 21st Illinois Regiment sat facing him. 'It's impossible,' said their spokesman. 'It would be murder to send us into battle under Colonel Goode.'

'You elected him yourselves,' the Governor pointed out.

The young man shrugged. 'That was our mistake. It was foolish, but it would be criminal to stick to it.'

'He takes the sentries into town and gets drunk with them,' said another voice.

'The townspeople are scared to death of the men. It's not a regiment — it's a gang of hoodlums.'

'But I've no other man for you,' said the Governor. 'Things

are pretty well organized now. I wouldn't know who to put in Goode's place.'

'My Aunt Matilda would do better,' someone muttered.

'There's the man who mustered us in,' said someone else. 'Captain Grant — how about him?'

The Governor raised his brows. 'Would you serve under him?'

'Yes,' said most of the committee. One or two said, 'He couldn't be worse, anyhow,' and the rest shrugged and fell in with the majority.

'It shall be Captain Grant,' the Governor said with a flourish, and picked up a telegraph blank.

Ulyss looked again at the telegram. 'Will you accept the command of the Seventh District Regiment?' That was all, as though a commission, a niche in the world, were as simple as ordering a consignment of hides. It was a good sign. He had not asked, he had known nothing of it, but it had come to him. He remembered the regiment, made up of sons of farmers and business and professional men. The 21st Illinois, and he its Colonel.

He had shown the telegram to his father, who said, 'It's about time.'

'I'll need a uniform,' said Ulyss. 'A uniform and a sword. I'll have to buy them.'

'Go ahead and buy them,' said Jesse. 'But don't come down on me for them.'

Ulyss set his lips, but he was not deeply annoyed. He'd get the uniform somehow — the important thing was his regiment. He left at once for Springfield and went to the Governor's office to receive his commission, his slouch but little improved, his face more impassive than ever because there was so much joy behind it.

'They're a rough lot,' said the Governor doubtfully. 'If they

ever knew anything about discipline Goode has let them forget
it. Do you think you can handle them?'

'I think so,' said Ulyss quietly.

The answer was not vigorous enough entirely to satisfy the
Governor, but it was not weak enough to leave him room for
exhortation. There were stories about this man that made one
uneasy, and everyone who knew him at all knew he was a failure.
Still, the officers of the 21st had chosen him themselves, and
there was no one else easily available. 'There's another thing,'
said Yates. 'As you know, the 21st is one of the regiments that
enlisted for ninety days. Now that they're going into the Federal service, for three years or the war, they feel that they're
released from their pledge, and plenty of them plan to go home.'
The Governor paused, but Ulyss said nothing. 'We thought it
would be a good idea to have someone talk to them, Logan and
McClernand for instance. But they're your men now. Will
you give your permission for the speeches?'

Ulyss hesitated, not to increase his dignity but from genuine
uncertainty. McClernand would be all right. He was a Democrat, but had resigned his seat in Congress to take the field himself in a holy crusade. But Logan —— They were having to
guard the bridges at night down in Logan's district on the river.
The people there were as shot through with rebellion as though
they did not have the advantage of living in a free state, and
they worshiped Logan in a body. Ulyss was doubtful of the wisdom in letting him speak to his men, who were apparently growing tired of the war and willing to listen to any chilly doubter.
Yet the Governor had suggested him, his name was coupled
with McClernand's —— 'All right,' said Ulyss.

They went out together to the regiment, Logan and McClern-
and and Ulyss. They talked, or at least the two statesmen talked,
of affairs in Washington, of the possibility of foreign intervention in the American quarrel, of the permutations and complications of states' rights, and Ulyss grunted politely on occasion.

He was thinking of his regiment, and these things were not in a soldier's sphere. His silence did not annoy the other two. They understood that war in a democracy does unpredictable things, may even make a colonel out of a clerk, which is a credit to America and a reproach to the tyrannies of Europe, but it does not necessarily demand that he take his place with solid men of affairs. They would talk to his regiment and go their way, on to battalions, brigades, armies of their own.

Ulyss's uniform was still an unsolved problem, but he had gone shopping in Springfield for the necessary tokens of his authority. He had wound around his waist a red bandanna handkerchief, and thrust through it a cavalry sabre. It was the wrong branch of the service, but it did well enough as a symbol. Strange to feel a sword at his side again. He threw back his shoulders and held his head high as he thought of it.

The regiment was drawn up to receive them, and stared happily at the trio. The handsome man who waved his arms around when he talked about glory would be McClernand. He was a good speaker, and they liked speeches. The big one with the black beard must be Logan. All of them had heard of Logan, and all of them were eager to hear from him. Then the other one, the little one with the brown beard and the red rag around his middle, must be their new colonel. They nudged each other and whispered in the duller portions of McClernand's speech, and their line wavered in cheerful unprecision.

Ulyss stared back at them, intently and with sudden keenness. It was obvious that their discipline and military deportment was not simply non-existent, but that they had a cheerful contempt for it. Yet there was no enmity in the eyes that surveyed their new commander. There was some derision, an enormous amount of curiosity, much interest. These men knew that Ulyss had been appointed in the hope of disciplining them, but they were not sullen. They looked rather as though they were challenging him to try a fall with them, after the fashion of their sports at home. They would do what they could to beat him, but they would accept defeat if they thought he fought fair. These were not such soldiers as were described in the books at West Point. Ulyss enjoyed his opportunity of looking them over at his leisure. He had never understood the books anyway.

With a rousing exhortation to the warriors of justice, the bearers of the sword of God, McClernand finished his speech and gave way to Logan. The men cheered with excitement, then quieted rapidly, for when Logan spoke his tone was compelling. His voice was not loud, but it seemed to carry without effort. His words were simple. He talked of the men who had revolted against the cynical corruption of an ancient world, and had braved the angry seas to build a new and beautiful world of their own. He told of how they had fought red savages, subdued the forces of nature, won free of the grasping hands of kings, conquered a continent for liberty, and founded a civilization as a brilliant example, the hope of the suffering peoples of the earth. That great achievement was threatened now. There were selfish, crafty men who sought to break it apart, to bring it down in ruins to crush the free man, and sell him back to a bondage as hopeless and degrading as that of the poor black man groaning under his master's lash. Were these young men before him, the sons of intrepid fathers, the guardians of their children's future, going to stand by in idleness? Were they going to invite the oppressor to make a mock of all that they held dear, or would they stand firm in one last glorious struggle to preserve their country forever? There was no need to ask. It was plain to see in the glancing of their eyes, in the set of their strong arms, that free men know how to preserve their freedom, that the Americans of this new age are worthy defenders of their fathers' faith.

The men shouted as one, cheered, shouted again on the borders of hysteria. Ulyss saw a few, lads who had deserted back-woods schools and stubborn farms for the call of adventure, weeping where they stood, unabashed, brimming over with a nameless glory. It was a long time before the tumult abated, and even then no quiet came. The men seemed unable to turn away to the drabness of life now that they had glimpsed great principles. Someone called, 'Speech! Speech from the Colonel!' and all the others took up the cry. Some wanted another taste of the spirits Logan had given them, others wanted to see their new commander try to match himself against that incomparable example. 'Speech, speech!' they yelled. 'Let's hear from you, Colonel!'

The little knot of officers and the two orators drew back and Ulyss faced his men alone, his hand dropped on the hilt of his battered sabre. The regiment was silent to hear him.

'Go to your quarters,' said Colonel Grant.

The House at the Edge of Town

CHAPTER TWO

LATENESS to parade, dirty guns, sloppy drill, intended
and accidental impertinence to officers, breaking bounds...
The transgressions of the 21st were numberless, and it seemed
to Ulyss that as soon as he had dealt with one he discovered
another. It was not easy work. He had no experience in the
command of a regiment, sometimes had to study in secret the
drill he was to teach to his men next day, and the 21st was on
the alert for any sign of weakness or uncertainty in him. But
he found that most of the men were wild rather from high
spirits and lack of training than from real viciousness, and

he found also a certain ability in himself that served him in the place of experience.

The worst of his problems was the few true incorrigibles of the regiment, men who had never in their lives accepted any law but their own code of force. They were not actually leaders, yet until they were subdued there could be no firm basis for discipline and order. The men who were biddable, ready to be molded, were eager to see what happened to these few rebels, half hoping to see them conquered, half resenting in advance the use of sheer physical domination, which was the only method they could imagine.

'Any bastard who touches me will welter in his own gore! He'll suffer unspeakable agonies and curse his mother that ever gave him birth! Any sniveler who lays a finger on me——' This was Mexico, perhaps the most refractory of the men. The group standing around him in apprehensive amusement came to attention as soon as Grant appeared, but Mexico continued his inebriate sentry-go with the magnificent unpredictability of a loose cannon on shipboard. He was not entirely unaware of his Colonel's presence, however, for his monologue shifted from mere colorful imprecations to profanity of great thoroughness and violence. One of the first things the 21st Illinois had learned from its Colonel was that he frowned on even so mild a word as 'damn.'

'Tie him up,' said Grant. The men knew that Mexico was almost as dangerous as he sounded, but four or five of them obediently rushed him, became a heaving tangle on the ground for a moment, then dragged him upright and bound him to a post. His bellows could be heard to the edges of the camp — 'I'll have an ounce of your blood for every minute I stand here——' He struggled against his bonds until it seemed that they or he must burst, but without effect, then subsided into swearing again, in oaths directed straight to his Colonel.

'Gag him,' said Grant, and returned to his tent without waiting to see that it was done. He stayed there, working on other things, watching the slow progress of his watch until the proper time for him to reappear. When at last he strolled outside he found everyone in sight ostentatiously busy on routine tasks, but most of the regiment seemed to have tasks in that part of the camp. Mexico still stood straining against his bonds, his bloodshot eyes focused on Grant the instant he came from his tent. There was something inhuman about the look of the man thus bound and gagged, and choking with raw fury.

Ulyss removed the gag and untied the ropes. Mexico stood over him, no longer swaying, his huge hands hanging loosely at his sides. 'Salute me,' said Ulyss. Mexico's right hand clenched, and he wavered a little on his heels. Ulyss stood still. Slowly the fingers straightened and drew together, and the hand rose jerkily to Mexico's cap. Grant returned the salute, and Mexico turned away, shambling at first, then running heavily.

In a few weeks the 21st Illinois was a respectable regiment. It knew something of company drill; its officers had learned to give orders and its men to receive them; it had become a thing in itself, a unit, rather than a group of men brave and afraid and pious and profane and independent. The 21st never became a machine on the European pattern, nor did any other regiment, North or South. There was always an elusive element in the men, appearing sometimes as the taking of unauthorized leaves because at home the spring plowing ought to be attended to; sometimes as the winning of battles because the men felt like fighting a little farther than they had been ordered; sometimes simply in the gaze of an enlisted man at an officer, respectful enough but curious and occasionally amused. This unpredictable spirit was still in the 21st, but its more abnormal eccentricities had disappeared, and Ulyss was filled with silent pride.

There was time for a visit to Galena before the regiment was ordered out. Grant did not bring with him his red bandanna and the sabre, and there was thus no outward sign that he did not still work in the leather store, but the townspeople knew. Some of the solid citizens who had scarcely nodded to the clerk stopped Colonel Grant in the street to talk to him and ask his opinions. That was pleasant, but it was pleasanter still to meet in his new dignity the men who had been kind to him, who had not been actual friends, but had at least felt that there might still be possibilities for him. There was E. B. Washburne, who represented the district in Congress, and who maintained now that any man with a discerning eye could have seen, as he had, that Cap Grant had the makings of a soldier and a credit to Galena. There was John Rawlins, the attorney for the leather store, whose friendly delight in Ulyss's success was a lasting warmth in the Colonel's heart. Rawlins was accounted one of Galena's foremost citizens, but he wanted to be a major in the army, and anxiously consulted Ulyss on his chances.

And there was E. A. Collins, a prominent business man. 'Look here, Ulyss,' he said. 'We're all mighty proud of you, but I know when you first get into the army there's a lot of expenses, and you haven't been able to put anything by. I've got three hundred dollars ——' So the uniform was ordered at last, and there was no longer any need for the lieutenant colonel to lead the 21st on its dress parades.

On the edge of town there was a house with a long, steep flight of steps leading up to it from the street. In the house were Julia and the four children, and there Ulyss found what pride could really be. Julia did not exclaim in open joy over his appointment; that would have been evidence that she had feared something else. But her face glowed all day long, and as she moved about the house she sang, unconsciously, almost constantly. To Ulyss music was a blur of unnecessary noise, but this music he understood, and it was beautiful.

When he came back to the house three-year-old Jesse was waiting, as usual, at the top of the steps. He stood balanced solidly on his baby feet, eyes bright, fists belligerently presented. 'Will you fight?' he demanded, as he had ever since he had learned to wait for his father's weary return from the store.

'I am a man of peace,' was the proper answer, 'but I cannot ignore a challenge.' Then came a combat clamorous with ferocious battle cries and inhuman threats, and ending, as always, with Ulyss lying in utter defeat on the floor while Jesse the victor bounced on his chest.

'You don't fight a bit better than you used to,' said Julia gravely. 'I don't know what the Governor can be thinking of, giving the 21st to a man who always gets beaten.'

'He knows the rebs haven't any generals like Jesse,' Ulyss answered between bounces. They smiled at each other, and in a moment he shook off his conqueror and stood up to face her. 'You don't mind?' he asked.

She was too puzzled to answer, and he explained awkwardly, 'Your father ——' He was not personally troubled by Colonel Dent's anger. That an old man had sworn melodramatically, 'There shall always be a plate on my table for Julia, but never one for a traitor,' was of no importance to the busy commander of the 21st. But Julia, who had grown up in the carefully Southern atmosphere of White Haven plantation, and was devoted to her father, might feel a secret bitterness over her husband's commission in the Northern army.

Julia laughed. 'He's an old man,' she said, as she might have explained some frightening noise to one of the children. 'You mustn't mind what he says, Ulyss. He just doesn't understand about things any more.'

'I just thought —— He's your father ——'

'You're my husband. I — I chose you myself.'

Little Jesse pulled hopefully at a worn trouser leg, and then at a full skirt, without result. People were always letting wars be interrupted. He wandered off, shouting, 'Dirty reb!' at the sinister, crouching legs of the sitting-room table.

The first assignment to the 21st of any importance was an order to move against a Colonel Harris, who was helping to keep Missouri in turmoil. As Grant moved out his regiment he remembered how desperately he had hoped for a commission, and he called himself a fool. He could discipline his men and see that they were properly fed and clothed, and lead them on the march, but had he forgotten that he must also lead them in battle? He was not afraid for himself. He had faced fire and had no fear of it, but he had never said to other men, Go forward; I am sending some of you to death, but go forward. Even that he could do, but suppose he sent them at the wrong time, the wrong place? Suppose he gave his orders to these young men who had no choice but to obey them, and they died obediently to no purpose? His mouth, closed firmly, was ashy dry, and as the regiment labored up the hill that commanded the rebel camp he knew that if he had true courage, moral courage, he would admit his unfitness and give the order to retreat. He was a coward, and could not speak. He tried to remember something of the techniques of battle, but the little he had ever learned escaped him now. The regiment had reached the top of the hill, and it was too late for anything but steeling himself to bear the disaster and disgrace that had come upon him.

The rebel camp was empty. It had been empty for several days, for almost as long as the 21st had been on the march. The formidable Colonel Harris must have retired rapidly as soon as he heard that a force was moving out against him. Colonel Harris had been frightened. Ulyss thought it over carefully, for the idea was new to him. Throughout his long march he had been thinking of the enemy as vaguely superhuman, fearless as archangels and not subject to error. He realized now, looking down on the emptiness where Harris had been, that the men on the other side were the same as the men on his own, with no more training, no more wisdom, no more indifference to a bullet whizzing by the head.

All around him the men were muttering in disgust at having marched twenty-five miles only to march back again without a fight. But Ulyss drew a deep breath, as might a man who had been hard pressed and found an indestructible weapon in his hand.

In this fashion the war got under way all across the country. People had said, There will be no war. Then there was war, and for a few weeks there was much excitement and the awesome knowledge that everything in the world had changed. Then, inexplicably, life went on very much as it had before, and nothing happened. Isolated regiments marched up and down in busy inconsequence, armies made tentative dabs at each other but never got close enough to scratch, occasionally there was a swift raid or a brush that left a dozen or so men lying on the ground. The young men who had volunteered by thousands asked in puzzled disgust, 'Is this all?' The women whose hearts had been high and singing when they stood in the streets to wave at the banners, whose hearts were tight and leaden when they sat at home making unthinkable bandages out of their trousseau sheets, laughed and said, 'Is this all?' Everyone knew it was not. Someone had loosed the beast, and there would be blood and pain and terror before he was caged again; but the heart is blind, and so long as it feels its way along familiar paths it is unconvinced by the shrill warnings of the mind.

Late in July people said there was going to be a battle. All that was needed was one big battle, and then the other side would see how stupid and downright impious it was to fight over the issue, and would go home quietly. It was more than three months now since Fort Sumter. The war should have been over by this time, and almost everyone was excited that now at last it was to be settled.

The battle was fought in Virginia at a railroad junction

named Manassas, and up and down a creek that ran close by, called Bull Run. Many men and an old woman were killed. The roads back to Washington were choked and piteous with young men running away, young men who did not know how to be soldiers. Not yet. The South laughed, unaware that Washington was in its grasp if it would but close its fingers. And suddenly there was the war, not ended, but just begun. Across the ocean the great men nodded and pursed their lips and began their long weighing of cotton and Jefferson Davis and policy against wheat and Abraham Lincoln and policy. And in the American States, United and Confederate, in the farms on midwest prairies, in graceful old houses under the warm sun, in banks and churches and camps, the people said, Just a little while longer, certainly before the year ends. It was necessary to say it, and after a fashion they believed it, but now even their hearts were afraid they lied.

The country was no longer a land with mountains, plains, and rivers as the setting for the life of its people, but as a setting for death. Mountains were walls of gigantic fortresses; rivers marked the division between two hostilities; and the wide plains were battlefields. In the few weeks following Bull Run this new geography was made clear. South and North were roughly divided at the line of the Potomac and the Ohio, intermingling in northern Virginia, Kentucky, and Missouri, which were to be torn not only by the recurring battles to which border territory is damned, but by the tortured conflicts in the heart of the people. In the west the Union commanders considered the Confederate problems of supply, and balanced the chances of attack on railroad lines, on rivers, on all the long lines of communication and supply necessary for the operation of armies on a continental scale. In general, however, the interest of the people was fastened on the hundred and fifty miles between Washington and Richmond. A railroad line is a cold thing to fight for, but men can die with a sense of glory in storming the capital of a nation.

In Washington preparations were made for the long, doubtful struggle this one was plainly going to be. Old Winfield Scott was gently put aside, and the army was rearranged with a gesture at organization. It was still a civilians' war. The enormous volunteer army had been raised by the states, and now the representatives of the states had much to say about its composition. E. B. Washburne was among the most active in this work. If there were to be new brigadier generals there must be some from Illinois; there should be one from Washburne's district.

'I'd suggest Ulysses Grant,' said Washburne. 'He's a good man, and he's done fine work with the 21st. Put the fear of God into 'em.'

'He drinks, though, doesn't he? Wasn't there something about his tour of duty in California? Seems to me I heard ——'

'Oh, he's over that by now. May take a drop now and then, but that's all.'

'He's not done any fighting yet, has he?'

'No, not yet, but you can't tell by that.' Washburne's tone became urgent. He believed in what he was saying, and furthermore there was no better candidate in his district. 'Grant can fight all right when he gets the chance. He was a regular, too, and that's pretty important with all these amateurs around ...'

The paper Ulyss was reading was still full of the echoes of Bull Run. Washington was almost in a state of nervous collapse over the narrowness of its escape. Too bad, Ulyss thought, that the capital had suddenly become a frontier town. It would be awkward to defend, yet the people would insist that it should be defended. The business of war would be greatly simplified if it could be run on military lines, uninfluenced by civilian prejudices.

On an inside page he found the item. The Illinois delegation in the House had recommended seven men to the President for promotion, and the first name on the list was Ulysses Simpson Grant. He looked at the article a long time, astonished, helplessly happy, but with a caution that came close to doubt. Possibly there had been a mistake, and even if there had not been, a recommendation was not the same thing as an appointment. It was very bad luck to allow himself to be pleased by something that was still unsure.

In the next day's paper the seven names had become four, the list that the President recommended to the Senate, still including Grant. Shortly it was confirmed, and the men of the 21st greeted Ulyss with regretful pride as 'General.' It pleased him to hear the word, so much that he was made awkward by it and could not return it with the proper easy indifference. It was a great thing to be a general. He did not understand why he had been promoted, since so far his military exploits had been making the 21st presentable and chasing rebel will-o'-the-wisps, but he did not question it, as he would not have questioned being overlooked. Things happened to a man or didn't happen, and either way there was no use wondering why. He was content in savoring his good fortune, and thinking how pleasant and unassuming and boundlessly proud Julia would be as the wife of General Grant.

A brigadier was entitled to a staff of two aides and an adjutant. The aides were easy enough to choose: one a young man from St. Louis; one from the 21st Illinois, a lieutenant named Lagow. He was a pleasant youth, easygoing, competent enough, with an open admiration for his commander that both pleased and embarrassed Ulyss. But the selection of an adjutant was not so simple. It was hard and responsible work, and Grant had not a wide acquaintance from which to choose. He would like to appoint Rawlins of Galena, who had a talent for organization and a selfless zeal for the Union cause, but Rawlins had wanted a major's commission, and Ulyss could offer him no more than a captaincy. Diffidently he made the proposal, and Rawlins accepted. He could not come at once, he said, because his wife was very ill with consumption, but he would take up his duties as soon as possible. He seemed pleased by the opportunity, and Ulyss had a happy sense that he had done Rawlins a service.

The appointment of Ulysses Grant as a brigadier general was predated to the middle of May. He had been ruling forms then, and beginning to despair, but now by military fiat he had been a brigadier general. The date, however, had far more than an ironic significance: by its arbitrary placement he was the senior of the other Illinois brigadiers, which was not at the moment of great importance to him, but was a mighty grievance to the other gentlemen. One of them swore that not even patriotism put him under the authority of a former clerk, and had to be sent to another department. Ulyss was unperturbed. He knew that volunteers made troubled citizens in the arbitrary democracy of the army, and he had not yet discovered in practice that seniority can sometimes be a greater asset to a commander than a dozen regiments.

Southern Missouri and southern Illinois were formed into the District of Southeast Missouri, with headquarters at Cairo, and Grant was put in command of it. When he first entered the district office he found it choked with citizens, demanding, complaining, suggesting, knowing perhaps that it was useless, but taking some comfort in the assertion of their rights before authority. He had a sudden, unwanted memory of McClellan's anteroom as he gave his name to the young man presiding over the turmoil, and the memory became too clear when the young man, who either had not heard the name or was too harried to realize it, waved the newcomer away to wait his turn with the others. Ulyss found a table and wrote out an order: he was taking command of the District of Southeast Missouri, effective at once. The young man took the slip of paper, caught his breath in surprise, and looked up at the shabby civilian who had given it to him. This was not what he had expected the new general to be, this bearded man with an undeniable slouch and clothes clean but shapeless, and ill fitted to him. But he looked again, at the blue eyes that now held the habit of command, and the mouth stamped with its assurance. He saluted hastily and rose, and with an answering gesture General Grant took his place.

Cairo was a river town, basing its existence on the Ohio and the Mississippi; its existence forever threatened by the Ohio and the Mississippi. Its people were river people: roustabouts, steamboat gamblers, pilots, merchants whose trade was carried in the twisting river channels. All of them were filled now with angry dismay, for the rivers were all but barred to traffic, and a peaceable man on his lawful journeys was likely to get a cannon-ball through the smokestack. Some cried out to the district commander for immediate opening of the rivers — surely the Union wasn't going to let a handful of rebels choke the life out of the Midwest? Some cried that the military organization was an outrage to the town and an oppression of free citizens — there would be no trouble if the armies went away and let things take their natural course. Ulyss said nothing to either side. These people did not know the real significance of the rivers, the possibilities that flashed from their long watery courses.

'Look how deep they cut into the South,' Ulyss said to Rawlins. Mrs. Rawlins's illness had ended in death, but her husband had reported for duty without wasting time for his personal grief, and Ulyss was finding him indispensable. He dominated the staff and ran the office with implacable efficiency; he was a shrewd listener; and he had a native ability that made him valuable even without military experience. Ulyss spread a map before him and followed the lines that stood for rivers with an eager finger. 'The Mississippi, of

course, but the Cumberland and the Tennessee too. Look —
the Cumberland flows by Nashville, and the Tennessee clear
down to Alabama and over to Chattanooga. The South's full
of rivers.'

'And the rivers are full of their forts,' said Rawlins gloomily.
He jabbed quickly at each of the dark spots that clustered up
and down the lines. 'Here's Henry and Donelson on the
Tennessee and the Cumberland. Just eleven miles apart there.
The damned rivers — they twist around so the rebels can
take every trick, like the world was made for them.'

'Maybe. But if they lost those forts they couldn't hold
Kentucky or West Tennessee. The river would take us right
down to the interior — we might even strike at the Mississippi
from there ——'

'If they lost Henry and Donelson. People say they're
impregnable.'

'That's so.' Ulyss said it regretfully, not only because it
might be true, but because he had no opportunity of testing its
truth. He was supposed simply to obey orders, which had to
do chiefly with keeping an eye on Confederate encroachments
in Kentucky. If it weren't for those forts there would be no
Confederates in Kentucky, but he had no authority to base
any action on that fact. He sighed and pushed away the map,
knowing that in a little while he would forget his helplessness
and pull it back again.

There was very little action that fall anywhere along the
thousands of miles of the indeterminate line, and almost none
in Grant's district. His men were restless and weary of a war
that consisted in drilling up and down the fields outside of
Cairo; and his aides began to drink heavily out of ennui, thereby creating tension on the staff. Rawlins felt that the war
was the visitation of an angry God, a national torment which
it was obscene to take lightly, and he abhorred drinking. He
would, he said firmly, rather see a friend of his take a glass of

poison than a glass of liquor. Grant admired his rocky character, and the intense conviction that burned in his pale face. Rawlins was always sure he was right, and that too Grant admired, for he himself was sure of only a few things.

In November the routine was broken for a few days by an order to go out and make a demonstration against a rebel camp at Belmont in Missouri. The operation was carried out, not very well, for the men were raw and the officers ignorant and overexcited, and the engagement was more than a demonstration without reaching the level of a conclusive action. Its greatest importance was in bringing the men under fire for the first time, teaching them that no battle is fought all at once, that minutes follow one another in straight and single line, each one only a part of the whole. Most of the men found that after the first shots they did not think nor feel, not really, not as they were accustomed. They thought, The line is moving forward. That reb there behind the bush — I can get him before he gets me. Swing wide here, don't want to step on the chap, maybe he isn't dead. That was Charlie. They felt the warm sweat starting under the blue cloth, the awkward fingers growing deft as they reloaded, sometimes a thump in leg or arm or body that became a licking flame of pain, sometimes just a thump with nothing after. Minutes, in a single line. Not again would they suffer the sick paralysis of the first time, and to them it was a truly great battle.

All those engaged felt so much excitement over having at last been in action that they could not see the proportions of what they had done. Rawlins was inclined to look with emotion on the dauntless lads who had burned the rebel camp, and to forget that the rebels had recaptured the camp and forced the blue army into a quick retreat. McClernand, who had been made a brigadier general at the same time as Grant, but was junior to him and now under his command, made fervent speeches to the men about the glory of their cause in general and their own matchless courage in particular. Grant himself spoke of the affair with some pride, even though its results were so obscure that it was necessary to explain them.

The whole of the North had a great need of a victory, of some bright event to think about instead of the disaster at Bull Run and the following weeks of inactive failure. The newspapers made one out of Belmont. They did not balance nicely just what it had accomplished: that was not the province of newspapers; and all they wanted was a triumph after so many months of frustrations not to be disguised by even the most unscrupulously optimistic. Certainly Belmont was a glorious achievement, and McClernand would be long remembered by his grateful country. Very few of the papers remembered that a man named Grant had been in command at Belmont, and even if they did they could tell nothing of him. He had simply appeared, without a background, without a personal legend to give color to his present exploits, with very little to say. McClernand had been a member of Congress, had forsaken his party to throw in his lot on the side of justice, had fought with all the glamor of an ancient warrior; and was gracious about interviews. And so the papers were full of McClernand, and of McClernand's men.

It was impossible for Ulyss to admit how much that misapprehension wounded him. For a day or two the battle had been called his, but then it had become McClernand's, and now so far as the papers were concerned he might almost as well have been in Galena. There was a bitterness in him that he could neither deny nor dispel, but he was rigidly determined that no one else was going to know it was there. His friends, Rawlins, Washburne, the officers on his staff, and most of those in the regiments McClernand did not command, were indignant for him, and suggested to him any number of reprisals, but they admired him because he would not move.

Ulyss knew it, and he would not sacrifice that respect however hot his anger rose in his throat.

Yet his friends could not keep a like silence. 'God damn it,' Rawlins cried, 'it's insubordination! McClernand says — McClernand did —— After his great victory McClernand —— The bastard! The damned, slinking, Judas bastard!'

Ulyss made no reply. He winced at Rawlins's oaths, but he had learned that his adjutant swore as inevitably as he breathed, and there was an unadmitted pleasure in the knowledge that even the phenomenally upright Rawlins had a vice.

'They don't even mention you. There's not enough decency in twenty of these sheets to make a handkerchief a gentleman would wipe his nose on!' Rawlins turned on Grant. 'What did you say to those mewling pups that came to see you this afternoon?'

'I told them,' said Ulyss with careful calmness, 'that I don't have time for newspaper fighting.'

Rawlins paused and considered, surprised at first, then slowly approving. 'Good,' he said. 'Better than good. It's goddamned dignified.'

Slowly the reorganization occasioned by Bull Run was completed. McClellan was summoned from Cincinnati to Washington to be general in chief — with the assistance of the President and the Secretary of War and anyone else with a theory and time to propound it. Fremont, Grant's immediate superior, was removed from St. Louis, where he had been ruling according to his will with no regard for civil liberties or even for policy, and replaced by a General Henry Wager Halleck. The middle name, said Lagow, was an error, for obviously there was nothing whatever of the gambler in the new general. He was exceedingly learned, methodical and cautious. He was a good administrator, but slow to agree to plans of action, for such phrases as 'inferior numbers,' 'lines of communication,' were dark, unalterable realities to him, military no-trespassing signs that only a criminally insane man would ignore.

Thus, according to immutable laws of impersonal experience, Halleck weighed the men over whom he had been put in authority. On one side were such men as C. F. Smith, who was under Grant at Cairo — a regular, an elderly man who had left his teaching post at West Point and served loyally under his former pupils, a gentle man, beloved and trusted and trustworthy. On the other side were the McClernands, volunteers always hasting forward with unsound schemes, with no conception of the successive complications of the art of war. Balanced precariously in the middle was Grant. He was a regular, which was automatically a point in his favor in Halleck's eyes, but he had got through West Point without the thorough and respectful knowledge of strategy and tactics that being a regular ought to imply; and there were troubling rumors of his years in California. Halleck kept a doubtful eye on Grant.

After Belmont Ulyss grew restless. McClellan and Halleck, and Buell in Cincinnati, were concerned about the relief of eastern Tennessee, suggesting and counter-suggesting, obstructing each other with considerations of sound strategy and not wasting noble fellows' lives, talking their way through November, December. How could any move be made, Ulyss demanded silently, while Fort Henry and Fort Donelson stood where they were, a peril to the rear of any Union force in Tennessee, a firm backing to the Confederate forces in Kentucky? It was so very simple a proposition, and yet his superiors argued 1861 to its close, and so far as he could see would still be arguing at the end of 1862.

Once he asked permission to go up to St. Louis to discuss the matter with Halleck, but it was refused. Then early in January, after a demonstration against Fort Henry, C. F. Smith told Grant that he thought the place could be taken.

'Henry's strong,' he said eagerly, 'but they've put another fort across the river, a little one that the gunboats could reduce. And it commands Henry.' The plan sounded feasible. It was absurd, Ulyss knew, to think of taking Fort Henry so simply, with the help of one of its own safeguards. But he trusted Smith's military sense, and he knew that military engineers can make astonishing mistakes.

This time Halleck grudgingly gave him leave to come to St. Louis, but received him coolly. Ulyss found it more difficult to begin than he had expected. It was always hard for him to talk to those who were not intimates, and now the consciousness that Halleck was not receptive made him more awkward than usual. 'It's about Fort Henry,' he plunged, wishing that his superior would lift his eyes from the desk.

It is as I thought, Halleck reflected gloomily. The man's no soldier — his very uniform shows he's a misfit. He stammers and gets his words twisted, and the pauses while he thinks of what to say get longer and longer. Doesn't seem to have been drinking, not today anyway, but of course he still does. A man who couldn't control his weakness even for the sake of staying in the army would be incapable of controlling it at all.

True, there was something worth considering in what he was trying to say. If Fort Henry could be taken — without risk, with regard to the maxims of warfare tested by generations — it would be a fine thing. But each time Halleck was tempted to give the stammered project real consideration he was hardened by the knowledge that such an expedition would necessarily be commanded by this Grant, a risk he did not wish to take. He could not accept the suggestion, but neither could he bring himself to cut the man short. He allowed him to finish and then sat searching for the words which would commit him to least.

In that long pause it seemed to Ulyss that Halleck had

scarcely heard what he had said. 'I'm sure it could be done,' he murmured, trying to put into his tone all the conviction he felt, but the words sounded flat, empty, tinged with the uncertainty of his reception. 'General Smith ——'

'Yes, yes,' said Halleck abruptly. 'You seem to have forgotten, General, that moving a force out from Cairo up the Tennessee would be a plain case of exterior lines — a situation disastrous ninety-nine times out of a hundred.' He had found it, the phrase that backed his reluctance to move into the perilous unknown, and he looked sternly at Grant, who would have tempted him into risk, as harebrained as a volunteer.

Dismissal was apparent in the set of Halleck's lips as well as in his gesture. Ulyss went back to Cairo, searching over his plan for the defects that had been so apparent to Halleck, feeling a mixture of resentment and growing self-distrust as he failed to find them. 'It's no use,' he said to Rawlins. 'Halleck seemed to think the idea was preposterous. He said it was a plain case of exterior lines.'

'What in hell's that?' demanded Rawlins.

'It means we'd have to go a longer distance to get where we're going than the rebs would,' Ulyss explained gingerly. He tried to remember what it was that made them too dangerous ever to be risked, but could not.

'That's nonsense,' said Flag-Officer Foote, who had come into the office to hear the results of the trip to St. Louis. He commanded the new fleet of gunboats that bobbed idly in the river, and he was strung with impatience to try out the possibilities of naval combat in the centre of a continent. 'Suppose we did have exterior lines? The point is, we can take Fort Henry if Halleck would ever stop reading books long enough to let us move.'

The words were wonderfully warming to Ulyss. 'But he won't,' he said, conscious that the tone of the talk had shifted from a report of failure to a conspiracy to further progress.

'He made it plain he didn't want to hear anything more about it.'

'You scared him,' said Foote. 'We'll creep up on him now, easy like.'

The next day Grant sent to St. Louis a full report of Smith's reconnaissance of Fort Henry. Four days later he and Foote sent telegrams stating that they could capture Fort Henry if they had permission, and the next day letters explaining exactly what they intended to do. Halleck, studying all these things in his office, was harried. He knew there were possibilities in the movement — if the exterior lines were compensated by sufficiently superior numbers, if it were not necessary to entrust the command to the unstable Grant, if one could only be sure —— He had told McClellan that if he had more men, say the greater part of Buell's Army of the Ohio, an attack on Fort Henry would be possible, but his suggestion had been rejected. Now here was Grant, persistent if not trustworthy, insisting that the thing could be done without extra men. And Foote and Smith, regulars of sound reputation, were backing him. They would be there to take the real leadership, even though the actual title was not theirs; it was possible that with their training and reliability they could achieve a success as noteworthy as Buell's Mill Springs. On the first of February Halleck capitulated and gave his permission.

In twenty-four hours Grant moved out from Cairo. Foote happily led his gunboats upriver; Rawlins swore joyously; Ulyss was neither deeply excited nor deeply apprehensive, though he had reason to be both. Since he had himself fought for this responsibility it was many times heavier than if it had been laid upon him by the independent decision of his superior, and he knew that Halleck would not condone a failure however justifiable. Yet his mind was too filled with the details of his work, the handling of his men, the timing of the attack, to leave room either for joy at having won his point or for fear of losing his battle.

It was as smoothly simple as a daydream. McClernand directly threatened Fort Henry, Smith moved on the small fort across the river and forced its evacuation, and Foote's gunboats made the Confederate position untenable. In a few hours the rebel commander withdrew his men with wise haste to Fort Donelson. The Tennessee River was open. The Union forces had a water highway all the way to Alabama, where for miles the Memphis and Charleston, one of the only two railroads that crossed the Confederacy from east to west, followed the riverbank. Another railroad, the line of communication for the rebel forces in Kentucky and Tennessee, crossed the river at Fort Henry, and the Federals celebrated their victory by cutting the bridge. 'There go the interior lines,' said Ulyss.

Sudden fame descended on the Army of the Tennessee. Belmont had been called a victory, however meaningless it was. Mill Springs had been a victory, but had led to little. But Fort Henry — anyone who could read a newspaper or look at a map could see what it meant. As the news spread across the North in that stormy February, the people wept and sang and marched in processions and asked eagerly about the man named Grant, the hero who had strode from the shadows bringing a shining flame of hope.

Rawlins, Foote, McClernand, Smith exulted also, and Grant was warmed by the pride of his friends and the applause of strangers. He telegraphed to Halleck, 'I shall take and destroy Fort Donelson on the 8th.'

River Gunboat

CHAPTER THREE

IT WAS raining. It had rained and snowed and thawed and rained again for days, and the men said that the last commissary mule dug out of a loblolly had come back speaking Chinese. Ulyss hoped that they could keep on joking. He had marched them up to the Confederate rifle pits encircling Fort Donelson, and was keeping them there, with no shelter, for he had no tents for them; almost no blankets or overcoats, for they had thrown them away with naïve impatience on their way from Fort Henry; even no fires, for none could be allowed on a line as close to the enemy as the one which they held. They milled about slowly in the freezing rain, and their commander's main hope of success lay in their ability to laugh while they waited.

'Come in,' said Ulyss to a knock on the door of the hut he

was making his headquarters. Rawlins pushed the door open
and silently handed his dispatches to Grant. The adjutant
was even more depressed than his chief by the repulse of the
gunboats that day. It seemed monstrous to him that a cause
that had triumphed with the easy inevitability of justice at
Fort Henry should be held to a stalemate at Fort Donelson.

'Anything new, Rawlins?' Grant asked quietly. He was
heavy with disappointment himself, and a little frightened, but
then he had known many failures, and his adjutant had had
the unquestioning optimism of the successful man.

'No,' Rawlins answered gloomily. 'The supplies General
Sherman sent up are unloaded. He didn't send any blankets.'

'It wouldn't occur to him that grown men would throw away
their equipment in the middle of February. If we stay here
much longer I'll have to see about it.' Ulyss hurried on to
divert the question Rawlins was about to ask, unwilling to
face immediately the problem of what he was going to do now
that Fort Donelson had failed to fall at the gunboats' command. 'I knew Sherman at West Point,' he said. 'He called
me Sam — for Uncle Sam Grant, you know. My family always
called me Ulyss, but he started Sam there, and I don't guess
any of the cadets ever remembered what my name really was.'

'He's certainly eager to help,' said Rawlins. He was touched
whenever Grant mentioned, always with the diffidence he was
showing now, the old days in the army, and his old friends.
He had never mentioned them at all in Galena. Now they came
up sometimes, once or twice after Belmont, quite frequently
since Fort Henry.

Sherman's dispatch was in Grant's hand, and he read it again.
'He says I can call on him for any men and supplies I need.
He says if I want he'll waive his rank and come himself.'
Ulyss's blue eyes glowed, and the straight mouth curved into
a smile above the beard. 'That's like him — Sherman was
always just that way.' He put down the dispatch and looked

up at his adjutant. 'Funny, the way things happen. Sherman was head of a military school in Louisiana, and now he's a Union general. Jim Longstreet stood up with me when I married Julia, and now he's the best man the rebs have. Simon Buckner lent me money when I came back from California, and now he's over there.' Ulyss nodded to where Fort Donelson lay behind its rifle pits.

'It's a shame,' said Rawlins sternly, 'that good men forget themselves enough to engage in a damned unrighteous cause.'

'Yes — of course.' Grant felt himself accused of backsliding by Rawlins's black, unwavering eyes. 'It's too bad.' Perhaps he ought to say more, certainly his adjutant expected more vehemence of him, but he could not. Buckner and Longstreet had been his friends. By the laws of war they were his enemies now, and he would so deal with them, but his personal law forbade him to forget that once there had been friendship between them, and that friendship was a bond not even civil war could break.

That night it grew steadily colder. The steel wind wailed up from the river, stiffened the bottomless mud into gray, jagged, impassable tracks; cut into the hearts of the men trying to sleep, and reduced life to the problem of existing from one ice-sharp breath to the next. In the morning the men rose, most of them, and moved stiffly to tend the guns too cold to touch, but there was no joking any longer. The laughter and talk had been frozen out of them, and Ulyss saw anxiously that all they had left was courage, and that would be next to go.

Flag-Officer Foote had requested Grant to come out to his ship. The commander of the gunboats had been wounded the day before, but apparently what he had to say could not wait, and Grant knew what it was as he hurried out in the bitter light of dawn. It was written in the faces of the men he rode past: McClernand's division, Wallace's, Smith's. They could not endure for long as they were. There must be combat and a quick decision, which Ulyss had tried already with no success, or a siege, with the equipment necessary to keep the men alive and functioning while they waited. A siege was what Foote wanted.

'We can't do it with the boats,' he said mournfully. 'It's not like Henry. It was nice and low there, and we could get at 'em, but here, up on that hill, they can do us more damage than we can do them.'

'I know.'

'I'd suggest that you dig in for about ten days. In that time I can get repaired, and try again. If I could get just one boat past them I could do in their communications ——'

The discussion lasted a long time. Ulyss knew the gunboats must be repaired, and that there could be no action until they were back in service, but he could not bring himself to make the final decision. He had lunch with Foote and accepted a cigar from him, then started back to the fort, to think over a decision he knew was logically already made.

As he reached the shore he saw Lagow laboring over the icy ruts toward him. 'McClernand's smashed up, sir,' he gasped. 'The rebs came out this morning, and they've been at us like devils ever since ——' Ulyss's cigar went out and grew cold in his mouth as he listened to the tale of disaster, and it seemed to him as he urged his horse over the spiky road that he had been caught fast in a nightmare, that he had been hearing Lagow's panicky words and seeing his chalky white face forever. He had not expected this. He had been certain that in this weather the Confederates would make no move, be glad enough to be left alone in their fort, and his only orders before he had set out had been that none of his commanders was to do anything to bring on an engagement.

'How did it happen?' he asked. 'Did McClernand ——'

It was very possible that McClernand had ignored the orders. Once before, as they had taken up their lines around the fort, he had conceived himself annoyed by a rebel battery, and sent his men in a whooping rush to take it. The battery was part of the main line, defended by the entire rebel force, and the men had had to fall back, except the large number of them that would never have to do anything again. It would be very like McClernand to ignore orders in another piece of gallant foolishness.

'No,' Lagow said promptly. 'We didn't do anything. They just came out on us this morning, thousands of 'em, yelling——' He shivered as he spoke. He was shaken and sickened by that day. Belmont had been a picnic with military sideshows, and Fort Henry a brisk affair of two hours with little close contact and an assured end. Lagow had never imagined what it would be to watch a whole division crumpled and swept back, helpless, not only uncertain of the end but seeing with terror what it might be.

Thousands of them, thought Ulyss. The phrase stuck in his mind, lacking any deep meaning as yet, but persistent, a far drumming signal he would understand when he came a little closer. He rode rapidly around the lines to McClernand's wing. Smith's division was lying quietly to its arms, ready, unshaken by the tumult that had continued all day. Wallace's too was quiet, but some companies showed signs of struggle, for being next in line Wallace had sent help to the threatened sector. But where McClernand's line should have been there was chaos. The division had not fled, Ulyss noted with relief. Whatever McClernand's faults as a general, he did hold the loyalty of his men, and his men were as brave as he. They had not run, but their ammunition had given out and they had found themselves facing the gray men with nothing but empty rifles or bare hands. They had fallen back out of their lines, out of range of fire, lost their formations, and stood now in hot discussion of what had happened to them. Some of them sat on boxes of cartridges.

Thought they were never gonna stop comin'... And he says,
You, Yankee, go back where you comes from, and he cries...
'Peared he was gonna stay out an' fight a week, he had so
much grub on him... I'd 'a liked to take one more shot at
the big one...

Ulyss reined in his horse and went back to one of the men.
'What did you say?' he demanded.

'It was the biggest stinkin' buzzard of a fight you ever saw!'
the man answered with enthusiasm, delighted to have a fresh
and willing audience. 'I was just sayin' to Jim, my messmate,
it was too cold to spit, when I heared a yell ——'

'No, no, about the food. You said something about fighting
a week.'

'Oh, that.' The man was dashed, and resentful that he was
not after all required to tell of his incredible day, and of the
series of miracles that had preserved him through it. 'I just
said that one of 'em, the one that fell right on top of me with
a hole in his head, looked like he was out for a real set-to.
He was totin' hardtack and sidemeat and I don't know what
all ——'

Then Ulyss knew. Thousands of them, Lagow had said,
and this man had seen that they carried food. They had not
meant simply to attack and demoralize one division. They
had been trying to get out. They had drawn all their strength
to the left of their line, issued rations to the men, and made a
thrust for freedom. 'Where is the enemy?' Grant asked an
officer.

'Over there, sir,' was the answer, with a gesture at the line
of Confederate entrenchments. They had gone back in then,
after they had broken down the wall that caged them. That
was strange, but Ulyss had no time now to ponder the tactics
of the enemy. He saw his opportunity, a shining one, but to
be grasped quickly before it dulled. If there were thousands of
Confederates in front of McClernand there must be only

dozens before Smith at the other end of the line. There was a pause now while McClernand's division lay spent and shattered and the Confederates incomprehensibly rested to taste their victory. The first to break the pause, Ulyss was sure, would seize the triumph that lay beyond it.

He gave orders, quickly, succinctly, for the thing was of such crystal simplicity that there was no possibility of complication, however great the necessity of speed. McClernand's men took form again and went back into the lines Wallace's division had been watching for them; word ran from man to man that the rebels had not come out simply to show how strong they were, but were trying to escape; and the blue men received the sudden heartening that comes with perception of the weakness that lies coiled at the roots of power. Smith's division, which the old soldier had held in quiet readiness all day long, moved forward silently through the abatis that protected the Confederate line, then in one rush swept over the skeleton force that confronted them. Fort Donelson lay defenseless, and every man on both sides knew that in the morning it would fall.

Inside the fort that night Floyd, who was in command, and Pillow, who did the commanding, and Buckner, who knew how to command, held a conference. It took a long time, for though they all knew what was going to be decided it was difficult to find the shielding words to cover the nakedness of the fact. Fort Donelson had to be surrendered in the morning and, as seemed even worse to Floyd and Pillow, somebody had to surrender it. Floyd could not. He had been Secretary of War when that meant simply a cabinet post, and in the North he was now under indictment for strengthening Southern arsenals in preparation for the war that was coming. He wished very much that he had thought of so doing, but he knew mere innocence would not protect him if he marched out into Union hands. Pillow would not. He felt it his duty to get away with as many men as possible. Buckner must. He was a good soldier, too good to say what he thought of the way the defense of Fort Donelson had been conducted, of the opportunities ignored while they still outnumbered the Yankees, of the failure to prepare sufficiently for that day's victory over McClernand, and of the fatuous withdrawal into their old entrenchments to send triumphant telegrams to Richmond. He respectfully bade farewell to his superiors when they slipped away southward on the river, then sat down to write a letter to Ulysses Grant.

The letter was brought to Ulyss before the sun came up. He wrote his answer at once, shivering in the dawn wind, grunting as he noticed that Buckner had fallen heir to the command when at last the orders were to be given by the other side. Commissioners to agree upon terms, Buckner suggested. That was nonsense, Ulyss knew, when Smith's troops were all but sharing the breakfast fires of the Confederates. He was impatient with the immemorial practice of setting formalities and long-winded courtesies in the path of the obvious. 'No terms,' he wrote rapidly, 'except an unconditional and immediate surrender can be accepted. I propose to move immediately upon your works.'

That was all. Buckner answered that the terms were unchivalrous and ungenerous, but that the distribution of the troops left in his command made it necessary to accept them. He had originally written, with thoughtless frankness, 'the condition of the troops,' then substituted 'distribution,' but did not trouble to make a fair copy. He knew as well as Ulyss the ceremonial nature of the sheets of paper whose main function was to stand for the battle in after years, when people had forgotten the cold wind and the pain and the dead. Buckner went down to meet the victorious commander. 'Hello, Sam,' he said.

'Hello,' said Grant warmly. 'How are you, Buckner?' He thought fleetingly of Rawlins's rigid condemnation of misguided men, but it did not matter. Buckner in the gray uniform of treason was a reality, but so was the Buckner in a blue uniform who had said, 'Here, take it, Sam, and get on home to your family. They need you.' To Ulyss it would have been a far more heinous treason to forget it. There was not enmity nor coolness nor even awkwardness between them. The number of men to be surrendered; the permission to bury the Confederate dead who had fallen with such pointless heroism in the last sally; all the myriad details that remain when the fine full word 'Surrender' has brought the curtain down, were settled with amicable speed.

'If I had been in command,' said Buckner in a low voice, 'you would never have got up to the fort the way you did.'

'If you had been in command I wouldn't have tried it that way.' They smiled at each other, and when Buckner took his leave Ulyss went with him a little distance, out of hearing of his subordinate generals and the members of his staff. 'Buckner,' he said hurriedly, in a tone just above a whisper, his eyes fixed tactfully on the wintry river below them, 'I don't know how it is with you — what you're going to do now ... Please allow me ——' Buckner looked down at his friend's outstretched hand, and saw in it a very worn leather purse.

The capture of Fort Donelson, Halleck telegraphed to Washington, was the achievement of General Smith. 'Promote him and the whole country will applaud.' Halleck was convinced that he believed it. If Smith had not been ready, had not carried out his orders so well, the fort might not have fallen for a long time. True, he did not give the orders — but he was such a good soldier, so fitted for command, so far beyond reproach of any kind. All Halleck's preconceptions, which stood to him for thought, argued Smith's cause against the single stubborn fact that Grant had been in command. But he lost, overwhelmed by the force of civil opinion unhampered by any knowledge of what ought to be expected of a soldier. The people of the North said that Grant was the hero of Fort Donelson, and overnight his name and his deeds were entered in the folklore of the war. Young ladies practicing the piano, small boys taking their turn in games, facetious men confronted with loaded dinner tables, said, 'I propose to move immediately upon your works.' Ulyss, once Uncle Sam, became Unconditional Surrender Grant.

The first gift to reach him was his commission as Major General of volunteers, and it was followed by an endless stream of articles ranging from gold watches through Rogers groups and antimacassars to an infinity of cigars. Someone had observed that cold stub that Ulyss had forgotten to drop when he came to see the turmoil of McClernand's division, and now cigars poured in on him from every Northern state. He smoked them, and his staff smoked them, at every possible opportunity, but they never reached the end of them.

Sometimes there was trouble with Rawlins about the gifts, and it always puzzled Ulyss. 'There's a man here to see you,' said the adjutant. 'He's got a bottle of brandy he says he wants to present to the hero of Donelson.'

'That's nice of him,' Grant answered. 'Ask him to come in.'

Rawlins stayed where he was. 'The bottle of brandy,' he said.

'What? Oh.' Ulyss was a little annoyed by Rawlins's instant, vigilant wrath whenever a bottle of anything appeared. 'Thank him for it, and give it to some of the men.'

'I'll be goddamned if I will. They're fighting for their country — they're men and know what they're doing, not poor stupid beasts to be poisoned into submission. I'll rot in hell before I give it to them.'

'All right, Rawlins. I expect you're right,' Ulyss interrupted. His suggestion had been a slip of the tongue, and he was faintly surprised that he was able to bring his adjutant to a stop so soon. 'Give it to the surgeons for use in the hospital, or throw it away if you like.'

'Why accept it at all?'

'I won't hurt the man's feelings,' said Ulyss in sharp exasperation. 'I can't refuse his gift even though I won't use it myself nor let my men use it.'

'It isn't only that it's liquor.' Rawlins still stood his ground. 'It doesn't matter what the gift is, I question if it's wise to take all these things. People are usually after something ——'

'That's ridiculous. I won't insult the man by making a fuss over a few drops of brandy. I'll see him for a few minutes.' Ulyss knew and appreciated Rawlins's thoroughgoing, if demanding, loyalty, and acknowledged his long-sighted wisdom in many things, but he refused to be led by his cold distrust of people. Grant, too, could be unyielding when a man had once played him false, but it was impossible to him to be as universally suspicious as Rawlins.

The interview was a little disappointing; somehow all the interviews with the callers who had poured in since the capture of the fort had been a little disappointing. Ulyss was not sure exactly what he had expected of them. It still embarrassed him when people praised him in his presence, but he had felt that citizens had a right to come and see their army fighting for their cause. Perhaps, deep encysted in his mind, was a desire to see for himself the approval in their faces, the admiration and respect that would sponge away so much that lay dark and heavy in his memory. He did see it in the stream of faces that passed him in those few days, but it was always worn thin to transparency by eagerness for something else. Everyone had come in excess of patriotic fervor to congratulate him, but in a few minutes' talk it invariably appeared that everyone had fine cheap beef to sell to the army, or wanted an interview for his newspaper, or had an infallible scheme to end the rebellion in three weeks. Nowhere was there the steady, proud appreciation that would expunge the years since California; nowhere except in Julia's face, and he could not see that. Ulyss was suddenly thirsty for Julia, filled with a childish desire to take Fort Donelson and lay it at her feet, and hear her say, 'Ulyss, how wonderful! I knew you would!'

This man seemed to be interested in trading with the soldiers, but he left without saying much about it, baffled by Grant's silence and the intent abstraction in his eyes. Ulyss turned to the papers piled in towering disorder on his table, and was still fingering them restlessly when Rawlins came in. 'More stuff has come,' said the adjutant. 'A bedspread, and four more boxes of cigars, and God knows what else.'

'Send them on to Julia,' said Grant without looking up. 'All except the cigars.' She should see that much of his triumph anyway.

'Don't you think ——' Rawlins began, and stopped. He was uneasy about his chief's simple acceptance of anything that anybody chose to send him, but he had learned that on certain things Grant stood immovable, and reasoning, expostulation, and outright pleading were of no effect whatever. 'There's some more correspondents outside,' he said instead.

'I won't see them,' said Ulyss. 'If I say white they print I said black, and if I don't say anything they print I said pink, with green stripes.' He pushed away the papers before him with an impatient gesture. 'Why aren't we doing something, Rawlins?' he demanded. 'The whole southwest is open to us now — we ought to be chasing Johnston, and pushing south before he can redraw his lines. What's Halleck doing?'

'Telegraphing Washington for re-enforcements,' said Rawlins.

Grant snorted. 'We've got enough men, if only somebody would tell them to move.' He stood up with sudden decision. 'I'm going down to Nashville and see what's going on. Telegraph Halleck that if he has no objections I'll leave in the morning.'

Rawlins went out to send the telegram, on his way telling the correspondents that the General would not see them. They were not surprised, for he frequently denied them, but they were annoyed, and wandered about talking to the subordinate commanders, to the men, even to the other callers on the General. They could not be balked of information by one uncooperative man.

No word came from Halleck, and Ulyss went to Nashville. He was stirred by his perception of all that could be done, for now that Donelson had fallen Tennessee lay open to the Union, Kentucky was cleared, and a vigorous thrust might even threaten Vicksburg where it lay in arrogant power on the Mississippi. But there was no thrust. Buell moved around Nashville, and Smith was occupying Clarksville, and Halleck was gravely discussing multiplied men and divided responsibility over the wire with Washington. McClellan wanted to know how many men Halleck already had, and Halleck asked Grant, and there was no answer.

This, thought Halleck, is exactly what I expected. The man may be able to win a battle, properly supported, but he can't be trusted. The newspapers said Grant was in Nashville. What right had he to be there? Why was he neglecting his duties at Donelson, and wandering about without troubling to ask permission? (Somewhere in the reaches of half-built telegraph lines, river and raw country between St. Louis and Fort Donelson dispatches were going astray, but Halleck, busily convincing himself that Grant was a menace to the orderly conduct of the war, hardly needed a misunderstanding to bring his alarm to the pitch of action.) Some newspapers in McClernand's district in Illinois, and in other places, were speaking vaguely of cases of liquor accepted as bribes, and of the convivial nature of a certain popular general. That accounted for it. Halleck had been expecting it, and he determined to move quickly to get the man out of the way, before to his bleared eyes one soldier appeared as two and he undertook expeditions with half the required force. He telegraphed McClellan that the old bad habits had reappeared. 'I am worn out and tired with his neglect and inefficiency. General Smith is almost the only officer equal to the emergency.'

In Washington McClellan read the dispatches regretfully. It was too bad about Sam Grant. He had never been much of a talker, and he didn't look like a man who would do anything in the world, but you couldn't help feeling sorry for him anyway. He loved his family so much. McClellan remembered how he had looked at the print of his son's hand — but he also remembered what he had said. 'Ulyshush — name' after me.' McClellan telegraphed Halleck: 'Generals must observe discipline as well as private soldiers. Do not hesitate to arrest him at once, if the good of the service requires it, and place General Smith in command.'

It was adequate authority, but now Halleck, uneasy in mind, wondered if perhaps it was not somewhat too adequate. He had not determined exactly what he wanted to do with his disturbing subordinate. All his inclinations were to stop the man's rise to power before he could damage the Union cause, but his impulse was weakened by a rigid sense of justice. To arrest and disgrace a victorious general because of his neglect of details would be an action hard to defend, even to himself. Yet to ignore that neglect would be lax, and moreover dangerous. Halleck hesitated a long time, seeking a solution that would conform to laws civil, military, or simply traditional, and appease his own fears without putting remorse in their place.

A movement to follow up the victory of Donelson was at last decided upon. It was not to be a campaign with a decisive intent — Halleck sternly forbade any action that might bring on a general engagement with Johnston; it was essentially only a raid up the Tennessee against the net of railroads that centred about Corinth in northern Mississippi; still it was a movement,

action with a definite purpose. Ulyss came back to Fort Henry,
where his headquarters had been moved, eager to set out again
with his men.

'I'd rather be moving against Corinth,' he told Rawlins.
'Looks to me like if we're after railroads it would be simpler to
go there, where they cross, than to nibble round the edges on
the river. But I'm not complaining — we're going to move,
and that's the main thing.'

'Halleck says we can't do anything about Corinth till all our
force is collected,' said Rawlins, without lifting his eyes from
the order he was writing out.

'I say it's a good idea to do something about it before
Johnston has all his own force collected,' Ulyss said mildly.
'Anyway — we'll make those railroads look like something had
happened to them.' He turned his cigar in order that it might
burn more evenly, and looked at it reflectively. It was March,
now, and would soon be a year since Fort Sumter. Last March
he had been working in the leather store. He let his mind dwell
on that fact for a little while, which he seldom did, but it seemed
safe now to let it rise up vividly, to taste the bitter monotony
and sour failure that had seemed like to last forever. Rawlins
swore abruptly at a blot, and Ulyss, recalled from a daydream
almost too clear, smiled at him, oath and all.

'Dispatch from St. Louis, sir,' said Lagow in the doorway.
Rawlins half rose to take it, but Ulyss was before him.

'Never mind, you're busy,' he said, tearing open the dispatch to read it aloud. '"You will place Major General C. F.
Smith in command of expedition and remain yourself at Fort
Henry. Why do you not obey my orders to report strength and
positions of your command?"'

With a gesture Rawlins dismissed Lagow, who needed only
the permission. The adjutant came then to his commander,
but Ulyss turned away, blindly stuffing the dispatch into his
pocket. 'Go away,' he said.

'For Christ's sake, sir ——'

'I said you could go.' Ulyss heard the reluctant closing of the door, then released the sobbing breath that choked him. Bad luck — how could he forget it, how could he trust so blindly to good fortune and not remember that disaster lies in wait forever? He shook as he stood, with the utter, unreasoning misery of a whipped animal. He had met despair before, and looked many times into the face of hopelessness, but he had never felt such blackness as this, for never before had he had so far to fall. He did not question causes nor feel anger, as a crushed man does not expostulate with an avalanche. There was but one thought clear in his mind: I was the victor of Donelson, admired and acclaimed throughout the North, and even yet I was not safe.

Slowly that thought formed a corollary. The victor of Donelson, Major General Ulysses Grant, was a soldier, still a soldier until positively dismissed from the service, and a soldier has duties to perform however sick at heart he may be. Ulyss sat down at Rawlins's table, moving steadily but very slowly, as one in pain will move to perform a necessary task. He wrote out the order assigning Smith to the command of the expedition; then, still more slowly, wrote his answer to Halleck. The words seemed to form not so much by conscious composition as by subconscious instinct, by a deep-lying, hitherto formless knowledge of what was due from a subordinate to his superior, and from a man to himself. ' ... I have done my very best to obey orders and to carry out the interests of the service. If my course is not satisfactory remove me at once. I do not wish in any way to impede the success of our arms.... My going to Nashville was strictly intended for the good of the service, and not to gratify any desire of my own. Believing sincerely that I must have enemies between you and myself who are trying to impair my usefulness, I respectfully ask to be relieved from further duty in the department.'

The letter written, exhaustion flooded over Ulyss. Strength of purpose and strength of body were alike drained out of him, and he was filled with raw, twitching nerves, so that such commonplace things as the order Rawlins had left half written, his worn blue overcoat thrown over a chair, even the inkstand, seemed mocking souvenirs of the happiness that had crumbled under him. He could not bear to look at them. More than anything else in the world he wanted indifference to them, some armor to keep every chance object from tearing at his naked heart.

Dimly he remembered that a day or two ago Lagow had offered him a drink. He had been too happily busy then to be interested, but now it was of no consequence to anyone or anything if he took it. Probably Lagow still had the bottle, hidden in his tent away from Rawlins's watchful eyes. Ulyss went to the door and looked out. It was dark, but he could see that most of the staff was gathered by the campfire, and there was only empty shadow between him and Lagow's tent. He walked over, found what he wanted and returned. A glass — somewhere there must be a glass. He found one on Rawlins's table, and filled it. The whiskey burned his tongue, brought no warmth whatever to his heart, but in a few minutes did dull his eyes somewhat.

He tipped the bottle to refill the glass, but Rawlins's hands, reaching from behind him, took both glass and bottle and crashed them into the fireplace. 'Don't be a fool, Rawlins,' said Ulyss wearily, without turning around.

'My God,' said Rawlins, almost softly, 'it's you who's being the fool.' He sat down across the table from his chief, and Ulyss saw his face in successive planes of black beard, white cheeks, black, burning eyes. He expected a tirade such as he had heard on several occasions before, but Rawlins said nothing.

In a few minutes his silence demanded an answer. 'I've given the order putting Smith in command,' said Ulyss. 'He's in charge as soon as you take it out. What difference does it make what I do?'

Rawlins swore, still in a tone that would have been gentle had it not been so vehement. 'You're in command,' he said. 'Smith will take the expedition for a while, but you're the commander of this district.'

'I tell you I'm finished. I've asked to be relieved.'

'Where? Let me see.' Rawlins read the paper that Ulyss pushed toward him, and nodded. 'Good. Subordinate, but manly and dignified. But, man, don't you see that Halleck can't relieve you? How are he and his brains going to look when he tries to explain that he let his best general go because a few dispatches were held up?'

'You don't understand.' Ulyss shook his head. 'This is the end. Someway or other, it's the end. I know it.'

'God in heaven, you don't know anything!' Rawlins cried. 'You don't know what's going to happen, no man does. You don't know, or you won't admit in evidence, the sort of man that Halleck is. You don't even know enough to keep away from that stuff, so you'll be ready when your chance comes again!' He gestured indignantly at the bright alcohol flame dancing on one end of the log. 'That's the only thing that will beat you. It isn't Halleck or McClellan or Johnston who can finish you. It's you, Ulysses Grant, and nobody else.'

Unwillingly, Ulyss met his adjutant's compelling eyes. He was crying out inwardly all the denials of hope he had learned in forty years of failure, but somehow he could not say them aloud with those black eyes fixed on his. 'Fight that battle now,' Rawlins was insisting, in the exalted tone of the fanatic. 'It will be a greater victory than Fort Donelson — it will mean more to the Union. Promise me you'll never touch a drink again till the war's over.'

'I promise,' said Ulyss slowly, almost helplessly. It seemed absurd that Rawlins should be forcing him to safeguard a career already ruined, but the man's angry vehemence lit a small spark of hope that could never have been kindled by sympathetic efforts at comfort. If Rawlins believed in him enough to be enraged with him, it was possible — just possible — that he might be right. Rawlins was a good friend to him. 'I promise,' said Ulyss again, and dropped his head on his arms.

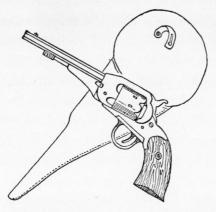

The General's Revolver

CHAPTER FOUR

Instead of relieving you, I wish you, as soon as your new army is in the field, to assume immediate command, and lead it to new victories.' The letter from Halleck reached Grant at Fort Henry a little over two weeks after his suspension. There were enclosures: an order from the War Department directing Halleck to investigate Grant's behavior, and a copy of Halleck's reply, a warm exoneration. 'As he acted from a praiseworthy though mistaken zeal for the public service in going to Nashville and leaving his command, I respectfully recommend that no further notice be taken of it.'

It was the General in Chief, then, who had so nearly wrecked Ulyss. He was not surprised. He thought well of McClellan, but McClellan's attitude toward him had been made clear in Cincinnati, and this was simply proof that it had not changed.

Ulyss did not consider anything else, Halleck's shift from peremptory coldness to a warm defense; or his own popularity; or the recent reorganization that gave Halleck complete authority in the west, not only over Grant and the Army of the Tennessee, but over Buell and Pope, of the Armies of the Ohio and the Mississippi. The important thing to Ulyss was not how he had been restored to favor, nor by whom, but the fact that he was again free to join his army in the field.

In those two weeks the Army of the Tennessee had gone down the river almost to the Mississippi line, and was encamped at a place of woods, swamps, and a few scattered fields called Pittsburg Landing. The army was to move on the Confederates at Corinth, but Halleck had forbidden any action until Buell arrived with re-enforcements, and Grant spent his time in impatient journeys between the Landing and Savannah, the little river town a few miles away where he expected Buell to come. The men were kept occupied by enough drill to teach the rawest to remember which was left and which right in times of stress. They were quite ready to move on Corinth without help, for they had a low opinion of the Army of the Ohio. In the first place, it was not the Army of the Tennessee, which would have been cause for condolence except that it was too stiff-necked to see it. Further, it was not the victor of Henry and Donelson, and could boast no more resounding a triumph than Mill Springs. Worst of all, it was brushed and polished and drilled without end. The tin soldiers, the bandbox battalions, maintained the unkempt Army of the Tennessee, had officers who said, 'Gentlemen, please to present arms.'

As March blew itself into April the camp was troubled by skirmishes on the picket lines and rumors of rebel forces along the railroad not far away. Ulyss was worried. He was quite sure that Albert Sidney Johnston, the Confederate commander, would not come out of his works at Corinth, where he had but to sit still to be attacked, and march twenty miles to do the attacking himself. Yet the pickets were always having to fire at small knots of gray men that glimmered for a moment through the undergrowth ... 'It's a lot of nonsense,' said Sherman, who had become one of Grant's subordinates after Donelson. 'There isn't any force of the enemy to amount to anything nearer than Corinth. They're just saucy, that's all.'

'I hope so,' said Grant doubtfully. 'But they might be going after our stores at Crump's Landing.'

'What for? I tell you, Sam, there's nothing to it. Remember, most of our men haven't ever held a gun in their hands before, and of course they see Johnston and a hundred thousand rebs behind every bush.' Sherman waved his arms about in large gestures that at once described and derided the spectres haunting nervous recruits.

'Guess you're right,' said Grant. If Sherman were unconcerned it was an absurdity to worry. Ulyss could not give his fears a definite basis anyway; they were simply apprehensions as vague and menacing as the swampy, tangled terrain between the camp and Corinth. 'It's getting late,' he sighed. 'I'd better be off to Savannah. Buell will likely be on hand tomorrow.'

'Maybe Halleck will let us move then,' Sherman grunted. 'No wonder the men are jumpy and think they see things. Anybody gets nervous with nothing to do but sit on his tail and think.'

It had been drizzling all day, but now as Grant came outside he found that the rain was coming in driving waves, occasionally illuminated by flashes of lurid lightning licking through the trees. His horse snorted uncomfortably, and picked his way over ground that seemed about to dissolve after days of such weather. Ulyss spoke soothingly to him, and left the reins lax, but the animal slipped on the spongy ground, floundered for a long moment as he tried to retain his balance, then fell heavily.

For a time Ulyss was not sure what had happened. He was dazed by his sudden impact on the mud, and as he was drawn from under the plunging horse he had a sudden fear that his leg was crushed. He withdrew his weight from it convulsively, and somehow made the journey into the nearest tent, leaning on the support of people he was too shaken to recognize. The surgeon came, and as his fingers moved over the leg Ulyss realized that only the ankle was injured. The boot was cut off, and it was decided that no bones were broken: the drenched mud that had brought him down had let him escape with a bad sprain. The ankle pulsed with pain, but in his relief Ulyss could almost ignore it. 'I'll go back to Savannah,' he said. 'Let me know if anything unusual comes up here.' Someone found him a pair of crutches, and he made his way to the steamer while the receding thunder echoed down the sky toward Corinth.

The next day the Army of the Tennessee had an unexpected addition to its rations. Rabbits and squirrels fled from the woods into the picket lines, where many of them were seized and welcomed as a variation on bully beef. They were roasted over the campfires and eaten while the men gazed with mild interest at the great numbers of birds circling restlessly over the trees. There was desultory firing during the day, and toward evening a brisk burst of it that resulted in the capture of a few prisoners. Sherman examined them. 'We're all here,' one of them boasted. 'The whole lot of us.'

'You're a liar,' said Sherman. He consigned the man to the guard, and sat down to write his report to Grant. 'The enemy,' he wrote, 'will not press our pickets far. I will not be drawn out far unless with certainty of advantage, and I do not apprehend anything like an attack on our position.'

In the morning the rain had stopped, and the early April sun rose clear and golden. It was Sunday, and in a few hours the chaplains would hold services for those who were free and

had the desire to attend. There was a church at Sherman's
position, but no services would be held there. The armies had
come, and with their arrival all the ordinary life of the countryside had ceased. A man cannot plow his fields between rows of
tents, nor sleep warm and quiet at night while the bugles call
under the uneasy stars, nor sing old hymns while there is the
sharp ring of orders outside. The armies had come: the people
had gone; and the service of God would not be observed that
April Sunday in Shiloh meeting house.

While the men were cooking breakfast one colonel sent out a
reconnaissance into the thick, meshed undergrowth. There
was a burst of firing, not the little spatter the pickets had been
keeping up for days, but a long roll that threw the blue men
back as if they had encountered a brewing tornado. 'What do
you mean,' his superior demanded, 'by trying to bring on an
engagement when you know we're not ready?'

'I'm not bringing it on,' the colonel gasped, 'it's here.' As
he spoke the undergrowth shook and spawned a line of rebels,
a long line that stretched from Sherman on the right all the
way down to the river. There was a pause, long enough for the
horrified eyes of the Union men to convince their unbelieving
minds, then there was no time for anything but firing into the
gray line, finding that any gap in it was instantly filled, firing
again, and trying to delay the backward steps as long as possible. There was but one sound that rose into the early morning
air, a single roar that swallowed up the short barking of rifles,
the bull-throated crash of cannon, the screams of men in fear or
pain or possessed by blind-eyed rage, and the occasional silly
ping as a bullet struck a tin pot tipped over on a smoldering
breakfast campfire.

The sound shook in the air above Savannah, and Grant heard
it as he sat at his own breakfast table. He was not really surprised. It was as if he had been waiting to hear it, with sure
knowledge that it was coming, yet a paralysis of preconceptions

had possessed him: he had waited, apprehensive, knowing what was to come, but doing nothing. He could not explain it even to himself, but he knew it was true. His staff officers were talking excitedly, running outdoors to listen and back inside to discuss. Ulyss finished his breakfast in silence. It had come, in spite of him and with his connivance, and it would continue in its ordained course regardless of what he did.

All that chaotic day he moved with this sense of playing a part that Destiny had written for him: whether he acted or abstained from acting, it had been so intended. He was a sensitive man, with an unending necessity for his own approval and the praise of others. He had had little of either, and as the frustrated years dropped behind him his fatalism had become as necessary a shield against himself as was his reserved, phlegmatic bearing against the outside. Thus he came to the battle he had foreseen and denied. There was in truth little he could do when he reached the field. It was too late then to attempt an order of battle, and the only clear facts were that the Confederates were trying to push the Union men into the river, and the Union men were resisting as best they could. Ulyss rode to every command in turn, all day long, but he knew that the issue lay with the grim, sweating men who swarmed through the bushes, never noticing when he went by, yet alert to see the gray forms that kept coming toward them, endlessly, with a relentless shove that might be resisted for a while but always ended in the loss of a few further yards.

Several officers, with the horrors of responsibility added to their natural terrors, fled to the rear and carried their companies with them. There some were assembled with other stragglers and sent back into line, but many made their way down to the riverbank and crouched there, inert, waiting from minute to minute for the nameless end. Yet on the whole the men, veterans and new recruits alike, stood well, for the cowards among them were restrained by those of steadier nerves.

It was the men under the bank that Buell saw when at last he arrived on the other side of the river. He met Grant on the dispatch boat, talked quickly of ferrying his men over, then looked at the fugitives, and the confusion on the bank above them. 'Have you any arrangements for retreat?' he asked.

'I haven't despaired of whipping them yet,' Grant answered. He had not, nor was he sure that he could. He was not sure of anything, but plans for withdrawal were as far from his mind as had been plans to prepare for Johnston. Buell looked at him doubtfully, and Grant went back to his rounds.

The hard-fought, yielded yards added to each other and became a lost mile. But it took a long time, while the day moved by, and at dusk Ulyss saw that at last the lines were holding. He had lost much, but not everything, and he was aware that the Confederate attack had reached its peak, yet was making no further progress. In the gathering shadows of night and the rain that was beginning to fall again, the armies reached a balance, precarious and certain to slip one way or the other, but a balance.

'It's like Donelson,' Grant told Sherman. 'Whichever one goes in first now will win. If we can start in the morning ——'

'We'll be first,' said Sherman. 'We've got 'em licked now.' All day long he had fought Johnston's main intention, to flank him and thus turn Grant's right wing. His men were recruits, but he had held them, retired in good order as he must, and rested now in the shelter of a swamp and flooded creek that ensured his safety. 'If they didn't get us today they certainly can't tomorrow, now that both Buell and Wallace have come up. They're finished.'

To be first in the morning, that was Grant's message as he visited each of his commanders for the last time that day. Darkness had put a stop to the noise as it blotted out the field, and there was little sound but the rain and the murmur of exhausted men. They were sleeping on the ground, heedless of the puddles that rose around them, for their tents had been abandoned in the first dismaying hour of that day. There was one log cabin still within their lines, but it was being used as a hospital. Ulyss sat down under a tree nearby. Now that it was quiet and there was nothing more to do till morning, he had time to think. He did not want to think. He would have much preferred to sleep, but the accumulated pain in his foot that he had been too busy to notice all day, and the accusations in his mind that had likewise been lying in wait for him, made a horror of his rest. Why had he not — entrenched his men, made more thorough reconnaissances, done anything whatever to protect himself against the possibility of attack? There was no answer. He had not, and he knew that the whiplash why would never draw an explanation, but he could not help applying it.

In a few hours, driven by his inner and outer misery, he took refuge in the hospital cabin. The surgeons were still working at desperate speed, even now at midnight. Dazed a little by the light, Ulyss sat quietly in the corner for several minutes before he really saw the place. He had smelled it at once, of course. No preoccupation could blur the transition from the rainy air of an April night to that thick atmosphere of blood and sweat and filth, breathed too many times by too many people. But Ulyss was fairly indifferent to smell. He sat waiting to dry off, looking straight ahead of him.

Slowly the moving shapes began to take form in his consciousness. Surgeons, working with exhausted intensity, their eyes on their hands but with a far, fixed look. Men, some walking, cradling an arm or holding a side; others carried in, staring with bright, fearful eyes, or apparently inert until they shrieked under the surgeons' hands, or really inert, to be glanced at and carried out again. Ulyss was fascinated by the speed of the process. It took but a few moments for probe, lint, bandages; even for the decision that some limb must be taken off and the swift motions that did it, leaving a man on the table and his leg, in fantastic separation, on the floor.

And then, suddenly, Ulyss's attention shifted from the process to the fact. These moving shadows were men; these gasping moans and occasional screams were the signals of pain that no courage could long deny; these shapes with an arm or leg missing were youths who would go henceforth crippled, never in all the years that they might live to be whole men again. Sickened to his very spirit, Ulyss fled the place and stumbled back to his tree. He lit a cigar and sat rejoicing in the rain and his injured foot, as tangible things that were his own discomfort, not a boundless horror oppressing him at once with pity and with guilt. It was some time before he could bring his shaken mind back to his immediate concerns, away from the larger truth that tortures a man with his own helplessness. He had always said that war was an ugly business, and he had no means of dealing with the complexities that lay beyond the strait limits of his province. It was not for him to question why these thousands of young men, and the other thousands in gray, should be delivered up to torment and the peril of death; nor for him to wonder what manner of nation was to be born in such travail. His function was to defeat Johnston, and that was what he thought of when he had contrived to thrust the scene in the cabin from his mind.

As dawn glimmered over the battle-torn trees Union skirmishers set out to find the Confederate line. It was almost all the way back at the beginning of the lost mile, and it did not hold with any firmness when the skirmishers were followed by the whole of the Union army. Ulyss knew now that Johnston was dead, having died in the most thoroughgoing futility in the front lines when he should have been directing from the rear, of a slight wound that drained away his life before it was found and stanched. But even had he lived, Ulyss thought, that second day would have taken the same course. Buell's army

was engaged, and so was Lew Wallace's division, which had
spent the first day hastening toward the battle by the wrong
road. Grant's strength was nearly doubled, and it swept back
the rebels with the same implacable force the rebels had used
against it the day before. By the middle of the afternoon the
Confederates could stand no longer, and broke into hasty retreat. Ulyss would have liked to pursue them, to make something more of his victory than the negative triumph of having
held his ground, but the churned mud of the roads was all
but impassable to tired troops — and he had held none in
reserve. Thus the battle ended as it had begun, without plan
and with little point, and he stood watching while the Confederate army fled back to Corinth to make it strong again.

After a battle, as inevitably as the burial parties, come the
newspapers. For a day or two they overflowed with joy. The
case seemed plain — a great battle had been fought, ending
with the rout of the rebels, and it was therefore a resounding
Union victory. Then, as they wished to fill in the outline with
details, the correspondents clouded through the camp talking
to soldiers, to privates and officers, to trained men and men
with theories, and the civilians' clear picture of a triumph was
shadowed by military considerations. The sound of firing heard
at breakfast became a tale of men captured in their beds;
Grant's absence at Savannah was first questioned, then condemned, then reported as a drunken stupor. In ten days the
battle of Shiloh plummeted from a glorious triumph to a shame-
ful disaster. That was what the newspapers said, intemperate
in either verdict; but men of knowledge and understanding
declared that the battle had been mishandled, badly prepared
for, ineptly conducted, and concluded in futility. It was given
at last the damning military label, Surprise.

It was true, Ulyss pointed out to his intimates, that Johnston
had come upon him before he knew it, but the Army of the

Tennessee had had time to form lines, the rebels had made no considerable number of captures until long after the battle had started, it had been a Union reconnaissance party that had done the first firing . . . He could not admit to himself that essentially he had been surprised. But the newspapers seized upon the label with no effort to weigh its importance, with no consideration of any mitigating factor, almost without remembering that the Confederates had not after all prevailed.

And the people could have no wider knowledge nor steadier balance than the newspapers had. The emotional tension that makes a war possible continues through it in hysteric joy at victories and hysteric fury at defeats, and the repressed uncertainty and dread of a war seeks someone to pillory, something tangible to be a whipping boy for the processes of history. Grant had been at fault, and it did not matter how seriously nor with what results. The very extravagance of the admiration poured out upon him after Donelson made it easier to condemn him now, and the public picture of him was swiftly redrawn from hero to drunken incompetent to butchering traitor. All through the North the journalistic howl was raised: Grant is drunk every night, and half drunk in the daytime. His men have no confidence in him. Hit Rawlins on the head, they say, and you'll knock out Grant's brains. He keeps his place only because of the muddleheaded officials who prefer a sodden West Pointer to the brilliant qualities of a McClernand.

It was impossible for Ulyss to defend himself, for he had but to open his lips to lose the last inner self-respect that was protected only by his silence from the raging journalists. Nor was there much that others could do for him. To old Jesse Grant, who had been reasserting his prideful fatherhood in Covington, this new blow was an outrage, an unfounded, malicious attack on his son the Major General. He wrote to the newspapers in protest, an old man's letters, querulous, rambling, compound of ill-informed defense and surprisingly capable invective, with the facts and beliefs expressed not always clearly allocated as coming from himself or his son.

Ulyss was in despair. 'He'll ruin me,' he told Rawlins. 'He starts out to defend me, but as soon as he gets good and mad he doesn't care what he says or does. He was always like that. I remember ——' He stopped, remembering too well Jesse's unbridled tavern talk, that had made Ulyss the butt of the neighborhood.

'Can't you stop him?' Rawlins demanded. 'Can't he be made to see that he'll get you into serious trouble if he goes on like this?'

'I'll try,' said Ulyss doubtfully. 'He isn't easy to stop — but I've got to try.' He wrote a letter, intending simply to make clear the fact that his standing could not be improved by published letters from his father accusing his fellow officers of stupidity, carelessness, and worse. But as he wrote, harried by his own consciousness of shortcomings, troubled by the newspapers' accusations, fearful for his future, his resentment of the past rose up in him and flowed into his words. 'I have not an enemy in the world who has done me so much injury as you in your efforts in my defense. I require no defenders and for my sake let me alone.' Ulyss did not look at the words again before he sealed the letter. He knew what they said, of his present trouble and of his old bitterness.

Thus Jesse was bound over into fuming silence. The only one of Ulyss's friends who could do him real service now was Rawlins, whose growing military abilities had not weakened his thorough knowledge of civil politics. He could do nothing about the newspapers, but he worked hard to make fast the bulwarks of influence against the raging tides of newspaper opinion. Washburne asked him a blunt question, and he replied with apparently equal bluntness. It was an outrageous lie, he wrote, that Grant had been drunk before, during, or after the battle. Grant was never drunk. He had not even

taken a drink since the beginning of the war. At that statement Rawlins hesitated for a moment. It was not precisely
true, not even of the weeks since Grant's despairing pledge
after Fort Donelson. Occasionally he took a glass of wine at
mess; once or twice, Rawlins was positive, Lagow had offered
him a drink and he had accepted. But in a larger sense, politically, he did not drink. Rawlins let the sentence stand and
cheerfully proceeded with his warm defense and confident faith
in the man whom Washburne had first advanced.

To Ulyss the important thing was not the savage outcry
against him, much though it hurt him when he thought of
Julia hearing it. Newspaper denunciations, however galling,
could not affect his work and his conception of himself. But
Halleck came down from St. Louis to take command in the
field, and Grant's position became almost intolerable. It need
not have been so: he had never questioned his subordination to
Halleck, and it was natural for a commander to leave his desk
and take personal charge of a campaign. At first Ulyss did not
understand that there was a greater significance in Halleck's
arrival. It took some subtlety to see it, for Halleck was not
taking advice even from those in his favor, but in a day or
two it was clear even to Grant's unanalytic mind that Halleck
was deliberately isolating him, and that the blind, deaf look
with which he was received was not given to the division commanders. The officers' reports of Shiloh went directly to
Halleck and were not even shown to Grant, who had commanded there. Halleck's orders went directly to Thomas and
Buell and Pope, and Grant, the second in command, not only
did not see them but was made aware that he was not supposed
to see them.

For a while, even after he understood, he tried to perform
his duties as a responsible officer. 'It seems to me,' he suggested
to Halleck, 'that if we keep the lines just as they are we're going
to have trouble getting by Phillips Creek.' Halleck was writing

something, but Ulyss had been given leave to speak and he stumbled on. 'I've been looking over the terrain to our right, and I think it would be easy to march General Pope that way at night. Then we'd have dry ground all the way to Corinth ——'

'Impossible,' said Halleck. 'Quite impossible.' That was all; no discussion of the plan, no statement of any objection to it. It's as though I had proposed flying, Ulyss thought angrily, or chasing mad dogs into Beauregard's army. He couldn't be more contemptuous if I had. Grant's cheeks above the beard reddened, and he stood struggling with a desire to demand a fairer hearing, knowing that by so doing he would but make his position worse, but tempted by despair.

General Thomas came in behind him as he stood thus in mutinous silence. 'Ah! Thomas!' said Halleck with animation. He rose and drew his visitor into a corner of the tent, and talked to him earnestly in low tones. There was no need for Ulyss to take his leave. Thomas had glanced at him once as though he were about to speak, but Halleck swallowed up his attention.

The bad time after Donelson was not as bad as this, Ulyss thought as he turned away. Then there had been charges against him, however obscure and unfounded, and their existence had made it necessary either to clear him or condemn him. But now there were no charges. Whatever faults he had committed at Shiloh were not of the kind for which an officer can be relieved from duty: therefore there was no necessary end to the limbo in which he had been placed; he must endure the degrading mockery of title without meaning, office without power, rank without respect, at Halleck's pleasure. It was difficult to meet people's eyes, to see the sympathetic indignation in his staff, the awkward discomfort in such colleagues as Thomas, the gleam in McClernand's glance.

His own staff tried to bear themselves as though the title second in command meant that he had a command, to ignore the fact that they seven were all who were bound to obey his

orders. It was not easy to talk of the new order of things without stumbling over the unexpressed comments that clustered
angrily about every subject. 'It's really a good thing to merge
the Armies of the Ohio and Tennessee — makes everything
simpler this way.' (Yes, certainly. But now the Army of the
Tennessee, that sneered at the bandbox soldiers, has lost its
identity, and marches under the orders of Thomas and Buell,
of the Army of the Ohio, and Pope, of the Army of the Mississippi.) 'We outnumber the rebs now three to one.' (Then why
don't we go down and chase them out of Corinth? We creep
forward every day and entrench ourselves at night as though
a corporal's guard of rebs could eat us alive.) 'The men call
General Halleck Old Brains.' (Maybe they're right. Maybe
the smart thing to do is to make up for too little entrenching
at Shiloh by entrenching every inch of the twenty miles to
Corinth. By the time we get there most likely the men will be
so mixed up they'll try to shoot the rebs with spades.)

Over six weeks after Shiloh the Union army entered Corinth.
For several days the men in the ranks who had been railroad
workers had been putting their ears to the rails and counting
the number of trains that were coming empty from the south
and returning full, but Halleck was not to be tempted from his
safeguarded course by mere suppositions. He closed in warily,
and pounced at last on an empty town. There were no Confederate soldiers in it: even the sick and wounded had been
removed in leisurely comfort while the Union lines were inching forward. There was no food, nor supplies of any kind.
There were no munitions. Halleck had been worried by the
cannon bristling about the town, but his gingerly approach
was not fired upon, and when the men came up to the guns it
was discovered that they were tree trunks mounted on wagon
wheels. Quaker guns, the men called them, with mingled annoyance and amusement. They were not grateful to Halleck for
the care with which he had husbanded their lives. They had

taken Corinth practically without loss, but apparently also without gain. The Quaker guns seemed to embody the laughter of the rebels, and however enraged the Union men were they could not but recognize the laughter, and sheepishly share it. It was a humor they understood.

Ulyss had had some hope that after a safe entry into Corinth there might be some change in his status, even a lifting of the silent ban under which he had been placed. But day followed day, and so far as he could see he had been forgotten. It was as though he were a prisoner of high rank, free of the camp, courteously treated by the sentries and his own staff, but excluded from the councils and responsibilities that would have given his existence a point. He waited with all the patience of a quiet man, but Halleck did not relent, and at last Ulyss felt that he could wait no longer. He would leave the department, no matter if he thereby relieved himself from duty and lost whatever the army might have held for him. Perhaps it would be less painful to lose it in the obscurity of Galena, rather than here under the eyes of the men he had commanded.

The boxes were half full, and Ulyss's headquarters already had an abandoned look, when Sherman appeared. 'What's all this?' he demanded.

'I'm getting out,' said Ulyss. 'I'm tired of standing in the corner with a dunce cap on my head. I'm leaving the department.'

'Don't do that.' Sherman tapped him on the shoulder so vigorously that Ulyss fell back a step. 'Stay here — you mustn't leave.'

'Why not? It's plain enough there's nothing for me here, the way things are, and never will be. That sentry over there has more chance of doing something than I have.'

'The way things are! That's just it. They won't stay this way. They never do, they can't.' Ulyss was kept stepping backward before Sherman's vehemence until he stumbled over a packing box and sat down on it, when his fiery friend stood over him, waving his arms to emphasize his points. 'The newspapers said I was crazy, just like they say you're a butcher, and I looked just as finished as you do. But then came Shiloh, and things were different. Something will come now, and things will be different again. If you leave the department you'll be fixed so it won't help when the change comes. You'll be the crazy one.'

'But ——'

'There's no use talking about it. It's perfectly plain. You may as well cut your throat.'

'Well — all right.' Ulyss ordered the boxes to be unpacked, and received Sherman's congratulations with a doubtful smile. His impulse was to go, for he had had little encouragement in trusting to the future, but at least there was the consolation of having a friend who could take so intense an interest in his affairs.

Sometimes, when he was with Sherman, he could forget his tacit suspension, talk of the campaign as though he had a voice in it, and laugh a little at Halleck's management of it.

'You observe,' Sherman commented, 'that we're going to hold Corinth. Maybe we'll lose Washington and New York, but we'll hold Corinth.' He gestured toward the placid country around the town, scarred in every direction by large new fortifications.

'Yes. It will only take about a hundred thousand men to hold it in this style.' Ulyss had smiled, but his eyes did not. 'Sherman, what have we taken this place for, anyway?'

'Because of the railroads,' Sherman chanted piously. 'The Memphis & Charleston and the Mobile & Ohio, crossing at Corinth, make it a strategic point of the first mil-i-tar-y im-por-tance.'

The tone was so exact an echo of Halleck's professorial manner that Grant laughed in the midst of his earnestness. 'But

what good does it do us?' he continued. 'We didn't beat
Beauregard. We let him retreat in a way that was a kind of
victory for him, so his men think they're pretty smart and the
civilians around here are bigger rebels than ever. All we've got
is the town, which is about as much use to us as — as the
Quaker guns. And all we do is build forts to hold it — and to
hold us. What good does it do us?'

'Rail centres are important, Sam.' Sherman had stopped
laughing, and he glanced curiously at his friend's face.

'Not as important as armies, or, in a war like this, the people
behind the armies. We could take every city in the South,
and tear up all the railroads, but unless we lick Beauregard and
the others, and show the people they can't possibly win, we're
just wasting our time and material.' Ulyss spoke with an open
eagerness that was unusual in him. His ostracism had given
him much time to think, to listen to the endless discussions
around the campfires, and he had come to the slow decision
that nearly all their affairs were ridden by unnecessary complications. The complex always troubled him, and he had
occupied his empty hours in hunting back of the swarming
details of what they were doing for some simple, guiding concept of what they should be doing. It seemed to him that he
had found it, and he was at once absorbed in his new conception
and appalled at how little it governed actual policy.

Something of his feeling spread to Sherman, whose imagination was easily fired. He ran his hand through his hair, and one
lock was left thrust up, a sure signal of excitement.

'Supposing,' he said, 'just for the sake of talking, that you
were in command here now. What would you do?'

'I'd move straight down on Vicksburg,' Ulyss answered
promptly. 'We've got plenty of men gathered here to hold what
we've got and still take Vicksburg before it gets any stronger.
That would cut the Shreveport and Louisiana, so the Confederates in the west wouldn't have any line to Richmond left, and

it would open the Mississippi clear down to Baton Rouge.'

'I thought you weren't interested in railroads and such like?'

'Of course I am. They're important, because they feed the armies and move them around. They're so important that the rebs feel like they've got to hold Vicksburg, and they wouldn't give it up without a battle. And when they lost the battle it would be a bigger blow to them than just losing the railroad. They'd lose men, and their people would lose confidence. And when I'd reduced Vicksburg I'd march on down to Mobile, and beat them again, quick, before they had time to pull together. The places are important because the rebs have to fight for them, but the most important thing is the fighting, again and again until they're licked and have to admit it.'

'We'd lose a lot of men ourselves,' Sherman observed. 'And we might not win all those fights.'

'But we'd have a better chance of winning than we do this way, tying ourselves to places that aren't any use to us, and giving the rebs all the time they want to get ready for us.'

'It's a good thing Old Brains doesn't hear you,' Sherman laughed. 'He'd likely die in a fit. All the same, as a crazy man to a butcher, I think there's something in it.'

'You said if I was in command,' Ulyss answered. The animation died out of his face and he fell silent. There was no savor in such talk when he remembered that it was simply an intellectual exercise, with no chance of testing it in the field. He was sure now that there was no chance. Halleck was not going to relent, and he would not be given another opportunity to prove himself or his ideas. The only positive action open to him was resignation, and that he would no longer consider, but late in June he did ask permission to move his headquarters to Memphis. There he could at least occupy himself with the routine duties of the department, and need not kick his heels in such conspicuous disfavor. He fully believed that his exile was as final as though he were actually leaving the department,

yet the difference satisfied Sherman, and perhaps it was enough
to propitiate the gods of chance in whom Sherman believed.
For himself, Ulyss had almost lost his faith in any luck but
bad luck.

In Washington there was a rising murmur: The man's too
slow ... No, that's caution — we don't want a lot of hotheads
running this war ... Too slow ... But a good organizer ...
Better at desk work than in the field ... Too slow, but we could
use an organizer, better here than there. ... The President and
his advisers pondered their decision for some time, knowing
how impossible it was to be certain of a man's qualities, for
those were days of sudden strains that could crack a character
along the line of an entirely unknown weakness. But the need
was plain: for wise co-ordination in Washington of the armies
operating from the Atlantic Ocean to the Mexican border; for
vigorous, imaginative action in the armies themselves. Halleck
was appointed General in Chief.

Thus, about three weeks after Grant arrived in Memphis he
received a telegram from Halleck ordering him to return.

'What do you suppose he wants?' Grant said to Rawlins.
'I hadn't noticed I was so important down there that he
couldn't get along without me.'

'God knows what he wants,' Rawlins answered. 'Maybe
he's going to restore you to active command.'

'Maybe he's going to ask me to resign.' Ulyss was incapable
of optimism, and he telegraphed to ask if he should bring his
staff with him, rather than risk the absurdity of appearing in
full force for an hour's conversation.

'This place will be your headquarters,' was the answer.
'You can judge for yourself.'

More puzzled than before, Ulyss returned. Halleck said
nothing, and let him hear from others of Washington's decision,
which automatically put Grant in command at Corinth.

In the two days before he left Halleck was made uncomfortable whenever he looked at Grant. He was not an unjust man. He had distrusted Grant because of his past record and a genuine fear that he was incompetent, had disciplined him after Fort Donelson because he had thought it necessary, and had kept him in suspension since Shiloh because that battle had been mishandled, and he had been unable to decide what action he should take. Now he wondered if he had been unfair, if he had been more stringent and demanding than he would have been with another general.

'I can't spare this man,' the President had said after Shiloh, when the newspapers were in full cry after Grant. 'He fights.' There was a certain recklessness in the statement that Halleck deplored, but there was also an element of truth. He would have liked to say something of this to Grant, but his whole nature recoiled from admitting such a personal note to a military relationship, and so, uneasy, apprehensive, and somewhat remorseful, he said nothing at all.

PART TWO

Mrs. Grant Escapes

Vicksburg, the Crossroad of the War

II. THE PERFECT CAMPAIGN

CHAPTER FIVE

AT CORINTH Grant, with a force reduced to the point of danger by what the newspapers called Halleck's pepper-box strategy, waited anxiously to repel a Confederate attack. Butler and Farragut had just taken New Orleans, and Pope had overcome the Confederate stronghold at Island Number 10.

Some were busy with forts, some with cities, some were taking the offensive and others defending, but all alike were concerned with the line of the Mississippi and the railroad that crossed it at Vicksburg. As soon as the river was opened the western half of the Confederacy would be cut off, and dwindle into insignificance; as soon as the railroad was cut the eastern half of the Confederacy would be deprived of the flow of supplies from Texas and the unblockaded coasts of Mexico.

The Confederates were pressing up through eastern Tennessee, that mountain country populated largely by Union sympathizers. Halleck had sent Buell to help, but had given him orders to repair the railroad as he went, and Chattanooga fell to the rebels while Buell was laying track for raiding parties to tear up again.

In the east it seemed for a little while as though Richmond might fall, and people felt that that would mean the end of the war, despite the uncertainty in the west and the Confederate victories in Tennessee. McClellan, who had been transferred to the command of the Army of the Potomac, worked up the James River all the way to the Confederate capital, and was preparing to close in when the enemy shifted commanders. A General Lee appeared, and began the defense of Richmond that came to be known as the Seven Days, a term whose very simplicity conveyed something of the magnitude of the events that sent McClellan reeling northward. Pope was hastily put in McClellan's place, but Lee and Stonewall Jackson defeated him in a disastrous second battle at Bull Run, and Washington once more lived in terror of capture. Lee turned north, however, and was at last checked in Maryland, but he was not pursued, and returned into Virginia, grave, courtly, remote. In those few months his name had become something more than the title of a man.

A new feeling began to appear in the North. It was not the simple impatience that had been felt earlier in the war, for there were some Union victories in the west to set against the dark record in Virginia. But Vicksburg remained in Confederate hands and Richmond would apparently be impregnable with Lee as her defender. People began to wonder if it would always be so: if what was won would have no meaning because of what could not be won. Perhaps Lee stood for an essential quality in the rebellion that would prove invincible, and all the Union efforts would lead only to tragedy. Few said the thing aloud, few even thought it consciously, but it was spreading in the dark.

Something of that shapeless depression also touched Grant, though not so fundamentally. It was a hot and trying summer in Corinth, for he had not enough men to undertake even a modest offensive, much less the sweeping attack on Vicksburg he had envisioned. There was nothing at all that he could do until the rebel forces under Van Dorn chose to attack him. Then, if he could defeat them, he would be set free, but he could not be certain of a victory, and in any case it irked him that the initiative must come from the other side. Sometimes he took a drink to break the sultry monotony, but once Rawlins saw him do it and raged for an hour, and thereafter Ulyss drank only when he was certain that his adjutant was not about.

Late in September Van Dorn struck, and was decisively repulsed. He was not altogether crushed, but he could no longer hold the Union men in Corinth, and Grant set off into the interior of the state. He went slowly, for he had a long line of communication back to loyal territory, growing longer with every mile he advanced, but at least he was advancing, and his spirits rose.

In November a young engineer named James Wilson joined the staff. He had served through the summer with McClellan, and Grant and Rawlins took great interest in the young man's first-hand knowledge of that dramatic campaign.

'I tell you,' he said as he described Lee's first movements, 'it was like we were fighting a different army, a new one. We got pushed back and back, whatever we did, and once we were almost surrounded ——'

'No commander's that good,' said Ulyss flatly. 'Only sometimes his men think he is, and that's when the trouble comes.'

In his turn Wilson was absorbed by the projected campaign on Vicksburg, yet he always showed a certain uneasiness when it was discussed. Shortly after his arrival, when the great supply depot at Holly Springs was mentioned, he drew a long breath and interrupted, 'I feel I ought to tell you, sir ——' He stopped, not abashed because he had cut short the talk, for there was no ceremony with Grant, but searching for some neutral presentation of what he had to say. 'When I was in Washington, before I came out, there was a good deal of talk going on ——' There was no point in putting in uncertain terms what he knew to be true, and he said flatly, 'General McClernand has received authority from the President and Secretary Stanton to raise an army and proceed down the river to Vicksburg — independently.'

'I'll be damned,' said Rawlins, slowly, reflectively; then, with sudden vigor, 'God damn him!'

'Are you sure?' asked Ulyss, with little point, for he himself was instantly sure. McClernand had been absent on leave for some weeks, and recently Ulyss had seen newspaper references to the volunteers being raised by that brilliant and popular general.

'Yes, sir,' said Wilson. 'A good many men in Washington know about it. General McClernand is personally acquainted with the President, you know. And both he and Secretary Stanton believe in the plan.'

'He's to raise recruits? Raw men?'

'Yes. He's raising them now.'

'What sort of man is Stanton?'

'Well — he's got the War Department much better organized, and there's not nearly so much dishonesty in contracts.

But — he's tempery. He doesn't like to be argued with, and he's got lots of ideas. He doesn't put much faith in regulars.'

'Damned fool,' said Rawlins, the volunteer staff member who had a regular's distrust of volunteer generals.

Vicksburg, thought Grant, was rightfully his to conquer, by all the logic of achievement, position, and rank, and it was a bitter thing to see it awarded to another man. But there was a worse thing than bitterness in his mind. Ulyss knew that McClernand could fight. He led his men in battle as if they were all heroes, and those who lived to come back worshiped their leader, but too few lived. He had no conception of generalship beyond the ringing word and inspiriting gesture; he preferred frontal assaults because they were more glorious; and he had a contempt for the chief elements of war: maneuvering, waiting, and outguessing the enemy. There were times when his methods were brilliantly successful, but they would not be against Vicksburg. That city, set high on its hills on the outer edge of a horseshoe curve in the river, so that its guns commanded the channel for fourteen miles, was not going to fall to a rabble of untrained heroes.

Thousands of men were being enlisted by McClernand's fiery words and the report of his deeds, thousands of youths without any knowledge of war. They would attack, and fall, and being McClernand's men they would attack again, and fall, until even they could bear no more. Their lives would be lost to no purpose, and for each one there would be a home in the North filled with bitter despair and indifference to the further progress of the war. It was this knowledge that deepened and colored Ulyss's sense of personal injury. He knew how McClernand could talk, and he was learning that Stanton and the President would listen eagerly to anyone who spoke for action. It was understandable; certainly there had been a heartbreaking number of times when battle had not been given, pursuit had not been made, and opportunities had been missed because of inertia. But this time it was the wrong action that was proposed, and there was no one in Washington who knew it. The President and the Secretary of War were apparently enthusiastic about it; Halleck — This was not a plan that Halleck would approve, and Halleck was General in Chief. Ulyss asked Rawlins to send a telegram to Washington. He did not mention McClernand in it, but simply asked how much authority he had to proceed with his campaign based on Holly Springs.

The dispatch was received by Halleck with fellow-feeling. Grant was not his ideal general, but compared with McClernand his faults seemed peccadilloes. Halleck had done his best to veto McClernand's proposal, but his best was little against Lincoln's hunger for victory and Stanton's imperial assumption that the Secretary of War had supreme command. Yet his cause had not been altogether lost. He had seen the secret letter of instructions to McClernand, and knew that it authorized him to make an expedition against Vicksburg, 'when a sufficient force not required by the operations of General Grant's command shall be raised.' A small phrase, but comfortably large in its implications. The letter was so secret that it had not been shown to Grant, McClernand's superior, and could not be now, but Grant had a right to know the limits of his authority. Halleck telegraphed to him that he had command of all the troops in his department, and could fight the enemy where he pleased.

'Where I please,' said Grant with satisfaction. 'Well, Pemberton's come out of Vicksburg with a good part of the garrison to meet me, and I'll keep him busy. Sherman and Admiral Porter can go on down by the river, and see what they can do while the rebs aren't home. The troops General McClernand raises will come in handy — in my department.'

'But damn it,' Rawlins objected, 'McClernand is to go by river, and he's senior to Sherman.'

'He's not there yet, though. And when he does come he won't be able to project around entirely by himself.'

'I wish we were all going by river,' said Wilson. 'The rebs couldn't break our communications by tearing up the water, anyway. That railroad behind us makes me nervous.'

'We've got to take some chances, and with the depot at Holly Springs we wouldn't be so bad off even if they broke the line north of there.' Ulyss knew that the matter was more dangerous than he was choosing to admit, but it could not seriously worry him so long as he was sure that the Vicksburg campaign would not be taken from him. There would be difficulties, some so great that they had been called impossibilities, but he had an illogical conviction that if he could control McClernand's pretensions he would inevitably, by land or water, take the fortress city.

Van Dorn burned the Holly Springs depot. Thereby he broke the Union line of communication, destroyed the supplies that might have made it possible for the Union army to stay where it was, and came close to capturing the Union commander's wife and son. Julia was bringing small Jesse down to spend Christmas with Ulyss, and had to be hurried away from the raiders in a box car. She was a little frightened at first, then remembered how Ulyss had explained to her that in war few things developed the way they were expected to. This affair must have upset Ulyss's plans, but he would think of something else. He was an important man now — even when he was in disgrace the criticism and invective were on a large scale. He had conquered worse things than a Confederate raid.

There was no such simple comfort for Jesse. His war, that had been so much fun in the days he had spent capturing Fort Donelson in the back yard, had become appalling when he had to flee before real rebels. They could upset his father's plans. He did not know the meaning of that night's confusion at Holly Springs, but he sensed that it was against his father's will, and his world was shaken.

The train ground and shuddered to a stop. 'We're here,' said Julia.

'Where?' asked Jesse. His hands were clenched tight, but his chin was set and his voice almost steady. Dreadful things had happened, and might still happen, but he was the General's son, and would remember it as long as he could.

'Where your father is,' said Julia, with supreme content. The heavy doors of the box car were pushed back, and Jesse saw his father. He looked all right. He was smiling, and hugging Jesse's mother just as he used to at home in Galena. Everything must be all right, after all. Jesse threw back his shoulders and swaggered a little, for he was the General's son.

'It's bad enough,' Ulyss was saying in answer to Julia's questions. 'It means I'll have to go a different way, and it won't be easy.'

'You'll do it, though.' She spoke not as though she were trying to reassure him, but reminding him of an accepted fact. 'You'll be the victor of Vicksburg — that sounds funny, the victor of Vicksburg ——'

'Maybe it's a funny idea,' he said, but smiled as he spoke. She knew nothing at all of his problems, nothing of the great danger in which he stood, but her glowing, ignorant confidence somehow lightened his own dark knowledge.

The citizens of the little town sympathized with him, smiling broadly.

'Too bad about Van Dorn burning up Holly Springs, General,' they said. 'We hate to see so many men starving to death — even if they are Yankees.'

'I know you do,' said Grant. 'So you'll feed them —even if you are rebels.'

'But we can't do that!' The smiles disappeared. 'You can't starve our wives and children ——'

'I think there'll be enough for you. Of course there won't be much left over for your rebel friends.'

'But we're private citizens!'

'You should have talked that over with Van Dorn.'

The wagons sent out to collect food and forage from the countryside were limited to a range of fifteen miles on either side of the army, but they were filled daily with no difficulty whatever. Ulyss had not realized how rich the country was in provisions, and after the two weeks in which his army was supported in this fashion it appeared that he could have continued it for two months. The fact sank into his mind, ready for reference. He was too busy to give it full consideration at the moment, but he recognized that it might one day be important to him.

It was not possible to take Vicksburg from the north. Ulyss had good proof that an attacking force in the interior of the state could not maintain its communications; and at the same time it was proved to him that a force on the river was equally helpless. Sherman tried to storm the Walnut Hills, the high bluffs that were the town's northern battlements, and he was thrown back with no gain whatever. Yet somehow it must be possible. Ulyss did not believe in impregnability. While he was making his arrangements to get his army safely back to Union territory his mind was concentrated on Vicksburg, on the hills that held it high and safe, on the bayous and twisted streams that were below the hills. There must be a way. He could not see it yet, when Julia and Jesse returned to the north he still could not see it, but she had said, 'Victor of Vicksburg,' and somehow he would put truth into her unthinking prophecy.

In the first days of the new year McClernand went south on his river campaign. He found Sherman and Admiral Porter already there, as Grant had planned, and although he ranked them he could not ignore them: he did not have the independence that he thought had been promised him. Very soon Sherman and Admiral Porter sent a letter to Grant. He should come and see for himself, they said. He should come and take command himself, or be guilty of massacre when Vicksburg was attacked under McClernand's command. Ulyss went, but he was not as disturbed as his subordinates. He knew that McClernand was no longer backed wholeheartedly by the supreme authorities in Washington. Perhaps Halleck had argued to good effect, or time and absence had dimmed McClernand's persuasiveness, or the President and Stanton had simply thought better of the plan, but for whatever reason there was no longer any question of the volunteer general's being independent of his superior. Grant was now authorized to relieve him, to supersede him with a junior in rank, or to take command of the river expedition himself. Thus secretly armed he appeared at the river camp, smoking in silence as he listened to the prejudices, complaints, plans, and fears of both sides.

'You can't let him have his head like this, Sam,' Sherman insisted. 'He talks about taking Vicksburg like the rebs were defending it with bows and arrows. He's drunk on storybooks, if you ask me.'

'His men fight well,' Ulyss observed with careful justice.

'No men on earth can fight well enough to make up for an ignorant general. Vicksburg isn't going to fall like Corinth, or even Donelson, Sam. There's four or five ways to try it, and it looks like they're all impossible.' His voice took on an awkward tone. 'I tried the Walnut Hills ——'

'That wasn't your fault,' Ulyss said quickly. 'You counted on my help, and because of Van Dorn I couldn't either give it to you or let you know I wasn't there. You've no call to blame yourself, Sherman.'

'It wasn't anybody's fault, but I was just stopped cold. I couldn't get any advantage at all. I tell you it's going to take plenty of thinking before we get in there, and the only brains McClernand has are for speeches. You can't leave him in command, Sam.'

There was much the same insistence from Admiral Porter,

who maintained that he might as well scuttle his boats and drown his men at once as drag out the process under McClernand's orders. Even the men under Sherman's and Porter's command thoroughly disliked the volunteer general, because of his obvious certainty that he and his men were the chief figures in all actions. McClernand himself said little. He made a few bitter remarks about lack of co-operation, but indicated that Vicksburg would fall to him anyway, to the glory of the Union.

It was a fact that Sherman and Porter had no confidence in McClernand. It was a fact that their attitudes were shared by their men. Ulyss was interested in facts, not in the validity of the reasons behind them. It was also a fact that he had planned ever since Van Dorn's raid to concentrate his forces on the river and take command of them himself, but it was good to be persuaded into his course by reason as well as inclination. He assumed command before the end of January. McClernand wrote him outraged letters, threatening him with the wrath of Washington, pitying himself as the victim of antiquated military prejudices, remarking on the current sad lack of disinterested patriotism. Ulyss ignored them.

The city of Vicksburg was protected by the river before it, and furthermore the river coiled through the country to the north and west in a system of bayous, lakes, swamps, backwaters, and smaller rivers that made up a terrain of muddy water and watery mud. To the south of the city there was dry land and good roads, so Ulyss was told, but however far he marched in that direction the river spread a broad and impassable barrier. There were no bridges, and the guns of Vicksburg swept the channel, keeping Porter's transports to the north of them. As Sherman had said, there was little to choose between the impossibilities of the various routes.

Soon after his arrival Grant went over the ground with his officers, searching for an opening that might give even a little promise. They found none, and returned gloomily to dinner on the headquarters boat. 'I never saw such country,' complained McPherson, one of the corps commanders. 'It looks like God forgot to finish creating it. How do people live here, anyway?'

'They grow webbed feet,' Lagow suggested. 'Didn't you notice the town of Duckport, down the river? Named after the outstanding family of the district.'

'They live in Vicksburg,' Sherman said morosely. 'They're dry and snug enough there.'

There was a faint snort from McClernand, who was maintaining the dignified silence of an injured man. 'There must be some way to them,' said Hurlbut, another commander. 'I never heard yet of a place that couldn't be taken.'

'We might dig a canal across the point,' someone suggested. 'It isn't entirely out of range of the guns, but the boats wouldn't have nearly so far to go under fire.'

'That's the plan the President favors,' McClernand vouchsafed. 'He knows how the river behaves, and that it would rather cut a new channel than not.'

'It was Butler's plan,' said Sherman. 'His man tried it, and the canal just eddied, top and bottom. It filled, all right, but with those soundings you could just about take a canoe through.'

'The river never does what you expect it to,' Rawlins commented.

'It will always break through a levee, if you give it half a chance.' Sherman leaned forward, his signal lock of hair standing upright. 'We could break the levee, and let the bayous fill deep enough for our transports.'

'But where will we be transported to?' McPherson objected. 'If the bayous fill their banks go under water, and how can we disembark troops in a flood?'

'How about connecting Lake Providence and some of the other damned puddles to make an interior waterway?' Hurlbut made the suggestion with a tinge of defiance. He too was a volunteer, and felt with McClernand that the regulars were edging them out of their rightful position.

'Maybe we could do it,' McPherson answered doubtfully. As an engineer, he had the fewest illusions among the commanders. 'It's possible, but even if we could get the channels deep enough and clear away the trees that are under water, and didn't get stuck anywhere in a swamp, we'd have to go over four hundred miles before we were in the clear.'

'There's another plan,' Rawlins said suddenly. 'There's more risk to it than to any of these, but there's a bigger gain.' He hesitated, and Sherman and McPherson urged him to speak his mind. McClernand glanced at Hurlbut and tightened his lips. It all depended, he thought, on whose friend a volunteer was. 'Well,' said Rawlins, 'it's agreed we can march the men south, till they're just across the river from good roads into Vicksburg?'

Sherman nodded. 'A couple of days, when the roads dry up, and we could have every man opposite Grand Gulf. But they can't swim across, Rawlins.'

'No, but they can be ferried across on boats,' said the adjutant. His usually pale face showed a line of red along the cheekbones, and his eyes were black flames. 'And we have the boats, too. If we ran the batteries with them it'd be dangerous as hell for a few hours, but once we got by we could get right up to the town, and God Almighty couldn't save it then.'

'You're crazy, man.' Sherman shook his head with regretful finality. 'That idea couldn't possibly work.'

'It might!' Rawlins insisted. 'I said it was dangerous, and of course it is, but it's not a piece of idiotic foolishness like the rest of these notions. It's got a plain purpose, and it can be done if we only have the courage of our cause!'

McClernand's compressed lips involuntarily loosened, and he tapped thoughtfully on the table. It was the sort of plan that appealed to him, the headlong dash, risking annihilation for the sake of brilliant victory. For its sake he could almost forgive the volunteer staff officer who was listened to, if not with approval, at least with a friendliness that had never been shown to the major general who was the intimate of presidents.

'It couldn't work,' Sherman said. 'Why, the rebs are sitting up there day and night, just waiting for us to try something like that. It isn't only losing the boats, or even the success of this campaign. A thing like that might lose us the war, with the bad luck the Union's had and the way people are beginning to feel. It's a risk we don't dare take.'

'It's a risk we've got to take,' said Rawlins. His voice had the timbre that came into it only in extreme earnestness, and it compelled attention even from the group that so disagreed with him. 'I know the meaning of victory or defeat too. And God knows I don't want to see men take their lives in their hands like this. But this war has got to stop, and the only way to stop it is to win it. We've got to do it, Sherman — no other plan gives us a chance. We've got to do it.'

The debate swept on, and Rawlins was overborne by the others under Sherman's leadership, but he was not persuaded. He was exhausted and shaking when the group at last dispersed, but still unalterably convinced that he was right. Grant gave orders that the canal across the point should be tried, and his adjutant could not protest, but the black eyes were full of reproach.

Ulyss went out on deck to smoke a last cigar before he went to bed. The river glimmered before him in the faint starlight, twisting down from the north, passing the lights of Vicksburg on her bluffs, leading south to firm land. It was after midnight, and very quiet. A dog was barking somewhere far off, and Grant's footsteps seemed loud. He stopped and leaned on the rail, looking at the dim water and thinking that he could still hear the words that had clashed around him all evening. He had said little. All the suggestions and their faults had been canvassed over and over for weeks, and he had gone through them so many times himself that they had been almost sucked dry of meaning. Even the proposal of running the batteries had been previously discussed by Wilson and Rawlins in his presence. Ulyss tried not to think of it, but it haunted him in this silent hour. He knew that eventually that was what he would do. All the other schemes were ingenious, complicated affairs that would serve to keep the men busy for a few weeks, until the roads on this side of the river were fit to march over. Then he would send the boats through the miles covered, yard by yard, by the batteries on the bluffs, with his future and perhaps the outcome of the war hanging on the result. It was true, as Sherman had said, that a failure here might lose the war, for after Lee's successes in the east a defeat in the west might break the will of a disheartened people. It was also true, as Rawlins had said, that no other plan had any real possibility of success.

It was easy for them to talk, Ulyss thought with sudden exasperation. Passionate as they were, they were concerned simply with policy, with the impersonal considerations of tactics. They spoke of risk, but it was not theirs. They did not peril reputation, the hope of the future that was still a new thing in his heart, Julia's happiness. They argued as if the responsibility of choice were theirs. Ulyss knew that the decision was already made, by circumstances and not by him, yet he alone must bear its burden. He had suspected it for some time, and in that afternoon's tour of inspection he had seen with remorseless clarity the necessity laid upon him. The other plans — he would try them, they would give the impression of busy purpose while he waited for the roads to dry, and there was always the chance that one of them might succeed against all likelihood. Then it would not be necessary to run the batteries, but he had not enough faith in that possibility to make it a hope. He sighed in resignation and threw away his cigar, watching the bright arc it made and shuddering with quick superstition when it hissed into oblivion in the river.

The canal was faithfully worked on, even after the Vicksburg guns made the dredges withdraw, but it was given up when the river rose and broke the dam at the upper end, yet refused to flow into the new channel. The interior route by Lake Providence was tried and abandoned, for it was plain that it would take months of labor to clear a way through that tangle of cypress swamps, and no amount of labor could prevent it from being easily obstructed again by small parties of Confederate sharpshooters. The levees were cut to fill the bayous, an action which resulted only in Admiral Porter's being besieged in his gunboats until Sherman rescued him and he could make his way back to the open Mississippi. The same pattern fit every attempt. If water was needed, the river fell; if the success of a scheme depended on dry land, the river rose and spread over the countryside. It rained so constantly that the men began to wonder, not that there was so much water mingled with the land, but that there was any land at all. They camped on the levees, watching the water rising on either side. Many suffered from malaria and smallpox, and those in good health stood in the puddles and gazed morosely at Vicksburg, high on her hills, remote as ever.

The truth about the Vicksburg campaign was discovered by the Northern press. The men were dying by thousands of disease and neglect. Plans were adopted aimlessly and abandoned for as little reason. The commander was a muddleheaded incompetent utterly unfitted for his great charge, and had lost the confidence of officers and men alike. There were stories of how he sat in sodden indifference to the waste of human lives of which he was guilty, stories presented in more detail in Washington, to the President and Secretary Stanton, who had so blindly broken the promise they had given McClernand. Early in April, as the roads at last began to dry, a visitor from Washington arrived at the camp. Mr. Charles Dana, Assistant Secretary of War, was accredited to General Grant as an observer. Ulyss was well aware of what he had come to observe, but was undisturbed by him. The dreaded and inevitable moment was very close now, and Mr. Dana's report to Washington could be of little significance. If the attempt were successful all former criticisms would be washed away, and if it failed they would be dwarfed by his final ruin.

His indifference was not shared by others. McClernand received the newcomer with silent satisfaction, but Wilson and Rawlins met him with disarming friendliness. Rawlins had his tent pitched next to theirs. Wilson was happy to act as secretary for Dana's dispatches to Washington. The three sat up to talk at night, and in their informal conversation Dana learned much about the problems of the last months, and received stirring hints of the future.

'You've come just about in time,' Rawlins assured him. 'Now that the rains are over things are going to start moving around here.' He made no direct statement of what he expected; he could not, for Grant had said nothing of his plans to anyone. But Rawlins knew his chief well enough to gamble on his intentions, and he gave Dana an impression of plans well matured and wisely considered, and that sense of possessing a military secret that warms the heart of the civilian.

There was a dance on the headquarters boat the night after Dana's arrival. Several of the officers' wives were present, including Mrs. McClernand, and the other feminine guests were recruited from the countryside, where there were a number of rebel young ladies who were willing to take advantage of their position as noncombatants. For the evening the war was a matter for badinage; rebellious beliefs a pretty waywardness in a young girl; Union convictions a romantic variation on man the ancient enemy. The new and temporary conflict was forgotten for a while in the old and endless one. Ulyss sat alone in an inner cabin, looking at a map, his fingers tapping the time of music he did not hear.

'You'll wear yourself out like this,' McPherson came in to object. 'Come out and join us, for a little while anyway.'

'Not tonight,' Ulyss answered, smiling at the young man. He was fond of McPherson, as was everyone who met him. 'Things are beginning to clear, and I just about see my way. Is Porter around?'

'No, he hasn't come yet.' At the mention of the Admiral's name McPherson's troubled eyes went involuntarily to the map on the table, that showed so clearly the loop of river and the batteries that swept it. 'Shall I send for him?'

'Time enough when he comes. Ask him to step in then.' Grant had seen McPherson's glance at the map, and the doubt and apprehension in his eyes, but he chose to say nothing. The young man went back to the dance, and Ulyss caught a glimpse of Mrs. McClernand sweeping through a waltz with her handsome husband, and a young lady from one of the riverside plantations teasing Rawlins. Ulyss smiled briefly at that. She would not know that as a rebel she embodied grievous error to Rawlins, and nothing more. Pretty little thing, too. She looked archly at the unbending adjutant, pouted for a moment, then gave her hand to Lagow for a polka, and slid from Ulyss's thoughts. Fourteen miles of the gantlet. He had spent the last few hours in a final attempt to find a way of evading them, or shortening them, and now he knew definitely that there was none.

When Admiral Porter came to him Ulyss told him of the project in very few words. It was simple to explain: it would be simple enough to do, if it could be done at all. The old navy man looked closely at the map, repeated Grant's outline of the plan, and nodded.

'Yes,' he said, 'that's the way to do it, clear enough. That's the way to use the ships, not get them stuck in a brushpile with rebs taking pot shots over the rails. I'll run the gunboats and steamers down for you.'

'The transports can't go as they are ——' Ulyss began.

'No, they'll have to be padded some. We can put bales of forage around the boilers — you'll need that below, anyway. There's just one thing ——' He hesitated a moment, then said bluntly, 'I don't like to order my men to make the run. They can get the ships ready, all right, but I wouldn't want to give a command for the rest of it — we might be wrong...'

'No, you can't order them.' Ulyss understood the scruple. Dangerous as the project was, it held no more peril than some of the desperate charges on a battlefield, but without the strung tension of conflict it was a very different thing. 'This is work for volunteers.'

The Admiral nodded, and the two rose to join the party in the large cabin. The dancers were resting now, and listening to Rawlins declaiming. Poetry was his pleasure and his release; the rolling periods of inspiration at once gave an opening for the fervor that throbbed if it was pent too close in his spirit, and dressed it in a guise to stir the more lethargic. When Rawlins recited a poem that moved him he commanded the attention of anyone within sound of his voice.

'The pith o' sense and pride o' worth,' he was saying as Grant and Porter entered, 'are higher rank than a' that.' His voice all but wavered as he saw the two and realized what their conjunction meant. Wilson saw them also, and with a quick gesture pointed them out to Dana. Sherman caught his breath in consternation; McClernand's eyes brightened. But even that significant entrance could not cheat Rawlins of his hearers. His voice rose, and his tone shifted with instant fire from philosophical discussion to exhortation: 'Then let us pray that come it may (as come it will for a' that), that sense and worth o'er a' the earth shall bear the gree...' There was a moment's silence when he finished, as though his performance too closely resembled prayer and prophecy for applause.

In the morning Grant informed his officers of his decision to run the batteries, and Sherman, concerned for his friend's reputation and for the existence of the army, could not keep silent.

'It's impossible,' he insisted. 'The ships will be destroyed, and Vicksburg will be lost to us. We can never do it.'

'We've tried everything else,' Ulyss pointed out. 'This is the only possible way to take Vicksburg from here.'

'We can't take it from here, then. We've at least proved that by all the swimming around we've done.'

'What would you do?'

'Go back to Memphis, fortify it and use it as a supply base, and march on Vicksburg through the interior of the state. We'd have to get clear down to Jackson before we turned, but we could be sure ——'

'That would be defeat,' said Grant. 'It wouldn't matter why we went back to Memphis. Nobody would bother to ask. They'd see that we'd spent three months down here and gone back no better off than when we came. It would be a bigger defeat than if the batteries got every one of the boats, without even the chance of victory. You know how enlistment has fallen off, and how discouraged people are. I'm not afraid to take the responsibility of running the batteries here. I am afraid to go back to Memphis.' He stopped, reddening a little at having spoken at such length. Ordinarily he never explained himself, but Sherman was his good friend, and however determined he was on his plan he would not receive a friend's protests with the unhearing indifference he gave to others.

It was obvious that the discussion was profitless, but Sherman, as dogged as he was concerned, expounded all his objections in a letter to Rawlins. He was like Grant, he thought grimly as he wrote, in taking the last chance even though it was plainly hopeless. The letter assured his friend and commander of his loyal support whatever the decision, but made very clear that he considered the present decision the wrong one.

'I make these suggestions,' he concluded, 'with the request that General Grant simply read them, and give them, as I know he will, a share of his thoughts. I would prefer he should not answer them...'

Rawlins gave the letter to Grant without comment. Ulyss read it in equal silence, and put it in his pocket, where all his papers, official, private, trifling, and significant, were stored until the resulting bulges hampered his movements.

The transports were prepared for their perilous journey by an armor of hay and cotton bales to protect the boilers, with sacks of grain to fill in the chinks. The sailors made them ready, but only a few volunteered to run the batteries in them. Grant called for volunteers from the army. He did not have an army of soldiers. His men fought and wore uniforms and more or less observed military organization, but to all of them the war was an interlude, grim or adventurous according to their individual temperaments and beliefs: they were workers on leave. Now there was work to be done on the river, and out of the ranks came the river men: the lordly pilots, the engineers, the captains and mates and deckhands. Many of them had long known Vicksburg, the military problem, as the first stop on the packet run from New Orleans, and had come to intimate knowledge of those fourteen miles of channel in the days when the citizens greeted steamboats with freight and eager passengers instead of shells. There were five times as many volunteers as were needed.

As the preparations were being completed Ulyss went to spend a day in Memphis, and Julia met him there, bringing him Fred, the first of their sons. 'It will be good for him to be with you,' she said placidly. 'Now that he's getting so big he ought not be with women all the time.'

'You're not afraid for him?' Ulyss was half reluctant to ask the question, dreading some womanly misgiving that would after all deprive him of his son's friendly, admiring presence. He was half eager to ask it, knowing in his heart what the answer would be.

'Of course not. He'll be with you, and I've told him he mustn't worry you by getting into mischief. He'll behave himself, I'm sure.' She dismissed the subject then, as if consigning her son to the uncertainties of a campaign were of no graver importance than sending him to school, and talked instead of the small events of home. Buck was growing so tall and smart, and everybody said that Nellie was pretty as a picture, and as for Jesse, it was a wonder to her where that child ever got the things he thought of. Grant listened to her with close attention, and shared her pride and pleasure, but he found afterward that he remembered chiefly the way she had talked, the short, emphatic gestures of her hands, the toss of her head as she repeated some remark of Jesse's. She was not beautiful. Her features were large and not delicately shaped, and her left eye had an erratic cast. She had none of that appearance of youth that adorned women of easier lives. Ulyss did not notice it. He never really saw Julia's face, in his mind or when he looked directly at her. He knew every line, every slight shift of expression, but what he saw was Julia herself.

When it was time for him to go he kissed her and assured her once again that he would take care of Fred. The boy was standing beside him, wide-eyed, holding himself so stiff that his neck ached, because he was practically a soldier.

'Take care of yourself,' said Julia. 'You look after him, Fred, so you're both in charge of each other.' She kissed them again, then watched them down the street to the levee where the dispatch boat was waiting for them. Ulyss was walking with his odd, round-shouldered gait that always made him appear as if he were about to stumble, the smoke of his cigar drifting behind him. Fred, holding fast to one hand, was now all but capering, and had obviously already begun his endless list of questions.

For a moment Julia let herself realize the gravity of the movement Ulyss was undertaking. She did not understand its exact nature, for he had said little of it, but she was aware that it meant more to him than any attempt he had made. She was afraid for him. It was not only fear for his life, so constant in her that she was scarcely aware of it, but fear for the light in his eyes and the set of his lips. He was so vulnerable now that he was happier. Julia shut her eyes to pray.

'Dear God,' she commanded, 'it must be all right.'

Burned Bridge in Big Black River

CHAPTER SIX

THE spring night was soft and warm. The air moved gently above the water, filled with an undefined sweetness of earth, and a low moon silvered the mists that clung to the ground and shredded slowly about the bushes. It was such a night as seems new and unique, yet carries in it the undertone of all the countless springs the earth has known: a strange setting for the boats silently jockeying into line, the crews absorbed in their duties yet each man knowing that he might face death within the hour. It was ten o'clock when Porter's flagship moved into the channel and began slipping downstream, followed by the gunboats and transports in single file. Ulyss felt as though each one were a card slipping from his fingers, in a game with a veiled opponent for higher stakes than he allowed himself to remember.

There was a pause, not to be measured by time, while the boats slid forward and the night was silent. Then a battery spoke, the one farthest downstream, but within comfortable range across the point. It was as if that single shot had been a question, answered by the crash as the whole line discovered the Union effort. Along the shore, that had been lost in misty shadow, there was a series of glows that spread and brightened and became houses roaring up in flame. As Sherman had once said, the Confederates had been waiting for such an attempt, and had prepared footlights for the drama. The burning houses lit the river in lurid red and yellow, with the long black line of boats in detailed relief. The light was cast upward on the city, and through the billowing smoke the citizens of Vicksburg could be seen, gathered to watch the spectacle.

The headquarters boat was run down almost to the line of fire, and stopped. There was little talking as Grant and his staff stood watching on deck. Everything that had been discussed was now to be answered by action, and the scene itself was too large for comment. Rawlins stood to one side, swearing in a steady whisper, an inverted prayer. Dana made a few ejaculations to Wilson, but was too absorbed in what he saw to notice that Wilson was too absorbed to answer. Ulyss smoked without tasting or smelling his cigar. His arm was around Fred's shoulders. The boy was trembling, not with fear, not with delight, but with a tension almost unbearable.

The gunboats attempted to silence the batteries, running up close under the bluff and shelling them valiantly, but with no effect, for the line of guns remained in full operation, mercilessly raking the ships attempting to slip past them. Yet as time crept forward the ships did make progress, working down one side of the point, farther and farther into the screaming maelstrom of shells, slowly making the turn and beginning the passage of the other side. Then one transport wavered, yawed crazily, and fell out of line. The watchers on the head-quarters boat gasped and leaned forward, as though by gaining a few inches they could see more clearly through the smoke and across the distance. For a moment the disabled ship was very hard to see, then another shell hit her, and she was swept with flame. 'The cotton round her boilers,' someone murmured.

'Her crew had time to get away,' said Rawlins. 'Thank God.'

They watched the blazing hulk drifting downstream, and waited helplessly for the others to meet her fate, but the slow progress of the line was not halted. By a little after midnight the gunboat that brought up the rear was exchanging fire with the last of the batteries, and all the ships had disappeared into the darkness to the south of Vicksburg.

'Wilson,' said Grant abruptly, 'come with me. I'm going down.' There was a rising murmur of talk now among the others, but he did not stay to share their speculations, the eager discussion of how seriously the boats had been injured, the hopeful question as to whether the plan was now on the way to success. He could not wait to wonder. The running of the batteries had apparently been successful, but he was afraid to accept it as a certainty lest he invite disappointment by hoping for too much. He must make sure. He was afraid: more afraid to believe in success now than he had been when the risk was still to be taken.

The boats were safe. Porter told him so when they met on the flagship in the early sunshine of that April morning. 'We're pretty banged up, of course,' said the Admiral. 'We were hit plenty of times, but no damage was done that we can't fix. That' — he rubbed his hands and smiled — 'was a night.

The rebs just about broke their hearts trying to stop us, and all they got was one transport.'

'You can ferry the men across, then?' Ulyss did not look at Porter as he spoke, but at the opposite shore, a different shore, of most gratifying solidity after the marshy indefiniteness he had been looking at for months.

'The boats will be fixed up good as new before you can get the men down here to put into them.' Then the two men looked at each other and smiled, silently. They had no need of pointing out how great was the advantage they had gained, and they were both aware of how much there was to be done before the advantage could be pressed.

The men marched down quickly, leaving behind only a small force to threaten Vicksburg and keep the garrison from interfering with the operations downriver. Even then, in mid-April, some of the roads on the low, swampy west bank were impassable, and the men made their way by detours and hastily constructed bridges, even by rowboats through the woods. But they arrived, filled with high spirits because they were at last to see action with some possibility of accomplishment.

It had been Grant's intention to cross the river at Grand Gulf, the first high ground with good roads into the interior, but the seven thousand Confederates occupying the town held stubbornly to their cannon, and the gunboats could not silence them. His next choice was Rodney, a village nine miles downstream. He was working on his orders for that movement when Rawlins came in to him, saying, 'There's a nigger out here with information. I think you ought to see him.'

The lines were always full of negroes who drifted in from the countryside to wait for whatever was going to happen next, excited and docile; they were walking problems in civil law, military convenience, and human necessity. Many of them had schemes of childlike grandeur that they discussed eagerly with any blue uniform that would stop to listen; but Grant knew that Rawlins would not interrupt him with one of these cottonfield Napoleons. He nodded, and Rawlins brought in his discovery.

He was a tall negro, with heavy, muscular arms and shoulders out of proportion to his long, thin legs. His head was set well on his neck, and his features had a clean precision that was a curious combination with his black skin. He gave Ulyss the impression of being mismated to himself, with body and spirit made up of parts so unlike that it was strange they should fit together at all. The man began speaking as soon as he saw that he had the General's attention.

'They say you goin' down to Rodney,' he said. 'No need of that. You can cross at Bruinsburg, three, fo' mile from here.'

The map on the table showed Ulyss Bruinsburg lying halfway between Grand Gulf and Rodney, but the contour lines indicated that the ridge he wanted was some distance back from the river at that point. In this region all the roads ran on the ridges.

'What about the roads?' he demanded. 'Bayou Pierre's in flood by Bruinsburg.'

'Road's all right,' said the negro without excitement. 'Good, high road. I been over it, many a time.'

If this was true it was valuable information. Ulyss became absorbed by the map, and Rawlins asked, 'Why did you come to tell us this?' He was not searching for a tale of horror and oppression. He had approved the emancipation proclamation that had marked the new year as a politic step in handling the danger of foreign intervention, but he had toward negroes a humanitarian indifference. Yet he was interested and puzzled by this man, struck by his assured interference in matters of strategy.

At the question the man drew a short breath, and suddenly the negro in his face predominated. 'Gonna win,' he said. 'Gonna win...' He spoke rapidly, in a very low tone, and

Rawlins could hear only an occasional phrase. There was
something about David, and the children of Ham, and a land
of milk and honey. The man shook, and as his eyes rolled his
aspect of a sober workman wore thin to show the jungle visionary beneath.

Ulyss looked up from his map and said, 'All right. If you're
telling the truth we'll go by Bruinsburg, and you'll have done
us a great service.'

The man quieted as quickly as he had flared. He ducked his
head and turned to leave, but at the door he paused and said
slowly, 'You're gonna win. It's in the Book.' He did not wait
for an answer, and disappeared into the crowd of negroes
shuffling about the outskirts of the camp.

The information was correct, and the Union army crossed
the river at last, unopposed, the men leaning on the rails and
gazing lazily at the water they had fought for four months. The
east bank, below Vicksburg. It seemed almost impossible to
Ulyss that he had reached it, but he had little time for the joy
of realization. The Confederates at Grand Gulf swarmed out
in angry desperation, and had to be disposed of before he could
even consider his next move.

(Save the ammunition. The rebs are 'way outnumbered,
we're bound to beat them, and every bullet that doesn't hit
one is a waste we can't replace. Save the ammunition. 'Keep
firing!' cried McClernand. 'I started this battle and I'm going
to finish it, and by God there's nobody on earth going to interfere with me!')

When Grand Gulf was cleared Ulyss paused to map his
campaign. There was Pemberton in Vicksburg, bewildered and
blustering. It would be simple to reach out and seize the town
— but if Grant did so he would present a beautiful opportunity
to the Confederate Joseph Johnston, who was somewhere in
the vicinity of Jackson, less than fifty miles to the east, with a
force of unknown strength. Pemberton might not see an op-

portunity, but Johnston was a brother of the Albert Sidney Johnston who had fallen at Shiloh, and was an able soldier. He would greatly enjoy the chance of catching Grant's army on both flanks at once and erasing it from the Mississippi scene. And since he was Pemberton's superior he might be able to extract co-operation from him.

If I meet them together I'll lose, so I must meet them separately. It was very clear to Ulyss. Johnston first, then Pemberton. He must move fast, fight fast, and even though he made all possible speed he might not be able to keep ahead of disaster, but he was determined to try. This time he was going to win — he felt it, so strongly that the risks he contemplated seemed to him of no great importance.

The worst of his problems was supply. He had counted on Banks, the Union commander in Louisiana, to reduce the downriver rebel garrisons so that he might base his supply line on New Orleans, but Banks said he could not render any effective help for some time. The line could not be based on Memphis now, for it would be impossible to run a sufficient amount past the batteries. No supplies. Forty thousand men in hostile country, and no supplies. Grant's lips tightened, then widened in a sudden grin. A supply line was also a tether. For two weeks after Van Dorn's raid his men had subsisted comfortably on supplies drawn from the countryside. They could do it again, and move the faster.

The plan was not discussed with anyone, for Ulyss scorned to take counsel with McClernand and the other hotheads, and knew that the wiser and better trained men, such as Sherman, would completely disapprove. It was necessary to inform Halleck of his intention, and the General in Chief would certainly be horrified to the bottom of his cautious soul; but it would take some time to get a message to Washington, and Ulyss hoped that his object would be achieved before the inevitable prohibition could come back to him.

In those days just before the army cut free from Grand Gulf and struck eastward, Rawlins watched his chief with growing interest, remembering the Brigadier General who had dreamed wistfully of taking Fort Henry. Now he was moving against the greatest Confederate stronghold in the west, using methods disapproved alike by his superior and his subordinates, knowing that if he failed the guilt of thousands of squandered lives would be on his head, and he would be forever ruined. Yet this man who so deeply mistrusted destiny, who had learned bitterly that almost everything to which he put his hand twisted from him into failure, was walking into hazard with an assured step, and looking confidently at his world.

One could not say that he was basically different from the man who had fallen into childish despair after Donelson, or the man who a year ago had endured under Halleck's continuing public displeasure for the sorry results of Shiloh. He looked as shabby as ever; his ideas were not essentially changed, only clarified by better knowledge of his materials. Yet there was a difference, so subtle that it all but disappeared when put into words, so vast that it transformed not only the man, but the pattern of the war in the west, and might affect the war itself. Rawlins saw it, as he was sure Grant did not, saw it and glimpsed its possible results, but put the vision away from him. The nation's anguish must come first: it was close to disloyalty to speculate now on what the issue might be.

Even in small things Grant showed a new, inflexible assurance. Wilson was concerned by the growing hostility toward McClernand among his brother officers, and felt that Grant should remedy it.

'He's a great patriot,' the young engineer earnestly argued with Rawlins. 'My family knows the McClernands, and they're fine people. Sure, there's times when he acts like a spoiled child or a lunatic, but we ought to remember that he was in favor of running the batteries when most of them said it couldn't be done.'

'He can't be trusted,' Rawlins objected. 'He'll throw men away on some big charge that doesn't get any place.'

'Maybe he does it because he feels that he isn't trusted. Maybe if General Grant fixed things up with him he'd be one of the best men we have — he's brave enough, and he's certainly loyal to the cause.'

'Maybe,' said Rawlins grudgingly. He disliked McClernand with an intensity he knew was probably unjust, but he was an accomplished politician, and he saw the wisdom in Wilson's suggestion. If Grant could be induced to become friendly with McClernand it would be just such a gesture as appealed to the volunteer general's overweening sense of the dramatic: it might in truth make him a valuable officer, might even dam the stream of slander that trickled steadily to Washington. For such a result it would be worth while to renounce the pleasures of righteous indignation. Rawlins went at once to Grant, before his antipathy to McClernand could weaken his sense of policy.

Silently Ulyss heard out his adjutant, and silently answered him. He only looked at him: a strange glance, unfocused, so that Rawlins could see straight into the blue eyes and find complete withdrawal, as though his chief had not heard, had not seen, and yet scorned him. Ulyss turned and left, quickly, for the suggestion that he barter friendship for loyalty outraged his deepest convictions. Friendship, once given, could not be withdrawn, and could not be given by reason: a politic friendship, a convenient, a pretended friendship, were blasphemous contradictions in terms.

Fast, move fast. Johnston saw his opportunity, as Ulyss had feared, and ordered Pemberton to come out of Vicksburg and fall on the rear of the Union army, a move that would have caught Ulyss squarely in a vise. But Pemberton, happily confident that the campaign was being conducted according to precept, informed his superior that he would cut Grant's communications and 'force him to attack me.' So he took seventeen thousand men and hunted with busy ferocity for a line embodied in the one messenger Grant occasionally sent back to inform the Washington authorities of his progress. And one rainy day Sherman and McPherson fell on Jackson and drove the Confederates out. Factories that had been supplying the Confederate army were burned; Johnston was not eliminated, but was thrown back so far that he could no longer co-operate with Pemberton even had that General been capable of co-operation; and the railroad that was Vicksburg's chief supply line was destroyed.

It was a highly satisfactory victory, and Ulyss was pleased by it, but he knew that it did not insure the final result. Pemberton still remained, Vicksburg would not drop into his hands without a hard and precarious struggle, and he received news from the east that made his success even more vital. 'There's been another battle in Virginia,' he told Sherman, 'and Lee won it. At a place called Chancellorsville — where's that?'

'South of the Rapidan, I think. They call that country the Wilderness — hell of a place to fight in.' Sherman looked at Grant's grave face and asked, 'Was it bad?'

'Yes. Hooker had started down for Richmond again, and now Lee's thrown him back across the river with heavy loss.'

'I know what that means,' Sherman groaned. 'We'll have to stick to Washington and say our prayers all summer. What's the matter with them in the east, anyway? Can't any of them beat Lee? He couldn't win more often if he were Napoleon.'

'I saw him a couple of times in Mexico,' said Grant thoughtfully. 'He was a good soldier, but not that good.'

'He beat McClellan, and Pope, and Burnside, and now Hooker.'

'He can be beaten,' Grant said abruptly.

'Maybe so,' Sherman answered. 'He'd better be.' Neither of them spoke of the effect of that disaster a thousand miles away on their own campaign. Both knew that it would make a failure here an utter catastrophe to Union morale, but it was pointless to discuss it. They were committed, and must hazard their fortune however much the stakes had been increased.

Fast, and faster. Pemberton, at last convinced that he was shadow-boxing, turned to face the audacious Yankee. It was too late now to join Johnston, but he took up a position that barred all three roads to Vicksburg, prepared to dispose finally of the suicidal force that had stolen success from the very lap of discretion. Grant drove him back, but there was little savor in that, for he had wanted to defeat him, so completely that he would surrender on the spot. Now he had fallen back to the Big Black River, the last line of defense before the actual entrenchments at Vicksburg, and must be fought again.

That night Ulyss bivouacked on the porch of a house that was filled with wounded Confederates. He kept his eyes closed, but he could not help hearing, and he saw as clearly as though he had risen to gaze through the window. These were rebels, that he had spent his day striving to bring to this condition. He was filled with angry sickness at the trick reality played. It was not fair that units in a gray line should be transformed at nightfall into men who suffered, who lay moaning, softly, helplessly, as sick children moan; or screamed with the shamed agony of those who can endure no more. This was not what he wanted. It was his endeavor to defeat an army, not to torment young men, yet the greater his success the deeper the suffering that produced it. He lay listening, wondering vaguely about the lives of the men beyond the wall: where they had come from, what their families were like, what they thought about the war; wondering briefly about himself, and whether power always has an alloy of guilt. He was glad when the light of dawn put an end to the profitless speculations that prey on a man lying alone in the dark, and set him free to go about his work. One month ago that day Porter had run the batteries.

As soon as it was light enough to see the Union army set out. The Confederates stood waiting behind a parapet, watching the blue men filter into sight through the bushes, pause, and take up new positions to give battle. There was some noise, but the early morning seemed very quiet, for the ears anticipated the crashing that was to come.

Someone touched Grant on the shoulder and said, 'Dispatch from General Halleck, sir. Forwarded from General Banks in New Orleans.'

Ulyss read it rapidly, more than half his attention on the battle that had almost begun. He knew what the orders were anyway, had known what they would be when he had respectfully informed the General in Chief of his intentions. He was to return at once to Grand Gulf, co-operate with Banks to reduce Port Hudson, and then march together on Vicksburg.

'Unfortunately I can't obey these orders,' Ulyss said with complacent regret. 'It's too late to withdraw now. General Halleck would not give them if he knew our present position.'

'They're very definite, sir,' Banks's aide objected. 'They don't give discretion. Port Hudson could be reduced now ——'

'Look,' Ulyss interrupted him. The brigade on the extreme right had raised a cheer and charged, with its commander in the lead, informally comfortable in his shirtsleeves under the warm May sun. It swept forward irresistibly, and Halleck's orders were trampled under its feet. The Confederates broke, but brought up short on the banks of the Big Black, for the bridges were burned. Many of the Confederates, caught between the river and the advancing Union line, surrendered; many swam the barrier; some were drowned.

Young Fred, who had joined shouting in the pursuit, felt the impact of pain in his leg and clutched at his horse's mane in confused shock and horror. Wilson was at his side before he could waver in the saddle, demanding, 'Are you all right?'

'I think my leg's mostly cut off,' said Fred rigidly, striving for the heroism of a soldier but afraid to look down and see the dangling limb.

'Can you wiggle your toes?'

The question seemed to Fred inane to the point of idiocy, but he tried. 'Yes,' he gasped.

'You'll live,' said Wilson with callous cheerfulness. He took the boy to a surgeon and had the graze dressed, then returned him to headquarters. Fred deprecated all inquiries, insisted that he felt no pain and that the injury could scarcely be called a scratch, but when he was entirely alone he said, 'I was wounded at the Battle of Big Black River Bridge,' and felt the bandage with thoughtful pride.

'If it is not too late,' Johnston wrote Pemberton, 'evacuate Vicksburg and its dependencies, and march to the north-east.' He saw that as the situation had developed the city was more a prison than a fortress, but hoped that if Pemberton could make a junction with him they could fall together on the Yankees and drive them out. Pemberton received the dispatch and called a council of war. In the last month he had been defeated over and over again, how much by Grant's perverse luck he could not estimate, how much by his own mismanagement he did not consider. But to admit defeat so openly as to abandon Vicksburg was more than his pride and convictions would allow. The city was the most important point in the Confederacy, he informed his superior. The railroad that helped to make it important was gone; Grand Gulf and Jackson and the line of the Big Black were gone; it would be necessary to give up the Walnut Hills; but he would hold on to Vicksburg. He took his men and sixty days' rations and retired within the entrenchments, trusting to the event.

The Union army threw bridges across the Big Black, the last to be constructed in that amphibious campaign. It would be a siege, thought Ulyss. He had hoped to avoid that, but now that he had no choice his mind fastened on its problems, of how to dispose his men, how to supply them. They had lived for the last month on an issue of rations for five days, and though they had been adequately enough fed they felt the deprivation of such things as coffee and salt and bread. They were not rebels, they complained, to live on hardtack or cornmeal. But he could supply them now, with a line from Memphis down the Mississippi to the Yazoo, and up the Yazoo to the Walnut Hills. It seemed strange to think of the Walnut Hills as a Union supply base rather than as a possible chink in the rebel armor. All his maps were reversed now, with his lines facing triumphantly west to the beleaguered city, instead of staring at it hopelessly from the other side of the river.

Sherman's men, marching from Jackson, reached the Big Black in time to cross it with the others. Grant had assigned to Sherman the extreme right of the besieging line, resting on the Yazoo bluffs, and they made their way there together. There was a great eagerness in both of them — boyish, for a few more hours had no significance in the long months they had waited, but irrepressible. They advanced with the skirmishers, so far ahead that they were under fire for a few moments as the Confederate outposts retired into Vicksburg. Then at last they came to stand on the Walnut Hills.

The ground fell steeply to the Yazoo and the bottomlands, that had been flooded last December when Sherman had stood below, looking up. From their present height they could see far out over the tangle of bayou and morass that had held them off so long, and could turn to see the Vicksburg entrenchments, well planned and formidable but not nearly so dismaying as the impenetrable swamps.

'Sam,' said Sherman suddenly, 'this is one of the greatest campaigns in history. I never really believed it had a chance. But now it doesn't matter whether Vicksburg falls or not — the campaign is perfect. It's a damned beautiful job, Sam, and I'm a fool.'

A Union Mortar

CHAPTER SEVEN

T HE great semicircle of entrenchments around Vicksburg was discouraging to see. Where the eroded hilltops followed a practicable line advantage was taken of it; and where the ridges radiated in the wrong direction the line was run from the head of one gully to the next, with triangular projections where a few men could enfilade any attack up the ravine. Ulyss had thought that after the successive blows he had dealt the Confederates in his progress from Bruinsburg to the Big Black, one final thrust might push them out of Vicksburg itself, and there would be no need to undertake a siege in the southern summer. His troops were scarcely assembled at the city before he ordered an attack all along the line, but he found that the opposing force was transmuted when it stood in the entrenchments prepared with leisurely wisdom weeks before. The men who had shown little resistance in all his encounters with them, who had fallen back with such frequency and speed that he had assumed they were demoralized, stood now immovable, and it was the Union army that fell back in bewildered resentment.

The Northern men were not happy when they stood at last before Vicksburg. True, they had won many victories, but they did not fully realize their importance; the strength of the fortifications in front of them was distressingly apparent; and their troubles affected them far more closely than their strategic triumphs. One evening when Ulyss walked out to inspect part of his line, a low voice remarked, 'Hardtack.' He could see the man who had spoken, a youth who stood quietly in his place looking directly at his general, not with dislike, but with respectful firmness. The comment was repeated, and spread all along the line. 'Hardtack!' the men cried, not leaving their places, but their eyes demanding an answer.

'The supply road will be open tomorrow,' Ulyss said quietly. 'Henceforth you will have regular rations, bread and coffee — and bacon,' he added, knowing the perverse dislike the men had taken to the poultry with which they had been largely fed for the last month. They raised a brief cheer, and he left them. He knew that this was but one, and the most easily redressed, of their grievances. If they must settle down to a siege, they were going to resent bitterly the process of digging themselves holes in the ground, and staying in them while they waited for the rebels to starve into submission. It would be resentment, not rebellion, but Ulyss wished that he could persuade them to accept the necessity willingly. He had not the personal affection of his men, as some generals had. McClernand could persuade his corps to do anything whatever with cheerful affection. The Army of the Potomac had loved McClellan whether he led them to victory or defeat; and it was said that the Army of Northern Virginia worshiped Lee with downright impious fervor. But Grant's men did as they were told respectfully, proud of themselves and their achievements, objectively proud of their leader, without warmth.

If he ordered another attack and it failed they could see for themselves that there was no choice but to accept the tedious discomfort of a siege. It was impossible to give such an order with the expectation of failure, and Ulyss knew that there was very little chance of anything else, yet there was a slight possibility of success. If he did succeed he would be delighted to have his beliefs disproved; and if he failed he would at least have better morale in his besiegers. He tried to give careful thought to his decision, but when at last he gave his orders it was more from the pressure of miscellaneous circumstances than of considered strategy.

The attack was to be at ten in the morning. It was preceded by the steady fire of howitzers and the thousandfold rattle of sharpshooters, but just before the order to charge was given the firing stopped. The silence was so deep that it thrummed, and men could hear their hearts beating like muffled drums for some ghostly quickstep. Then the blue soldiers surged forward in one long wave, cheering, feeling themselves invincible in their first unopposed steps. But the Confederates stood quietly in their entrenchments until the blue line was in full range, then fired into it with methodical regularity. Men wavered and fell; others went on, still deceived by their first sensation of irresistible success; others continued because, having once started, they were incapable of reasoned decision. The Confederate fire continued in regular volleys, and in a few moments reversed the current. The blue men turned back, again not because each man decided that he must, but because he had no choice, was caught in that tide of battle made up of thousands of drops in themselves inconsequent, but in mass overwhelming.

Some of McClernand's men reached the Confederate parapet and clung there for a time. He informed Grant that he had gained the rebel entrenchments and if re-enforced could break the line.

'I don't see it,' Ulyss said, almost to himself, watching the unshaken gray men holding fast. 'It looks to me like those

that have got that far are caught and can't get back.' He
waited, but McClernand sent him another call for re-enforcements, and he had no choice but to comply. Ulyss sent a
regiment, and told Sherman and McPherson to assault again,
hoping that McClernand might after all be right and one
good blow would turn the day.

The assault was repelled more quickly than the first. Ulyss
watched it thrown back, thinking that each man who fell,
jerking and spinning like some disjointed doll, died to no
purpose, because McClernand believed more in his desires than
in facts, and he himself had not acted on his own better knowledge. He said nothing, but he did not forget. When night
came the men who had reached the parapet could make their
way back, reasonably safe from the sharpshooters, and it was
demonstrated to every man in the army that Vicksburg could
be taken only by siege.

As that eventful month ended the fifteen-mile line was constructed, and the army that had concentrated on speed for so
long settled down to do nothing but hold fast. It was bored,
and very uncomfortable as the remorseless heat of summer
closed in, but it knew that eventually it must win, and it was
willing now to wait. And the men knew that inside the city
their grasp was being felt. As the siege dragged on the opposing pickets became well acquainted, exchanged news, and sometimes sat down together to talk through the long, hot nights.

'You're no good,' a Confederate would remark. 'We got two
hundred thousand percussion caps today, right under your nose.'

'How'd you do that?'

'Never you mind. Yankees ain't the only ones that are
slick.'

'We're slick enough to beat you. Why don't you give up and
have something to eat? I hear tell mule meat's not so tasty.'

'Why don't you make us? Come over and pay us a call, any
time — glad to see you. Hear about Lee goin' north?'

'He won't get very far. You rebs can't fight worth a damn outside your own state.'

'Go on and think so, if it pleasures you. General Lee can get clear up to Canada if he wants.'

'How about Antietam?'

'How about Chancellorsville, and Fredericksburg, and the Seven Days? You can't whip us, there's no sense trying.'

'We are whipping you. You can't get anywhere, with every one of your states able to secede again if it don't like the way things go.'

'That's a constitutional right ——'

'Constitutional my Aunt Betsy. Who ever heard of a country fixing things so it could fall apart?'

'States' rights ——'

'Common sense ——'

'I reckon we'd better stop, or we might fight.' They separated and went back to their posts, but the discussion was always renewed. The men were curious about each other. Many of them had never left their own districts before, and an Illinois farmer who thought in terms of corn found it interesting to hear of raising cotton as a tenant on an Alabama plantation. Such talk had a certain awkwardness, however, and usually shifted quickly to the catchword issues of the war or the embroidered boasting at which both North and South were adept. They found it less disturbing to talk of their political differences than of their personal similarities.

Ulyss had no objection to the odd acquaintances his men were making. He knew that a certain amount of fraternization is inevitable when two armies are held for long in close and more or less quiet contact, and he had some hope of his men's confidence in victory discouraging the rebels with whom they talked. He was always willing to use a psychological weapon.

The most annoying of his problems, now that the supply line was established and the necessities of the situation had been illustrated to the men, was his relations with McClernand, which were becoming increasingly difficult. The volunteer general carried himself with gloomy aloofness at conferences, and apparently resented the least exertion of authority by Grant. The inaction of a siege was not his conception of war, and, said Sherman, he was growing sulkier day by day as Grant grew more secure in victory. Sherman and McPherson not only disliked him but thought he was becoming a positive menace. They would have liked to see him relieved from duty, but Grant was reluctant to take the step. He had no charge to make against him save incompatibility, and removal for such cause would be hard to defend politically, for it was well known that McClernand was a zealous and brilliant fighter. He could do it if he wished: his two best corps commanders urged him to it; Dana, who had come to keep an eye on Grant because of McClernand's accusations, was now indignant about McClernand's conduct; and Grant had received a dispatch from Washington empowering him to remove 'any person who, from ignorance in action or for any cause,' troubled him, and holding him responsible if he failed to use the power. Apparently Halleck's conception of McClernand had prevailed over Lincoln's friendship and Stanton's predilection for volunteers.

Yet Ulyss held his hand. Eventually, he knew, he would probably do it. In his delay there was no forgiveness, and he would have acted at once had there been any likelihood of a battle in which he would need self-forgetful co-operation. But in the static conditions of a siege McClernand could do no harm, and it pleased Ulyss to savor the unaccustomed taste of powerful magnanimity. Wilson, with the hopefulness of well-bred youth, believed that the two might yet be reconciled, and Rawlins, with an eye on the Illinois newspapers that McClernand controlled, was against any hasty action. 'I cannot afford to quarrel with a man whom I am obliged to command,' Grant blandly answered the impatience of Sherman and McPherson.

There was a rigid etiquette surrounding McClernand at Grant's headquarters, carefully including him in all conferences, and wording every communication to him with the utmost diplomacy. It left him fuming helplessly on one side of the barrier, while Grant took his confident time on the other.

Johnston was still hovering in thwarted hunger in the interior of the state. Halleck had promptly sent re-enforcements to guard against him and to help hold the long line of siege, and if Johnston were to raise a comparable force he must draw men from the operations around Chattanooga. But Ulyss feared that perhaps for Vicksburg's sake even the Confederate successes in Tennessee would be jeopardized, and he kept a nervous watch on the crossings of the Big Black. One of them, at Hall's Ferry, was under McClernand's command, and Ulyss sent him word to strengthen it. It was a trivial order, but as usual Ulyss had it phrased with care, and sent it by Wilson. McClernand had been known to pause and talk with Wilson, as though the friendship of their families had some weight against the young man's position on Grant's staff and graduation from West Point. The volunteer general had just mounted his horse when Wilson arrived, and he turned gracefully to hear him. He was a handsome man, no less so with his eyes dark and lips tightened in expectation.

'General Grant's compliments, sir,' said Wilson. 'He thinks the outpost at Hall's Ferry might properly be strengthened now that Johnston is coming up, and suggests that you send a detachment ——'

'I'll be goddamned if I will!' McClernand shouted in sudden fury. Wilson blinked and drew back automatically, at first filled with simple amazement. McClernand's face was fiery, and his hands trembled on the reins. He had scarcely heard Wilson's words, only enough to add the last bitter drop to his resentment of his subordinate position, and to release a flood fed by the chill underground stream of his knowledge that even as a subordinate his tenure was precarious. 'I'm tired of being dictated to!' he choked. 'I'm supposed to be in command of this division, but I've no more authority over it than Jeff Davis has. I won't stand it any longer! You go back and tell General Grant that he and the sniveling bastards on his staff can go straight to hell and rot there. By God, if any more of your damned outfit comes around here to give me orders I'll send him back in a basket!' He did not stop, he could not, but in his rage he was soon incapable of constructing sentences, and took refuge in involved and increasingly comprehensive oaths.

As he listened Wilson's fingertips grew cold, and his breath came short and fast. He had heard McClernand abuse Grant before, but seldom with such passion, and never with such sulphurous attention to his staff. The young man had sincerely hoped for peace between the two commanders, and had blinded himself to the obvious indications that it was impossible, but he had youth's touchy sense of personal honor, and now as McClernand swore directly at him he forgot all the extenuations he had tried so hard to remember. The first time the volunteer general paused for breath Wilson said, 'General Grant wants the outpost at Hall's Ferry strengthened.' Then, with his duty officially discharged, he hurried on: 'General McClernand, I can accept a lot of things for the good of the service, but I don't have to let myself be sworn at, not by a major general or anybody else. If you say another word of that kind I'll — I'll pull you off your horse and beat the boots off you.'

McClernand had not realized how inclusive his fury had been, and now as he looked at Wilson's white, rigid face he was repentant. Not for what he had said of Grant, that was but an inarticulate fraction of what he felt, but he had not meant to offend personally this young man whom he liked, the son of a friend. There was a pause while he readjusted himself and Wilson sat waiting, tensed to carry out his threat.

'I beg your pardon, sir,' said McClernand frankly. 'I'm your

friend — I hope you're mine. I didn't mean to swear at you.
I was simply expressing my intense vehemence on the subject
matter, sir.' Wilson did not smile nor relax, but McClernand
put out his hand. 'Please accept my apologies — come and
have a drink on it.'

'I don't drink, sir,' said Wilson coldly. He bowed and rode
off on his way back to Grant's headquarters, so stiff in the saddle
that he seemed several inches taller. McClernand's rejected
hand dropped limply to his side. He was flushed again, for he
too had his pride, but there was more than anger in his heart as
he watched Wilson ride away. He did not understand what had
happened to him, how it was that the war in which he had meant
to take so great a part had been transformed from the gold
of an opportunity for glorious deeds into the dead leaves of
bickering and personal frustration.

In the first days of the conflict he had been admired as a
Democrat who put the integrity of the nation above his party
prejudices; as a man unwilling to talk while others bled, who
had taken the field himself to bear witness to his sincerity in
battle. He had meant to anneal the love and respect given him
into lasting fame. Now his men still loved him, but he seemed
to have no longer the trusting friendship of the President; he
had lost his place in the eyes of the people; his once brilliant
future depended now on the decisions of a shabby little man
with a pedestrian mind. Wilson, a young man such as those
who had once given McClernand their wholehearted devotion,
cleaved now to the upstart general. McClernand swore again
as he thought of it, but he could not smother with rage the
puzzled pain that gnawed at him.

Grant looked up when Wilson came back to report to him,
surprised to see the young man's nostrils drawn thin in anger,
for Wilson was ordinarily of an even and mild disposition. The
aide repeated the scene as exactly as he could, then waited for
Grant's wrath to fall at last on McClernand's head. He could

see the bearded lips twitch, and expected a brief, forthright decision, but Grant began to laugh. He rarely laughed at anything, but now he choked with mirth, increased when he looked at the respectful bewilderment in Wilson's face. Such an unusual sound attracted Rawlins, and when he came in Grant sobered and said gravely, 'Tell him, Wilson. Tell him — like you told me.'

The adjutant found nothing humorous in the story. His anger was as swift and thorough as had been Grant's merriment, and he turned indignantly to his chief, whose eyes still twinkled.

'What action are you going to take?' he demanded.

'None, right now.'

'Goddamn it, you can't do nothing about it! He ought to be court-martialed — he ought to be shot. If you let it go discipline will be shot to hell ——'

'You observe,' Grant said to Wilson, 'he isn't cursing. He's just expressing his intense vehemence on the subject.' He laughed again, with happy abandon. He knew exactly what McClernand thought of him, and was not greatly concerned about what he said in a private conversation, but he bore him a gleeful gratitude for having given him so neat a weapon. Wilson's lips curved; he gave a glance of compunction to his friend, then laughed with his chief. Rawlins hesitated longer, then smiled briefly. He was not a lighthearted man.

There were visitors to camp. There were always visitors whenever the army camped in one place long enough to be found. Politicians, soldiers' relatives, newspaper correspondents, traders, members of the Sanitary Commission, ladies of forbidding aspect on vague but pious missions, other ladies not so forbidding. Most of them were filled with energetic patriotism, and some were important enough to demand personal attention from the commanders. Governor Yates of Illinois came down, and fastened on Ulyss, crying that he would have a place in history because he had signed Grant's original commission.

'I knew we could expect great things of you,' he asserted, 'but, General, you have exceeded even my expectations.' He was an awkward guest, for his praise was too high for quiet acceptance and too vehement to allow deprecation, and Grant took refuge in showing him over the Union line. Perhaps if he walked more he could talk less. They went out to Sherman's sector, for that ground was so broken and shielded by undergrowth that there was least danger to the casual visitor, and Sherman was happy enough to do the honors. Grant drew aside, smiling a little as he listened to Yates's questions and Sherman's answers, full of detail that the Governor did not understand but was flattered to be given.

Then Sherman's unconsciously penetrating voice was saying, ' ... his idea alone. I opposed it — I thought it was suicidal. I wrote him a letter about it, with every objection I could think of, and he's never mentioned it nor told me what a fool I was to write it. The credit's all his, and anybody else who tries to take some of it is a damned liar.'

The thing was so unexpected that Ulyss was glad he stood where no one watched him. He had been satisfied with Sherman's praise when they stood together on the Walnut Hills, and it had not occurred to him that the matter would ever come up again. The letter, written to Rawlins, was not an official document, and when Ulyss had found it on going through his pockets he had destroyed it. There had been no necessity for anyone but Sherman, Rawlins, and Grant ever to know that it had been written. Now Yates knew, and eventually anyone who had any interest in the affair would know. Sherman had cheerfully and of his own will sacrificed some part of his reputation to his friend. Ulyss was moved, and he waited some time before he could join the others with his customary quiet bearing.

The days slipped by in hot and dreary procession. Ulyss sent Fred north, afraid that he might catch the swamp fever, although the boy insisted that he could bear the discomfort as well as his friends in the trenches. There was an absurd loneliness at headquarters when the boy had gone, for Ulyss had not realized how pleasant it had been to have him chattering and asking too many questions and getting involved in difficulties all over the terrain. Perhaps Rawlins was right, and women and children had no place on a battlefield, but Grant felt that he could wait with more patience if Julia and his children were with him. He knew what the end of the siege must be, but it was hard to sit idle until it came, wondering how long it would take, wondering if after all it would be of much significance. Lee was marching north, all the way up to Pennsylvania, people said. If he were not stopped ——

As Grant sat working on his report one evening Sherman and McPherson came to call on him. There was some formality in their bearing, and Rawlins, who came in behind them, looked even graver than usual. His eyes were angry, but showed also a certain satisfaction. 'What's the trouble?' Grant demanded.

'I want you to see something,' said Sherman. Ordinarily he spoke his mind at length and expressively, and his sparing words now seemed doubly portentous.

He handed Grant a St. Louis newspaper, some days old, for it was still giving follow-up accounts of the investment of Vicksburg. Ulyss had no difficulty in finding the article that so disturbed his officers. There was a heading, 'Address to the 13th Army Corps' — McClernand's division. Ulyss read it, and raised his brows. The Thirteenth, he learned, was an army of berserk warriors who equaled, if not eclipsed, the heroes of old; and their leader, who loved them as their father, was staunch to defend their fame. This was not in itself new, for McClernand's men were frequently thus assured. Ulyss continued. The Thirteenth, in its assault the day before — that would be the day of the first attacks, when Ulyss had learned they were useless — had gained the rebel defenses with a valor to be envied by the centurions of Rome, and had it received adequate support could have conquered Vicksburg and dealt a mortal blow to the Devil-begot rebellion. Support had been denied by a leader of more craft than imagination, and by brother officers who put personal jealousy above the interests of their tortured country. But the Thirteenth, undaunted, would come eventually to glorious triumph over not only its enemies but its self-seeking friends.

Ulyss grunted. Sherman said, 'Did he show that to you before he sent it north to be published?'

'No.'

'There's a rule, isn't there,' said McPherson, 'that any publication must have your approval?'

'Yes, there is,' Rawlins answered him. 'McClernand knows it, too.'

Ulyss dropped the paper on his littered table, and lighted a cigar. 'I'm going to relieve him,' he said calmly through the smoke. 'At once.'

'That's not enough,' Rawlins said over the instant agreement of the other two. 'Goddamn it, you could arrest him for less——'

'I quite understand your vehemence on the subject,' Grant said slyly. Rawlins flushed, but his eyes, black with outrage, did not waver. 'But I'm just going to relieve him — that's enough, I think.'

The constraint went out of the meeting as sentence was thus passed, and McClernand, past and present, was reviewed and wholeheartedly condemned. Grant listened, and joined in occasionally, but he did not give full expression to his grievances, remembering that he was judge. There was an enormous relief in him to know that he could at last put an end to the long half-covert, half-publicized antipathy. The end of that tangled thread lay in the newspaper on his table, but it coiled all through the Vicksburg campaign, stretched backward to

the precarious weeks after Shiloh, through Fort Donelson and
Belmont, to its beginnings on the day Grant had taken command of the 21st Illinois. Ulyss recalled that day very clearly,
and how he had stood before his men dwarfed by the fame and
assurance of his companions. Now Logan was with him, a subordinate general who did good work but had little contact with
his commander; and McClernand was being stripped of his
place by Grant's decision, not to be questioned nor resisted.

Wilson came back from a night tour of inspection while
McClernand's downfall was still being discussed. 'I think the
rebs will make a sortie on the left in the morning,' he said
cheerfully. 'Our line is crowding them there some, and they
don't seem to like it.' Ulyss nodded, but the others had not
readjusted themselves in time to make a comment, and Wilson
sensed their preoccupation.

'What's the matter?' he asked. 'Is there any news?'

'McClernand's slit his damned throat at last,' said Rawlins
with satisfaction, 'and he won't have any more wind to crow
with.' He showed the aide the incriminating paper, and told
him of the action that was to be taken. Wilson read rapidly,
the lines of his young face growing hard and almost pinched.

When he finished he looked up at the group around him. 'Is
the order written?' he asked.

'Yes,' Rawlins answered. 'It's all ready to be delivered first
thing in the morning.'

'That might be too late,' said Wilson. He spoke jerkily because his lips were drawn so tight. 'If the rebs do make a sortie
in the morning it will be on McClernand's line. You know what
will happen then — he'll throw them back, and be a tin-pot
god again with all the papers falling down to worship, and his
men cheering him every time he puts his nose outdoors.' Wilson's voice was high and thin with vehemence. 'Let me take
him the order, now, before anything happens.'

'But it's almost midnight.'

'No matter — let me go.'

Grant started to make a gesture, but stopped midway. He was not sure that Wilson's proposal was fair — but did the ceremony surrounding the order make so much difference? He said nothing, and without his protest Rawlins told the young aide to go ahead.

The road down to McClernand's headquarters was suffused with summer starlight, and Wilson could ride at a swift pace. There was little sound save the hoofbeats of his horse and the regular boom as Porter's gunboats on the river dropped a shell into Vicksburg. The young man thought of little as he rode. In the few days since their last encounter he had forgotten all that he had once striven so hard to remember about McClernand, all the ties of family friendship, political sympathy, state origin; and in his mind the volunteer general no longer stood for a person with ordinary virtues and human faults, but was a caricature, a figure painted in broad, unshaded colors by anger and prejudice and impatient circumstance. Wilson was pleased to see that there was still a light in McClernand's tent when he arrived, but he would have roused the general from bed if it had been necessary.

McClernand was writing at his table, and looked up when he heard Wilson's voice respond to the sentry's challenge, but he said nothing as the young man entered. One refused overture was enough for him.

'General Grant's compliments, sir,' said Wilson, and handed him a folded paper.

The brief lines were quickly read. General John A. McClernand was hereby relieved from command for publication of an order without first clearing it through army headquarters, and was directed to go to Illinois and wait there for further instructions.

McClernand looked up at Wilson, who had tried so long to reconcile him to the pettifogging Grant. 'You know this order relieves me?' he asked.

'Sir, it relieves all of us,' said Wilson as he saluted and withdrew.

McClernand did not trouble to resent the youthful impertinence. His mind was suddenly vibrant with plans: There was a man who dined with the President, and knew how to put in a word where it would be remembered. And another man, whom McClernand had known in Washington and who was under obligation to him. There were dozens of men, hundreds of men, each one a sensitive place that would respond to pressure applied in just the right way. This one would see the point most quickly if it were thrust at him — 'It's a regular conspiracy, they've been working for months to get me out of the way.' That one would need a more gentle introduction — 'I don't care at all for myself. One man is of no importance when we're fighting for our noble cause, but if it's one man who commands seventy thousand others, his conduct should be above question. Now, I happen to know ——' It would be easy, so easy. There was something close to intoxication in McClernand as he thought of how easy it would be, and he joyed in it, striding up and down his tent with his head thrown back and his eyes alight. If he stood still, if he stopped even long enough to curse Grant, he would realize that the threads of influence were no longer his to weave, that he had come to the inglorious closing of both his careers, and he knew it.

'Give us a plug, Johnny?'

'Mm. Got any bread?'

'Sure. We got lots of it.'

'Fair exchange.' The two men stuffed their mouths and leaned in hot indolence on their rifles. The Confederate had a strange look of age in youth, for scurvy had rotted his gums and thinned his hair, and there was foul decay in his breath. 'God, I wish I was out of this,' he muttered, searching anxiously to see if any crumbs had fallen on his unbuttoned coat.

'Come on over. It's just a step — there's nobody around.'

'I'm no deserter,' the man snapped, but was too hot to take serious offense. 'I reckon Vicksburg's yours, though. There's talk of gettin' us out in boats. I like boats,' he said reflectively. 'To home, I got one. Go fishin' in it — smooth an' easy an' quiet on the bayou. Most always cool there, and lots of shadders.'

'You'll be goin' north in boats.'

'Maybe . . . might as well be in prison one place as another. God, I wish I was out of it . . .'

Up from the picket lines, out of the spies' reports, came information of the desperate pass in Vicksburg. Johnston was very close to the Union force now, almost laying siege to the besiegers, but he could not attack because the Union defensive positions would hold him to a stalemate, and thus he could give no real assistance to Pemberton. His presence was an annoyance that Grant was content to endure until Vicksburg fell. It must fall soon. It had been defended heroically, but now there was no more food, and no more strength, and no more hope. There was not even a possibility of escape, for Porter was keeping close watch on the river. Grant made preparations for assault, knowing that the starved defenders could not resist it, hoping that they knew it too and would not try.

They did know it. In the morning of the third of July a white flag appeared over the parapet, and two officers advanced under it toward Grant's headquarters. The sputtering fire along the line was silenced, and men stood in the quiet and whispered to each other. It was a rather pathetic letter that the truce party presented, showing an old man's stiffnecked pride and blind faith in his preconceptions, but Ulyss did not see that. He was merely impatient with its ritual nonsense of proposing commissioners, and he saw nothing but mendacious bravado in the lines, 'I make this proposition to save the further effusion of blood, which must otherwise be shed to a frightful extent, feeling myself fully able to maintain my position for a yet indefinite period.'

'If General Pemberton wishes it,' said Ulyss, 'I'll meet him in front of McPherson's corps at three this afternoon. There's no use bothering with commissioners. I haven't any terms but unconditional surrender.'

General Pemberton did not wish it, but he had no choice. The misery of his men had become an almost tangible weight, pressing him forward on a road he had no desire to take, but must trudge step by step because he had not seen in time the crossroads and forks that would have taken him to happier goals. He came to meet Grant and sat down with him under a shapeless oak tree, puzzled and resentful that now in his old age he must go through the elaborate humiliation of surrender to a man whom he had first known as an insignificant quartermaster in Mexico. He was greeted pleasantly enough, but his pride choked him nevertheless.

'What terms will you give,' he asked stiffly, 'if I surrender my army to you?'

'I told you — unconditional surrender,' Ulyss said quietly. 'You can be assured that we admire men as brave and patient as yours. They'll have from us all the respect due to prisoners of war. But — I have no other terms.'

'The conference might as well end, then,' said Pemberton, following his desire of the moment, and denying his certain knowledge that in the end he must swallow the terms Grant offered and his pride with them.

'Very well,' said Ulyss.

'General Grant,' interposed one of the attendant Confederate officers. 'Perhaps we can reach a solution — will you allow me to talk it over with one of your officers?'

'Go ahead,' Grant answered easily. He waited with Pemberton while the two subordinates consulted. He knew the game was his, and he had enough patience to allow a certain amount of squirming by his opponents. Pemberton sat in almost complete silence, pulling up blades of grass, realizing that he had been delicately superseded and resenting it, yet not unwilling that someone else should do for him what must be done. The Confederate officer returned to them suggesting that the defenders of Vicksburg should be allowed to march out of the city with the honors of war.

'Impossible,' said Grant, standing up with a gesture of finality. It could be genuine if he chose: he could attack or prolong the truce, treat or demand, as he would.

The little group of men in gray, knowing how wholly the matter depended on his will, looked at him anxiously. One of them asked, 'Will you write us your final terms, sir?'

'My terms are ——' Unconditional surrender, he had said. It would be simplest to cling to that and not trouble to consider it further, but perhaps there was an alternative. Not the unconditional release involved in that odd phrase, 'the honors of war' — that was impossible. But there might be a compromise that would at once sweeten the inevitable for the Confederates and relieve the Federals of a few troublesome problems, without actually affecting the result. 'Yes, I'll send them to you by ten tonight,' said Ulyss. Thoughtfully, he went back to his headquarters and summoned to him the corps and division commanders who were within reach. Almost half of them, including Sherman, were some ten miles away, confronting Johnston.

'Gentlemen,' said Ulyss, 'I want your suggestions as to the surrender of Vicksburg. The decision is mine, but I want to hear what you think.' He outlined the letters that had been exchanged, and that afternoon's interview, and concluded, 'What have you to say?'

They had much to say, but most of it could be expressed by unconditional surrender. They liked the phrase, feeling that the two words summed up their power, and put the proper crown on their long campaign.

'But,' said Grant, 'have you thought that if we insist on that we'll have to send thirty thousand men north to Cairo? We've got better uses for our transports than hauling rebels.'

'You can't turn 'em loose,' someone objected hotly.

'I can parole them till properly exchanged, and there's a commissioner in Vicksburg to do the exchanging. If we send them north they'll simply have to be taken east and exchanged at Aiken's in Virginia. Why spend all that money when we can do the same thing here?'

'But here they'll go straight back into the army.'

'I don't think so,' said Ulyss stubbornly. 'I think they're sick of it, and won't have any more. Lots of them live around here, and when they go home sick and discouraged they'll spread the feeling.' Ulyss always believed firmly that Confederate morale was precarious. Almost all his officers disagreed with him, but, as he had warned them, the decision was his. He wrote Pemberton proposing to parole all thirty thousand men. The old man boggled at a few last details, and then, late at night, agreed.

The white flags drooped along the parapets in the hot morning sunlight. As the Union men filed past the Confederates they looked at each other with sudden shyness: looked, and glanced hastily away, and looked again. The Federals marched in to the central square of the city, exchanged the banner on the flagstaff, then stood together, thousands of men in blue, to sing 'Old Hundred.' Ulyss stood looking about him, with a greater sense of strangeness than he had ever felt on simply entering a place that he had never seen before. This was Vicksburg, that Vicksburg which had been the centre of his thinking and planning and dreaming for almost a year. And it was just a town, a little southern town on the river, with houses for people to live in, and streets for them to walk on, and churches where they married and buried each other and met with decorum on Sunday mornings. Vicksburg.

On that Fourth of July the Pennsylvania hills around Gettysburg rang with the monstrous salute of cannon, and Lee met tragedy at last. But at Vicksburg the day was celebrated by silence, a deep, spent stillness to mark the end of a storm; the deeper for its unsounded indications of the storm that was to come.

PART THREE

The Gunboat Arkansas

The Battle of Lookout Mountain

III. 'THE COUNTRY TRUSTS YOU'

CHAPTER EIGHT

MY DEAR GENERAL: I do not remember that you and I ever met personally. I write this now as a grateful acknowledgment for the almost inestimable service you have done the country. . . . I thought you should go down the river and join General Banks, and when you turned northward, east of the Big Black, I feared it was a mistake. I now wish to make the personal acknowledgment that you were right and I was wrong.' The signature, 'A. Lincoln,' was curiously detailed, in an almost feminine script. Ulyss read the letter many times, more pleased by it than he himself knew. It was good to be told how important the fall of Vicksburg was, for in the reaction after long effort he sometimes felt that the victory was paltry when measured by the operations he wanted to undertake next, and was forbidden to try.

Again it was Mobile that filled his thoughts, and such a movement seemed now doubly important, for the Confederate General Bragg was making a serious threat in Tennessee. If Mobile fell the Union forces would be in Bragg's rear and make his position untenable, and even if the city could not be taken the campaign itself would wreck the rich supply regions of the deep South, on which both Bragg and Lee were drawing. But Halleck said no. 'He seems to find it easier to say no than yes,' Grant snorted. 'Maybe there's something wrong with his throat.' He fumed in disappointment, but there was nothing he could do either to overcome the obstinate caution of the General in Chief or to prevent the official orders that let his army dribble through his fingers. A division to Missouri, a brigade to Natchez, a corps to New Orleans. Every summer, thought Ulyss, his army melted, his organized, veteran force was spread thin over half a dozen states; and every autumn and winter must be spent in collecting and shaping it again.

Vicksburg was quickly brought to life. The citizens came out of the caves in the hills where they had lived during the bombardment, and set about repairing their houses. The merchants made the most of the blue-uniformed market that had been thrust upon them. The paroled prisoners were marched away, with the Union army drawn up in a double line to see them go. There was no cheering. The blue men looked at the long gray ranks a little sadly, for they understood, being so much alike, how it would be to lose. Sherman disposed of Johnston's threat, and then for a while the war seemed reduced to lounging about the hot Vicksburg streets, or hunting guerrillas who never allowed themselves to be found.

'As a Yankee, Miss Hurlbut, it must have been painful for you. Did you get full rations, such as they were?'

'My hosts are my friends,' the girl answered Grant's aide nervously. 'I think you should remember that they are now your hosts. I shouldn't like to see the hospitality of the South put the courtesy of the North to shame, Lieutenant Lagow.'

'Well said!' another aide applauded. 'Lagow, you're ambushed.'

'It's a pleasure,' the Lieutenant said indolently. 'So lovely a copperhead can even besiege me, if she likes.'

'I — I'm not — you're ——' The girl turned aside, too proud to withdraw under fire, too disturbed and angry to make an adequate defense.

Rawlins had been watching the group on the piazza from the doorway and now came forward. 'Lagow,' he said crisply, 'I believe you have something better to do than tormenting ladies.'

'Yes, sir.' Lagow saluted, and began defensively, 'I didn't mean ——'

'I know. You never mean, but you always do.'

The Lieutenant saluted again, his lips rigid, bowed to Miss Hurlbut and withdrew. The girl swept him an elaborate curtsy, with her eyes lowered not so much for modesty as to hide the tears in them, then turned to the rail and looked out over the river in its haze of heat. The other aide had effaced himself on Rawlins's arrival.

'I beg your pardon, ma'am,' said Rawlins, 'for him, and for the staff. He's a light-minded cub.'

'I had thought,' she said, still with her back turned to him, 'that I would receive from my countrymen the same consideration that I had from Confederate officers. They never forgot that I was a stranger here, nor that I was a lady.'

'No apology can excuse him, ma'am,' said Rawlins. 'I can but assure you that I'll see to it myself that he doesn't annoy you again.' She curtsied to him silently, and moved off down the porch, her figure erect and somehow touching in her swaying skirts. Rawlins looked after her thoughtfully. He knew little about her, save that she was a New Englander, and had come down to this house in Vicksburg before the war. What she was to the planter family with whom she lived was not clear. Some sort of governess, probably, since her stay had exceeded even the expansive southern notions of entertaining, but obviously a friend too. When Grant had moved his headquarters to the large, airy house she had been introduced simply as 'Miss Hurlbut,' with the implication that her footing was the same as the others'. The planter treated the war as a remote annoyance not to be mentioned at a gentleman's table. His wife was supposed to be a Unionist, but she never mentioned the subject, and Rawlins had decided that they were both sunk so far in tradition and the pattern of a genteel life that they were incapable of genuine emotion even on the wrong side of the question, and he had at first lumped Miss Hurlbut with them.

But there was a difference. She spoke in a decisive New England tone that was not like the southern vagueness, nor yet like Rawlins's midwestern twang. Her eyes had a shrewdness that had nothing in common with the feminine calculation of Vicksburg's young ladies, and her face an unaltered gravity when theirs shifted from soft grief to careless gaiety with the unpredictable rapidity of their own southern skies. Most of all her difference appeared when she talked with the young men of Grant's staff. Where a southern girl would have laughed, she frowned in earnest thought; where a southern girl would have made a teasing attack, using sober words as social bagatelles, she spoke of concepts in serious analysis, and when she was teased about them was angry and bewildered. Rawlins was not sure how far her convictions varied from those of her friends, but he was certain that her way of thinking was alien. She was no girl to cope with the gallantries of young men taking their leisure after a long campaign. Rawlins swore thoughtfully as he watched her go, and went in search of Grant.

Ulyss was in his room, smoking a cigar and watching the small, peaceable traffic on the river at the foot of the bluff. 'Well, Rawlins?' he said as he heard the other enter.

'I want to say something.'

'Mm?' Grant turned to face him.

'Now that I'm chief of staff there are some things that are my responsibility that used to be only my annoyances. There are some members of the staff who seem to be unable to see their duty as soldiers.'

'Who is it now?' Grant asked somewhat defensively.

'Lagow,' Rawlins answered grimly.

'What's the matter with him? Doesn't he get the returns in on time?'

'He does the office work well enough, but — he hasn't enough weight to be a member of your staff, now. Goddamn it, he acts like the war was a kind of picnic — I found him this morning annoying Miss Hurlbut.'

'How do you mean — annoying?' Grant frowned.

'Teasing her — twisting her words — he had her almost crying.'

'Can't she look after herself?' Grant's instinctive anger was stilled, but he was increasingly puzzled. 'I haven't noticed that the rebel young ladies need much protection from our officers.'

'Damn it, she's not a rebel!' Rawlins shouted. 'She comes from Connecticut — she's serious-minded — she ought not be forced to have young pups forever yapping at her heels ——'

Grant dared not let his amazement appear fully in his face.

He knew that Rawlins was easily stirred to passionate objection, but the man had never before taken on himself the obligations of chivalry. Even if he had been by nature gallant he had always had too deep a sense of his superior's importance to bring such matters to him. But here it was, and Rawlins's eyes blazed as if he were demanding a court-martial.

'Well,' said Grant helplessly, 'tell him to leave her alone. Do what you like about it — I'm going to New Orleans.'

'New Orleans?' Rawlins's suspicions stirred even in his preoccupation. 'I thought General Halleck refused permission ——'

'He told me to confer with Banks,' said Ulyss woodenly, not meeting the other's eyes. 'That means I go to New Orleans.' Rawlins let his silence shout his objections, and Ulyss chose to ignore them. He had a right to relax for a while, to forget for a few days the everlasting pressure of men and measures, to appear in that city where his name had grown enormous. Rawlins had no right to assume that such a pause would amount to an orgy. 'I'm going down,' he said flatly. 'You and Sherman can look after things here. Sherman can draft the orders — and you can protect Miss Hurlbut.'

A long whistle from the river interrupted Rawlins's retort. Both men turned automatically to look out, although the sound was common enough. What they saw was ordinary too, yet their breath caught, and it was as if a long sigh rose up from the city. There was a steamboat in the channel, a commonplace packet moving down the river as thousands like her had done. Yet she was the first, the first since war had choked the river traffic. She was the concrete symbol of what had been achieved, and as the swishing beat of her paddlewheel echoed against the bluffs it seemed to evoke other echoes, of the guns that had made her passage possible. Rawlins and Grant watched her southward out of sight, in silence.

The next day Grant left for New Orleans, and Rawlins became regent in all but formal title. There was little to do, for there was almost no action after the fall of Vicksburg, but Rawlins took his responsibilities gravely, and did not hesitate to make use of his authority. One evening soon after Grant's departure the chief of staff intercepted Lagow and demanded to know where he was going. Rawlins had seen Miss Hurlbut withdraw to the slight coolness of the porch, and intended to make sure that she be undisturbed.

'I'm off duty,' the young man snapped. 'I don't think I'm accountable to you for my free time.'

'I'm chief of staff,' said Rawlins evenly, 'and in authority here in General Grant's absence. I have a right to an answer to whatever question I please to put to you.'

'I don't admit that,' said Lagow. He spoke as if he were reading the words, or repeating them from memory. 'I have the honor to offer you my resignation, sir.'

'You're quite right,' said Rawlins promptly. 'I have long known that you were not well suited as a soldier, that you misunderstand the requirements of military ——'

'I certainly do. I had assumed that an army was an organization for fighting, not an ingenious form of slavery for white men.' Lagow withdrew in dignity, and Rawlins smiled slightly as he watched. The opportunity had come, as he had known it must, and he was too well pleased to be troubled by its paltriness. A frivolous young man may have been good enough on the staff of an inconspicuous brigadier, but he would not do as an aide to a man who had grown great in the land, and was marked to grow greater still. From the first Rawlins had set himself against Lagow and the others of his stamp, with apparently unjustified vehemence, because from the first he had glimpsed the possible destiny of his stolid chief, and had felt himself drafted in its service.

He stood now in the wide, empty hall, thinking of that destiny, of the tangled and perilous road by which it had come and of the ambushes that still lay ahead. There was so little of the drive to greatness in the man whom greatness had chosen. He had no presence: strangers were likely to think first of how they might use him, not of how they could serve him. What ambition he had seemed fulfilled by the praise of his friends, and the calibre of the friends seemed of no consequence to him. He had no genius, only a peasant common sense singularly undisturbed by the subtleties of learning or imagination. Yet circumstance itself fought for him. The distrust of wiser men, the intrigues of more ambitious men, the follies of his own shortcomings, could hamper him, occasionally seem to defeat him, but they always fell away and advanced him one step farther. Rawlins wondered why, but even he could not isolate the effective factors in the vast welter of chance, hidden qualities of character, necessities of the time, and nameless compulsions that shape a man's life. He but knew that Grant was marked for the future by a fortune with a taste for paradox, and that such men as Lagow must be cleared from his path.

It would be much easier, thought Rawlins, to make a career for himself than to watch over Grant's. He had in himself the wisdom, the knowledge of manipulation — and, God knew, the ambition — that Grant must draw from other men; but he was not chosen. It was his part to stand here and survey the pattern, fitting the daily details against the years-long motif, while Grant took his pleasant ease in New Orleans like an ordinary man, receiving praise and flattery with apparent indifference, but delighted by them as is a child by an unexpected indulgence. Great man. Rawlins was suddenly weary, drowned in abrupt fatigue, a mood that came upon him as swiftly as his phases of invincible exaltation. He walked out to the porch, thinking that the breeze from the river might clear his mind, and in any case too tired to climb the stairs to bed.

He had forgotten that Miss Hurlbut was already there. He would have excused himself when he saw her, but she said frankly, 'Don't go. You must be very tired — do sit down, sir.' His hesitation could not stand against her pleasant reception and his great weariness, and he dropped into the chair she indicated.

'I am tired, ma'am,' he admitted, 'but I did not intend to disturb you.'

'You don't, I assure you. I was but taking the air — the heat has been very troublesome today.'

'Very.' He paused, and there was nothing in her silence to demand that he continue. She was there, a misty, white figure in the darkness, but her presence was rather a soothing companionship than a compulsion to talk. When he spoke again it was because he wished to, because his obscure curiosity about her rose above his lassitude. 'Do you miss your home, ma'am, these hot days?'

'Yes,' she answered simply, 'but no more than I do at other times. In February, for instance — it never seems right for spring to come then. February has always seemed to me almost another word for snow and cold. But it is beautiful here' — she made a gesture of deprecation — 'and they have been very kind to me.' Her last words were not so much relevant to what she had been saying as to the unspoken meaning of his question.

He said nothing, and in a moment she asked directly, 'You feel very strongly about the war, don't you, sir?'

'I do.' His tone was impolitely emphatic, and he added, 'But if you would rather not discuss it ——'

'I don't want to argue about it, but I should like to discuss it. It has been most difficult for me to decide what I feel. I have seen so much kindness and fine feeling ——'

'Goddamn it — I beg your pardon, ma'am' — to her start of amazement — 'but G — but kindness and fine feeling can't disguise error nor excuse a crime.'

'Crime?' He could not tell if the slight edge in her voice were a result of his outrageous breach of manners or of the tension of debate. 'These people do not conceive that they are criminals, Colonel Rawlins. They feel that they are defending the right, and their homes, and that the invaders are the criminals. This is what I have found so difficult. How is one to say where the right lies when both sides are so convinced that it is theirs? The ministers here pray for victory in the cause of liberty, and so I presume do those in the North. The young men I talk to, the serious ones, are just as sure, blue or gray. They even use mostly the same words ——'

'Ah, but Miss Hurlbut.' Rawlins leaned forward, and forgot that he was supposed to be engaged in decorous talk with a young lady. His mind seized on the substance of hers, and his words were neither slowed nor softened by doubts of the strength of her understanding, nor by the deference due to her sex. 'The same words, but do they have the same meanings? You know there can be only one right, and therefore one side must be wrong.'

'Yes, but ——'

'You would ask how to test them. Think of the meanings of the words, of their sense to those who speak them, not their sense to you. When a rebel says "liberty" he means liberty to tear down all that it has taken years and thousands of lives to build. He means the liberty of destruction, the liberty of death ——'

'You are vehement, Colonel Rawlins. You are most persuasive, but you are not discussing, you are preaching. I have heard gentlemen here say that the North cants of liberty and means the liberty of one group to impose its will on another, a liberty limited and exclusive, to be doled out at the will of tyrants, and they call that the liberty of death.'

Horrified, Rawlins kept silence for a moment, knowing that if he spoke at once he must offend her beyond all remedy. 'Do you believe that?' he asked at last, painfully.

'I neither believe it nor disbelieve it, Colonel Rawlins. I

agree with you that there is but one right, but I am sure that it is not to be found with passion. The meanings of words — they are really only passions, sir, they have no content beyond the beliefs of those who speak them.'

Rawlins could have cried aloud his hot denial, stormed and raged at her as he did at Grant or any other man who slipped from the appointed paths of thought, but even in his appalled anger he was aware that if he did his cause would be indeed lost. She would oppose hardness with hardness, vehement certainty with a contempt that would grow into a negative certainty. If he would convince her he must give her battle on her terms, for she could not be forced to accept his. She had left him one opening, had agreed with him that there was but a single truth — Rawlins could feel his cheeks growing hot in the darkness as he marshaled his words to slip through that one undefended point, suppressing the blasphemous shock troops that usually led his assaults.

'There is another way,' he said with great care. 'If you won't admit the meaning of words — I differ with you there, ma'am — you can also find the truth by the results.'

'I don't follow you, Colonel Rawlins.'

'I mean that you can look to the results of men's actions if you will not judge them by their words. We of the North are fighting to preserve our country, and to make it one great nation — free and indivisible, the President says. Think of what it will mean when we stand united again! In a little over a hundred years we have accomplished miracles, although we have been racked with bitter divisions all that time. When the divisions are healed there will be no limit to our power. We have all the rich west for empire, and such men as corrupted Europe cannot match to be its masters. The world has never seen such strength as ours will be, for the wealth of men and the wealth of mind and the wealth of land will all be ours ——' He stopped, realizing that he had been ranting again, but this time she did not chide him. She sat motionless and intent, and although he could not see her face in the dark he felt that her eyes were on his, cloaked in the secret intimacy of night. He remembered that he sought not to charm her but to convince her, and with an effort turned from the glory of his vision back to the line of his argument.

'The South is fighting against that ideal. Oh, I know they don't see they are mistaken. God knows — I'm sorry — it's impossible for men to fight as they do if they don't think they have the right of it. But the tragedy, the damned black crime of it, is that all this suffering and death is squandering the lives we need for our future. Because the South is blind our country is torturing itself, like some ghastly, pitiful madman. If the South won, God forbid, it wouldn't mean simply that the nation that should be one would be two. The nation would be nothing. It would be a living thing cut in half, so that the spirit was gone out of it and the two parts had no future but decay.'

'Perhaps you take too gloomy a view, Colonel Rawlins.' Her uncertainty had lost much of its assurance, but she had not yet surrendered. 'Perhaps the division is irreparable, and the future that you dream of was never really possible. If that is so — and neither you nor I can be certain — then the tragedy and the crime is to go on killing each other for the sake of something that never could exist. And' — he would have spoken, but she would not stop for him — 'and even though it might be possible, I wonder if it is worth what we do to get it? Would it not be better to be content with little, to sacrifice power and place in the world and glory but to keep men alive? Life would be almost the same as it always has been if the Ohio were the boundary between nations instead of states, or even if each state were a nation by itself ——'

'Men cannot live like that, Miss Hurlbut,' Rawlins said quietly. He could be calm now, for he felt that he had overcome the intellectual resistance in her. This last objection was a matter of emotion, rising from the feminine heart that fastened so passionately on certain aspects of life that it had no strength for the vague, distant compulsions which men felt. 'Think a moment. Can you really imagine a truce which said nothing of principles, but simply declared that the issue was not worth fighting over? Can you imagine men going home to till their fields and — and rear their families, content never to think of anything more?'

'No,' she admitted slowly, 'I can't. But — Colonel Rawlins, war is wrong! It's cruel and stupid — I've seen things, here, in June ——' For the first time the thoughtfulness in her voice gave way to emotion, to a loathing and sick fear that filled Rawlins with protective pity, and touched him with guilt. 'There's nothing right about it — truth can't come out of such a thing, and surely no truth could have made it necessary!'

There was no refutation he could make. In her terms she was right, and it would have taken a brute or a cynic to deny her terms. Rawlins was neither. Yet he knew that the matter was not so simple: men like the President, possessed of a tolerance so wide and insight so deep that his spirit was clawed by tragedy; like Grant, who was as sickened by the sight of suffering as any woman; like himself, who loved his country with all his heart and held a man's life sacred, had seen war coming, and accepted it, and furthered it now with every power of body and spirit.

'Miss Hurlbut,' Rawlins said slowly, feeling his way on a path strange to him, that he was not altogether willing to take, 'war is wrong. I suppose it's always wrong, without exception. But — sometimes it comes upon us — it's — it's a visitation that can't be avoided. Many wars you can trace to some definite greed, to a man or group of men with the souls of criminals. I think they're not possible now, with governments that represent the people, for selfish calculation is powerful only in individuals, not in masses. Mobs do wrong things, but they do not deliberately think wrong things ——'

It was so easy to talk to her that he was tempted to expand this detail, but he held strongly to his course. 'So one sort of war has disappeared. But I'm afraid that the other sort will not be abandoned for a long time. The war of ideas, such as we are fighting now — no one wanted it, no one thinks it right and proper, but it came, and no one could avoid it ——'

'Wise counsel,' she said abruptly. 'There were wise men in our government, Northerners and Southerners too. If they had really believed that war was wrong, the worst of crimes, they could have found a solution ——'

'Who would have listened?' he asked gently. He had given her the pain of seeing the illusions supporting her beliefs, and he felt he must protect her now, draw her in from the icy world of objectivity, and wrap her in his own warm assurance. 'Who would have stopped to consider compromise? Sometime in the future men will say, If that had not been done, if so and so had said such and such, it would have been different —— They will be wrong. The war was coming, it had to come for a thousand different reasons, and God never made the man wise enough to turn it aside. When it is over we will see what we might have done to avoid it, but we could not have seen while there was still time. Not enough of us could have seen. War is wrong, yes, but this one is here, and our task is to give our whole strength to the side of right.'

'It's a horrible picture you draw,' she said with a shiver. 'Men killing each other, a whole nation suffering, to no purpose, because we have no choice ——'

'Ah, but there is a purpose. You must not forget that. The means is horrible, but the end is glorious. We fight because we have not the wisdom of gods, to find another way. We make a blood sacrifice, but the greatest horror would be to make it in vain ——'

He stopped, afraid that to her his vehemence might seem bombast. She sighed, and in a moment rose. 'It's very late,' she said. 'I have been worse than thoughtless, Colonel Rawlins — you were so tired, and I have allowed you no rest.'

'You have given me a great pleasure, ma'am. I but fear that I have tired you, unmercifully.'

'No.' The single syllable carried so much sincerity that any elaboration would have seemed empty. 'Good night, Colonel Rawlins. I hope we may talk again.' He bowed over the hand she gave him, and when she had disappeared he sat down again, staring at the warm darkness in confused exaltation. The evening seemed to him full of incident, despite its quiet. He had done nothing, but his thoughts had been of such significance that it was as if they were tangible: the strange, alloyed gold of Grant's future, the steel of war, and something else he could not see clearly, a touchstone on which to ring all else to find its worth.

Neither Rawlins nor Miss Hurlbut was conscious that the staff watched their growing friendship with gleeful curiosity. Rawlins had domineered over the aides with such single-minded thoroughness that it was a joy to them to see him drawn along the path of ordinary men. 'Wish I had a young lady to protect,' one sighed. 'It seems to make things so much easier. These defenseless rebel misses are mighty hard to get into the garden, and then all you get is a giggle and a slap.'

'If he heard you you might as well kiss your commission good-bye.'

'No fear — he's too busy kissing his submission.' But he lowered his voice, knowing that if Rawlins did overhear him he would be fortunate to escape with a mere discharge. There was an unusual gentleness about the chief of staff, an abstraction that came upon him even when the war was being discussed, but he would have no mercy on anyone who commented, however harmlessly, on either himself or the young girl who so interested

him. The staff might laugh, and bet on how long it would be
before the dénouement, but was careful to do so only in private.

Living in the same house, it was natural that the two should
often meet, and not unnatural that casual meetings should
become strolls through the garden; excursions to the summer-
house that commanded the whole sweep of the river; long intimate hours on the porch. They talked sometimes of their
homes, of what their lives had been before war had so whimsi-
cally altered them, but often of nothing at all, sitting together
in friendly silence. Rawlins told her of his wife, and how consumption had licked away her life as the war began, and of the
three small children she had left to him. Miss Hurlbut's sympathy was unfailing, and most sweet. He found it easy to talk
to her of things that troubled him, and when the news came
that Grant had been injured in New Orleans he told her of his
anger and dismay with a frankness that would have been indis-
cretion had she been an ordinary woman.

'I might have known that's what would happen,' he stormed.
'Damn it — I am sorry — it would have been all right if he'd
stayed here where he belongs. Now the newspapers will start in
again ——'

'But he wasn't — there was nothing discreditable about it,'
she pointed out. 'His horse fell on him, it might have happened to any man. It might have happened to him here.'

'I don't know,' he answered. 'I'm d— I'm sure I can't tell
what really did happen. Just rumors is all we have. That —
outfit he had with him wouldn't let me know anything, of
course. Irresponsible idiots.'

'But they're staff officers? They're General Grant's friends?'

'That doesn't mean anything. God knows how he chooses
his friends. He associates with men like Wilson and me, and
then goes off with some tosspot with nothing to recommend him
but a knowledge of poker and of how to tell him the things he
wants to hear. By God, sometimes it's more than a man can

stand.' He was too disturbed to notice the oath, and did not
see her lifted brows calling for an apology. He strode at her
side, angry, resentful of the refractory nature of the material
he sought to shape, but with his anger and resentment re-enforc-
ing his determination. She did not fully understand why he was
so troubled, but she guessed enough to flush her cheeks with
excitement and fill her eyes with admiration of him.

The newspapers did tell of Grant's accident with some in-
nuendo, but in his fear of it Rawlins had forgotten Vicksburg.
That campaign had made Grant a glittering hero, the trusted
friend of the President, the terror of the Confederacy, and it was
no longer possible to criticize him with any abandon. Ulyss
lay in bed and read over and over how his horse had shied at a
locomotive and fallen on him, and the nation might thank its
God that he had been spared. Perhaps he was safe now from
the everlasting journalistic sniping, or at least no more exposed
to its accusations and violent criticisms and three-quarter libels
than any other man. The possibility somewhat comforted him
even in his uneasiness over what Rawlins was going to say. He
could no longer pretend to his chief of staff that the jaunt to
New Orleans had been entirely for the purpose of conferring
with Banks. It had taken too long, and his enjoyment of the
city was too well known.

Even now that they were dulled by repentance his memories
were pleasant: the rippling thunder of horses on the racecourse;
the theatre twilight with something glittering and gay on the
stage, and the little waves of applause when he entered his box;
the companions he had found, the men who admired him with
pleasant frankness, who knew how to play with that relaxation
of body and spirit which Rawlins condemned. It had been a
bright and carefree world. Ulyss had not thought to question
what lay behind the shuttered windows of so many old houses,
behind the rigid faces of the citizens who hastened through the
streets. It had not occurred to him that New Orleans' pride

had been equaled only by Charleston's, and that the city he had
seen, built of racecourses and hotels and theatres, and peopled
by Federal officers, cotton speculators, and Northern adventurers, might not be all of New Orleans. He had enjoyed his
stay so much — it was malicious luck that accident fought on
Rawlins's side.

As soon as he could be carried Ulyss ordered a steamer and
went back to Vicksburg. His holiday was over, and he might as
well return to face his chief of staff's righteous wrath. But it
was not Rawlins who waited at the steps to direct his bearers to
his room. It was Julia. He could say nothing when he saw her,
could only clasp her hand, and even when the men had gone and
he had drawn her down to him he said only, 'You.'

'Of course, Victor,' she smiled. He looked puzzled at the
name, and she laughed outright. 'Don't you remember last
Christmas? I said it sounded funny then — not any more.'
She sat on the edge of his bed and talked with an odd ring of
childish happiness over the deep pride in her voice. 'I thought
I knew all about the way people felt while I was still up North,
but I didn't know anything at all. Victor, you ought to see
this place. It's so full of things ——'

'Things?'

'Presents — unbirthday gifts. I think everybody in the
world has sent you something. Books and furniture and millions of cigars — the children are going wild.'

'Are the children here too?'

'All of them.' She stopped laughing, and looked at him almost with shame. 'My dearest, I did believe, but I never
dreamed — I'm so proud ——' She hid her face on his shoulder,
and he thought he heard her murmur again, 'Victor...' He
held her fast, knowing that he had never fully realized his
triumph until now. The singing of his troops as they stood in
the square, the President's letter, the applause and admiration
he had been given in New Orleans, were pale and tasteless be-

side this moment. It was some time before she drew away, and when she did he thought there were tears in her eyes, but she went to unpack for him, and when she returned there was nothing in her face but gaiety.

The children were summoned — Nell and Jesse from the garden, Fred and Buck from the sentries' quarters, where Fred had been renewing old comradeships. Small Jesse was at first a little shy with his father, but soon had to be restrained from bouncing on his father's chest. The other three chattered without awkwardness, as confident of his interest as they had been at home in Galena. Ulyss looked long at each one. Fred and Buck seemed to be all that boys should be, noisy, confident, happy in their world. So far as he could see they had not the feeling he had known in his own childhood, the gloomy knowledge that all that he did was forced on him by other wills, that however much he disliked a thing he had no choice but to do it and suffer its consequences. His children always assumed that any unpleasantness would be removed from their paths, if not by their mother certainly by their father.

There was something strange about Nellie, and Ulyss's eyes returned often to her until he realized that she was going to be beautiful. The thought almost shocked him, and even in his pride he was a little awed by it, until she pulled Jesse's hair and then defended herself with mundane vitality. Julia separated them, scolded them mildly, and comforted them with a promise of something from the pile of presents downstairs. Then Fred and Buck had to be included, and all four went off whooping. Ulyss lay and listened to their shouts, trying to remember what the place had been like before. He could not. His staff headquarters, a house in a captured city — it was neither. It was his home, with Julia and his children, and could never have been anything else.

The slow weeks of his recovery preserved that illusion. There was very little that called for his decision, and the long, hot days were marked chiefly by how much he was able to move, how long he could sit up, how far he could walk again. The war was so distant that it did not exist while the children chattered around him and Julia lifted her eyes from her work to give him a swift, warm glance. Even Rawlins did little to jar on the muted content of that time. His reproof was silent, to put a heavier burden on Grant's own conscience, and they quarreled on but one occasion, when Rawlins came to Ulyss to protest against the accumulation of gifts, still mounting every week.

'They're pouring in,' he said, 'from everywhere — and from everybody.'

'Well?' Grant knew all about them. He had not yet been able to go downstairs and inspect all of them himself, but Julia described each arrival to him, and showed him the more unusual items.

'I question the wisdom of accepting them,' said Rawlins carefully.

'What do you want me to do? Send them all back? I can't do that, when people have taken so much trouble to give me pleasure.'

'That isn't always the motive.' Rawlins struggled to keep his objective tone, and failed. 'Goddamn it, don't you see how it works? The really valuable things down there are all from people who expect a return, the speculating bastards, and ——'

'I don't take bribes, Rawlins.' The very quiet of Grant's tone was menacing.

'Of course you don't — send them back, for Christ's sake.'

Ulyss said nothing, simply looked at Rawlins, and the chief of staff recognized defeat. He rarely encountered that icy, empty gaze, but he knew that it put an end to all argument. There was much that he could command in Grant, many liberties he could take that would have destroyed the friendship of another man, but against this ultimate resistance he was helpless.

Other disagreements not so serious had left him ruffled and chilly for days, and it was when he was little affected by this one that Grant began to notice a difference in him. 'What do you suppose is the matter with Rawlins?' Ulyss asked Julia. 'He's not like himself — he seems to have something on his mind.'

Julia looked at him and laughed. 'You've seen that much, Victor. Why don't you look a little farther?' She nodded to the gardens gray in the moonlight, where Rawlins had disappeared some time before. 'He doesn't go walking by himself, you know.'

'Not — but who — Miss Hurlbut?' Grant's amazement made his emphasis almost a shout.

'Hush, dearest, it's indelicate to yell like that. Yes, of course Miss Hurlbut. Why not?'

'But Rawlins ——' Ulyss remembered his friend's demand that the girl be protected, and his disbelief wavered. 'It just doesn't seem possible,' he murmured.

'I don't see that. Poor man, a widower and all. I think it's sweet.' Julia nodded placidly, and Grant suppressed a laugh that might have seemed to her lacking in the proper feeling. He had almost forgotten that Rawlins had come to him straight from his wife's deathbed. He had almost forgotten that he had ever known Rawlins as a citizen, and that he could be one again. The man had been so absorbed in the war that it had seemed impossible for him to have capacity for any other emotion. Yet it was true that the blaze in his black eyes was now a softer light, and Grant, once he saw the possibility, took it as a certainty. He had not long to wait for proof: early in September Rawlins announced quietly that Miss Hurlbut had accepted him.

'I've heard of gentlemen laying siege to their ladies before,' said one impertinent spirit on the staff, 'but never so literally.' Rawlins gave him a cold look, and the young man subsided. The chief of staff was not in the least softened by the romantic achievements of John Rawlins.

Thus the time of respite was rounded out, but in the third
week of September the little oasis of illusion was swept away by
the news of Chickamauga. Bragg had turned on the Federals in
Tennessee, defeated them, and penned them hopelessly into
Chattanooga. The Union loss of life had been enormous, but
worse than that was the loss of the Union prestige that had risen
from the Confederate defeats in early July. The people had fed
on the triumphs of Vicksburg and Gettysburg, but when their
first hunger was dulled they began to suspect they had feasted
on Dead Sea fruit. Lee had been defeated at Gettysburg, and
for a time the awe around his name had faded, but he had been
allowed to withdraw without pursuit, and had regained all his
stature when he stood once more on the red Virginia earth.
Vicksburg had fallen and the Mississippi was open, yet the war
showed no sign whatever of coming to an end. Now there was
news of the desperate case in Chattanooga, where men were
living on mule meat and facing the knowledge, daily more clear,
that they must soon abandon the town. If Chattanooga were
lost almost all the achievements of the war in the west, the
only Union achievements of importance, would be imperiled.
Was it worth while to fight when even victories were in essence
meaningless?

Ulyss was not really surprised when he received orders to
come north. He had not consciously expected them, but even
his habitual refusal to speculate on the future could not keep
him entirely unaware that a bad situation was likely to be given
to the attention of a victorious general. His injured leg still
made traveling difficult, but he took his staff and set out at once.
His family, Rawlins's astonishing engagement, the pleasant
summer days by the river, vanished as completely as though
they had been fired from the cannon at Chickamauga.

At a station on the way his train was halted just as it was
pulling out. 'The Secretary of War,' a breathless messenger
gasped. 'He's here — by special train.' Grant turned, curious

to see the man whom he knew so well, and did not know at all. For a long time Stanton had been a prime factor in his plans, yet defined only by what others said of him and by deductions from his acts. Peremptory, short-tempered, cantankerously honest, and devoted to the Union — but what else?

A man swung up the steps with a breathless air, as though disaster were close on his heels, seized on the staff surgeon, and exclaimed, 'Ah, General, I knew you at once by your pictures.' The doctor indicated Grant, but did not hide his amusement quickly enough to avoid being given a look of angry disapproval, as though he were guilty of petty treason in also wearing a beard. Stanton came to Ulyss and almost without a greeting plunged into his concern over Chattanooga. He had no new information, but the facts as he set them forth overflowed with catastrophe. Ulyss watched him more than he listened to him, marking the broad brow, heavy nose, thin lips, strangely combined in an almost childlike countenance.

'And so,' Stanton concluded, 'I have here two orders. You may read them, General, and take your choice.'

The two were almost the same. Both created a new Division of the Mississippi, Major-General Grant in command, to include all operations west of the Alleghenies, with the exception of Banks's command in the southwest. Ulyss's eyes were warm with approval, unaffected by his own appointment. Here was an end to the exasperating jockeying to reconcile three independent divisions, with success in one always nullified by failure in another, and no possibility of a unified plan.

One order made no changes in existing commands. The other relieved Rosecrans from duty at Chattanooga and put Thomas in his place. Ulyss hesitated. For a long time he had seen excuses for Rosecrans, but his shortcomings were now straining tolerance. Thomas was a good soldier, beloved by his men, trusted by his superiors, and his behavior at Chickamauga had been the one comfort to the Union side. Ulyss remembered, with shamed unwillingness, that Thomas had been one of Halleck's trusted commanders in the weeks after Shiloh. No matter. He could forget that now, surely.

'I think this one is best,' he said, handing the paper back to Stanton. The Secretary nodded and swept into an exposition of his own theories on what should be done. Grant scarcely listened. He was thinking of the new division, his command, stretching from the eastern mountains to the Mississippi, from the Ohio to the Gulf. His. He wondered suddenly what had become of the letter he had written to the War Department two years ago, saying that he thought he could command a regiment. There had never been an answer.

Confederate Carbine and Union Musket

CHAPTER NINE

THE peril of Chattanooga was clearly written on the road-side. This was the only line of communications, but almost every loblolly held an abandoned wagon, and the carcasses of starved mules frequently marked the end of another attempt to bring rations through. It was raining, had been raining for weeks. Even when the downpour stopped for a while the sound continued as the water dripped from trees and bushes, falling to the soaked ground almost with a splash. Grant's horse slithered gingerly over the track, snorting nervously as he slid, and sometimes Ulyss could feel him shiver.

Impossible to rely on this line, thought Ulyss. Messengers could get over it, but transporting food in any adequate quantity was out of the question. And food Chattanooga must have. Men might starve for a little while with cheerful fortitude, but they reach very quickly the point where a piece of bread outweighs glory, pride, and courage together. Ulyss did not like to think how close that point might be, and what it would mean if the balance that rested on it dipped to the Confederate side. Chattanooga gone, the line of rebellion re-established on the Ohio, Vicksburg and New Orleans perhaps made untenable, the people of the South reassured and triumphant —— He was touched by panic, and reined his thoughts back firmly. It must be that the long, difficult day and the pain of his injured leg had overtired him, that he should trouble himself with such profitless ideas.

'Much farther to Chattanooga?' someone asked the guide.

'Naw — two miles maybe, maybe less.'

Two miles — it seemed a long distance, with the uncertainties of rain and darkness gathering over the sodden earth, but Ulyss rode on. The group was silent, too weary and wet even for complaint. Time was marked only by the muttered comments of their guides and occasional pauses to make sure of the road, and when at last they saw a few lights before them and the road began dropping to level ground they were astonished to hear the guide say 'Chattanooga,' as though they had forgotten that their journey had a goal. They could see little of the town. Houses, the clatter of cobblestones under the horses' hooves, a few soldiers hurrying through the cold rain. Most of them had no overcoats, and there was a gaunt look about them. They glanced with cool curiosity at the group of strange officers, and Grant heard his name, not shouted in welcome but passed in identification from one man to another.

When he reached Thomas's headquarters he had to be lifted from his saddle, and he limped into the house. Thomas came to meet them.

'We did not expect you tonight, General,' he said. 'Such a long journey, and with this weather ——'

'I know,' said Ulyss, 'but I came through.' He had not meant to stop there. He had intended to say something of his

admiration of Thomas's work at Chickamauga, and the coura-
geous stand he was taking in this beleaguered town. But the
words died unspoken, without a reason that Ulyss understood,
for they would have been sincere. He respected Thomas as a
soldier and a man, yet seemed unable to speak to him with
even ordinary freedom. It was not that they disliked each
other, but a genuine understanding between them was made
impossible by circumstances stretching back far beyond their
births. They stood looking at each other for a moment, Grant
soaked with rain and spattered by mud, stooping more than ever
in weariness, twisted a little to favor his aching leg; Thomas
erect and immaculate, not only by reason of material circumstances but with the stamp of Virginia breeding and an antique
code.

The pause was broken when Thomas offered his superior a
chair by the fire and ordered food. He urged Ulyss to borrow
his own dry clothes, and grew cordial as he met the clear
demands of tradition. Ulyss ate, but refused his host's other
courtesies, maintaining his silence until the members of
Thomas's staff arrived. Then a map was spread out on the
table, and Grant saw his problem.

'That's the main trouble,' said W. F. Smith, Thomas's
engineer. His bald head caught the light dully as he leaned
across the table and ran his finger along the furry lines that
stood for mountains. 'Bragg's got both Missionary Ridge and
Lookout, one on each side of us, and Lookout's so high he can
control even the north bank of the river. It's practically a
siege.'

'The men are as hungry as if it were,' a Captain Porter
agreed.

'Just how do your supplies stand?' Ulyss inquired. He had
said nothing while the others introduced themselves and talked
of their situation. Now, slowly, he was beginning to understand
not only the details of the problem but the nature of the men.

Smith was assured and soldierly, perhaps a little abrupt in speech, but with an obviously thorough knowledge of his work. Young Porter talked with ease and wit, and there was in his eyes an indication that he was more than just a good-humored and competent young man. All the staff members made their devotion to Thomas plain. There seemed to be a feeling between them that had a warm, subtle difference both from the loyalty required by the military code and from the affection such men as Wilson and Rawlins had for Grant.

It was Thomas who answered the question. 'I could say we have no supplies, and it would just about be true. The men are on half-rations of hardtack and superannuated meat — they call it beef dried on the hoof. We've had no small rations at all for a long time, and almost no medical supplies. A wagon train almost got through to us across the river, but Bragg's cavalry got hold of it. Since then there hasn't been anything.'

'Ammunition?' said Ulyss.

'There's enough for one day's battle,' said Porter. 'No more, here. But there's plenty at Bridgeport.'

That town was forever being mentioned. Bridgeport was on the railroad. Re-enforcements sent to relieve Chattanooga, but holding off because Chattanooga could not feed them, were at Bridgeport. Ammunition in plenty was at Bridgeport. The town was plainly the key to the supplies the Army of the Cumberland so desperately needed, and also to the offensive on which Grant hoped to send that army, but Bragg's force seemed to bar all communication with the place. It was almost due west of Chattanooga, and on the other side of the river, for the Tennessee here flowed in a particularly perverse line. The guns perched on Lookout Mountain could sweep any of the customary routes between the two towns.

Something might be done — there was always something that might be done, given daring and imagination and luck. But Ulyss could not be certain of the morale of these men.

It was possible that the great blow of Chickamauga, followed by the slow abrasion of hunger, had so weakened the blade that it would break in his hand. 'Are there any plans for retreat?' he asked, bluntly putting his uncertainties to the test.

'General Rosecrans had considered this line,' said Porter, putting his finger on a red and blue mark on the map. Grant scarcely looked at it. He knew it was a good enough line and might be held for a short time, but Bragg's men with the weight of victory behind them would break any line once they started for the Ohio. He was not really interested in arrangements for retreat, but in what effect the suggestion would have on the men before him.

It had been an entirely reasonable question, an inevitable one, and comments on the answer were not called for. But as Ulyss looked at the faces around him he found the answer to the question he had not asked, and he was well pleased. Smith could not keep silence, and leaned forward over the map.

'There's another plan to be considered before retreat, General,' he said. 'We've been thinking that at this point' — he indicated the place where Lookout Mountain rose sheer from the river — 'it would be possible to get men by at night without the rebs seeing us, and surprise them at Brown's Ferry. Once we have a foothold in Lookout Valley we could open up the line to Bridgeport, and hold it, easy. The base of the mountain itself would protect us from the guns on the top.'

'You'd have to cross the river twice, the way it lies,' said Ulyss. He was not so much making an objection as stating it in order to hear the solution.

'We have boats — the men have been making them for weeks.' Then all the others began to talk, and from their swift, eager words Ulyss gathered not only the details of the plan but evidence of how long and carefully it had been prepared. In outline it was very simple. As usual, in this war

fought across the width of a continent, the river greatly complicated the movement, but Smith had set up a sawmill and kept
the men busy making boats to ferry themselves across. The
night attack was risky, but if well executed it would break
the encircling Confederate ring, and it had a good chance of
success.

'It's a fine plan,' said Ulyss at last. 'You command it, General Smith. It was your idea, and you know most about it.'
The light of satisfaction in Smith's eyes was reflected on the
faces of his comrades, and the group dispersed with as much
confidence as though the project had no element of risk at all.
Ulyss went to bed, exhausted, but with so many thoughts
crowding for his attention that it was some time before he
slept. He approved of the plan Smith had already set so far
on its way, he was sure it would be effective, that the Army
of the Cumberland would be fed and made capable of offensive
action again. He had some vision of what that action could be,
and satisfaction in the thought of another triumph to sap at
Southern pride, a most important Confederate resource.

Yet, with all his approval of the plan, admiration of the men,
and hope for the future, there was another feeling in his heart,
unformed, nameless, but very close to loneliness. It was a
great honor to have been put in command of all the armies west
of the mountains, and to be called on to save Chattanooga. He
appreciated it, and took pleasure in the fact that he had risen
so high that it would have been strange had he not been thus
honored. But he seemed to have lost something. He had no
clear notion of what it was nor where he had lost it; it was only
that power and success did not seem the same as they had when
he had dreamed of them, when he had first tasted of them
after Fort Donelson. Then victory had been a personal joy,
something he could give to Julia as recompense for the drab
years, something he could sense warm in his heart and bright
in his friends' eyes. But now, when his triumphs were resound-

ing, his delight in them shrank as they grew. There was so
much to be considered, so many factors to balance and compromises to make, that he had no time any more to stop and
think how happy he was. His friends' praise was like the
public's applause, pushed by the burden of his affairs too far
away to warm him.

As he twisted impatiently on his bed he remembered the look
of Thomas's officers when they turned to their commander.
They loved him, with the straightforward masculine love that
sometimes shines out of the bloody battle clouds. Perhaps,
thought Ulyss, that was what he did not have — not what he
had lost, for he had never had it. Even Rawlins's cross-grained
affection was not comparable, nor Sherman's fiery and vivid
friendship. The shaggy and unceremonious Army of the Tennessee had understood him, but had not loved him. He was
proud of all these things, yet he felt that night that the dust
of distance had filtered over them and obscured their bright-
ness. His feet were set at last on the road to success after so
many years of wandering, and it seemed a diverging path,
with few companions on the way.

Smith's expedition to open up the supply line was carried
out with smooth success. The Confederate outpost at Brown's
Ferry was surprised and overwhelmed; two forces from Chattanooga and one from Bridgeport combined efficiently; and the
line, part river and part road, was opened. Supplies began
pouring over it, and for a day or two it was unmolested. The
surprise of the movement was one of the chief elements in its
success, for Bragg had been deeply convinced that the situation was his to command, but he was quick to see that the
Federal action was far more than audacity. Chattanooga
hungry had been a prison for the Federals: Chattanooga fed
could become a very dangerous base.

Longstreet was sent out to reoccupy Lookout Valley and

restore the imprisoning wall, and with so much at stake on both sides, the engagement was fought with all the passion of a major battle. Longstreet had the greater numbers: the Union men the more vital necessity. For some hours the two forces were in almost even balance. The soldiers were absorbed in their work, too busy with details to be affected by the terror of the whole, but the Union teamsters, waiting in the rear, had no such armor. It was their work to get wagons back and forth over roads half dissolved by rain and cut to pieces by troops, and to struggle with the demonic vagaries of mules. It was no part of their duty to stand in range of fire and wait for the result of a highly uncertain battle, and they left that place. Deserted, the mules in their charge also ran away, but, being mules, they ran in the wrong direction and charged straight for Longstreet's men. The Confederates looked up to see huge shapes galloping through the smoke with breakneck heroism; someone shouted 'Cavalry!' — and the line broke. The supply line was not attacked again. The victorious mules were rounded up and returned to their wagons, and the quartermaster respectfully recommended to Grant that they be brevetted horses, for gallantry in action.

Then for a time there was quiet. There was plenty of food, and the men lost their grim listlessness as they ate. Bragg still held the hills before them, and obviously there would be hard fighting soon, when Sherman came up and Grant could set his plans in action, but meanwhile nothing happened. In the early days the prospect of a battle even several weeks off would spread tension through a camp, but now the men paid little attention to it beyond long, lazy arguments on just what was planned.

There was an Indian-summer informality in the army. Once an outlying picket called, as Grant passed, 'Turn out the guard — the commanding general!'

'Never mind the guard,' said Ulyss.

He had not intended to stop, and was walking past when he heard the cry of the Confederate picket on the other side of a little stream, 'Turn out the guard — General Grant!' He turned to see the group of gray men standing at attention and surveying him gravely. He saluted and passed on. He was within pistol range, but there was a distinction between war and murder.

'Shorty,' said one of the Confederates succinctly as they fell out of ranks. The Union pickets laughed. They had no great liking for their commander. It was plain, however much courtesy and military deportment tried to conceal it, that he and Thomas were uncongenial, and the men loved Thomas. They pointed out to each other at length that the plan for opening the supply line had been set in motion before Grant took command, and they resented the newspapers' admiring chorus that Chattanooga was being fed within five days of Grant's arrival. Some of the men believed a rumor that Grant had said the Army of the Cumberland could not fight.

Ulyss sensed something of this feeling, and it seemed to him that the farther east he came the more of it he found. He understood it, remembering how his own Army of the Tennessee had resented Buell's men, long ago before Shiloh, knowing that it would take time and a victory before he was truly accepted by the men as head of all the western armies. He regretted it, but he had graver difficulties to concern him. He was impatient with Thomas, who seemed to have little concept of warfare involving whole armies, and who certainly had no liking for him. Hooker, his other commander, had been sent out from the Army of the Potomac, and seemed to think that fact of greater weight than mere rank until Rawlins interfered.

'Impertinence!' the chief of staff snorted. 'He's a ——' He stopped heroically to rearrange his words in accordance with his promise to his betrothed, then continued straitly. 'He's as insufferable as if he didn't have Chancellorsville to

think about. He seems to believe that any private in the Army
of the Potomac outranks a general from the west.'

'Lots of people feel that way,' Ulyss said thoughtfully.

'It's the damnedest conceit I ever heard of,' Rawlins exploded. 'These easterners think nobody is as good as they
are — God knows why, when they've lost almost all their
battles. They're a pretty poor lot, it seems to me ——'

'No,' Grant interrupted him firmly. 'They're fine men —
no better anywhere in the world. It's true they've been defeated a lot, but I think they've never been fought to a finish.
You shouldn't sneer at them, any more than they should sneer
at us. That's one of the main troubles on our side — we're too
much divided. Our armies are like a team of balky mules, wasting most of their strength pulling against each other.'

It was a very long speech for Ulyss, and its conclusion surprised even him. He had intended simply to counterbalance
Rawlins's vehemence, but as he spoke he remembered with
equal vehemence the many opportunities that had gone un-
seized because the Union armies did not cooperate. He was a
little embarrassed at having criticized something beyond his
field, and turned away as if to search for a paper in the chaos
of his desk. Thus he did not see the look in Rawlins's eyes,
first of resentment at having been corrected and reproved, then
of calculation.

In those troublesome days of contending with Thomas's
courteous but unalterable limitations and Hooker's fractious
self-importance, Ulyss rooted his patience in his expectation of
Sherman's arrival. A battle must be fought very soon, for
Burnside, whose command was in desperate case at Knoxville,
where Longstreet had gone to pin him down, could be relieved
only by sweeping Bragg from his position at Chattanooga, and
thereby cutting Longstreet from his base. It was a complex
problem that was apparently little understood in Washington,
for Grant's busy days were punctuated with telegrams from

Stanton or the President bringing Burnside's peril to his notice, as if it were not his hourly concern. It would be of no help to send Burnside men, since he had not enough food for those he had, nor could supplies be taken through to him. Plainly Burnside's battle of Knoxville must be fought by Grant at Chattanooga, however obscure the relation appeared to Washington. Ulyss explained it regularly, and waited for Sherman.

Missionary Ridge was the key to his plan. That long, narrow, and steep hill was the wall of Bragg's fortress, protecting his railroad and base at Chickamauga Station, and there were two lines of rifle pits stretched along its face. So long as it could be defended Bragg could not be dislodged: so long as Bragg held his position he covered Longstreet at Knoxville. The ridge, then, must be taken. Ulyss planned for Sherman to attack its north end and turn it if possible, so that Bragg must either lose his base on the railroad or weaken his defending force on the ridge itself. Hooker was to clear out the Confederates on Lookout Mountain, and then attack the south end of the ridge. When Bragg's centre had been sufficiently depleted to meet these threats on both wings, Thomas was to make the frontal assault. The plan was simple enough, but it involved moving thousands of men back and forth over the streams that laced that mountain country, and the autumn rains had set in. Pontoon bridges pulled and groaned on the rising waters, some fixed bridges collapsed, and Sherman's advance was delayed for day after rainy day, while Ulyss answered frantic telegrams from Washington. The President and the Secretary of War were sleepless over Burnside's plight, and Ulyss's heart grew heavier as he watched every rainy twilight close in, knowing that the lost day had made the situation yet more desperate. Burnside himself sent a dispatch inquiring, with cheerful disregard of the possibilities, if he should give battle at Knoxville to keep Longstreet from sending men to Bragg.

Shortly after the middle of November Sherman arrived at last. He swore at the weather, slapped Rawlins on the back and inquired about his approaching marriage, strode up and down the room smoking excitedly while the plan of battle was explained to him, and it seemed to Grant that he brought victory with him. After the difficulties with Thomas and Hooker it was heart-warming to go over the terrain with Sherman, to watch the quick eyes that saw so many factors, the decisive, spirited gestures. Sherman inspected the river crossing he would have to make to reach his position, whistling in concentration, and returned his field glasses to their case with a thump. 'I can do it,' he said, and Missionary Ridge seemed less steep, not quite so high, with fewer men to hold the rifle pits that scarred its sides.

As the two generals returned they were observed by dozens of men who were apparently absorbed in other affairs. 'That's Sherman,' was the word, frequently with the addition, 'Now we'll be taught how to fight.' It was well known that Grant was expecting most from Sherman's part in the project, and the men of the Army of the Cumberland looked after them with curiosity and resentment, repeating to each other rumors of the great contempt in which Grant held their own division.

There was still much to be done, and always there was a swollen river to bar the way wherever men had to be moved. But the troops were brought into position at last, despite the continuing rain and mist that hid men from each other and obscured their places. It rained all during the time of preparation, and it rained the first day of the battle, when Hooker seized Lookout Mountain in a magnificent assault, and Sherman advanced on his end of Missionary Ridge. Grant was well pleased with the gain, but he knew that it left the central problem untouched. Missionary Ridge was still before him, and the day that was dawning was the one for which he had been planning over a month.

The morning was clear and blue, such a morning as he had forgotten existed. As he rode out to the vantage point he had chosen he found that all the ridge stretched before him in the sparkling air, its steep slopes dark with cedars and glistening with the naked trees of winter, and marked in long horizontal lines by the Confederate rifle pits. The lambent air of the autumn morning gave clarity and precision even to distant details, and from where Ulyss stood with Thomas opposite the centre of the ridge he could see all the way from Sherman at the north end to Rossville Gap at the south, where he expected Hooker to appear; he could watch small gray men moving about the two lines of rifle pits and the bristling line on the crest; could even see Bragg's headquarters high in the glistening sky, with toy staff officers riding busily back and forth. It was as though he looked at a gigantic setting for some pageant, and in the flooding brilliance of that light the figures that moved forward and dropped back were not men nor soldiers but actors.

Yet as the day was transmuted from diamond morning to golden noon the pageant failed to follow its script. Sherman fought valiantly but made little progress, for Bragg shifted enough detachments to hold him fast. Ulyss had considered that possibility, and had planned to meet it with an attack by Hooker on the other end of the ridge and one by Thomas on the centre, but Hooker had missed his cue and was not in his place. Rawlins brought a message to Grant and gloomily watched him read it. Hooker's command was barred from action by a creek where the Confederates had burned the bridge.

'They're rebuilding it?' Ulyss asked.

'Yes, but it takes time.' Rawlins coughed hollowly in the reek from a cannon that was being pointlessly fired nearby, and his hot, dark eyes lifted to the ridge. 'We can't afford time,' he said. The words were unemotional, but Ulyss felt the drive of desperation behind them. Rawlins was always tense in battle, as if he went down to contend with the powers of darkness in the person of every blue soldier Ulyss commanded forward, and of late his fanatic absorption had been a mounting fever.

'We're not beaten yet,' Ulyss said, with the more assurance to cover his concern. 'Hooker will come as soon as he gets his bridge built, and I don't want to send Thomas's men in till then. Bragg can throw them back if he doesn't have to meet an attack on his left at the same time.'

'How about Sherman?' Rawlins demanded, with the petulance of a sick child who refuses to be comforted. 'He's being smothered, and we're doing nothing.'

'Sherman will come through in fine style,' Ulyss said with his accustomed confidence in his friend, but betrayed himself by a nervous start as the neighboring cannon fired again. 'Have that thing stopped,' he said, in a tone of cold anger that summed up all his dismay at the precarious state of his battle. Thomas, who had been standing nearby, quietly gave the order, and the cannon ceased barking at the ridge. The comparative silence only emphasized the spluttering roar from Sherman's command, rising or falling occasionally but never advancing. Rawlins coughed again, an oddly heavy sound, passed his hand wearily over his face and rode away.

It was soon necessary to send re-enforcements to Sherman, and Ulyss, holding to his original view of how his plan would develop, believed for a moment that they would enable his friend to turn the ridge. But Bragg on the heights could see the movement clearly, and met it swiftly. Thus stalemated, Grant commanded Thomas to assault. He had heard nothing more from Hooker, and the face of the ridge was still very strongly held, but if the Army of the Cumberland could occupy the first line of rifle pits it might yet give Sherman an opportunity to break through. It seemed to him an insufferably long time before the order was obeyed.

Then at last Thomas's men moved out to the ridge. After their long inaction the order to charge was a relief even to those of uncertain courage, and they felt obscurely that behind them stood Thomas, for whose sake they resented many things. There could be no talk as they sped forward, and little conscious thought, but for a long time they had been discussing Grant's supposed opinion of them, and that day they had been watching with a certain satisfaction his beloved Army of the Tennessee getting nowhere.

Of these diverse and inarticulate factors was made a momentum that sent them across the field and into the first line of pits in blind disregard of the singing sleet of the Confederate fire. Their orders were thus fulfilled, and brilliantly, but they were no longer an army to obey orders. They did not remember what the command had been, and responsible officers could not make themselves heard. There was no hesitation at the first line of pits, and gray men and blue poured together into the second. The hill was steep, crowned with strong defenses, but these considerations had no more weight than orders. Each man was seized with an individual, irresponsible impulse that sent him surging onward in collective irresistibility. Not until they had swept over the crest and sent Bragg fleeing in amazed horror down the other side did they lose their impetus. Then some fired happily at the Confederates, out of range, and others turned to look back. Hooker had come up, and was shattering all that was left of Bragg's army. Sherman had broken through when the force confronting him had lost its backing. There were no longer any Confederate eyes to look down from the heights on Chattanooga, and in the valley the deepening blue of twilight drew the curtain.

The General's Stars

CHAPTER TEN

I'LL be back as soon as I can,' said Rawlins, 'but I'm afraid that won't be before the first of the year.'

'Don't hurry,' said Grant with solicitude. His eyes were troubled when he looked at his chief of staff, who had grown even thinner of late, and whose cheeks had a flush not entirely warranted simply by a bridegroom's happiness. 'You need a rest. You're entitled to it, for your wedding.'

'I think I can safely take a few days, but my duty's here.' The rasp in Rawlins's voice became a cough. 'There's a lot of things to be done now.'

'I don't know — there's always a slack time after a battle. You rest while you can. Maybe in the spring we can move on Mobile.' So many times he had said it, so many times been held back — perhaps this time, with his growing prestige, he could break free...

Rawlins did not listen to the familiar recital of the advantages of the movement, but sat watching the repeated choppy gesture as Grant dropped his hand on his knee, wondering how innocent this man was of his future. Grant read the papers, sounding the temper of the people and using that knowledge in his military calculations. Reading, he could not fail to see the mounting talk of himself, the adulation as extreme and sometimes unjust as had been the condemnation that dogged him before Vicksburg. His name darkened Thomas's and Smith's and Burnside's, just as it had once been shadowed by McClernand's and Sherman's and Buell's, and in the newspapers' songs of praise there was the growing theme of the coming year, 1864, election year. He must have seen all this, but he was either dissembling his interest with the skill of a great actor, which Rawlins did not believe he possessed, or he did not really make a connection between the gigantic Ulysses Grant of the newspapers and himself.

The matter was of more than abstract interest to Rawlins. He felt that his stewardship of Grant's career was a heavy responsibility, and he had seen long since what end it might have, some day, when the long processes of development were complete and the proper moment had come. But it was not his first responsibility. It was after all but one man's life, and however important it might be it had no weight as against the life of the nation, to which it was dedicated. It was possible that Grant might one day be president, but if he left his work on the battlefield half done to take that office he would turn traitor in Rawlins's eyes. Unlikely as it was that he would consider it, the mere possibility haunted Rawlins, and he had determined to make certain before he went away.

'Likely you're right,' he interrupted Grant's exposition. 'Biddy Halleck will probably agree to it now, and there's not much to stand in its way — unless election year makes a difference.'

'Election year?' Grant's puzzled tone delighted his friend.

'Yes — with all the talk that's going on it's hard to be definite about anything.'

'I don't see that it has anything to do with us — unless we need a victory to shut the mouths of the copperheads.'

'Well' — Rawlins tried to say the crucial words as indifferently as possible — 'suppose you were nominated?'

The look on Grant's face was one of startled embarrassment, and nothing more. 'That's nonsense, Rawlins,' he said at last. 'I'm a soldier, and everybody knows it. That stuff in the papers — they've nominated just about everybody except a nigger. Besides, Lincoln's only had one term. Why make a change?'

'I don't think we ought to,' said Rawlins with disingenuous frankness. 'He seems to me the best man for the place.'

'Of course he is. Who wants to put in a Democrat who thinks the war's a failure, or a Radical who wants to give niggers the vote? What's got into you, anyway?'

'I just spoke without thinking. It gives you a queer feeling to have an election in the middle of a war. God knows I wish it were over and we could go back to things the way they were. What do you want to do, when the war's over?'

There was a long hesitation before Grant answered, and when he spoke he kept his eyes on his hands. 'I'm a major general now. If everything goes well here, maybe after the war — I'd be assigned to the Pacific Division. I'd like to take Julia out there — it's beautiful . . .'

Rawlins hid a smile. This was the ambition of the only consistently victorious Union general, to return in triumph to the place where he had known failure and humiliation. The one thing he thought he wanted, and most certainly that thing he could not have. The fame and power of victory were waiting for him, but not the simplicity of peace. Rawlins rose and said good-bye, reassured, but touched almost to pity.

Outside, the winter rain was beginning to glaze over the streets, and the thin wind of the mountains drove it into Rawlins's face. He coughed, and tried to shrink into his coat as he hurriedly made his way to his quarters. It was true that he did not feel well, was almost ill when he stopped to think about it.

A few nights ago there had been blood on his handkerchief, and for a panic-struck moment he had seen the white, haggard face of his dead wife. He had gone to the staff surgeon, thinking rigidly of nothing at all until he was reassured: ' . . . run down . . . possibly a bronchial affection . . . rest, and don't worry . . .' Well, he could rest now. For a few days he would go back to life, and forget the strung, harried existence that was war. Perhaps when he came back he would not feel so harried. Rest, and don't worry.

For some time Grant forgot his last talk with Rawlins, or remembered it only as the fantasy of a puzzling man. But shortly he received a number of visitors who had not the usual requests to make, and he began to see that Rawlins's notion had not been altogether fantastic. Newspaper gossip is one thing, and elaborately vague proposals from accredited party members is another. There was almost nothing definite said, but in half an hour or so of conversation it was clear to Ulyss that precision waited only on his word. After the first interview it did not take him so long to understand. Democrats and Republicans alike began by talk of his glorious achievements, and progressed to wordy, obscure remarks on how desperately the nation needed a leader of proved worth. That was the place where a word of deprecation, even a conscious look, would bring the discussion to flattering concrete terms. Ulyss sat with silent lips and silent, blank eyes, and in time his callers stammered into silence too. The General's bearing was worse than a refusal: it made awkward, guilty boys of them, and none of them knew how to withdraw from it with any grace.

The matter filled Ulyss with amazement and shock. For nearly three years now the nation had been at war against itself, and he believed that the coming year would bring a decision. Yet the people were absorbed in politics, originating and spreading criticism of their leaders, daring to call into question not only the conduct of the war but whether it should be continued at all. To Ulyss the thing was as outrageous as though his enlisted men gathered to criticize his battle plans. He would have liked to say something of this to his callers, but he could not trust himself to speak with any force to strangers.

There was one, however, to whom he could speak. On an evening late in December Wilson announced a Mr. Jones, and Grant recognized an acquaintance from Galena. He knew him but slightly, for Jones had been a man of great importance, but he did know him. He seemed in no hurry to speak, and Grant's mouth set as he thought that this man too was on the same disloyal errand.

'I've just come from Washington,' Jones said at last, 'and I've been out of touch. How are things going here, General?'

'Well enough,' said Grant curtly. He would have stopped there, but the other's quiet waiting led him to add, 'I hope to move on Mobile in the spring, as soon as we can clear Longstreet out of east Tennessee.'

'A magnificent plan,' Jones nodded, 'and I'm sure you'll carry it out with your usual success.' It was the familiar opening move, and Ulyss regretted that he had been even so slightly cordial, but his caller's next words startled him. 'Mr. Lincoln places a great deal of faith in you.'

'The President?' Ulyss said with a blankness approaching stupidity. He was not surprised at what his caller had said, but was astounded that he had said it.

'Yes,' Jones continued evenly. 'I've known Mr. Lincoln a long time, years before he attained his present great office, and he sometimes confides in me. It is very gratifying to me as his friend to know that there is someone he can trust, and that someone a man from Galena.'

'The President has many close friends,' said Ulyss, with a slight frown, still afraid that perhaps he was being led into a trap by a more adroit hunter than he had yet encountered.

'Abe Lincoln had friends all over the country. President Lincoln has mighty few, General, and when he goes to bed at night he can't be sure that he'll have those when he wakes up in the morning. How could he be?' Jones dropped his formal, wary tone, and spoke rapidly, with a sincerity to convince even the doubtful Ulyss. 'A President's whole life is to decide things, and whatever he decides there's dead sure to be thousands of people who think he's wrong, and try to fight him. Not just Democrats, but men of his own party. Maybe they're the worst. He not only has to fight the rebs, and the copperheads, but the Radical Republicans, and if he's defeated —— That would be a disaster, I think. He has to have another term to finish his work, and his friends feel that for the country's sake his work must be finished.'

Then at last Ulyss understood. 'Of course,' he said. 'A man has to finish what he's begun. The President same as anybody else — same as me. I wouldn't think of stopping for anything else before the war was fought to an end.' He paused, unaccustomed to the methods of indirection, then added, 'I'm a soldier — he's the President. We each have our own jobs.'

Their eyes met, and Jones nodded. His commission had been carried out, but he stayed a little while. He mentioned Galena, but soon found that Grant had no great desire to reminisce, and shifted slowly to talk of Washington and the complex tangle of affairs there. This was a subject of which Grant had little knowledge, and he listened with bewildered interest. A cabinet with more dissent than cooperation, and at least one member reporting its deliberations to its enemies. A Congress already considering measures of reconstruction, and denouncing the President as a traitor because his plan was less stringent than theirs, and he had dared to use his veto against them. A party reluctant to face the traditional renomination. Days and nights dissonant with criticism, pleading, reproach. Compromises interpreted as weakness, and firmness as tyranny. To

Ulyss, whose only experience of public life was military, it was
a nightmare world that Jones described. He had thought of the
President as the head of the state, the occupant of an office with
definite and unquestioned duties. Now for a moment he saw
him as a man whose office was always being shaped, never quite
the same from dawn to dark; a man storm-whipped — and
lonely. Ulyss had long known the loneliness of failure, was
beginning now to know the loneliness of success, and fleetingly
he glimpsed what it must be for the man who was success and
failure at once.

Word began to spread in the newspapers that General Grant
had declared he could not be a candidate for president. His job
was to finish fighting the war, he had said, and until that was
done he could not even consider anything else. No one knew
exactly where the rumor came from, but it appeared in approxi-
mately the same form in many places, and when the correspondents came to the General he confirmed it.

'How about after the war?' they asked. 'Would you accept
a nomination then?'

'No,' he answered, remembering his talk with Jones. 'I'm a
soldier, not a statesman.'

'Wouldn't you accept any office at all?'

'I'd like to be mayor of Galena long enough to build a sidewalk from my house to the station.'

The correspondents had their story. Ulyss had meant nothing by his final remark, had not even known it was in his mind
uutil it was spoken. The necessity of saying something, the
momentary memory of Jones and the sub-memory of the Galena
where he had known him, combined to produce a few facetious
words that he promptly forgot. But the newspapers did not
forget. The sentence made a neatly satisfactory conclusion to
an interview with the famous soldier, and on that foundation
the figure of Grant the modest and self-effacing man was raised
beside Grant the imperturbable and relentless warrior. Rawlins,

reading the account at breakfast while his bride watched him fondly from across the table, nodded in satisfaction.

Soon after his decision was made public Ulyss was summoned to St. Louis by a frantic telegram from Julia. Fred, who had not been well for some time, was gravely ill. As Ulyss's train rattled and jerked over the prairies it seemed to him to repeat over and over, 'Send for the family . . . send for the family . . .' That was what they did when someone was dying, that was what they had done now. He tried to think of it coolly, without denying the probabilities, as he thought of dangerous campaigns, but he could not. Death was a suspended sentence on his soldiers, a commonplace factor in his calculations: it had no place in the other category of his life, where Julia and the children were supposed to be happy, and safe. Fred. The feel of the boy's tense shoulders when they had stood together to watch the running of the batteries at Vicksburg. The absurd white plowhorses he and Dana had found for mounts in the campaign, and the odd, warm friendship that had been between the boy and the observer. The wound he had received at the Big Black; his original panic followed by exaggerated indifference. These things were the boy Fred, and it was impossible to imagine him lying still, meeting in a hushed room the blackness that he faithfully believed he had faced on the battlefield. Death was for soldiers and old people, not for boys, not for Fred. But Julia had sent for him, Julia who was capable and self-sufficient and not easily frightened. Send for the family . . . send for the family . . .

She was waiting for him where the ferry came in. 'Not much change,' she said without waiting for him to ask. 'It's pneumonia.' He took her in his arms, and for a fragment of an instant she relaxed there, trembling; then she was grave and composed again, with her terror showing only in her eyes.

White Haven was thick with quiet when they arrived. Ulyss had always thought of the place in connection with the young

Julia and his love of her, but now it had no meaning apart from the sick boy upstairs. Colonel Dent greeted him soberly, the servants moved mournfully about, even small Jesse was subdued except for his welcoming shout when he saw his father. Ulyss went upstairs to see his son. Perhaps then his sense of unreality would go, and he could face the thing as he was accustomed to face catastrophe, shielded by fatalism. But there was no reality in the pinched young face on the pillow. It was not Fred. There were shadows in it of the child Fred had been, and it had the form of the young man Fred would be, but nothing at all of the present Fred. Ulyss choked and turned away. Julia took him downstairs and stayed with him a while before she returned to her vigil.

Colonel Dent talked to him, at first with a kindly wish to distract him, and then because the old man wanted to talk. He had evolved a compromise between sentiment and pride. By position and inheritance he was a Southern sympathizer, but with his son in the Union army and his son-in-law its most conspicuous general his rebellion was chiefly a poetic emotion. He talked now with happy inaccuracy of Lee's campaigns, with apparently complete adulation until he added, with unabashed illogic, 'Of course, when you meet him it'll be a different story.'

'I won't meet him,' Ulyss responded dully. 'It's the Army of the Potomac that opposes him, and it's not in my division.'

'It'll be all one when you're lieutenant general.'

'There's no such grade.'

'There will be, all right. And when the bill's passed you'll be appointed, never fear. You're the only man they've got who has a chance against Lee...' The voice went on and on, but Ulyss did not listen. He tried to think of what the lieutenant generalship would mean. He knew that it was not simply an old man's fancy. There had been talk of it, not only by newspapers but by such weighty men as Washburne. Lieutenant

General Grant, the first since Washington. It had no meaning. Nothing had a meaning while his son lay ill upstairs.

For several days Ulyss waited miserably. People came to see him, dispatches came for him, there was a considerable demand on his time, but he was not conscious of anything but waiting. Julia might perhaps have comforted him, but he could not take her from Fred's side. He wandered over the house and the wintry fields, alone or accompanied by Jesse. The child's chatter at least demanded no response, and there was a certain comfort in watching him — not all his sons were to be taken from him.

Then one morning he saw Julia coming out to him, walking quickly. He ran to her, not because he was eager to hear her news, he was afraid to hear, but to relieve her the faster of what she must say to him.

'It's all right,' she called before he reached her, and he stopped short.

'You mean he's going to get well?' He was incredulous. He had not even tried to hope: that had seemed a needless twisting of the knife that could not be turned aside.

'Of course he is. He slept well, he's breathing easier, and the doctor says he's out of danger.' She spoke as though she had never expected anything else. Ulyss was humbled, and for a moment he felt that her courage to meet the catastrophes of living was greater than the courage of his men who charged cheering into death.

With Fred recovering, there was no good reason to hold Grant any longer from his headquarters. Rawlins had returned there, and Ulyss thought he could feel his chief of staff's impatient disapproval even at that distance. But the people of the city were planning to give a dinner for him, and Ulyss stubbornly determined to stay for it. He knew that Rawlins regarded such functions as idle, vainglorious, and wasteful encroachments on the time and dignity of a soldier, but Rawlins had no true realization of what such a dinner in St. Louis meant to Ulyss.

As he sat in his place and looked at the guests gathered to do him honor he saw them as headings in the account of his failures, drawn up now to be paid in full. Colonel Dent, who had vowed never again to receive his traitor son-in-law. The man who had taken Ulyss into the real estate business, and eased him out again. The man whose vote had lost Ulyss the county surveyorship. The head of the university where Ulyss had wanted to teach mathematics, and had been refused. Dozens of leading citizens who had ignored the shabby farmer carting wood over the country roads, or treated him with the brusque kindliness given to a failure whose sin is rather ineffectiveness than a positive crime. They were all there, the landowners, soldiers, business and professional men. They looked at Ulysses Grant with respectful curiosity, and the knowing among them murmured of how close the presidency had come to this man, and of how Washington sources had assured them that the lieutenant generalship bill was a sure thing. In a few weeks Grant would have supreme command, except for the President, of all the Union forces. Ulyss looked back, without rancor. These people had on the whole not been unpleasant to him, and if there had been more tolerance than faith in their attitude he did not blame them. He could not have expected them to believe he would ultimately succeed when his own belief had been worn down by the years to crumbling dust. It was enough that they had come today.

He was startled when his contemplation was interrupted by cries for a speech. He stood up, trying desperately to think while they cheered him, but as usual his throat closed and he seemed unable to recall more than a dozen words. Too soon the noise stopped and the guests sat waiting.

'In response,' he began, his voice sounding thin and distant. He cleared his throat and began again, 'In response it will be impossible for me to do more than thank you.' His hearers

still waited, but when he sat down abruptly, his cheeks red
above the beard, they realized that his speech was finished.
They cheered again then, and laughed, friendly, approving
laughter. It was a good speech, fitting precisely with the man
they had come to know in the last few years, the great soldier
whose deeds spoke for him with Attic eloquence, who was too
modest to elaborate them with his own tongue.

'U. S. Grant and son, Galena, Ills.' Fred, still hollow-eyed
after his illness, quivered with pride as he watched the words
entered on the hotel register. The clerk had turned away while
the formality was observed. A desk clerk at the Willard in the
chaotic Washington of wartime had neither time nor energy
to be curious about a stooped, ill-dressed man and a boy. The
clerk saw Mr. Dana of the War Department hurrying toward
him, and let the new arrivals stand while he waited to learn
the will of that important personage. But Dana swept by him,
thumped the bearded man on the shoulder, grinned at the boy,
and shouted, 'Why, General Grant, we hadn't expected you
so soon!'

Then it was impossible to see or hear anything. The lobby
was crowded, and at the words everybody in it clustered about
Ulyss. He found himself surrounded by shifting faces, with
strangers pumping his hand, pounding his back, pressing ever
closer to him. He had for a moment a desperate desire for
flight, but he was imprisoned by a curious and enthusiastic
wall, and forced to stand his ground. Questions were shouted
at him, but it was impossible to answer, or to do anything but
stand still and let himself be touched and looked at until the
unoccupied population of that part of Washington had satisfied
its interest in the man who was to be lieutenant general.

It was over an hour before the crowd weakened enough for
the hotel manager to escort the General to his rooms. Dana
accompanied him, and chuckled as he watched Ulyss wiping

his face and pulling vaguely at his clothes. They were not really disordered, but he felt by instinct that he had been mauled.

Dana remarked, 'So besieged, even you must surrender, General.'

'I've been surrendering till I have no arms left,' Ulyss grinned, but quickly sobered. 'I didn't know it would be like this,' he said.

'What did you expect?' asked Dana. 'You're a famous man. You've just been appointed lieutenant general. Did you think people wouldn't pay any attention when you walk by?'

'I didn't think,' said Ulyss. He looked from his window down to the swarming streets, deep mud being churned yet deeper by the passage of army guns and ambulances, loaded wagons, private carriages, occasional riding horses. The people on foot, mud-spattered to their heads, cursed and threatened by teamsters, jostled recklessly by others of their own tribe, plunged blindly forward as if they were resigned to their peril. 'I guess I'm not much used to cities.'

'Washington is like nothing on earth right now,' Dana agreed. 'For one thing, it's overloaded with soldiers to protect it, has been ever since First Bull Run. They say a man threw a stone at a dog on Pennsylvania Avenue the other day and hit three commissioned officers. Then the contractors, and office-seekers, and anybody in the country with a lunatic idea — that's leaving out lots of people, including Congress and the regular population.' Fred was listening to him with bright-cheeked interest, but Ulyss frowned heavily. 'Of course,' Dana added, 'you get used to it after a while, and never think anything about it. Are you planning to make your headquarters here?'

'No,' Ulyss answered, with so much emphasis that he sounded violent. 'Not here — I'm not meant for a place like this. I belong in the field.' There was an unreasoning reluctance in him to stay in this teeming city. He was assured now in his

own setting, in the military world where authority and responsibility were neatly defined, and a man's work was plain
before him. He felt something close to terror at the thought
of exchanging those clear limits for this place, this meeting
point for the thousands of demands, intentions, and desires that
make up a nation, controlled only by the uncertainties of civil
order.

'No,' said Ulyss again. Not so loudly this time, not so much
a protest as a vow.

'Where, then?' Dana spoke so casually that Rawlins would
have been suspicious of him, but Ulyss did not notice. 'West,
or east?'

'I can't tell yet.' Grant's brow cleared as he returned to
familiar ground. 'I've not had time to make plans for all the
armies — the only thing I know for sure is that there ought
to be one plan for them all to work on, not a different campaign for every corps. If it works out right, and I can, I'd like
to make my headquarters in Tennessee. That would be the
centre — and I'm a western man.'

Nodding, apparently in complete agreement, Dana began
to talk of the affairs of the Army of the Potomac. He spoke
casually, not in the least as if he were explaining a delicate
situation or arguing against Grant's intentions. But Ulyss
received an impression of the Army of the Potomac that he
did not at the moment fully realize. Meade, a good soldier
but with a certain rigidity which prevented him from pro-
gressing beyond adequacy, a courteous and considerate general
except during a battle, when his temper came so close to the
demonic that his own aides avoided him. Warren, another
good soldier, but a comic-opera reversal of Meade, gentle and
unruffled on the battlefield and at any other time an impossibly
rasping associate, either as superior or subordinate. Sedgwick
the beloved, the gallant warrior. Behind these were the shadows of McClellan, of Hooker and Pope and Burnside, the

leaders who had taken the Army of the Potomac and spilled its blood to no avail; and behind them all, vast, incalculable, legendary, was the shadow of Lee. Dana's comments demanded no answer, and Ulyss made none. He was scarcely conscious of how much he had heard, nor that far back in his mind, where his plans were being formed, the eastern end of his line was assuming a troubled importance he had never given it before.

That evening Ulyss went to the White House to see the President. He had been told there was a reception scheduled for that night, and had expected that there would be other callers, but he had not imagined that there could be so many. The walks were crowded with people, shabby, richly dressed, with the pride of station in their bearing, or the half-arrogant, half-suspicious bearing of those who sought for station, or the simple curiosity of sightseers. Remembering the crushing crowd in the lobby that morning, Ulyss would have much preferred to withdraw and pay his respects another time, but that meant turning back, and his superstition was stronger than his aversion. He let the tide carry him into the house and to the door of the East Room. There the narrowed channel held back the stream for a moment, and he had his first glimpse of Lincoln. Tall, gaunt, dark, as his pictures had indicated. Ugly, as the pictures also said, but with something else in his face that no picture had shown and Ulyss could not define.

It was only a few seconds that Ulyss had to look at him, for then the President's gray eyes found the short, bearded man in the doorway, and he said, 'It's General Grant!' The words were not shouted, and the room had been clamorous, but they made an instant's silence that mounted into a buzz of comment, and a path was cleared for Ulyss.

'This is indeed a pleasure,' Lincoln said as he shook hands. He talked easily, warmly, so that it was not necessary for Grant to say much in reply. Ulyss had to hold his head back to see the President, for there was a difference between them of eight inches in stature. Even so close he could not be sure what element he had seen in Lincoln's face. Something — dark? light? — that was in no other face around him, that could not even be traced to a given feature, not to the small deep-set eyes nor the high lined forehead nor the mouth compound of stubbornness and sensitivity. Perhaps it was the look of the man himself, a man so set apart from any whom Ulyss had known that he had no way to measure him. As he spoke in the familiar midwestern tones Ulyss remembered suddenly what Jones had said: 'Mr. Lincoln places a great deal of faith in you.' That was an obligation, and must be discharged unfailingly. Ulyss could serve this man, and if he did not fully understand him it would not matter.

In a few moments it was necessary to turn Grant over to the others who were waiting restlessly for the President to relinquish him. Ulyss had thought that nothing could be worse than the morning's experience, but this time he was in real danger of being crushed, and Lincoln suggested that he stand on a couch. He stood there, a living monument to himself, and felt his cheeks grow hot, but woodenly kept his place. It was easier if he left his eyes unfocused, but he did glimpse Lincoln's quiet smile, and the look on Secretary Stanton's face, of cold curiosity and something too close to jealousy. Ulyss looked away. He understood Stanton well enough.

Before Grant left Lincoln drew him aside for a private word. 'When I present your commission to you,' he said, 'I'll say a few words, not a speech, but just a sentence or so.' He apparently did not see the appalled look in Grant's eyes. 'I'll give you a copy of what I'm going to say, and you might have an answer ready.' Then he did smile, with open understanding. 'I'm going to read my piece.'

Then I can read mine, Ulyss thought gratefully. He had heard that the President was tactful.

Julia and Rawlins were waiting for him when he returned, having come down on the evening train from Philadelphia. Fred had been told to go to bed, but his eagerness to hear of his father's call on the President was too great to allow obedience. He stood by his mother and listened, and their eyes were wide and bright while Ulyss told them of how Lincoln had recognized him in the crowd, of his warm reception, and how he had been rescued from his admirers. Wife and son prompted him with rapid questions, and their pride lit their faces. Rawlins listened too, sitting a little apart, half-swallowing his coughs so as not to interrupt.

This was what must be, he knew. He had seen long ago the path the undistinguished brigadier would take, and had set himself to lead him on it, to clear it for him, to keep his own eyes on the goal Grant had not enough imagination to see. It had been plain to Rawlins that a general with this one's habit of aggressive military thought, and plodding persistence, was likely one day to be given supreme command, for the North had need of a man who could use superior force as a sabre to break through the brilliant fencing of the South. Properly managed, Grant was an almost inevitable choice. Rawlins had managed him, and had now the double satisfaction of successful work and fulfilled prophecy.

But he had not foreseen that when this moment came he would feel the man he had come to think of as his ward slipping from him. He had not remembered that as Grant advanced from brigadier to major general to supreme command he would be enfolded with successive layers of military formality, and his relations with a subordinate must stiffen, however receptive he might be, however determined Rawlins. Moreover, Rawlins felt, Grant was not as receptive as he once had been. Since Vicksburg there seemed to be a new element in him, a greater confidence in success, a more peremptory habit of command, that made him less malleable. This, too, was inevitable, and proper. A succeeding man does not allow for failure in his calculations; a commanding general does not question his own authority.

The very nature of his task, thought Rawlins, would make it more difficult the closer he brought it to completion. Why not abandon it in its present stage? There was a naïve pride in Grant's voice tonight, a certain complacence in his bearing. Other offices, perhaps greater than the lieutenant generalship, might come to him, but he did not know it, and they would not make him happier than he was now. Rawlins would be glad enough to call his work done, to fight the war without any speculation on what was to come after, to fill his busy mind with thoughts of his wife Elizabeth. He had come to Grant straight from the death of his personal life, and the cloudy destiny of his superior had been an interest into which he could pour all his patriotic energy and nervous ambition. Now he had a wife again, and it would be sweet to plan only for his own life with her. He thought for a while of how sweet it would be, but not for long. He was a realistic man, and knew that he could no more turn from Grant than Grant could turn from his future.

In the morning Ulyss with his wife and son, and Rawlins, went again to the White House. He was to receive his commission that day. Knowing that it was merely a formality, and with permission to read the only speech it would be necessary to make, he thought very little about it, but smoked quietly and looked for indications of spring in the glossy bushes of early March. When spring came he could move his armies, all of them, from Meade's on the Rapidan to Banks's in Texas. But Julia's hand was tense on his arm. She said nothing at all after they left the hotel until just before they reached the sentries in front of the White House, and then she gasped:

'I'm so nervous, Victor — I swear to goodness I wasn't half so upset the day we were married.'

'It doesn't mean anything,' he assured her. 'The President will just hand me the commission, and that will be all. There's nothing to be nervous about.'

'It's a very great responsibility,' said Rawlins behind them. 'The President's in giving it, and yours in taking it.'

There was a group of people waiting for them: Wilson, who had been transferred to the Cavalry Bureau, now come to see the honoring of his former chief; all the cabinet; Halleck, pleasantly friendly, with no indication that he resented the transfer of whatever substance his office had possessed to this man whom he had taken so long to trust. A few others whose standing or influence entitled them to witness the final unification of the Union command.

The President was announced immediately after Grant's arrival. He came in quietly, with no pomp of office in his bearing, but the gravity of the occasion was in his eyes. Greeting the assembly, he advanced to Grant. There was a folded paper in his right hand, and another slip in his left, at which he glanced as he spoke.

'General Grant,' he began in a clear, low voice, 'the nation's appreciation of what you have done, and its reliance upon you for what remains to be done in the existing great struggle, are now presented, with this commission constituting you lieutenant general in the Army of the United States. With this high honor devolves upon you also a corresponding responsibility. As the country herein trusts you, so, under God, it will sustain you. I scarcely need to add that, with what I here speak for the nation, goes my own hearty personal concurrence.'

The commission was put into Grant's hand. He bowed and drew forth his own slip of paper, striving to give to his voice and words the grave clarity there had been in the President's.

'Mr. President, I accept the commission, with gratitude for the high honor conferred. With the aid of the noble armies that have fought in so many fields for our common country, it will be my earnest endeavor not to disappoint your expectation. I feel the full weight of the responsibilities now devolving on me; and I know that if they are met it will be due to those armies, and above all to the favor of that Providence which leads both nations and men.'

For an instant the commission was immeasurably heavy in Ulyss's hand. He realized then that the armies so consigned to him were not weapons but men, and that failure now would be no longer simply a personal humiliation, but a blow to his fellow man, a bitter tragedy to the nation. For a flash of eternity he was stiff with icy panic, then his moment of perception passed. He had been commissioned lieutenant general, and he knew what he must do.

PART FOUR

Ruins of Richmond after the Fire

IV. FOLLOW TO THE DEATH

CHAPTER ELEVEN

NOT cities, not railroads, not positions, but armies. Not
Richmond, not the Richmond, Fredericksburg & Potomac, but
Lee. The problem was the same, and the answer was the same,
whether the example was a minor campaign in the Mississippi
Valley or the conduct of the war across the breadth of America.

It was the people of the South who must be subdued, and fundamentally the Southern people was embodied in Lee. For three years the North had cried 'On to Richmond!'; for three years Northern victories had seemed almost barren because Richmond still stood. Richmond, Ulyss saw, was of importance only so long as Lee was bound to protect it, and therefore bound to it.

The simplicity of the fundamental conception made simple all the vast strategy of the war. Lee must be defeated, again and again until he was incapable of any resistance whatever. The Army of the Potomac would do that, by moving on Richmond and forcing the Confederate general to fight for the place. Lee had parried other such attempts by raids on Washington up the Great Valley of Virginia: this time a Federal force under Sigel would operate there and close the valley. Lee was fed by the broad, fat, unravaged fields of Alabama and Georgia: Sherman would move down to Atlanta, preventing Johnston from sending any help to the east, and destroying Lee's supplies and communications. 'You I propose,' Ulyss wrote his friend, '. . . to get into the interior of the enemy's country as far as you can, inflicting all the damage you can against their war resources.' The pincers on Johnston were to be completed by Banks, moving on Mobile and then striking northward. Last of all, the Army of the James under Butler would directly threaten Richmond while Lee confronted the Army of the Potomac. There were two thousand miles of front involved, and half a dozen armies, but the plan was in essence single and uncomplicated: a gigantic turning movement pivoted on the few miles of Virginia soil that Lee was forced to defend. Pressed on all fronts, it would be impossible for him to send or receive re-enforcements, and the plan of repeated engagements rather than maneuvering for positions would mean snowballing casualties that Lee could not replace.

'There'd be casualties on our side too,' Rawlins said doubt-

fully as soon as he saw what was in Grant's mind. 'We've
lost more than Lee in almost every action.'

'We can replace ours,' said Grant calmly. 'Now that the
draft law's working there won't be much trouble about that.
But the rebs haven't got any more men big enough to tote a
gun. What they lose, they lose for good.'

'Even so — it'll be a damned bloody business on both sides.
If you sent the Army of the Potomac to Richmond by water,
or even struck straight down from the Rapidan instead of
fighting Lee in that God-blighted Wilderness ——'

'Then Lee would be at Richmond before us, and we'd have
to sit down and starve him out. I don't want a siege if I can
help it. It may come to that, but if we don't fight him till he's
bled white first he'd have enough men to make a detachment
to threaten Washington, or re-enforce Johnston. I can't have
that.'

'There'll be more lives wasted in a campaign like this than
in all the rest of the war,' Rawlins persisted.

'Look here, Rawlins,' Grant said with annoyance. 'This is
the way I'm going to fight the war. We've got more men and
material and money. Why not use them? Maneuvering all
over the map, with a dab here and a dab there, is idiotic if
you've got the force to do anything else. If we did that most
likely we'd win in the end, but it would take us several more
years, and by that time the people might be so sick of the war
they'd listen to the copperheads. Even if they didn't we'd lose
more men in dribbles, by skirmishes and sickness and so on,
than we would in a few big battles to wind things up in a hurry.'

A duller red shadowed the color in Rawlins's cheeks, but he
said nothing more. He was revolted at any plan with the
avowed purpose of killing as many men as possible, and had
fought with every argument he could find, but found none
strong enough to affect this assured and authoritative Grant.
He was homesick for the Army of the Tennessee, where, if he

did not always win his case, he was at least never cut short
by the brusque reminder, 'This is the way I'm going to fight
the war.'

Grant's first intention, to make his headquarters in the west,
to go back to the terrain and men and methods he knew, disappeared so soon that he almost forgot he had ever had it.
Lee was in the east, and he was to be fought and defeated by
the Army of the Potomac. Ulyss, with the responsibility of the
whole entirely on his shoulders, could not add to his burden the
detailed leadership of a single organization, but neither could
he stay at a distance, trusting the vital thrust of his plan
entirely to other hands. He determined to make his headquarters with the Army of the Potomac, so that he could meet
shifting events hour by hour and see that his orders were
obeyed at once; but to leave the actual command of the army
in Meade's hands.

The arrangement was awkward, but in dealing with Lee
Ulyss dared make no other, and Meade was loyally cooperative. 'You must not feel obligated to keep me here, General,'
he said. 'If you would rather have another man to work with
you in my position, Sherman, for instance —— This campaign
is too important to be interfered with by consideration of
personalities. I'll do my best wherever you want to place me.'

'I've no intention of making any change,' Grant assured
him. 'You're the commander of the Army of the Potomac,
you know the men and they know you. I wouldn't think of
substituting anyone else.' He hesitated, then added with a
frankness brought forth by Meade's selfless attitude, 'I would
have liked to put W. F. Smith in at the head of the Army of the
James. Butler's a good enough administrator, but I'd rather
have a soldier.'

'Yes,' Meade nodded. 'But in an election year ——'

'That's what the President said.' Lincoln had made clear
why it must be so. Ben Butler had reached his rank because

he was a clever politician, and it would be foolhardy to relieve
him before the election. 'Well,' Grant consoled himself aloud,
'with Smith as second in command he can't go very far wrong.
He'll keep Lee worried about Richmond, and he can hold the
James, so if we do have to lay siege we'll have the river for a
supply line.'

'Do you intend to besiege Richmond, General?'

'Not if we can wipe up Lee before he gets there. But maybe
we can't, and then we'll need the James.' Ulyss smiled slightly.
'We're moving the fourth of May — we'll find out then.'
Meade nodded but did not speak. Both were thinking of the
Wilderness, that region of scrub growth and matted thickets,
where so many Federal attempts had been defeated that the
place could be considered as the first outwork of the Richmond defenses, a hundred miles away. There Grant would
meet Lee, and find an outline of the answer to the question the
nation was asking.

The tall Confederate commander haunted him. His name
seemed written on the maps, inscribed with bold triumph at
Manassas, Fredericksburg, Chancellorsville, and at all the
little villages clustered about Richmond where McClellan had
first encountered him. Many officers in Washington spoke of
him with a respect colored by awe and an odd affection, as if
they were forever distinguished simply by having fought him.
They tried delicately to indicate something of his quality to
Grant, having seen too often the bloody results of ignoring it,
and even the common soldier made the same inverted boast.
Any talk of Grant and his triumphs was certain to be cut short
by the comment, 'He hasn't met Bobby Lee,' made by some
enlisted man with a look of grim pride, ignoring the fact that
his point was likely to be proved with his life.

He's mortal, thought Ulyss. He did good work in Mexico,
but so did other men, and nobody made a hero out of him then.
Now even the papers on our side call him a greater Napoleon

every time his pickets have a skirmish. He's mortal, and so are his men. But mere logic could not erase that name.

The plans were kept as secret as possible, for even highly confidential matters were likely to be fully recounted in the Richmond newspapers. Stanton was angry that they were not entrusted to him, but fussily cautioned Grant against telling the President of them. 'He tells everything he knows,' said the Secretary irritably. 'He's got no conception of keeping a military secret.'

Lincoln gave Grant the same caution. 'Don't tell me what you're going to do,' he said with a slow, slightly twisted smile. 'People are always trying to pump me, and it saves me an awful lot of temptation if I just don't know.' The traces of the smile stayed on his lips, but his eyes were grave and searching as he added, 'And I won't tell you what to do. It's a good idea to wait for military advantage, but we haven't got all eternity to fight in, nor the treasures of Croesus to fight with.' He had spoken sternly, but his tone softened. 'I've watched you, and you know that. There won't be any executive orders for you — we can both have a rest.'

It was an assurance that Ulyss was glad to have, and he nodded. Army men had long been impatient at the peremptory orders issued to them by the civilian President, but although Ulyss was pleased that there would be no such orders for him he understood well enough why there had been for others. The policy of delaying action until it could be had on the most advantageous terms annoyed him as much as it did the President, and he had never been so learned in his field that he could forget the non-military factors of money and civilian morale, factors which sometimes outweighed in his deliberations the technicalities of position and force. Thus it pleased him that the President promised him no interference, but did not surprise him.

The entire campaign was to be set in motion on the fourth

of May, from Sherman in Mississippi to Butler in tidewater
Virginia. The preceding weeks were a blur of work to Ulyss,
for there was not only the main outline of his strategy to be
determined, appointments to be made, orders to be given, but
his personal affairs to be considered, ranging in importance
from the fine new gloves that Julia gave him so that he might
make a fitting appearance, to the selection of his new staff.
Rawlins had offered his resignation, with a half-resentful,
half-wistful punctilio.

'I'm not a trained soldier,' he said. 'Now that you're lieutenant general you ought to have a West Pointer in my place.'

'Why, that's impossible!' Grant protested. 'I can't let you
go, Rawlins — I couldn't get along without you ——'

'I guess you could,' said Rawlins, but at length allowed
himself to be persuaded. It was not only Grant's friendly
insistence that held him, but a sense that it was truly impossible
for him to remove himself, that he was bound to Grant despite
the growing distance between them. And it was now such a
staff as he was glad to head. The young Captain Porter who
had been at Chattanooga had attached himself to Grant.
Adam Badeau, who had been a journalist before the war, was
now a most efficient military secretary to the lieutenant general.
The engineer was O. E. Babcock, darkly handsome, with strong
white teeth and eyes as black as Rawlins's own, though with an
entirely different glint. Most of the lightweights had disappeared as Grant had progressed, and the staff as a whole
almost came up to Rawlins's standards.

In the last days of April Ulyss paid his final visit to Washington. The arrangements were complete, and Meade had his
orders, the vital point of the campaign. 'Lee's army will be
your objective point. Wherever Lee's army goes, you will go
also.'

Lincoln said good-bye to his general quietly, and Grant
crossed the street to the war office to make his farewells to the

Secretary. Stanton was still annoyed that Grant had not consulted him on the plan of campaign, and but little consoled that the President had not been consulted either. He believed firmly that the War Department had complete authority over commanders in the field, and in his person at least ought to have authority over the Commander in Chief.

'I suppose,' he said stiffly, 'that you've left Washington strongly garrisoned?'

'No, I couldn't do that,' Grant answered quietly.

'Why not? Why not?' Stanton's eyes were instantly dark with suspicion, and cold with the old terror for the city that had ridden its inhabitants since the first battle of Bull Run.

'I need all the men I can get. Washington's best defense is keeping Lee too hard pressed to threaten it.'

'That won't do at all. It's contrary to my plans.' There was unquestioned finality in Stanton's voice, and an undertone almost of satisfaction at having caught his headstrong subordinate in suicidal error. 'Washington can't be left wide open like that. I'll order the men back at once.'

'You can't do that,' Grant said, not in protest, simply in level statement of a fact. 'I need the men where they are.'

'And why can't I?'

'I believe I rank the Secretary of War in this matter.'

It was said, and they looked at each other in silence for a moment. Grant's eyes did not waver. There was no defiance in them, nor curiosity, nor arrogance. There was not much interest. Stanton's eyes were blazing, and he was held quiet only by the realization that against the other's calm an open exhibition of anger must appear as weakness. 'We'll take it to the President,' he threatened.

'That's a good idea,' Grant nodded. 'He ranks us both.'

They crossed to the White House and went directly to the President's office. Lincoln looked from Grant's quiet face to the Secretary's pinched lips and hot eyes, and raised his brows.

Stanton said curtly, 'State your case, General.'

'I haven't a case,' said Ulyss mildly. 'I'm satisfied.'

'Mr. President,' Stanton cried, too outraged to struggle any longer for concealment, 'this man wants to turn the town over to the rebs. He's stripped the garrison and sent the men down to the Rapidan. Even supposing he should beat Lee, what good will that do when we're murdered in our beds and the Capitol's in flames?'

Ulyss watched the President. He had been promised freedom from executive orders, with the implication that without them he would make speed. He was gambling that the promise would not be revoked in order to slow him down. Lincoln sprawled in his chair, watching his infuriated Secretary reflectively.

'Now, Mr. Secretary,' he began when Stanton at last spluttered to a stop, 'we've been running things our way for three years, and we haven't very much to show for it. We sent across the mountains for Mr. Grant, as Mrs. Grant calls him, to run things for us, and I reckon we'll have to let Mr. Grant run things his way.'

Stanton turned and left the room. There was genuine pain in his face. Lincoln sighed as he looked after him. 'I'll have to fix that up,' he murmured.

'Fix it up?' said Grant. 'Fix what up? You're his superior ——'

'I'm President, and he's my Secretary of War. He's a good Secretary, Mr. Grant, you know that. He's honest and devoted to his country. There's times when he's a mite too attached to his own lights, but I can't let the usefulness of a good man go to waste because he isn't perfect. I'll have to find something to ask him about, so he can tell me what to do.' He smiled, the slow, illuminating smile that touched his ungainly face with beauty. If there was weariness in it Ulyss was too puzzled to notice.

Far down the sleeping lines there was a sound that swept up in a long wave, borne by the tide of drums and crested by the bugles' silver calling. The dawn of the fourth of May was rose and gold behind the feathery trees. Ulyss stood before his headquarters drawing on his gloves, uncomfortable of body with his trim new uniform firmly buttoned and his waist bound twice over with a silk sash and a gold-striped belt; uncomfortable of mind with a tight, airless sensation, as though he might have forgotten to breathe.

Across the little river before him was the Wilderness, and somewhere in the Wilderness was Lee. He could not be seen, nothing could be seen but the mat of scrubby bushes and entangling vines topped in places by a cedar or a sweet gum. Once off the few ill-defined roads a man would be invisible behind such cover, a whole army could be invisible. The ghost of Stonewall Jackson, shot by his own idolizing men, testified to the tragic confusion of battles fought in this place. Here Hooker had crossed, and been thrown back across the river with crushing losses. Burnside had tried to avoid the place, and gone down by Fredericksburg, where his men had been piled in walls of death ten feet high and the rebels had cheered the heroism of the countrymen they were killing. McClellan had gone all the way around by sea, and Lee with Richmond at his back had all but annihilated the Army of the Potomac. Pope had not even got this far. Ulyss pulled uneasily at his tight collar, and smoothed his gloves. Today a new chapter was beginning, and he knew that in it the end of the story would be foreshadowed. If he could get through the Wilderness and give battle in the open on the other side, or if Lee chose to give battle in this tangled terrain, and failed, the war would be over, however many months and lives it might take to accomplish the inevitable. But if Lee threw him back — Ulyss shook his head. He was not coming back across this river.

Already the men were crossing, rank after eager rank, looking curiously at the dark thicket on the other side of the bridges. They also glanced up at Grant and his staff as they passed. Washburne had come to see the beginning of the campaign, the ultimate responsibility of the man whom he had sponsored, and it was his figure that most interested the men, for his black civilian dress underscored him in the group of blue-uniformed officers.

'It don't look so good, boys,' somebody shouted. 'The old man's brought along his private undertaker.'

'He's come to bury the Confederacy,' someone else protested. 'He's goin' to preach the funeral sermon in Richmond next week.' The men around the two laughed, and the sound spread far beyond, even to those who had not heard the original remark, but laughed because they heard others laugh, and it was a pleasant sound in the warm May sunlight.

By late afternoon the army had crossed the Rapidan, unopposed. 'Lee's been surprised,' said Ulyss with warm satisfaction. 'He hasn't fired a shot — he must have been expecting us to come by his left.' So much for the Lee-worshipers. The great military genius had let a hundred and twenty thousand men steal a march, and perhaps by the time he had recovered his presence of mind he would have to meet them in the open. Even the Wilderness did not seem so formidable at close range. It was only trees and bushes. Close-growing and troublesome to pass, certainly, but no more than an ordinary forest if it did not hide Lee.

The telegrams from other fronts were also encouraging. Sigel was moving down the Valley; Butler had started up the James toward Richmond; Sherman was advancing toward Atlanta and expected shortly to give battle to Johnston. The fourth of May, that portentous day, had passed in quiet efficiency. Grant went to bed early, for whatever he hoped he could not be certain that tomorrow would not bring battle to him. Washburne remarked that Napoleon had been content with four hours of sleep, and Ulyss snorted that he didn't believe it, that he must have taken naps during the day. Another heroic legend, he thought. People persisted in attaching them to generals, as though it weren't ordinary common sense that counts most in war.

Somewhere back of a thicket Lee sat in his tent. To hold on, that was the important thing. To stretch out the war by every possible means until those people wearied and let their unwilling sisters go. It would not be easy to hold on against Grant. Longstreet knew him, and respected him. 'That man,' he had said, 'will fight us every day and every hour till the end of this war.' Every day and every hour, with two men in blue to one in gray. If his crossing of the river had been contested he might have been long delayed; he could not have been defeated. But once entangled in the Wilderness, where he was a stranger and the gray men had fought until they were familiar with every bullet-riddled bush, he might be wiped out altogether. To hold on ... every day and every hour ... to hold on.

In the morning it began. There were shouts, and the eldritch rebel yell from behind the bushes, and then the long roar of a battle no one could see. The field of Shiloh had been obscure, and some of the actions before Vicksburg had been confused, but this was chaos. Men could not advance in line, a ten-foot gap destroyed communication, sometimes a break a mile wide went unobserved. Trees were topped by the ceaseless artillery fire, and fell on men feeling blindly toward one another in the drifting powder smoke, through the undergrowth. Here was no tide of battle, no massing of force in planned strategy, but an unordered raging of living men stepping on the faces of the wounded and the dead.

It was Lee's intention to annihilate the Union army: Grant's either to annihilate the Confederate force or inflict great losses upon it and throw it back. He had not expected to be attacked in the Wilderness when his crossing of the Rapidan had been

uncontested, had believed that the Confederate commander
had been outwitted. Lee had not expected to find such obstinate resistance — other Federal armies he had dealt with here
in his own fastness had not been so hard to persuade. All day
long, while the men fought with their hands, the two commanders balanced their intentions and their surprise, and neither
prevailed.

Early in the morning of the second day, the Union general
Hancock swept forward a long distance, and for a while Ulyss
thought he might snatch a brilliant gain from the clawing
struggle. But very soon the reports brought to him were less
encouraging, and then grew so bad that he could not deny the
day was turning against him. Hancock struggled to keep his
gain, but the gray pressure forced him back, and accident
brought Lee a horrible ally. Fire started licking at the brush,
and the wind expanded it and bore it down on Hancock's men.
Their log breastworks, flaming, fought them back as remorse-
lessly as bullets. And as they retired the last notch of insane
horror came, for the dead rose and twisted in the flames, and
the wounded shrieked and tried to drag themselves away, and
shrieked, and then were still.

Ulyss sat and whittled. Push rapidly away from him to point
one end, pull rapidly toward him to point the other, cut it in
two, throw it away, pick up another. His new gloves were worn
through at the fingertips. There was little he could do. Listen
to breathless messages, send re-enforcements to the places that
sounded most seriously menaced, wait for the next aide with the
shadows of horror in his eyes. There was little he could see,
except the gray, acrid smoke drifting through the bushes. He
whittled, grimly quiet.

It was a small thing that beat down his shield at last. One
officer came to him choked with the tale of disaster that could
not be fully measured on that impenetrable field, and was pushed
beyond endurance by the stolid manner of the general from

the west, who had been accustomed to brilliant victories over little men.

'General Grant,' the officer cried, 'this is a crisis — it has got to be taken seriously! I belong to the Army of the Potomac — I've fought Lee before, and I know his ways. He's going to throw his whole army between us and the Rapidan, and cut our communications ——'

Dropping his cigar, Ulyss stood up to shout with sudden exasperation, 'I'm sick to death of hearing about Lee and what Lee is going to do! You all seem to think he can turn a double somersault and land in our rear and on both our flanks at the same time. Get on back to your command and think a little about what you're going to do yourself!'

The officer saluted and withdrew, with the wooden look of the trained soldier who knows that even a stupid superior must be obeyed. Ulyss sat down and reached for another stick. There had been a joy in letting go for a moment, but it was hard to hold fast again.

It was harder still as the second day ended but the battle continued, lit by the smoldering brush fires. Hancock had been forced all the way back to where he had started in the morning, and now Sedgwick, at the other end of the obscure line, was assaulted. Reports which would have been alarming by day-light were appalling in that lurid darkness. The right has been rolled up, Sedgwick is captured, the rebs are burning the wagon trains... Ulyss listened, gave orders for re-enforce-ments, directed that a new line be drawn, and waited, trusting that his sense of military probabilities was more exact than the possible truth of what he heard.

In a few hours the truth came to him: Sedgwick had been thrown back, there had been several hundred captures, but the line held. Ulyss went into his tent to bed. His staff officers dropped on the ground in the immediate sleep of exhaustion, but he could not. Two days he had fought, with all his strength,

with all the vigor of superior force and fresh determination.
But he had been met by something new to him, a power that
did not come from numbers, nor position, nor even from a
devotion to a cause, for he had not found it in the west. He
would not name it, but he had been forced to feel it, and it had
fought him to a bloody and bitter stalemate. He had been so
certain of victory, and in its name had risked so much ——

Suddenly his thoughts escaped his wearied will, and he lay
helpless while his unrelenting memory brought him pictures of
those two days. He had tried in his trips along the lines to see
only positions, the balance of wings and centre, the terms of a
military problem. He had turned away his face and set his
jaw when he came on other things. But now they came to
him, and he was forced to see. He saw the men: the look of
surprise on the face of a boy whom a bullet had struck; the
agonized, inching crawl of a man with a shattered leg, and his
long scream when the flames crawled faster; the lined, set
mouths of the men still unwounded; and their eyes when they
looked at him. The men of the Army of the Potomac. He
had promised to lead them to Richmond. Had he brought
them to Chancellorsville again?

Ulyss tried desperately, but will and shame were not strong
enough, and he sobbed. He turned on his face and covered his
mouth with his hands, but he could not stop, and the sounds
tore at his throat. There was a hand on his shoulder, and he
knew that he had the humiliation of a witness.

'Get out,' he choked.

'No,' said Rawlins quietly. He stayed where he was in
silence, until at last Ulyss grew quiet enough to hear him, and
then he said, 'It's over now. It's bad, but it's all over.'

That was true, and it soothed Ulyss as only the accomplished
fact could. He knew that Lee had now withdrawn into his
entrenchments on Mine Run, and he had no intention of
assaulting him there. The battle of the Wilderness was over,

the ghastly little pictures were of the past, and the past cannot be altered. 'The men,' said Ulyss, turning aside his face and trying to rub away the marks on it. 'It was the men, burning ——'

'Yes, that was horrible.' There was no softness in Rawlins, none of the unthinking pity that would have refrained from driving in the point. 'But now that you've proved it to yourself you won't do it again. We didn't win, but after all neither did Lee, and when the men have been rested you can start again, by a different way ——'

'No,' said Ulyss suddenly. He spoke automatically, as soon as the talk shifted back to his plans, away from the human beings involved. 'We won't rest, we won't stop. We'll move by the left, toward Richmond.'

'But the men ——'

'I told you once what I thought, that the Army of the Potomac had never been fought to a finish. This time it will be. The battle's over, but its result isn't decided yet. If we stop and go back now we've lost. If we go ahead we've won.'

'But you can't ask men who've been through a fight like this to go right on. It's damned inhuman ——'

'We'll wait through tomorrow. If Lee wants to come out and try again he can. If he doesn't we'll pull out in the dark and high-tail it for his precious Richmond.' Rawlins tried for a while to argue, but it was as if Grant did not hear him. Then the chief of staff turned and left, shaking with anger, aghast at the mistake that was about to be made, and sickened by his own helplessness.

Lee did not stir from Mine Run next day, and the exhausted Army of the Potomac was told that as soon as darkness came it was to move. The men murmured about it, not looking at each other. Back across the Rapidan, or to Fredericksburg, or to some other place where they could sit down and think about the fourteen thousand men they left behind them in the charred thickets. All to be done over again.

As twilight thickened over the torn trees the men rose stiffly, and formed as well as they could to limp back by the road they had come. There was a fork in the road, and when they reached it the officers turned, unbelievably, south. There was a rapid whispering in the ranks, and then, as every foot they marched confirmed their goal, a long, high cheer that no caution could suppress. This was what had never happened before, a break in the pattern of battle, retreat or standstill, winter quarters. They had fought and they had not won, but they were marching south. They cheered, and one of their bands struck up 'Ain't I Glad to Get Out o' the Wilderness,' and they laughed. There was a burst of inquiring fire from the rebel lines, and they cheered that too. Even the wounded by the roadside, still waiting for the stretcher-bearers, added their cheers, and those who could hobbled a while with the others on the way south, and only the dead were quiet.

Crossing the James

CHAPTER TWELVE

THERE was some confusion about it. Lee thought Grant
was retreating to Fredericksburg, and Grant thought Lee was
falling back on Richmond, and they met at Spottsylvania, which
had once been a courthouse and a centre for the quiet country
around it, and was now only a name in the desolation that was
the area between the Rapidan and Richmond. The meeting
at that place was partly accident, but the forces that brought
it about held true: Grant was fighting, day by day, his first
consideration not so much victory as chipping at the rebel
army; and Lee was holding on.

They fought bitterly, the armies massed so close to the
breastworks on one part of Lee's line that men were pulled

bodily back and forth across it, and a bayonet thrust blindly through the logs was certain of its target. That part of the line was called at first the Mule Shoe, but it was rechristened the Bloody Angle. The men fought there for hours in the rain and crimsoned mud, stopped only by darkness. That night a band on the Confederate side began playing, softly, but it could be heard far up and down the lines. The notes faded off slowly, and then a Union band responded. Both camps were quiet in the rainy darkness, listening.

'What is it?' Grant demanded when he saw his staff stand silent, with an odd look in their eyes.

'They played "Nearer, My God, to Thee,"' Rawlins answered with set lips.

'We're playing the Dead March,' Porter added.

'I see,' said Ulyss, and was silent also. Music was inexplicable to him, but he understood well enough the music that night. It was fitting that some prayer should be said over that place where men had been killing each other with their naked hands, and the musical instruments were the only things untouched by guilt.

Having fought, the armies moved south again, Lee grimly hastening to a well-chosen stand, and Grant as grimly hastening to meet him there. The Army of the Potomac no longer cheered as it marched. It was spared the sick despair of futility it would have felt had it been led in the other direction, but there was no exaltation in the way it took. For one thing, it rained almost without pause, so that the men were never dry nor warm, their clothes were sodden-heavy on them, half-liquid roads made labor of every step, and there was not even dry fuel to cook their food. But worse than their soaked discomfort was their knowledge of the nature of their work. Every day there was fighting, brisk skirmishes as opposing lines felt out each other, cavalry brushes, or set battles that lasted for several days and sent the casualties mounting into the ghastly thousands. And these were not battles such as had been fought in other campaigns, struggles for some specific point that was held or lost and the issue settled. The purpose of these battles was to kill as many men as possible.

That was not what was said of them. There were always the surface strategic considerations of Richmond, the Virginia Central Railroad, the Shenandoah Valley, but beneath them was the real purpose. None of the battles ended in clearly defined victory or defeat, and their importance was measured in the casualty lists. How many men had Lee been deprived of, how many irreplaceable men? How many men had Grant lost? Was it enough to weaken his drive, to fan the horror of the North high enough to call him back?

The Army of the Potomac, having fought Lee for three years, knew that in the main this was the method necessary to defeat him, and accepted it. The morale of the machine was firm, but the spirits of the men could not be high. They slogged doggedly southward, under a leader they now trusted, but who could not warm them. They had insisted, 'He hasn't met Bobby Lee,' and had waited for him to be ruined. Now he had met Lee, over and over, and they said, 'Ulyss don't scare worth a damn,' and waited for him to kill them in his progress.

'This isn't war,' Rawlins shouted at Grant. 'It's murder. You used to do a little planning, to think about how to use your forces, now you do nothing but assault. Comstock's got at you, with his everlasting "Smash 'em up" ——'

'Comstock has nothing to do with it. Lee's army has got to be finished, or the rebellion will go on forever.'

'There's more than one way of finishing it. Does it ever occur to you that those things piled up in the field aren't logs of wood, but men? Some of them aren't dead yet, God knows how you let them get by, but they're stacked up with those that are ——'

'Rawlins,' said Grant with tight lips, 'perhaps you'd like to give the orders to this army?' It was not fair, and Ulyss knew it, but then neither had his friend been fair. He made no gesture of apology when Rawlins spun around and left him, but sighed to hear his cough, even that constant sound full of heartsick indignation. It was really too late now to be annoyed with Rawlins for stating his views too vigorously, but his friend's strenuous disapproval deepened the loneliness that was closing on Ulyss. Porter's admiring loyalty, Babcock's eager service, could not take Rawlins's place. Nor could his certainty of ultimate victory over Lee take the place of the clean satisfaction he had felt in the Vicksburg campaign.

The isolation of success, that he had begun to feel some time ago, had now worked into the fabric of his days. It had been forced on him by circumstance, without his knowledge or intention, and he seemed unable to escape it. It was not altogether his fault that interviews with Rawlins, once straightforward and heated but rewarding, so often ended now in the cold comments of a superior to a presumptuous subordinate. It was not his fault that his men looked to him with unexcited loyalty, and reserved their affection for lesser men.

Once, riding forward with Babcock, he came upon a wounded man lying by the roadside. The sight was common enough, and horrible enough, but the eyes that looked up at him were not ordinary. They were the eyes of a child, belied by the tense jaw under the beard, and the clenched hand over the wound that bled purple on the blue uniform. Ulyss reined in, despite the sickness that seized him, compelled by the commanding meekness of the eyes. As he stopped a dispatch rider behind him swerved out to pass, riding through a puddle that splashed gouts of mud into the wounded man's face. Ulyss started to dismount, but Babcock forestalled him. The aide's handsome face bent for a moment over the man, and he said something, but the sound that came from the man's throat was not speech, and the eyes filmed and closed.

'The poor fellow's gone, sir,' said Babcock, with exactly the right blend of sorrowful comment on the tragedy of war, respect for the heroism of a nameless soldier, and admiration for the general whose great heart took note of even the least of his men. Babcock had a nice appreciation of epic drama. Ulyss rode on without waiting for him to remount. The thing was wrong, it was not the way it ought to be, but he could not tell exactly what was wrong and certainly he knew no remedy, and so he went forward on the road he found before him.

Southward by the left. Four weeks of May and a week of June, and Richmond was in sight, but so was Lee's army, in front of it. Once more the armies met, at a place that had been named Cold Harbor for a forgotten reason, yet with a prescience of the number of lives that would come to port there. It took twenty minutes to shoot down six thousand men, but it took two days for most of them to die, lying in the summer sun while the generals exchanged notes about stretcher-bearers. Another attack was ordered, but when the hour came the men lay still and the guns were silent. It was not mutiny. It was simply a tacit statement that that part of the campaign was finished, and the leaders must think of something else.

Ulyss said little. He had taken a risk, basing his orders on the memory of Donelson, when of two exhausted armies the first to strike found victory, and of Missionary Ridge, where men had accomplished the impossible. The result puzzled him. It had seemed clear to him that the Army of Northern Virginia, that had sidled south with him for over a month, never taking the offensive, draining away day by day in casualties and deserters, had lost its morale. He had been proved wrong. He rued his attempt with all his heart, but there was nothing to say about it now.

The people of the North found much to say. They had been shouting, 'On to Richmond!' for over a month, and been assured of victory. Now they had got to Richmond and found it impregnable. The town could not be taken, Lee's army could not be defeated, and what was now to be said of the man who had promised both these impossibilities, and wasted fifty thousand men in failing? The newspapers said it, with passion and authority. Butcher: drunk, conceited, incompetent butcher who had put a corpse or a cripple into half the homes of the North. Not even the parts of the plan not under his direct supervision were succeeding: Sherman was striking down through Georgia, but had not been able to draw Johnston into battle, and had not reached Atlanta; Butler's advance up the James was a futile affair that was no real threat to Richmond; Sigel had not succeeded in definitely closing the Great Valley to the Confederates.

The cry that Grant should be relieved was loud in the land, and beneath it was a growing murmur that no one should be put in his place. Let there be an end to acclaiming geniuses who turned out to be bunglers. Let there be an end to killing all the young men for the sake of a lot of well-fed niggers and stiffnecked rebels that nobody wanted anyway. Let there be an end.

The nominating conventions were held that month. The Democrats said the war was a failure, and to continue it was a crime, and named as their leader a man whose courage could not be impugned, whose word had weight in the matter: McClellan. The Republicans said the war was being won, and to abandon it would be cowardly and a betrayal of the dead: they renominated Lincoln, and gave him for companion a man named Andrew Johnson, a loyalist from Tennessee who had been a Democrat. The Radical Republicans held a convention of their own, saying that the war might still be won if the leaders in Washington understood the necessary sternness, and they proposed Frémont.

All this came vaguely to Grant's ears, but he paid little attention to it, for he had a problem to consider. He could not take Richmond as things were, for its defenses were too strong, and its supply line too well based on the little railroad town of Petersburg. Butler had been told to occupy Petersburg, but had corked himself into a peninsula on the river and was boasting of the strategic advantages of the place where he had been immobilized. The man had brought to the battlefield the passion for obscure intrigue and showy methods that had made him a power in his ward in Boston, and the intimidation of the civil population, the discomfiture of West Point officers, and political threats against the President were as important to him as any military advantage. Grant, in appointing W. F. Smith to be his second in command, had hoped that Butler would content himself with his dark-lantern politics and leave the precise military thinking to his subordinate, but the politician fancied himself as a soldier too.

'The man's impossible,' Smith told Grant. 'He's a child on the battlefield, and as visionary as an opium-eater in council. His idea of war is digging ditches to turn rivers from their courses, or blowing up whole divisions with a bag of powder, and when such plans don't work he blames every West Pointer in sight. He never made a move toward Petersburg. The brilliant General Butler was going to capture Richmond the shortest way ——'

'I know,' Ulyss cut him short. Smith was a good man, but he had no sense of the optimum in criticizing his superiors. 'It's unfortunate that Petersburg wasn't taken in May, but we can take it now. This campaign has been fought as far as it can go by assault — we'll have to move now on supply lines and bases, and hold Lee that way.'

'I think that's a good plan,' said Smith, his eyes level but not quite focused on Grant's. 'General Meade made a dreadful mistake at Cold Harbor. It ought not be repeated.'

Ulyss made no direct reply, but he could not prevent the slow flush that came to his cheeks. He dismissed Smith as soon

as he could. He had a low opinion of Butler and no trust in
him, but he felt a twinge of sympathy for a conceited man
exposed hour by hour to Smith's tongue.

The Army of the Potomac disappeared. It pulled out of the
Cold Harbor lines and vanished into a forest, where a few
cavalry pickets guarding the roads were as a mountain range
to hide it. Beauregard in Petersburg, on the other side of the
James, sent vague and uneasy telegrams to Lee, who received
them with like uneasiness. It might be that the Union army
was crossing the river, but it might be that it was withdrawing
to another base for an attack on Richmond. He could not be
sure, and without certainty he dared not move with all his
force on either assumption. He waited for three days in that
obscurity, trying to balance both threats, holding on, cold and
lonely in the enormous shadow of his responsibility.

On a bluff overlooking the James Ulyss stood to watch his
army cross. It was a brave and beautiful pageant, with the
beauty that almost never touches war after the parades of
newly enlisted regiments. The river was broadly blue in the
June sunlight, and the pontoon bridge across it seemed more
an adornment than a bond. The gunboats guarding the up-
stream approach floated as lazily as pleasure craft, and at this
distance the regimental flags were bright, gay banners, un-
dimmed by the rents and grime of a hundred conflicts. A
dozen bands were playing, to add the final holiday touch to
the maneuver, and the men were singing again. 'We are coming, Father Abraham, one hundred thousand strong,' they
sang, and they lamented with vengeful vigor for old John
Brown, on whose grave the stars of Heaven were looking kindly
down. One regiment waiting its turn was celebrating its commanders. 'General Grant he's down in Dixie, and ready for
the foe. Do you think he'll give up Dixie? Not though it takes
all summer, No! And where is Picayune Butler? He's gone to

Dixie town, and there he keeps a-stirring the Secesh up and down. Our flag shall float o'er Dixie, the Red, the White, the Blue. We'll ne'er give up till Dixie sings Yankee Doodle Doo...' There were other versions, but this bright morning seemed not the occasion for them.

It ought to be over soon, thought Ulyss. We can fall on Petersburg before Lee knows we've crossed the river — and this time the Army of the James will be led by Smith, not Butler. When Petersburg goes Richmond must follow, and Lee will surrender. I said all summer, but by the first of July it will be over.

He tried to picture the world when the war should be over. The thousands of men below him dispersed, gone back to the varied lives they had suspended in order to be cast all together into the military mold. For himself, Julia again, every day and not in hurried moments months apart, his children, growing up with gradual and unnoticed changes, not four strangers each time he saw them. He would still be a general, he supposed, but the thought of sitting in a Washington office, concerning himself with the paper supervision of a peacetime army, was as unreal to him as the thought of occupying himself in the merchandising of hides in Galena.

The truth of his life seemed centred in these months of camp and battlefield; in thinking of the set, definite problems of the work to which he had come almost by accident but which nevertheless was peculiarly his; in dealing with his fellows on the clear lines of authority and accepted responsibilities. Another life, such as civilians and soldiers unoccupied by war must lead, was inconceivable to him. But it was also inevitable, and the approach of final victory was bringing it closer. Ulyss stopped thinking about it, since it was a troubling problem that it was not yet in his power to solve, and turned from the panorama of his army still under arms, still dedicated to a task yet incomplete. It was time he went to his new headquarters at City Point, to wait for news of Smith's movement on Petersburg.

Porter came forward to him with a telegram from Washington. There had been dozens of them: from Halleck, objecting to moving the army across the river, terrified once more for the capital's safety; from Stanton, giving suggestions with what he hoped was the force of orders. But this one was from Lincoln, the man who would sit up all night wrestling with himself over signing a death warrant for some deserter, yet who had given his full trust to the general who had lost fifty thousand men in a month. 'I begin to see it. You will succeed. God bless you all.' Ulyss put the telegram in his pocket, looked once again at his beautiful army, and set out down the hill.

In Petersburg that night Beauregard stood listening. He was almost too intent on hearing any sound from the Federals who confronted him in the darkness, or from the re-enforcements he had at last demanded, to realize with his emotions the danger in which he stood. That afternoon his outer defenses had gone, and Petersburg lay open and helpless. Its entrenchments were manned after a fashion, sparsely: here a boy out of military school, his young jaw clenched in nervous courage, his eyes bright and restless; there an old man, slow and stiff of movement, free and unreasonable of opinion, but with eyes lit with pride that life still claimed him, if only for death. Robbing the cradle and the grave, Butler had snorted of these ultimate defenders of Richmond. It was true. This was the South's last hour, and she came to it with all her possessions, with youth and age and love and hope and pride, with the singleness of feeling that was her glory and her defeat. The little army strung through the Petersburg entrenchments was great in symbol, but its military meaning was paltry, and Smith's regiments could blot it out at any moment.

Yet Smith did not move. Beauregard waited through the late afternoon, into the night. The moon rose enormous and pale gold, a fitting ornament for the Southern June sky, a dangerous light for the work to be done on Southern earth. A man could easily see into Petersburg from the Federal lines, as easily as he could walk the distance. But Smith did not move. Beauregard, listening, at last heard a sound, from the town behind him. Lee's men had come to make another stand. It could be a long one this time, for they came in force to hold the lines, and from the moment they filed silently into the entrenchments Smith's possibility of attack became Grant's necessity of a siege. A few hours' delay had canceled a three-day advantage and added months to the war.

Butler said that any soldier whose intelligence had not been motheaten at West Point would have succeeded. Smith said that any soldier who knew his business would consolidate the success he had already gained and not throw away lives in the headlong fashion of Cold Harbor; he had been promised Hancock's support, and Hancock was slow in coming. Hancock would have attacked had he been in command, but he was ill from his Gettysburg wound and had waived his rank. Butler and Smith quarreled. Meade and Warren quarreled, and Hancock asked for an official inquiry, since he apparently was being held partly to blame. The energy that had not gone into an attack on Petersburg was expended in bitter warfare among the Union generals, and Ulyss was kept too occupied in soothing them to think very much of what they had lost for him. He assured Hancock that he was in no way at fault, complimented Meade on his generalship, smoothed the irascible Warren. But between Smith and Butler no mediation was possible. They hated each other, and no amount of discussion could convince either of them that he had been wrong, or that the other might conceivably at any time have been right. One of them must be relieved from command. Smith had been in error at Petersburg, but Butler was constantly in error, and Grant wrote Halleck that he wanted him relieved.

The order arrived promptly, and Ulyss sent it to Butler. With equal promptness Butler arrived at City Point. 'General Grant is engaged at present,' Porter told him, with a hope that delay might induce him to go away obediently.

'He'll see me,' Butler snapped.

'Perhaps you could talk to General Rawlins,' Badeau suggested, looking helpfully over his glasses. Rawlins had a temper to match a savage politician's. 'He could take a message to General Grant.'

'I'm talking to Grant himself, now,' said Butler. His tone was brusque, but there was a disquieting lack of rage in it, as though he were too assured to be angry. He walked past the aides and Rawlins, and into Grant's tent. Ulyss looked up to see who came upon him thus unannounced, and reddened. He had felt it necessary to relieve Butler, but ever since he had made the decision he had been troubled by the memory of Lincoln's reluctance to do anything about him. The best interest of the Army of the James was obvious, but beyond that there was another interest, how big and where threatened Ulyss did not know, that might not be the same. Ulyss was uneasy, as always when he had to deal with something he did not understand, something not defined in straightforward terms.

'Did you write this?' Butler asked, thrusting at his superior the order of dismissal.

'Not in those terms. I — asked that it be made.' Ulyss was amazed to hear his own tone. This was not the way in which he was accustomed to speak to the officers he commanded. He was seldom overbearing, but he had never been conciliatory. He felt that he was humiliating himself, as he had not been humiliated even in the dark years, for then his pride had at least been safe from violation at his own hands. But Lincoln had trusted him, and he knew that Lincoln's trust covered more than a military campaign, more than his own self-respect.

'Why did you ask for it?'

'General Butler, the situation in the command of the Army
of the James is impossible. General Smith is a soldier only, but
you have great talents for civil life also, so you would not be
lost to the nation ——'

The smile on Butler's face was a detached appreciation of a
blunt man's attempt at diplomacy. He still smiled as he sat
down on the edge of the table, and while he spoke he played
absent-mindedly with the order. 'You bet I wouldn't be lost
to the nation,' he said affably. 'I could raise a stink from here
to California. I would, too. Now, General, there's no reason
why we shouldn't understand each other. That big-mouthed
bastard Smith won't wipe his nose till he finds the right chapter
in Jomini to tell him how, but you're a man, and we can get
along all right.'

Call the guard, Ulyss's instincts were shouting. Have him
drummed out of camp as Meade did the newspaper correspond-
ent, but let the placard on Butler read 'Slimy.' 'There are
reasons,' said Lincoln's voice in Grant's mind, 'political reasons,
why I delay doing anything about him.' This is my punishment, thought Ulyss. It was necessary to suffer this nudging
intimacy because he had ignored the warning the President had
given him. He should have done nothing. The President had
warned him, and the President knew the strength of those other
interests that puzzled and frightened Ulyss. The lieutenant
general said nothing, and kept his eyes fixed on the order, folded
into halves, fourths, eighths, and smoothed flat again in
Butler's plump hands.

'You know,' the friendly voice was continuing, 'I'm not
exactly a stranger in this man's country. You ask anybody in
Boston who Ben Butler is, and they can tell you. Ask in New
Orleans' — with a chuckle — 'they call me Beast Butler there,
but they can't deny I stopped all the pretty rebel gentlewomen
from spitting on our soldiers, and made the place fit for a God-
fearing man to live in. Ask in Washington — ask any place,

all over the country. Yes, sir, there's scarcely anybody doesn't know Ben Butler.'

The contemplative, casual tone disappeared, but was not replaced by a threat. There was rather the matter-of-fact inflection of a friend reasoning with a hot-headed youth. 'Now, General, there's an election coming up in November. I guess you think it's pretty important for Old Abe to be re-elected. I wouldn't know — I was a Democrat, you know. But I do know that it'd be damned hard to get him in if somebody started telling a lot of people that politics in the army was pushing out the volunteer officers, so as to cover up the mess the West Point men had made of the campaign. It don't look well, you know.'

He paused, but Ulyss made him no answer. Ulyss said nothing at all, and his eyes were empty of meaning, but he knew in his heart that this time there was no strength in his withdrawal. It had served him well at other times for other issues, but then the decision had truly been his. Now circumstances made it for him, and this man knew it. He was not abashed and stammering, as others had been when they waited for a response from Grant that did not come. He went on talking, easily, as though he had not stopped. 'Of course I agree with you that the situation in the Army of the James is impossible. Nobody can work with a subordinate who shoots off his mouth instead of his cannon. He even goes around saying you depend on me for a liquor supply. It's disgusting, the sort of mind he's got.' Butler shook his head sadly. 'Well, General, I won't take up any more of your time. I just wanted to make sure that we understood each other, and I'm sure we do.' He left at last, and Ulyss tried to breathe a sigh of relief, but he felt no relief.

It was not bluster. The Democrats who had chosen an active part on the Union side had an enormous effect on the vast mass of the undecided. McClernand had been one, and had carried

with him into the war hundreds of people to whom his decision
was a weightier factor than their own unguided consideration of
rights and wrongs. But McClernand had belonged to a world
of prairie and new farms and independent men, the world that
had produced Clay and Benton, and Lincoln himself. Butler
was a politician of a different stamp, a new character in the
national drama. His power was rooted in the poor of the cities,
the men who had masters, who gave their strength to the factories and the armies to build a world not for themselves.
They had rioted desperately in New York when the draft was
introduced, and had been drafted just the same. They had
but one power, the ballot, and they did not know how to use it.
Butler told them how, and they listened, for he and those of
his new race were the only people who ever troubled to tell
them they were strong. He knew how to make them promises,
and how to find excellent reasons for not keeping them if it
were inconvenient.

And they were strong. The sum of their individual hopeless
weakness was an inert might greater and more terrible than
the sum of many powers. It lay ready for the use of any man
who knew the means of grasping it. Butler could use it to his
own ends. He had not been threatening, but telling the truth
with unswerving frankness. The order was still lying on the
table where he had left it, soiled and crumpled and forgotten.
Ulyss reached out and slowly tore it into small pieces, destroying with it something of the pride he had carried with him since
he had stood in the central square of Vicksburg.

Soon after the lines of siege were drawn Lincoln came down
to visit the camp. He was quiet and tired, save when he talked
at his homely ease to the young men who gathered eagerly
about him, but the camp seemed to rest him even in its turmoil.
It was at least different from the unordered, shadowy conflicts
of Washington.

'I feel mighty close to the army,' he confessed. 'I'm even going to set myself up in the prophecy business for it. Every time we win a big battle I know about it the night before — I have a dream.'

'Must be a pretty strenuous dream, Mr. President,' Porter laughed. 'Do you dream about all the crucial places? You might let us know by telegraph, and we could make right sure your dream would come true.'

'No, I don't dream about fighting.' Lincoln had been fairly indifferent when he began speaking, but now his eyes lighted and his voice dropped a little to the full tone he used when he spoke of things that touched him deeply. 'It hasn't anything to do with war, it just comes before a victory. I think I'm standing on a boat, all alone. It isn't really foggy and it isn't really night, but it seems so, for nothing is very clear and the boat looks strange. I'm coming in toward the shore, but I don't know what shore it is, and I can't see what's on it. It's not much of a dream, boys, the main thing about it is that it can't be described, but every time I have it we win.'

There was a murmur from the group around him. All of them were accustomed to the wartime flood of tales about premonitory dreams and visions, but this was not a story for brief, puzzled wonder or a cynical smile. They were silent a moment, not so much because of the uncanny quality of the dream, as because it had been plain to the least perceptive of them that the President had been speaking of a thing he valued far beyond the telling. To him the meaning of the dream could not be put into halt and limited words: it was one small fragment of the unearthly beauty of the spirit, that lies hidden even from its possessor. It was Lincoln who ended the quiet, beginning in his usual drawl, 'When I was a boy in Illinois ——' and gently breaking the spell he had unintentionally cast.

During his visit he rode out to inspect some portion of the lines. He was a good enough horseman in technique, but in appearance he was grotesque. From his tall black hat to his twisted black broadcloth trousers he was plastered with dust, and the whole of him seemed several feet too long for the horse he rode. But the men, who called the spruce General Meade the goggle-eyed snapping turtle, because he wore glasses, saw nothing at all humorous in the sight of Lincoln. He was theirs. Their love of him did not set him apart in a hero's magnification, but took him into their hearts and clothed him with an affection few of them had given their fathers. They stood in ranks and cheered him, and shouted promises to bring him personally every stone and brick in Richmond.

Then Grant suggested that he go to see the negro troops. These regiments had been raised on a principle of consistent equality, but their exploits were given romantic admiration in the North, and their existence was a grim horror in the South. They too cheered the President, but they could not keep ranks. They crowded around him, sobbed and sang and ejaculated, and broke away to tell less fortunate comrades that they had touched him, with their own dark hands. Lincoln said little. He could not make speeches to these men pointing them to glory and assuring them that henceforth the conscience-stricken world would right the wrong it had done them. He was a wise man, and knew that the word freedom is easily enough written and proclaimed, but the fact freedom entails the years-long labor of altering the social fabric, with its daily disappointments and hourly terror of futility. He sat still and looked at them, and his eyes were dark.

It was a pleasure to Ulyss to have the President with him. Lincoln never asked about his plans, but he had a quick interest in what had been done, and an understanding of the fundamentals of the problem that seemed to make lighter the task of the future. Even the retention of Butler and Smith's dismissal lost some of its soreness in Ulyss's mind when he remembered that by humbling himself he had done a service to the President. He knew that Lincoln was concerned about the November election, though he scarcely mentioned it. He seemed to prefer to talk at his ease about things that had little to do with either the war or his office, and just as he did not ask for information he did not volunteer advice.

Not until he was leaving did he make his single request. 'I don't know much about it,' he said, 'and the job you're doing satisfies me. But I do hope you can finish it with as little bloodshed as possible.' Ulyss nodded. A strange man, he thought, with his tender concern for every life, yet approving this relentless campaign, where ruthless men like Stanton and Rawlins faltered; with his shrewd practicality that took advantage of every twist of temperament to turn a man to his purpose, yet putting a visionary faith in an obscure dream. A strange man, an incomprehensible man, but Ulyss wore his trust with more pride than he took in the three stars of the lieutenant general on his shoulder.

CHAPTER THIRTEEN

Build a high wall all the way around Richmond, pump water from the James inside, and everyone in the city, including Jeff Davis, will be drowned. Fill shells with powerful snuff, and the rebels will be so overcome with sneezing that they can be disarmed at leisure. Give the Union armies bayonets a foot longer than the Confederates'. There seemed to be no end to the suggestions, each of them urged by some commonplace man who could not see why his simple, infallible idea was not at once adopted. 'It's a wonder,' said Ulyss, 'that nobody has thought yet of infecting our bullets with smallpox.' His own idea for the reduction of Petersburg and Richmond was constant raiding against the railroads that were feeding Lee from the south, and slowly, steadily stretching his lines leftward around the invested town, a movement which Lee with his thin forces could not forever match. It took a long time. Everything was taking a longer time than Ulyss had expected, yet at least some progress was made, so slowly that it was invisible to the rest of the country, but enough to hold him to the line he had chosen.

There was one proposal for bringing the siege to a quick end that was something more than a jest around the mess tables. A regiment from the Pennsylvania iron country wanted to mine the Confederate lines, and blow them up so thoroughly that Petersburg could be taken before the rebels all came down again. Grant was doubtful about the plan even in its more coldly sober presentation, and Meade was wholly against it; but it would give the men something to work on and might have some success, and at length Grant gave his approval.

Late in July the mine was ready to be exploded, and preparations were made for the assault. The men were instructed to charge at the instant of the detonation, to occupy that section of the works before any help could be sent from the unshattered portion; and some troops were marched busily back and forth across the James to give the impression that Richmond was to be attacked, and force Lee to withdraw men from the Petersburg defenses. The choice of the assaulting troops was left to Burnside, who commanded that part of the Federal line, and he allowed his commanders to draw lots. There were capable men among them, but the lot fell to one who paled, whose lips twitched loosely when he saw it in his hand.

Half-past three was the time chosen for the explosion, and Ulyss and his staff stood together in the darkness waiting for it. The twenty-ninth minute of that hour was centuries long, but the thirtieth was an eternity, for the explosion did not come — and after that time raced toward dawn and failure. The fuse had been lit at the appointed moment. Perhaps it had gone out, or perhaps it had encountered an obstruction which it was burning through, and was waiting to crash the earth in on anyone who came to investigate. The light of a summer day began to flood upward from the east, and undaunted birds heralded it as if it were not a calamity.

The men from Pennsylvania, desperate for the success of their plan, would wait no longer. Two of them crept into the black hole they had dug, and forward into a silence that seemed to roar louder than the crash they expected. They found a break in the fuse, repaired it, relit it, and came back into the full light of morning.

Then it came. Ulyss felt a shock as though someone had struck at his head from the inside, and the earth seemed to slide under his feet, then a section of it rose straight into the air and stayed there, a pyramid balanced on its point. It was possible to see men, and fragments of men, suspended in it. For apparently a very long time the pyramid kept its shape, then it fell wide and far, with a gigantic, nightmare thunder. There was an enormous hole where that section of the Confederate works had been, and the gray men stood aghast and shaken.

This was the time when the blue regiments had been ordered to sweep forward and through the broken line. But there were difficulties. The man whom lot had chosen to lead them sat behind the lines, drinking whiskey to give him courage that was strong enough only to keep him where he was until he had another drink. The front ranks had wavered and drawn back, in fear that the collapsing pyramid was going to fall on them. The abatis had not been removed, and the Federals had to crawl through their own defenses. And there was a weakening shock in what they had just seen. Few men are altogether proof against the sight of impossibilities, strong to go forward with their accustomed force when they have just seen the earth and

other men spinning skyward in agonizing conjunction. The
blue men moved, and they fought, but they also stopped sometimes to drag a gray man still alive from his grave in the
powdered soil. When they reached the crater the explosion had
made they could easily skid into it down its crumbling sides,
but could not make their way up again, having no firm foothold anywhere, no protection from the fire the Confederates
were pouring into them from the rising ground beyond. And
yet more and more of the Federals came, streaming over the
edge of the crater and then caught in the solid mass. Soon the
living had no room to lift their arms in defense, and the dead
no room to fall.

Failure again. It was plain to Ulyss while the direct commanders still did not see it, or perhaps saw it and went on
throwing men into the crater with that sense of defeat that
dares not recognize itself. Failure it was, and the only thing
that anyone could do about it now was to stop it. Ulyss set out,
grimly silent, with a cold feeling in his heart despite the blazing
sun that seemed to suck at every fibre.

Confusion everywhere, bewilderment, the sense that something was wrong without knowing how wrong it was.

'Why aren't you moving?'

'My orders were to follow that brigade, and it's not moving.
Will you order us to go now?'

'No.'

Farther on, and other questions, and other answers, but
always the ultimate answer of error somewhere. Close to the
front lines the massed and milling troops made progress slow,
but it was not so crowded beyond the breastworks, where the
singing bullets stirred the dust. Ulyss left his horse and started
out in the open territory. He had to reach Burnside, and he
went the shortest way, with no more thought for the bullets
spurting around him than he had for the July sun pounding on
his head.

'The opportunity's lost,' he told Burnside when he found him and climbed back over the parapet. The general would have exclaimed and talked awhile about the risk the commander had taken, but Ulyss gave him no chance. 'We can't possibly win now. Don't send any more men in, and bring back those that are out there.'

'Oh, now, General, I don't think things are so bad. If we can hold on a little longer, and send in re-enforcements ——'

'They'd be slaughtered too. I said withdraw the men.'

The order was given. It was obeyed, in due time, after colored troops had added their black bodies to the stacks of white ones in the crater, after Meade and Burnside quarreled with bitter eloquence, after nearly four thousand men were lost. It was over, a finished thing so far as the armies were concerned, but it was not finished for a long time in the newspapers. The Richmond papers exulted in a great victory, and so it was. The Northern papers growled of defeat, new evidence that the campaign was a failure, the war was hopeless.

Ulyss went back to his slow pounding at the railroads, hoping for something from that, knowing that so long as he held Lee fast time itself fought for him. He could see that, see beyond the small frustrations and heavy disappointments of the days to the slow, inevitable progress toward victory of the months. But the country could not see. It was as certain of defeat as it had been certain that war would not come, and this was election year. In Washington Lincoln, who believed more firmly in the sacredness of the will of the people than he ever had in God, foresaw his defeat, and made preparations to cooperate with the new president to bring the war to a victorious end before the March inaugural. The people ruled, and were ruled in turn by their fears and uncertainties and ignorance. It was a hard balance to strike between their will and their interests, and the problem scored new lines in the face of the man who thought too clearly.

Before the fiasco of the crater Lee had made one more attempt
to raid Washington, sending Jubal Early up the Valley. There
was a panicky day when Early's hard-bitten men engaged the
Washington garrison, but Grant had sent re-enforcements,
and the raiders were driven off. Halleck and Stanton, however, were not to be calmed. Several divisions must be sent
to succour Washington, Grant himself must come to take
charge of them, the fate of the Union was at stake ... 'That's
exactly what Lee wants,' said Ulyss in exasperation. 'If we
pull out and go to sit on Washington, he can afford to send men
west, and then where will Sherman be? It's all nonsense anyway — Early can't do anything with the Washington garrison
re-enforced.'

'You can't blame General Halleck, though,' said Rawlins
slowly. 'It's damned nerve-racking, always expecting a raid
and having to keep the city crammed with soldiers.'

'Well, it's annoying to have our plans here upset every other
month by a howl for help from Washington. That's a dodge
Lee has used too often.' Ulyss thought it over, and gave his
orders. There was no unusual departure in them, simply a
renewed application of his first article of faith: not cities, not
supply lines, but armies. 'I want Sheridan put in command
of all the troops,' he wrote Halleck, 'with instructions to put
himself south of the enemy and follow him to the death.
Wherever the enemy goes let our troops go also.'

It was a good plan, Ulyss knew. Sheridan was a dauntless
fighter, had enough superiority in numbers to ensure a decisive
victory over Early, and could so devastate the Valley that no
army could possibly survive there. The plan was so good, and
its result so assured, that Ulyss had almost forgotten the matter
while he had been absorbed by his hopes, fears, and repentance
for the crater.

Then, early in August, he received a letter from the President. 'Please look over the dispatches you may have received

from here, even since you made that order, and discover, if
you can, that there is any idea in the head of any one here, of
"putting our army *south* of the enemy," or of "following him
to the death," in any direction. I repeat to you that it will
neither be done nor attempted unless you watch it every day,
and every hour, and force it.'

Ulyss went north, and forced it. Halleck submitted, as he
needs must to superior authority, and Stanton, overruled, could
do nothing more, but he fumed in his dissident heart. Sheridan,
released from their restrictions and given the complete freedom
Ulyss had intended him to have, made a complete success of
his campaign. Even that did not permanently quiet the fears
of Halleck and Stanton, but the victory was a clear indication
of the future to men of less fixed notions. Grant knew what it
meant, as he ordered back the men he had sent to Washington,
which no longer had need of them, and used them for the
leftward extension of his lines. Lee knew, as he struggled and
schemed to meet that extension, and every day faced the growing problem of stragglers. The gray lines were holding, with
heroic grimness, but not all the men had the abundance of faith
or the lack of imagination to be heroes. Some went home.
Those who were caught were tried and executed, but others
went the next day, and the next.

On the picket lines the Richmond and Washington papers
were daily exchanged. 'You got an awful lickin' at the crater,'
a Confederate said affably as he handed over his copy. 'Why
don't you give up and quit pesterin' us?'

'You know why. We're winning.'

'You're a liar. Still and all, this war's a terrible thing, now,
ain't it?'

'It is that.'

'No reason for it go on if we quit fightin' each other. Couldn't
go on.'

'That's a fact.'

'You were licked bad at the crater, weren't you?'

'Yes, but ——'

'We fought better'n you, didn't we?'

'You ——'

'Just as good, anyway. Every damn bit as good.'

'Yes.'

'This war is sure a terrible thing. Killin' each other, the way we're doin', it ain't Christian.'

'You're Goddamn right it ain't.'

'I reckon we'd better stop the war. After all, it's just you an' me fightin' each other, and I'm willin' to call it settled if you are.'

'It's a deal. Come on over.'

'Look out. I'm a comin'!' He dodged across the space and landed somewhat out of breath but entirely composed. There was no defiance in his face, but a hard assurance in his level eyes and the line of his jaw that any question of his courage would start his war over again.

The officer who questioned him before sending him behind the lines was interested. There was no one type for the men who drifted across the torn space between the breastworks. Some were boys who had come to war with trumpets ringing in their minds, picturing battles with bright waving banners, and men dying gracefully, with small, delicately red wounds in the breast. These found any escape preferable to continued living in the dusty ovens of trenches, with the latrine stench green and loathsome and pervasive, and the everlasting prospect of a skirmish that might make jawless, disemboweled travesties of whole men. Some were cowards in the classic sense, men of oblique minds and little spirits, to whom death was neither glorious nor an unpleasant necessity, but simply something to be avoided at whatever cost to personal integrity or outer responsibilities. Many were like this man, neither shaken nor craven, ruled only by the native, toughly individual logic that can found or uproot a political party, begin a revolution, end a war, with the same simple, good-humored force.

'Where are you from?' the officer asked.

'North Ca'lina. I got me a farm there, up country.'

'How'd you come to join with the rebels? Did you own any slaves?'

'Not me. I got all I can do to feed me and my woman, let alone a nigger.'

The officer was young, new enough to the Petersburg lines for enthusiasm, and not very busy. 'Why, then?' he persisted. 'Why were you with the Johnnies, when this war is being fought for you just as much as for the negroes?'

The man looked at his questioner, kindly, with a disbelief so complete and unexcited that it was impossible to resent. 'Well, now, I'll tell you,' he said comfortably. 'Th' was a conscription officer, one o' them slack-twisted, loose-belted, toggle-jinted kind o' fellers, come along an' told me I'd have to get into the ranks and go to fightin' for my rights. I told him I'd as lief have 'em all, but I wa'n't strenuous about it. Then I got to thinkin' that our side was losin' a good many battles, an' maybe I'd better jine an' kind of even things up. I notice South Ca'lina can start a lot, but she has to get the old Tar State to do the solid work. So I come an' fought, but lately I've been gettin' to feel peacefuller and peacefuller every day.'

'You've decided right,' said the officer, trying to put into his voice all the mature wisdom and authority that he felt this straggler had somehow stripped from him. 'You can go now. I expect you can find work in Philadelphia or New York or almost any place. There's a lot of new things being started — we'll make this country hum when the war's finished up.'

'Reckon I'll go west,' the man answered, unimpressed. 'I'll get me a homestead and bring my woman out. I don't like niggers and I don't like Yanks, and the poor old Tar State's gonna be chock full of both.' He went out, whistling the 'Bonnie Blue Flag,' and looking with contemptuous pity at other men still swarming around their little holes in the ground.

Many Washington officials found occasion to visit the camp, and Ulyss and his staff duly escorted them over the lines, explaining the dispositions as far as the civilian mind could follow. Seward, the Secretary of State, was one of them, and Ulyss found him difficult to talk to, for his own notion of foreign affairs was a vast fog wherein loomed the danger of English intervention, and little more. They discussed the recent destruction of the Confederate cruiser *Alabama*: 'Funny kind of neutrality England has,' Babcock observed. 'Standing by to pick up the *Alabama's* men, as if we'd been going to let them drown. She just couldn't bear to see her precious Johnnies go to prison for carrying on like pirates ——'

'Other things must be considered,' Seward said judiciously. 'Picking up the men was unwarranted, and letting the *Alabama* clear from an English port in the first place was inexcusable, but we've laid our complaints before their government on both points. The English are slow, you know, and particularly slow when they've got to admit they've done wrong. And there is a distinction between the English and their government. Palmerston and Russell have favored the South, but the people —— Remember the big mass meetings held for the Union in cotton-manufacturing towns, where our blockade of the South is taking the bread out of their mouths. Read what Bright is saying ——'

What is a nation if not its government? This was an intellectual hurdle that the military group did not care to scale. They discussed Maximilian's adventure in Mexico: 'I've had a long correspondence with Napoleon's ministry on the subject,' said Seward, 'pointing out that no foreign government has a right to interfere with the institutions of any American nation, and entering a vigorous protest against the presence of a French army on Mexican soil.'

Not enough. To these men reared in unconscious and ineradicable suspicion of Europe, Seward's words sounded as though they came from a State Department document, and seemed as thin and easily destroyed as the paper the document was written on.

'It seems to me,' said Ulyss, 'that the Mexican business is really the foreign part of this war. When the rebellion is over, and I've a notion that won't be very long, we'll have a veteran force in the west, all trained and under arms. We could march straight down to the border, Confederate divisions right along with ours ——'

'I hope it won't come to that,' Seward said hastily. 'We're doing all we can to settle it without war, or the threat of it. And I think the people of this country will want the army discharged as soon as possible. History would go to show that such a large force, once raised, isn't easily disbanded, but tends to struggle for power even against the government. I don't think so myself, but the possibility has to be considered ——'

The staff burst into angry, instant protest, undeterred by Seward's official position or by his personal disavowal of the theory. Ulyss said nothing, for the distance between military and civil authority seemed to him so wide and obvious that it was not worth discussing. The army was raised for the purpose of fighting, and had nothing to say of government, which was the affair of Congress and the President and was run by elections. But the others shouted in hot denial, and Rawlins was so angry that he stood up in order to swear with more freedom. Not until the subject was dropped, with what was almost an apology from Seward, did the chief of staff sit down again in his place by Ulyss.

He began to cough, as usual after one of his fits of passion, and put his handkerchief to his mouth. Ulyss glanced down and saw the spot on the cloth, bright, beautiful red in the firelight. Rawlins rose and withdrew, and Ulyss, with a word to Seward, hastened after him.

'It's nothing,' said Rawlins, almost savagely, when his friend reached him and caught his arm. 'It's just the same old bronchial affection. Breneman says it's nothing.'

'Have you — seen marks before?'

'Once or twice.' Rawlins coughed again, and put the handkerchief back into his pocket without looking at it. He pulled impatiently at the arm Ulyss was holding. 'It doesn't mean anything, I tell you. I — I think I'll go to bed.'

'Look here, Rawlins.' Ulyss tried to speak with no overtone of concern, but his voice sounded pinched nevertheless. 'That cough has been hanging on a long time, and while you work the way you do here you can't get rid of it. Why don't you go home on leave for a while?'

'I'm needed here,' said Rawlins, but he did not draw away.

'Of course, but the rest of them can do your work well enough for a while, and now that the mining notion has failed there's not likely to be much doing for a month or two. If you take a rest now, while things are slack, you'll be completely restored in time for the break when it comes.' Rawlins said nothing, and Ulyss added, as delicately as he could, 'And there's Mrs. Rawlins — you said she won't be coming down in the fall with Mrs. Grant ——'

'She isn't coming because I told her not to,' Rawlins snapped. 'I don't approve of women cluttering up the camps.' He pulled away from Ulyss and moved off toward his tent. 'I'll think about it,' he said. Then he stopped, and turned to call back, as graciously as he could when he was admitting that he was ill, 'I guess maybe it's a good idea.'

In a few days he did consent to go on leave, and departed to Connecticut, grumbling, unreasonably bad-tempered, with an

oddly unhappy look in his eyes. Ulyss was astonished to discover how much he missed him. There had been no deep
intimacy between them for months, but they had established
a fairly smooth relationship since the crossing of the James, for
that shift in tactics had put an end to the series of hammering
assaults that had roused the chief of staff's desperate protests.
But now that Rawlins was gone, and there was something odd
about the days because they were not punctuated by his
cough, Ulyss began to feel that his friend had been very important to him even though their friendship had been strained.

The rest of his staff was proud of Grant's work and of their
part in it, laughed with him over the small jokes of their
routine, sometimes even argued with him, diffidently, but always he was the General, set apart, not because he willed it but
because his responsibility built a wall around him. Rawlins
could not climb it either, but he was not impressed by it, and
stood waiting for the day when it would fall. Ulyss found himself eager for Rawlins's return, yet sometimes dreading it,
afraid to hear the cough and see the thin cheeks, definite proof
that all his easy assurances had been lies.

There was the sound of shouting in the General's cabin,
fierce shouting, but mingled with high, gleeful chuckles.
Porter, coming to the General with a handful of early dispatches, stopped short outside to listen. 'It's the family,' the
sentry volunteered. 'Miz' Grant an' the kids, they come in
early this mornin', and been raisin' hell ever since.' Porter
smiled before he remembered to emphasize in his own bearing
the deportment the sentry had forgotten. He tapped on the
door and was not heard, tapped again, then hammered until
someone shouted to him to come in.

Grant was lying on the floor, with Fred holding to both legs,
Buck involved with one arm and Nellie with the other, and
small Jesse circulating over the whole. As soon as the aide

entered the girl tore herself free and fled to a corner, trying to
smooth her skirts, her lips trembling with embarrassment and
a remainder of mirth. Mrs. Grant rose from her chair, remarked without excitement, 'Children ——' and separated
the struggling group with an impartial hand. Ulyss shook himself, introduced Porter to his family, and accepted the dispatches. He was not in the least embarrassed. He was happy,
and he read the dispatches with the air of a man who turns from
large concerns to deal with an insistent trifle. Porter talked for
a while to Julia, and found in her the same ease. She and
Ulyss were a man and his wife with their children around them,
and the uniforms, the military bareness of the room, the shuddering of the guns in the distance, were out of place, not they.

The camp at City Point soon grew accustomed to its domestic
overtone. There were difficulties, as when an aide had to rescue
Jesse from the line of fire and gallop to the rear with him, in
terror that he would be seen and his haste interpreted as a
measure for his own safety; or when Fred went fishing and was
picked up by the Union pickets as a spy, and could not convince his captors that he was the son of the General. But there
was also the pleasantness of Julia's visits to the hospital and
the cabins of those who fell sick, her suggestions to the mess
orderly, her quiet face at table. Battles past and yet to come
were still hotly fought at meals, with no effort to entertain her
or choose subjects to amuse her, and she listened with unaggres-
sive interest. Sometimes she and Ulyss had discussions, maintained with the same gravity that the others had.

'I'm moving Sherman's million down the Pecos to Mobile,'
he said largely. 'Then we can take Guadeloupe in rear.'

'But don't forget Jackson in the Great Smokies,' she answered. 'He has only eight hundred thousand men, but with
his fleet of gunboats he'll cut you off at Lexington unless you
guard the fords of the Housatonic.' It was a joke never screwed
to the point of laughter nor relaxed to serious meaning, an elab-

orate game played between them that the others were welcome
to watch. Sometimes, while their quiet voices piled chaos on
confusion, they looked at each other, and then they glanced
away quickly, shy and reddening.

In Georgia Sherman and Johnston had spent most of the
summer in a series of brilliantly cagey maneuvers. Johnston
took up one position after another in the tumbled hills, was
flanked out of each and contrived to retire without giving
battle. He could not prevent Sherman's advance, but he did
preserve his force as a constant menace. Sherman's line of
communication was constantly raided and constantly repaired,
until the thwarted Confederates maintained that the Yankees
carried even spare tunnels.

The generalship on both sides was excellent, but to Jefferson
Davis, who had Lincoln's habit of interference without Lincoln's
shrewdness in appraising men, Johnston's strategy seemed over-
cautious to the point of cowardice. Johnston was replaced by
Hood, who promptly gave battle, and thereupon Atlanta fell,
the Confederate force could no longer offer any important
resistance, and the whole of the deep South lay open to Sherman. 'As soon as your men are sufficiently rested and preparations can be made,' Ulyss wrote his friend, 'it is desirable that
another campaign should be commenced. We want to keep
the enemy continually pressed to the end of the war. If we
give him no peace while the war lasts, the end cannot be far
distant.'

'I can make the march,' said Sherman, 'and make Georgia
howl.'

The fall of Atlanta, and Sheridan's successes in the Valley,
did much to lessen the people's despair over the inconclusive
efforts in Virginia. The autumn rains damped down the fires
of the summer's political campaigns; in the autumn chill
the fundamental question stood forth clearly. The Radical

Republicans had withdrawn their ticket, and but two candidates, two alternatives, remained: McClellan if the war was to
be abandoned; Lincoln to continue it. And in the autumn quiet
the voice of the country was heard, commanding Lincoln back
to the White House.

'It's a great thing,' Ulyss told Julia. 'We were afraid of
trouble, bad trouble.'

'I don't see why. There's always fights at election time,
and parades, and some windows broken maybe, but you all
were talking about riots and sending whole regiments to keep
order. I never did see any sense in it.'

'We couldn't be sure,' said Ulyss. He knew that his tone was
defensive, and should not be, but he could not help it. Julia's
illogical belief that nothing bad would happen was so often
right that it gave her an unfair advantage. 'We've never had
an election in circumstances like these before. Rawlins says if
there'd been real trouble at the election we'd have lost the war,
no matter if Lee surrendered his army the next day.' Ulyss
had not understood the remark, but it clung to his mind.
Rawlins had always been given to obscure comments with an
elusive spark of truth in them, and had made them more often
than ever since his return from his two months' leave. His
cough was slightly improved, but his mood seemed no
lighter.

In a week or so Lincoln came down on another visit, and
Ulyss congratulated him on the double victory of a peaceful
re-election.

'Yes,' Lincoln said. He did not smile; and he did not look
directly at Ulyss, but fixed his eyes on some object so distant
that his gaze was plainly turned in upon himself. 'Yes ... I
didn't think it would turn out that way.'

'It had to, I think,' said Ulyss. The President's bearing
made him feel that comfort was more nearly appropriate than
congratulations. 'Without any big defeats just before election

day, the people were bound to realize how necessary it was to keep you in office.'

'I wonder,' said the President abruptly, 'if anything is necessary. I wonder if we ever really know what we do, or why — or if we would ever dare do anything if we knew what all the results would be.' Ulyss had never heard that dark, almost bitter tone before, and it struck him into puzzled silence. In a moment Lincoln laughed, and began telling a story of Stanton and a plot he thought he had discovered, returning to his customary drawl as simply as he would have changed garments.

That evening Ulyss told Julia of the incident, and she nodded. 'I don't imagine he has a very easy time of it,' she said softly. 'You know, I said something about the election to Mrs. Lincoln, and my land, how she did fire up! She said you were scheming to be President, and I dreamed day and night of the White House, and I don't know what all. Poor Colonel Badeau heard all of it, and squirmed so —— As soon as I could get a word in edgewise I told her neither of us had any such idea, that all I asked of God was that you should finish the war and be safe. And do you know, she calmed down right away and sort of preened herself, and said there was no reason I shouldn't think about it — it was very nice in the White House, and had lots of advantages. I believe the woman's touched, I do, really.'

'She's sick,' said Ulyss softly. He thought of Lincoln's 'Now, mama,' and remote pitying eyes when Mrs. Lincoln's outbursts created an unbearable awkwardness. Ulyss suddenly drew Julia to him and held her fast, as a miser derives a pleasure from the heaviness of gold in his hands that he cannot find in merely looking at the shining pieces.

Winter came down over Petersburg, and the men who had sweated and labored for breath in the heat of the trenches now shivered and coughed in the wet cold of the trenches, but they held fast. There were no more assaults, but week by week the lines crept farther to the left, closer to the vital railroads, nearer to the complete encirclement that meant the fall of Petersburg, the taking of Richmond, the crushing of the rebellion. In those weeks Ulyss grew stern and preoccupied. Hitherto, when it had been a matter of day-to-day advantage, his fatalism had tempered his concern, but now that it was a question of the final victory his hope bred monstrous fears. Suppose Lee should work free of Petersburg overnight and strike south? That might mean another year of the war, and in another year even the vital balance of morale might be altered. Suppose Hood turned on Sherman in Georgia, and that spectacular campaign ended in ruin? The questions hammered at Ulyss, and he could not quiet them with his old calm of common sense and the probabilities of the case. His desire was too great to be warmed with probabilities.

CHAPTER FOURTEEN

THE progress of our arms, upon which all else chiefly depends, is as well known to the public as to myself, and it is, I trust, reasonably satisfactory and encouraging to all.... Neither party expected for the war the magnitude or the duration which it has already attained. Neither anticipated that the cause of the conflict might cease, even before the conflict itself should cease. Each looked for an easier triumph, and a result less fundamental and astounding. Both read the same Bible and pray to the same God, and each invokes His aid against the other.... The prayer of both could not be answered. That of neither has been answered fully.

The Almighty has His own purposes.... Fondly do we hope, fervently do we pray, that this mighty scourge of war may speedily pass away. Yet if God wills that it continue until all the wealth piled by the bondsman's two hundred and fifty years of unrequited toil shall be sunk, and until every drop of blood drawn with the lash shall be paid by another drawn with the sword, as was said three thousand years ago, so, still it must be said, that the judgments of the Lord are true and righteous altogether.'

The voice was quiet, with no overtone of anger or of exultation. It was stern, as much with the acceptance of responsibility as with condemnation. It was a sombre inaugural speech to be made by a re-elected President in the last poised weeks before the end of a war, but it fit the mood of the nation. Victory seemed so close that it obscured the bitterness of conflict, but it was not yet close enough to reveal the joy of triumph. Men could see clearly on that March day, more clearly than they would again for a long time.

The preparations for the ultimate conflict had all been made, and waited now only for clear, dry weather. Lee had been given supreme authority over the Confederate forces, and had promptly restored Johnston to command. That general was hovering in the Carolinas, not strong enough to put a stop to Sherman's depredations; but if Lee could break through to him there was a chance that their combined forces might prolong the war. Grant had rid himself of Butler at the first opportunity after Lincoln's electoral victory; and Sheridan had come down from the devastated Valley, eager for further exploits. Everything was ready — everything but the weather.

At night Ulyss lay listening to Julia's quiet breathing, to the rain tapping on the roof, to the footsteps of the sentry, most of all to something he could not hear: the movements of Lee's men in Petersburg. If in the rainy dark they slipped from him —— He knew they could not, that the bottomless roads of spring barred escape for them as well as barred advance for the Union, but he listened nevertheless. Sometimes the rain trailed off for a little while, and he wondered if he might begin a move tomorrow, or the next day. In her sleep Julia put out her hand to him, and he took it without thinking. What if Lee pulled out of Petersburg tonight?

Late in March Ulyss ordered over half his force moved to the left, to envelop Petersburg altogether. It was too soon, he knew. There was only a thin crust over the mud, but he could not wait.

'I had thought,' Lincoln said to him, 'that maybe you were going to wait till Sherman could join you.' The President had come down to see the beginning of the final move.

'No.' Ulyss shook his head. 'Sherman's done enough. His campaign was brilliant, and everybody knows it. The Army of the Potomac has been fighting Lee for nearly three years, and it can whip him. If we waited now for Sherman there'd always be people to say that Lee wasn't licked till the westerners got after him.'

'I see. The country's split up enough as it is.' Lincoln laughed, but soon grew grave again. 'Is it going to work?' he asked quietly.

'I think so. If we can cut Lee off from the Danville Railroad, we've got him. When he can't get south he'll have to surrender.'

Neither said anything more. Everything had been said, over and over until the words were dry of meaning, and there was only action left.

The day the troops moved out, Ulyss kissed Julia good-bye in the doorway of their cabin, oblivious of the number of people who watched them and noted it as a touching scene in the proper tradition. Julia clung to him a little, but her lips were steady. 'Be careful, Victor,' she said.

'I'll be back soon,' he promised her. He heard his words as little as he had heard hers. There was an automatic tenderness in him when he touched her, but he was not thinking of her now. She knew it, and smiled a little as she watched him go, but her hands were tight and aching at her sides. Not until she could see him no longer did she look about her, and then she saw the President standing as she had, staring after Ulyss, his long hands pulling at the lapels of his coat and his eyes two dark pits beneath his jutting brows.

It was a relief to the men to be on the march again and to have done with the burrows they had lived in for the last nine months. For the first time since the early days of the war they felt that victory was close, and at last the grimness went out of them. There were no more stragglers, and the rear guards, deprived of their function, were restless because they were not allowed to push forward to the front ranks as the others did. There was singing again: sad elegies on the deaths of lonely pickets; long, ribald, and exact ballads of the deserter who arrived home unexpectedly and what he found there; and always the marching songs that drummed the length of the columns and back again. Even when the rain came down once more and dissolved the roads and soaked the men, they were not essentially dampened. They corduroyed their road before them, and when officers passed they shouted for pontoons and inquired when the gunboats were coming up. Sometimes they marched all night, for Lee was fighting with the brilliance of desperation, and it was not easy to keep his escape cut off and to re-enforce quickly the weak spots he discovered. Sometimes they were not fed, for the commissary wagons had difficulties in keeping up with the speeding army over the sketches of roads. But exhaustion and hunger belonged to the stagnant trenches and indecisive campaigns, and could not touch them now.

The southern end of the Confederate line rested on Five Forks, and it was there that Ulyss chose to strike. At Five Forks he could turn Lee's right, or if Lee detached enough men to hold the place Grant could march into Petersburg through

his centre. He remembered Donelson, long ago when the war
was young and the men were raw and he himself had known
very little except that with a given number of men, if they are
massed at one place they must be spread thin at another. Much
had changed since Donelson, almost everything had changed,
but mathematics is unalterable, and mathematics would bring
down the South to defeat. Ulyss knew it, and formed his plans
around that irresistible weapon. Lee did what he could to meet
them, knowing that his best was nothing, hoping that chance
might give him the opportunity that was not to be found in
logic. Slightly less than one man to two at Five Forks; about
one to five in front of Petersburg. There was little to hope for
there, but the convictions of the living and the sacrifice of the
dead demanded that he hope.

For some time the issue at Five Forks was not clear. Sheridan
and Warren had been supposed to cooperate in the movement,
but Warren was delayed by the abominable roads and by an excess of caution, so long that he was almost useless. Sheridan,
angry at the lack of support but willing enough to have the entire credit of the victory, dismounted his cavalrymen and used
them as infantry. They fought with the impetus given by an
assurance of victory, but their gray opponents had the angry
obstinacy of defeat, and held firm for a long time. Then Sheridan led his own charge, and the Confederate line broke. Lee's
right was crushed, and the railroads that had fed him in Petersburg and could have carried him southward were barred to him.

Porter rode back to Grant with the news of victory, working
as best he could through the marching troops, who had lost form
and discipline in celebration. He began shouting as soon as he
came in sight of the headquarters camp, and when he dismounted he thumped joyfully on the Lieutenant General's
back. Ulyss recovered his balance, and as soon as he could
make himself heard demanded, 'How many prisoners?'

It was difficult for Porter to isolate a single fact from the glory of the whole, but he answered in a moment, 'About five thousand, sir, maybe more, not much less.' Ulyss nodded. Five thousand prisoners, five thousand men who need not die in the last bitter days of a hopeless cause. He was more pleased by that knowledge than by the victory itself. Quickly, now, to the next step. The end was coming, and it might as well come fast. He wrote his dispatches himself, for all his aides were much too busy asking questions of Porter to take dictation. He ordered an assault from end to end of the line, and shortly the batteries began their deep, crashing roar, like the sound of legendary monsters in the night.

The staff was ordered to prepare for a ride to the front, and Badeau and Porter withdrew to their tent. 'I know you're excited, and all that,' Badeau said in friendly criticism, 'but I don't think you should have drunk anything today. After all, it's a pretty solemn thing ——'

'Do you think I'm drunk?' Porter demanded wrathfully.

'No, not exactly, but clapping General Grant on the back ——'

'What?' Porter's amazement was so great that it took all the force from Badeau's accusation.

'You did, I saw you.' Badeau nodded as he pulled on a boot. 'That's why I thought you were drunk.'

'Well, I wasn't. I haven't had a drop since New Year's.'

'Oh — I did wonder how you could get excited enough to do a thing like that. You're usually — ow!' Badeau stumbled back to the bed, and stared at his feet. One of them had been wounded almost two years before, and since then he had worn a steel boot on it. It was naked and unprotected now, and the boot was on the sound foot. Porter laughed and Badeau swore, and then they laughed together, an odd sound while the bombardment crashed for miles to either side of them.

All night long the guns roared, and at daybreak the Union men poured into the Petersburg defenses. Fort Hell and Fort

Damnation, known officially as Gregg and Whitworth, fell to them, and by mid-afternoon the whole of the outer line was theirs. Then the commanders came to Ulyss with bright eyes, and suggested that the inner line be assaulted. It could be taken, they knew, and by night Petersburg would at last belong to the Union.

'No,' said Ulyss. 'They're bound to evacuate the town to-night. We'll make no assault until dawn. If they're still there, then it can't be helped.'

'But they'll get away!' the commanders protested, remembering the long dread that Lee might slip from them, remembering how often he had wrought from failure the key to a new success.

'How can they, now that they can't get at the railroads any more? Petersburg and Richmond were lost at Five Forks. Lee knows that. He's not going to waste men trying to defend them if we give him a chance to get away, and once he's away we'll cut him off, and he'll have to surrender.'

'We could make sure of him now,' said the more stubborn.

'We're sure of him anyway. We could get him today, but only by killing a lot of men who don't have to be killed. There'll be no assault, not until five in the morning.'

There was none even then, for by morning the Confederates had gone. The long trenches were empty, the replaced line around the crater was quiet, the early sunlight threw undisturbed shadows on abandoned bombproofs and redoubts. The town, too, was empty, streets swept clean of life between the blind house fronts; the only token of the living a starved and savage cat prowling on its lonely affairs, leaping sidewise into the shadows when a group of Union cavalry clattered by. Ulyss stood with Meade and looked at the town they had fought so hard to win. It seemed almost a pointless victory, as meaningless as a scrap of paper with the writing on it washed away. The significance of Petersburg had been in her railroads that

stretched southward into unravaged country; in Richmond to
the north, which that day was falling to the Union; most of all in
the men who had fought for her and had now spilled out into
the countryside, gray uniforms on their bodies, gray frustration
in their minds, and the gray taste of failure in their mouths.
Some of them were still in sight, crowding into the roads that
led westward along the Appomattox River. They were within
artillery range, but Ulyss gave no order to fire. He was sure of
his result now, and had no longer any genuine fear that the control of events might be twisted from him. His only uncertainty
now was how long it would be before the climax came. He
knew what it must be, and certainly Lee knew also, yet the
bloodless, formal words of acknowledgment would be the only
fundamental defeat of the South, and no one knew how many
more lives must be paid before the words could be bought.

' . . . follow him up now,' Meade was saying. Ulyss had not
been listening, but he shook his head.

'No, we won't follow him, we'll get ahead of him,' he said.
'His only chance is to get on the Danville Railroad with a clear
line south. We'll get there first, and then we'll have him whatever he does.'

There were no more comments from Meade, and he gave the
orders to march the men out of town as quickly as they came in.
His had not been an easy part in the year since Grant had taken
supreme command. He was a capable man and a good soldier,
but his title had been empty and his position subordinate and
galling. He had done well. He had given his best to the cause
he believed in, had thereby furthered the fame of another man,
yet still stood by what he had said in the beginning: 'This campaign is too important to be interfered with by consideration of
personalities.' If he had his resentments, if he felt that his
worth had been slighted and his name half obliterated, he said
nothing of what he felt, and acted on what he believed. 'This
campaign is too important.' He remembered it again now, while

Grant was deciding what was to be done with Meade's army. He was right, probably, and right or not he had the authority.

In those crowded few days Ulyss never forgot the President, still waiting at City Point, following the uncertainties and successes and further uncertainties in the telegrams Ulyss faithfully sent him, hoping for much but burdened with his too clear knowledge of responsibility. 'If we would ever dare do anything if we knew what all the results would be.' Ulyss was not given to such doubts, but he had seen in Lincoln's eyes the darkness that they bring to a man. Surely here was a result not even Lincoln in his heaviest mood could question. Ulyss telegraphed to him a suggestion that he come to Petersburg.

They met on the porch of one of the deserted houses. There was no melancholy in Lincoln that day, and there was the light in his face that Ulyss had hoped to see. 'I had a sort of sneaking idea you were going to do something like this,' he said as they sat down together. 'I was betting you'd work Lee out of Petersburg some way, but I wasn't sure how soon.'

'I could have told you,' Ulyss confessed. 'There wasn't any danger of it leaking out — Lee knew very well what we were doing as soon as we began to move anyway. But — you've had so many disappointments. I was pretty sure, but I couldn't be positive.'

The President nodded, and his slow smile was more fervent thanks than all his words had been. 'I don't care,' he said. 'I wouldn't mind if you kept the capture of Petersburg a secret between you and Mrs. Grant, so long as you captured it. What are you going to do now — go on to Richmond?'

'I think Weitzel will march in there today — I hope to get that news before you leave. But I'm not going up myself. It doesn't matter any more, or Petersburg either, now that Lee has pulled out. The towns were important only as long as Lee tried to hold on to them.'

'Where is Lee now?'

'Heading west, to Farmville or thereabouts. He'll try to get south, to Johnston, and to a source of supplies, but we'll cut him off.' Ulyss told his plans in detail, delighting in being entirely frank with this man to whom he had for so long denied all information. 'And then he must surrender,' he concluded, and paused, touched again by the unreality of that inevitable result. Surrender — it must come, and soon, but Ulyss could not picture it.

'And then what, I wonder?' said Lincoln. He grew thoughtful, staring at his hands locked around his bony knee. 'That will be only half the job. Getting the Union really working again, with all the states present and accounted for, will just about take another war in Washington.'

'I think,' said Ulyss slowly, 'that most of the Southern people will be loyal, once Lee surrenders. There's been a good deal of distress and dissatisfaction. Some fanatics, of course, and the big slaveowners, but they're ruined anyway. And the North has been fighting for union. Who'll make trouble?'

'Think a minute,' Lincoln answered quietly. He spoke without anger, simply mentioning facts which existed and must be dealt with, much as Ulyss would speak of the strength and dispositions of an opposing army. 'Think of how many different ideas there've been about how to fight the war. There're ten times that many about what to do when we've won it. Have we conquered the South, so she's a sort of colony? Has she demoted herself, so those eleven states are more like territories? Or has she just lost an argument, and is still part of the Union, same as ever?'

'The Constitution,' said Ulyss uncomfortably.

'It doesn't say anything about this directly. It can be interpreted, but we've already had one war because we couldn't agree on the interpretation.'

'But that was because one side didn't care about the Constitution. Congress is full of lawyers, and they can figure out now just what has to be done ——'

'The trouble is that Congress is full of people.' Lincoln laughed, then frowned. 'Sumner came to me before the nominations last summer, and said he was going to work for somebody else unless there was a more vigorous prosecution of the war. He made quite a speech about it. I think he meant prosecution in both senses — his idea is that Southerners are criminals, and have to be punished like criminals.' Suddenly the President dropped his foot to the floor, and threw back his head with a determination more cold and steely than Ulyss had ever seen in him. 'I won't have it. I won't see this country torn apart like that when we've gone through four years of hell to hold it together.' He relaxed then, and grinned. 'I told him it was a pretty big hog we were trying to catch, and it wouldn't be easy to hold on to it. There'll have to be a fight to get things done the way they should be, but I think people will see it as soon as the war's over and they can settle down again. And nobody will get killed no matter how hard we fight. That's something.' He smiled the rare smile that Ulyss had never forgotten since he had first seen it, that seemed always a new and beautiful thing whenever it came.

'I'm sure it will work out all right,' said Ulyss. He had only vague notions of just what the problems were, but he was comforted by the assurance in Lincoln's manner, and pleased that, troublesome as they seemed to be, he was not so burdened by them that he could not feel the happiness of the present victory. That was the important thing. Lee must soon surrender, and then everything would be settled. Perhaps not at once, perhaps there would be a few trying months of readjustment, but there were wise men in Congress who could handle it, and Lincoln could handle them.

It was time for Ulyss to take his place with the armies that

were marching rapidly westward, and he made his farewells.
As he rode down the sunny, empty street, he turned several
times to look back at the ungainly figure he had left on the
porch, and each time there was a long-armed wave in return.
Ulyss had gone but a short distance when he received a dispatch
from Weitzel, who had entered Richmond unopposed. 'I'm
sorry,' said Ulyss half to himself as he stared at the sheet of
paper. 'I'd hoped it would come while I was with him.' It
would have pleased him to give the news to the President himself, to say, 'Richmond has fallen,' and see his eyes light with
sudden pleasure, see his smile take that light and so gild his face
with it that one forgot he was ugly.

Ulyss remembered the cries of 'On to Richmond!' that
smoldering night in the Wilderness; the fascination there had
been in his distant view of the place from Cold Harbor; this
whole past year when his every action had been affected by
thought of the city, the capital of the Confederate States, Lee's
charge. Now he cared very little. Richmond had fallen, Davis
and his cabinet were fleeing in pathetic futility to Danville, but
therefore Lee was bound no longer. Not cities, but armies.
'Have the news circulated among the men,' said Ulyss, handing
the dispatch to Babcock. 'We must hurry forward.'

Richmond was burning. No one knew exactly why, but it
was burning: the government buildings, the warehouses, the
factories, all the tokens of a nation that had tried to be. The
people came into the streets and stood watching, anything,
everything: the fat ugly flames that belched in gutted interiors,
and the thin flames that fluttered in the shattered windows,
silvery in the sunlight and bright orange when the smoke hid
the sun; the blue soldiers and the civilians who fought the
flames; the negroes and the very poor who swarmed about the
supplies that had been dumped from the warehouses; the James
River, dun with its reflection of coiling smoke and its powdering

of drifting ashes. Men stood in the streets rigid, with hands clenched and eyes fixed; women white and graceful, drawing on memories of family tragedies for the deportment proper to the end of a nation; young girls trembling and in tears, but conscious of the drama that had swept away the order of their lives and faced them with an unknowable future. Men stood in the streets puzzled and staring, aware that change had come, resenting it, welcoming it, and not knowing at all what to do with it; women nervous and shrill-voiced; children running and shouting as though the end of a world were a game and destruction their delight. The negroes stood together, men and women and children, or slowly sifted through the chaotic streets. The currents of their individual pasts were dammed now, and not they nor anyone knew what channel would lead their race into the future. They were stranded in the present, without great joy, without grief, waiting for a new pressure to replace the one that had been lifted from them.

In the fields by Richmond a man was plowing. He guided his ramshackle mule back and forth, swearing when the animal swerved or stopped with the stubborn whim of its kind, glancing only occasionally at the smoky clouds that half hid the city. It had started to be a fair day, but with all this burning there was a haze over the sun, and an odd smell in the air that almost hid the sweetness of the earth in April. Still, the sun and the spring weather were there behind the smoke, and the ashes that drifted on the wind and caught in the furrows wouldn't hurt the ground. The season was getting on, and a man must do his plowing when he can.

'Cavalry gi'n out ridin'.' 'Jine the infantry and give them pore dumb beasts a rest.' The marching columns shouted in blithe derision at the dismounted horsemen. One man broke step to cavort in elaborate imitation of a showy rider, and the sergeant who should have kept order laughed with the others.

Ulyss too smiled as he lay on his elbow in the grass and watched
them pass. Sometimes they recognized him and raised a brief
cheer, in recognition of his success and their prowess; sometimes they saw in him and his staff simply a group of exhausted
cavalry, and took the opportunity for a gibe. Either way
pleased Ulyss. The spirit of his men was all but tangible to him,
and it was a greater assurance of victory than all his precise
calculations. They knew. They marched tirelessly, fasted
without complaint, some of them died almost casually in the
daily skirmishes with Lee's desperate men, because they
knew.

The country they marched through was beautiful as they had
forgotten country could be beautiful. War had not been here.
The fields lay in smooth furrows, untrampled, with no fresh
trenches to mar their surface, and no weeds springing up over
the wounds of last year and the year before. Unmolested trees
were leafing out in the pale green shades of early April, and
peach orchards drifted pink on the hillsides. Houses were inhabited, and farm dogs came to bark at the outrageous novelty
of men by thousands marching on the roads.

Porter and Babcock were arguing, not with great heat but
persistently, about some detail of Sheridan's campaign in the
Valley last September. Grant listened idly, thinking how trivial
the discussion seemed, now that the end of fighting was so near
and all their lives were to be cut short and begun again on
different paths with different goals, and yet how impossible it
was to speak of that. Perhaps it would be easier for these young
men, perhaps their thoughts did not stop at Lee's surrender,
stubbornly refusing to look into the blank beyond. He himself
was centred entirely in these days, these hours perhaps, before
word came from Lee. The Ulysses Grant who would move in
his body thereafter would be a man as strange to him as Cap
Grant of Galena. He looked at his aides, wondering about them,
and suddenly they too were strangers. Then he saw Rawlins,

and as their eyes met there was for a moment the understanding there had been between them long ago. Ulyss smiled a little as he rose and brushed hastily at his blouse. 'We'd better be moving,' he said. 'If another company of infantry catches us we'll be disgraced for good.'

Lee is at Amelia Court House. Lee is at Farmville. One by one Lee paused at the little villages, and hurried on, trying to keep ahead of the Union armies that were always, not in his rear, but a little to the south of him, barring his way to Johnston. One by one the points where he had ordered supplies were blocked, or the Union raiders got there first and burned the wagons. The Army of Northern Virginia had no hope in any real sense, but it was not yet hounded to the point of making the step between the hopelessness of knowledge and the hopelessness of acknowledgment. Grant waited from expectant dawn to triumphant midnight, but the essential victory, a word from Lee, did not come.

Short of that there were many satisfactions. The flow of Confederate stragglers was unchecked now, and whole regiments melted overnight. Sheridan's ebullient dispatches were an almost unbroken tale of success. There was even criticism of Lee's obstinacy from his own commanders. Ulyss heard of it when he visited a field hospital at Burkesville. He disliked visiting hospitals, but he went, as if by hurting himself to make amends for the guilt that had been forced upon him. This one was like all the others, with the same shattered men, the same odors, the same whimpers and clenched teeth and brute indifference. But to Ulyss this one had a greater horror than any that he had seen, greater than the first, greater than the leaking cabin at Shiloh, greater even than the wholesale bloodiness of the Wilderness. He was sickened when he came out, and stood breathing the cool damp air of evening as though it could wash from him his memory of that quarter hour. 'There's no need of this,' he said, half in apology, half angrily, to the doctor who had accompanied him. 'The war's ending, and everybody knows it, but some of those men have been maimed for life when the fight has really been settled ——'

'I know.' The doctor's troubled voice had the Virginia softness. 'But it's a hard thing to say you've been whipped. I went today to see General Ewell after he was captured — he's a cousin of mine. He was pretty bitter. Said that once you had crossed the James, last June, there was only one ending the war could have. Said that if Davis had amounted to anything in the way of brains he'd have sued for peace then, when the South could still claim concessions. Now it's lost anyway, and it isn't strong enough to ask for anything.'

'That's true,' said Ulyss eagerly. 'The rebels are beaten, and the longer they won't say so the worse they make it for themselves.'

'Of course, but you see ——' The doctor's eyes were dark, but he smiled a little. 'Maybe it's like two boys having a fistfight — one of them has to say uncle, but the one who's losing doesn't think he's really whipped until he's said it, and there's a kind of boy who will wait to say it until all his teeth are knocked out.'

'War isn't a fist-fight,' said Ulyss with some sharpness. 'A man as smart as Lee knows there's a difference between dead men and teeth.' The comparison seemed to him callously frivolous, considering the rows of half-crushed human beings he had just inspected. But it stuck in his thoughts because it annoyed him, and slowly he began to see the truth behind the trivial metaphor. He had never seen a small boy of any courage admit defeat until he was so commanded. War is not a fist-fight, but it was possible that in its adult horrors there was some carryover of childish standards. Eventually Lee must surrender, and possibly that hour might come more quickly if it was not necessary that he make the first move himself. Ulyss thought of it for a day, reading the dispatches that told of the destruction of supplies intended for Lee's men, of successive barriers on Lee's route, and in the evening he wrote a letter.

General R. E. Lee, Commanding C. S. A.

The results of the last week must convince you of the hopelessness of further resistance on the part of the Army of Northern Virginia in this struggle. I feel that it is so, and regard it as my duty to shift from myself the responsibility of any further effusion of blood, by asking of you the surrender of that portion of the Confederate States army known as the Army of Northern Virginia.

'Holler uncle,' Ulyss said to himself as his messenger galloped away, but he did not smile, and he did not think of the term again. This was a sober hour, and there was an icy queasiness in him while he waited. A year ago he had scoffed at the tale of Lee, had insisted that the man was human and could be defeated, and had proved his point in the tortured progress from the Wilderness to Five Forks. But now that victory was his, Ulyss saw in Lee, the man, the stature he had never conceded to the Confederate general. He had dealt with Buckner, and with Pemberton. He had never dealt with Lee, and he was beginning to feel something close to awe.

Late that evening Lee's answer came. He was not hopeless, he said. (But he knew his men were dying in a hopeless cause. The statement was not made, but could be seen behind the reserved phrases.) What terms did General Grant offer? Ulyss answered early in the morning: ' ... peace being my great desire, there is but one condition I would insist upon, namely: that the men and officers surrendered shall be disqualified for taking up arms against the Government of the United States until properly exchanged.' He paused there, thinking of those men and officers and their long and shining record as an army, of the Seven Days and Chancellorsville and Gettysburg and their stubborn struggle against himself. Lee's army, and the army's Lee. It would be a bitter thing for a man to arrange personally for the disintegration of something so much a part of him.

Ulyss added, 'I will meet you, or will designate officers to meet any officers you may name for the same purpose, at any point agreeable to you, for the purpose of arranging definitely the terms upon which the surrender of the Army of Northern Virginia will be received.' A cumbrous and awkward sentence, but there was in it an escape for the man Lee if he chose to accept it.

Then nothing happened. All that day the armies maneuvered westward as though no letters had ever been written, and Ulyss sometimes wondered if they had. His head ached with sick violence, so that the words of dispatches weaved up and down and blurred before him. He rode doggedly forward, trying to direct his men and make intelligible plans, but there was no reality in anything but the pain that writhed in his head and seemed to coil through his very bones. His staff was solicitous, and plastered him with mustard when they halted for the night, but their nursing had no effect. He was glad when they let him alone and he could lie down in the dark to wonder why he had not heard from Lee.

The staff slept all together on the floor of another room. The more phlegmatic went to sleep at once, recognizing the importance of their own exhaustion, but Porter, Badeau, and Babcock stayed awake and discussed in whispers all the possible reasons for Lee's silence.

'For God's sake shut up,' Rawlins snapped. 'Lee will answer, he's got to. And you're keeping the whole army awake.'

'Suppose he gets away somehow?' Badeau persisted.

'Do you think he can fly? You remind me of a bunch of scared old women.'

They were silent then, and slept after a fashion, but even the early sleepers woke at the sound of a sentry's challenge. The letter from Lee had come, and it was brought to Rawlins. 'This is it,' he said, and stood staring at it for a moment. His eyes were dark and his cheeks flushed, but there was uncertainty on his mouth. 'I hate to wake him,' he confessed. 'It may be only another delay, and he needs his rest.'

'Maybe he isn't resting,' said Badeau. 'He was looking for this.'

'I'll have to see.' Rawlins crossed the hall and cautiously opened the door to Grant's room. Porter brought a candle, and the light cast upward on Rawlins's face made it a black and white mask, the glowing eyes half closed and the thin lips parted; the brow and cheek bones pale, finely modeled structures above the flowing darkness of the beard. Rawlins listened, and Porter looked from him to the letter in his hand to the candle's flickering flame, and the night wind crept about their ankles like the shadow of winter.

'Come in,' said Ulyss, 'I'm awake. I couldn't sleep with my head like this.' He was sitting up when they entered, his eyes wincing from the light, but his hand extended for the letter he knew they had brought. '"In mine of yesterday,"' he read, '"I did not intend to propose the surrender of the Army of Northern Virginia, but to ask the terms of your proposition. To be frank, I do not think the emergency has arisen to call for the surrender of this army; but as the restoration of peace should be the sole object of all, I desired to know whether your proposals would lead to that end. I cannot, therefore, meet you with a view to surrender the Army of Northern Virginia; but as far as your proposal may affect the Confederate States forces under my command, and tend to the restoration of peace, I shall be pleased to meet you at 10 A.M. tomorrow on the old stage road to Richmond, between the picket-lines of the two armies."'

'Lee still means to fight,' said Ulyss heavily.

'You can't treat for peace,' Rawlins snapped. 'You haven't the authority.'

'I know. It's impossible.' Ulyss folded the letter with elaborate and unseeing care, and sighed.

'He can't get away,' said Porter, assuring himself as much as the others. 'We've got him, whatever he says.'

'He's licked all right,' Ulyss answered absently, 'and he knows it. But I'd hoped——' He stopped. He might as well forget what he had hoped, forget once more that his materials were men, and wastage was lives. 'I'll answer in the morning,' he said, and lay down again.

'Maybe you can sleep some now,' said Rawlins, and his fingers brushed Grant's shoulder as he went out. Ulyss could hear the talk in the other room where the staff was discussing the letter, low but persistent, like the sound of the blood in his head. He had done what he could, whatever happened now was not his fault. He kept his thoughts fixed rigidly on that point, and held his body rigidly in its place. Pain lay in wait for either of them should they move.

In the morning he dictated the necessary answer to Lee. No authority . . . equally anxious for peace . . . terms well understood . . . difficulties settled without the loss of another life . . . The words rose out of his mind and said themselves, the formal, pointless closing of an effort that had once held life. He rode forward then in his ordinary routine, but his disappointment blackened the sunlight.

At Appomattox Station were provisions for the Army of Northern Virginia. Not many, but enough to last for a little while. Lee's men swept hungrily into the place, but between them and the rations they found Sheridan. They charged, taking the last desperate chance, but the Union cavalry, instead of standing firm, wheeled to right and left and disclosed the whole of the Army of the James behind it. The Confederates stood still and looked, and in a moment a white flag fluttered above them.

A messenger came to Grant where he was riding doggedly forward, too far behind the lines to know that the firing had stopped. Lee was waiting where he had said he would, to do what he had said he would not. 'I now request an interview, in accordance with the offer contained in your letter of yesterday ...' Ulyss had scarcely time to wonder while he wrote his answer and sent it off by Babcock. A temporary truce, the messenger had said, and he was so far away —— He rode as quickly as he could, thinking more of the renewed firing he might hear at any moment than of what he was going to do.

'How do you feel, General?' Porter asked with the concern he had shown all morning.

Ulyss stared at him a moment, then put his hand uncertainly to his head. 'It doesn't ache any more,' he said with some surprise, and added with a sudden grin, 'I guess I feel pretty good.'

It was Sunday, and there was a Sabbath look about the town of Appomattox despite the gray army clustered in the valley below it, and the blue army thick on the low hills around it. The dust stirred gently in the quiet street, and there was a decorous silence in the houses. Babcock rode up and down looking critically at the scene. He had been told to find a suitable place for the meeting of the generals, and with the setting of history in his charge he was hard to please. One suggestion he rejected, but he was at length satisfied with the house of a gentleman, a cool and roomy building with a long porch across its front. It was just right, Babcock knew. Simple and self-respecting, without the picturesqueness of more vulgar quarters, or the grandeur that European commanders would find necessary. He gave a last approving look at the miscellaneous chairs and tables on which he had conferred immortality, then left the room to Lee.

'That's Traveler, General Lee's horse,' Porter almost whispered as Grant and his staff reached the house. They all stared at the animal, but the Confederate orderly glared at them and they turned their eyes decently away. Nothing could be looked at, for men were wearing their pain in their faces, in drawn lips and dry, hot eyes. Nothing could be said, for one does not chat-

ter to heartbreak. The Union men dismounted in silence, and
Ulyss advanced up the steps and into the house where Lee was.
His dread that the surrender would not come, and his joy when
it did, had alike disappeared. He was depressed. He had
wanted peace and victory, and had forgotten that to get them
he must first humiliate a gallant man. The house was as quiet,
thought Ulyss, as though there had already been a death in
it.

A door opened, and Ulyss automatically accepted the silent
invitation. A man stood up and came toward him. Tall, grave,
immaculate, the gleam of a dress sword, eyes shadowed but
steady. 'General Lee,' said Ulyss. Their hands met, firmly
and briefly, and they sat down together. 'I met you once in
Mexico,' Ulyss said, 'when you came over to visit Garland's
brigade. I've always remembered you — I think I should have
recognized you anywhere.'

'Yes,' Lee responded. His voice was quiet, somewhat measured. 'I know we met then, and I've tried very hard to remember you, but I couldn't recall a single feature.' There was nothing ironic in his tone, but a rather puzzled note. He looked
now at Grant, and Ulyss was conscious of his uniform, old and
mud-spattered, with only the stars on his shoulder to distinguish him from a private. He wore no sword at all, much less
one so intricately beautiful as Lee's, and he knew that his head-
ache must have left sooty marks around his eyes and a pallid,
unwashed look in his face. He was not greatly concerned.
There was a difference between him and Lee, in temperament,
beliefs and methods, so deep that a greater conformity in exter-
nals would only emphasize it.

'That was a long time ago, Mexico,' said Ulyss. He talked
eagerly of it, for there was some comfort in letting Cerro Gordo
and Vera Cruz obscure for a moment Five Forks and Appomattox.

It was Lee who said the words that Grant found difficult. 'I

suppose, General, that the object of our meeting is fully understood. I asked to see you to ascertain upon what terms you
would receive the surrender of my army.' Long words, and
stately, as though they had been rehearsed, but they were said
at last.

'My terms are about what I wrote you,' said Ulyss slowly.
He wished fleetingly that Lee had accepted the opportunity that
had been offered him of appointing an agent for this final encounter. 'The officers and men to be paroled until exchanged,
and all arms and supplies to be turned over to us.'

'Yes, that's what I expected.'

'Our letters showed pretty clearly what we would decide
when we met. I hope that on this basis the war can be stopped,
and there need be no further loss of life.' Ulyss spoke at some
length on this subject too. There must be something more to
think about than defeat and finality. There was no joy in
triumph when he looked at Lee's eyes, and for the sake of the
Confederate general as well as himself he tried to look beyond,
to the glories of peace in a reunited nation. Lee listened courteously and sometimes assented, but was not to be swerved
even in thought from what he had to do.

'If you will put your terms in writing, General Grant, I will
sign them.' Ulyss knew then where the greatest kindness lay.
He wrote rapidly, setting forth in the required phrases the conditions he had proposed, unchanged until he reached the section
on surrender of arms and ammunition. There was no need for
the officers' swords and delicately ornamented pistols to be
turned over to the United States Government. He excepted
the side arms and personal property of officers, then finished
the formal letter as had been agreed.

The change at last drew a smile from Lee. 'That will have a
very happy effect,' he said, and Ulyss felt a slight tinge of
warmth. Lee found a word left out, and borrowed a pencil from
Porter to set it right. The young staff officer stood fascinated,

watching his pencil gain historic significance with every twirl in the gray general's fingers.

'There's one other thing,' Lee said slowly as he finished the letter. 'Our army is organized differently from yours. With us, the privates own their mounts. Will they be allowed to keep them?'

'Not according to these terms. Only officers' property is exempted.'

'Yes. I see that is so.' Lee sighed, almost imperceptibly.

There was a pause, and Ulyss looked out of the window, thinking of the plowed, receptive fields he had seen on the way from Petersburg, and of other fields: the weed-matted clearings that were Virginia's farms from the Rapidan to Richmond; the burned and desolate swathe that was Sherman's track from Mississippi to North Carolina. Officers' side arms were useless ornaments of no significance, but the horses and mules remaining to the men who had been Confederates were vital tools.

'I'll tell you what I'll do,' said Ulyss. 'All this is new to me — I didn't know your men owned their own beasts. I suppose most of them are small farmers, and they couldn't possibly get in a crop this season to feed their families unless they have horses. I won't change the terms as written, but I'll instruct the officers who take the paroles that if any man claims to own a horse or mule he can take it home with him to work his farm.'

Lee smiled again, and the shadow in his eyes lifted for a moment. 'That will have a better effect on the men than anything else,' he said. 'It will do much to conciliate our people.' He directed the only aide who had accompanied him to draft his acceptance of the terms, and then both documents were copied. During the pause Grant introduced to him Sheridan and Ord and most of the Union staff, who had been standing silently around the walls. Someone made a joke, and Lee bowed, unsmiling, acknowledging its existence, not accepting it,

not disapproving it. Over the murmured words the scratching
of pens on paper was very clear.

'General Lee,' Ulyss said suddenly, 'I left my camp several
days ago, and haven't seen my baggage since. That's why I
don't have my sword today — I wear it as little as possible.'
He was unconcerned about his appearance in itself, but so far
as it might be interpreted as disrespect he felt that it must be
explained.

'I wear mine most of the time,' Lee said with a nod, 'when I
am among the troops.' There was as little of criticism in his
words as there had been of apology in Grant's.

The letters were finished at last, and signed. Lee made his
farewells and went out to the porch to leave. The orderly was
slow in bridling Traveler, and Lee stood waiting, silently looking down into the valley where his army was. Three times he
struck his hands together without knowing what he did, without
seeing the groups of Union officers in the yard, and the sound
was flat and heavy in the quiet. Not until Traveler was led
before him did he withdraw his eyes from the distance on which
they had been fixed. He put out his hand, and the gray horse
lipped it gently, and then at last he swung into the saddle.

Ulyss and his staff had waited indoors, giving what solitude
they could to the man from whom they had taken the hope and
justification of four years. But they had not allowed for delay,
and came forth just as Lee mounted. Ulyss looked at him,
knowing that all the words had been said, and were useless; all
the acts were past, though no one yet knew their meaning.
Ulyss took off his hat in silence, and his officers ranged behind
him swept off theirs. Lee raised his in wordless acknowledgment, then turned down the hill to his men, gray and erect.

The quiet of the Sunday afternoon was shattered by the
sound of cannon. A roar, and a pause, and another roar. A
hundred-gun salute in honor of victory. 'Have that stopped,'
Grant said abruptly. 'The Confederates are our prisoners —

we can't celebrate in front of them.' He mounted and rode rapidly back to his headquarters. Wherever he looked he saw Lee's eyes, and in his ears Lincoln's voice questioned over and over, I wonder if we ever really know what we do ... And then what, I wonder? Ulyss rode faster, because he did not know the answer.

PART FIVE

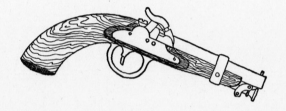

Grant's Special Train on the Rebuilt Southern Railroad

V. THE END OF THE BEGINNING

CHAPTER FIFTEEN

I THINK it would be a good plan for you to play "Dixie."
I always thought that it was the most beautiful of our songs. I
have submitted the question of its ownership to the Attorney
General, and he has given it as his legal opinion that we have
fairly earned the right to have it back.' Lincoln laughed with

the people who came to cheer him at the news of surrender, with the sober purpose of attacking with that kindly laughter the forces of bitterness and hatred that had not been surrendered. The Southern people must become citizens again whenever they wish. When one tenth of a state's voters in 1860 come together to set up a loyal government, that state must function once more in the Union. The Southern people are Americans, brothers still in the bond that cannot be broken, and if there is to be any punishment at all it must fall only on the few who led them into rebellion. Lincoln spoke to the people, gently and steadily, not with the heat of argument but as though he were expressing their thought, and those who heard him believed they had that thought.

He had so little time. In these first days after Appomattox the spent nation was incapable of anything but celebration, hysteric with joy that the past was finished, forgetful that there must be a future. Men got drunk, and cheered, and marched up and down the streets of Washington, and did very little thinking. Almost no one had ever considered that the end of the war was not the end of the nation's problem. Lincoln had. Lincoln had been thinking for months of this last and most dangerous phase, and from his basic beliefs he had wrought a plan that he was determined should be accepted. He worked as quickly as he could in the few days that the people, relaxed and acquiescent in victory, would cheer every and any word he said; and anxiously counted over the few months that Congress would not be in session. So little time in which to do so much, but it was all he had, and he must make it suffice.

It was strange to Ulyss to see the urgency that Lincoln felt, and it made him a little envious. The President seemed to see so much to work for, but Ulyss had been filled with blank restlessness since he had parted from Lee. He had come back to Washington with all possible speed, disappointing his staff,

who had been hoping to see again some of their friends who had
been fighting in gray. His reason had been that as general in
chief it was his duty to slow the purchase of military supplies,
put an end to recruiting, bring to a stop the enormous and
complicated machine of war that had been dragging the country
forward. His officers covered their disappointment and applauded his public-spirited thrift, but Ulyss knew in his heart
that his reason was an excuse. What was he to do, now that
he was not fighting Lee? With what relish could he wake in
the morning, with no campaign to concern him; with what
satisfaction go to bed, with an unchanged day behind him?
He tried to absorb himself in the details of an office that was
losing its vitality, but too often his thoughts escaped him and
fastened on Lee, riding off to tell his army that it did not exist.

At a cabinet meeting to which the President invited him
Grant saw more clearly the problems of peace. 'I think it's
providential,' said Lincoln, 'that the rebellion was crushed just
as Congress adjourned.' He spoke casually, but his eyes marked
the faces that turned toward him; Seward's emphatic nod,
Stanton's thin, curled lip. 'If we're wise we can get the state
governments going again and order prevailing before Congress
comes together in December.' He spoke less casually, with the
tone Ulyss had heard him use at Petersburg. 'There must be
no bloody work after the war is over. No one need expect me
to take any part in hanging or killing those men, even the
worst of them.'

'How about Jacob Thompson?' Stanton interrupted. 'He's
trying to get away to England, but I know exactly where I can
catch him ——'

'If you've got an elephant by the hind leg and he's trying to
run away, it's best to let him go.'

'Oh, rot!' Stanton snapped. 'I suppose you'd say that about
Jefferson Davis too?'

Lincoln laughed. 'Once in a town in Illinois where I was

practicing law I found a little boy crying in the streets. I asked him what the trouble was, and he pointed to a very poor specimen of the coon family he was pulling along at the end of a string. He said, "Mister, that coon has given me a heap of trouble. He's nearly gnawed the string in two — I just wish he'd finish it. Then I could go home and say he'd got away."' Stanton snorted, but most of the others laughed. Lincoln continued in a tone closer to severity than Ulyss had ever heard him use: 'Frighten them out of the country, open the gates, let down the bars, scare them off. Enough lives have been sacrificed.' He looked at each man, and said slowly, 'We can't expect to have harmony and union if we can't forget our resentments.'

There was no answer, and the President turned back to his discussion of the Southern states. Grant listened for some time to the talk of how quickly the new governments could be set up; of methods of circumventing the Radical majority in Congress; of the thorny question of negro suffrage, which Senator Sumner was trying to insert in every context. Whatever their disagreements, they all spoke as though there were not an armed man in the country. As soon as he could Ulyss said diffidently, 'Mr. President, I haven't heard from Sherman, so he hasn't come to terms with Johnston yet. It might be some time before the war is actually over ——'

'That's all right, General Grant.' Lincoln nodded in friendly assurance. 'It can't be very long — in fact, I wouldn't be surprised if we heard today. I dreamed of my ship again last night, and that always means a victory. This time I could almost see what the shore was — maybe I did see it, and just couldn't remember when I woke, so it must be a big victory.' Stanton muttered something, and Lincoln smiled at him, and shortly adjourned the meeting. He detained Ulyss, saying, 'Mrs. Lincoln and I are going to the theatre tonight, and we'd be very happy to have you and Mrs. Grant come with us.'

'I'm afraid we can't,' Ulyss answered with genuine reluctance, for he disliked denying any request of Lincoln's. 'I've promised Mrs. Grant to go with her to Burlington this evening, to see our three oldest children in school there. If I can possibly finish my work in time I can't disappoint her.'

'People would be so pleased to see you, you really ought to come.'

'I think I can get along for a while without having anybody pleased to see me,' Ulyss grinned, remembering the crowds shifting up and down the streets, pouncing on any known figure as an excuse for a demonstration. 'But I'll talk it over with Mrs. Grant, and if she's willing to stay over we'll be happy to come. Or if she feels like she's got to see the children and I can't get away to go with her, I'll come alone. I'll let you know.'

The plan satisfied Lincoln, and Ulyss stopped by his hotel to see what Julia thought of it. He was willing enough to go, but he suspected that she would not be held a moment longer than necessary from Burlington. She came toward him as soon as he entered the room. 'Ulyss,' she said, not giving him time to speak, 'while Jesse and I were having lunch today there was a very queer-looking man watching us. He moved to a table close to ours, and seemed to be trying to hear what we said ——'

'Did he annoy you?' Ulyss frowned.

'No, not what you'd think of as annoying a lady, or I'd have called the manager. But he frightened me a little, Ulyss. He looked so strange ——'

'He had big eyes,' Jesse explained. 'He was a big black man and he leaned over like this — look at me, papa, like this ——' Jesse's imitations were generally applauded, but this time Ulyss gave him no attention. Julia had been frightened, and he was concerned by that, however trivial the cause.

'There's no need for alarm, my dear,' he said. 'It's troublesome, I know, but right now this city is full of people with no manners and not much sense. You know how it is in the streets.'

'This was different, Ulyss. There was something about this man's eyes.'

'Maybe he was a little addled,' Ulyss admitted, knowing that Julia's fears were never to be soothed by scouting their origin, 'but there's plenty like him — there's a man over on Seventeenth Street who thinks he's found a gold mine in Anacostia, but he's harmless too.'

'Big eyes like this,' Jesse persisted.

'Forget him, darling,' Julia said to her son. 'Papa says he wasn't important.'

The words were the exact truth, and there was no irony in the tone, but Ulyss felt that his reassurances were dismissed as firmly as the child's persistence. 'The President wants us to go with him to the theatre tonight,' he said abruptly.

'Oh, no, Ulyss, do we have to?'

'No, I told him I didn't think we could, but he seemed so much in earnest I decided I'd talk it over with you again.'

'Ulyss, I don't want to. I want to go on to see the children, and — and I've already talked about it with Mrs. Stanton. They were asked, and she told me she was afraid to sit in the same box with Mrs. Lincoln unless I'd go too, but I told her I wouldn't.'

'Aren't you ladies a little hard on Mrs. Lincoln?'

'Do you remember our dinner, when she started screaming that Mrs. Ord was trying to get Mr. Lincoln away from her? I wouldn't want to risk sitting in a box with her — anything that happened there might just as well be on the stage.'

'All right, you go on to Burlington.' Ulyss knew that much of what was said about Mrs. Lincoln was true, and had seen too many incidents himself to defend her. But he was not so ruthless as Julia. To him the darkness in Lincoln's eyes seemed more important than the darkness in Mrs. Lincoln's mind.

'Aren't you coming too?'

'I will if I can, but there's a lot of work still to be done.

I'll get on to the office now, and if I can't finish in time I'll come up by the late train.' He kissed her, but she frowned a little when he had gone. They had not disagreed, not really —— She spoke sharply to Jesse, who was making faces at himself in a mirror, and began packing with the vigor of an uncertain mood.

It was raining, a purposeless drizzle that made the sidewalks clammy without washing them clean, and made the crowds short-tempered and uncomfortable without dispersing them. Ulyss found the interior of army headquarters scarcely less damp than outdoors. There was still no word from Sherman. He was disappointed, without good reason, but he had half shared Lincoln's conviction that the ship dream was a sign of victory. His desk was more clogged with papers than ever, and he sat down to work at them doggedly, but the effort to fix his attention was out of proportion to their importance. It was a relief when Rawlins came in and he could turn from them to talk of the cabinet meeting that morning.

'I don't know,' the chief of staff said doubtfully. 'It's a good enough plan if it works, but it may not work, and Congress is sure it won't.'

'Lincoln thinks Congress hasn't anything to do with it, except to seat the Southern representatives as they come in.'

'That's a matter of opinion. The Radicals say reconstruction is the concern of Congress alone, and they're in the majority.'

'Do you think the President is wrong?' Ulyss was troubled by Rawlins's comments. Lincoln had said it was a good thing Congress was in recess, and Ulyss, who thought about it only when Lincoln reminded him, had assumed it was a good thing. But Rawlins's doubtful words reminded him of something else, that Congress was elected by the people to voice the will of the people, and the President was the chief executive of that will.

'I'm not sure he's wrong,' Rawlins answered slowly, 'but I

think maybe he's too trusting. Not all Southerners are Lees.'

'They're not all criminals either,' Ulyss said with a vehemence the greater for the uncertainty that was growing in him. 'The President says he's not going to stand for any bloody work when the war's over.'

'There's a difference between bloody work and justice.' Rawlins was not arguing. There was no light of passion in his eyes, and he spoke quietly, as if he were simply showing his friend that there was a choice of methods. 'The war has lasted four years and killed thousands upon thousands of men. It's utterly ruined half the country and put an almost intolerable strain on the other half. Certain men are responsible for the war. Should they go scot free?'

Ulyss did not answer, for he did not know. He looked out of the window, across the gleaming street to the War Department grounds and the faint shapes of the trees that stood around the White House. It was not late, but the rain had brought an early twilight. It was a horrible city, Ulyss thought suddenly. Once off Pennsylvania Avenue you were mired in the ugly and unpaved side streets; once lift your eyes from the set duties before you and you were lost in the thorny maze of theory and belief, political pressure and personal prejudice, a maze that led nowhere to a definite answer. Ulyss stood up abruptly. 'I'm going to catch that train with Julia,' he told Rawlins. 'Oh, yes — send the President a note saying I'm sorry I can't be with him tonight.' He caught up his coat and the most urgent papers, and hastened out, glad to have the excuse of hurrying to catch a train. Rawlins stood at the window, watching him run down the steep outside steps, fingering his beard reflectively.

'Puff-puff, puff-puff, clickety, clickety, clickety-clickety,' Jesse said, over and over, trying to imitate the train switching on the next track. Julia hushed him absent-mindedly. She was used to it, and since they had been given a private car no one else was there to be annoyed. Someone entered, and she looked up in surprise, but when she saw Ulyss she rose and ran to him, with as much gladness as though she had not seen him for a long time.

'I thought you couldn't —— ' she began. 'Oh, Ulyss, I'm so happy you could come!'

'I brought along the things I couldn't leave,' he said, glad that she was not inclined to question him and make him think why he had changed his mind so many times that day.

'Papa, papa,' Jesse was chanting, 'there was another man. Papa, he came to look at us, and mama was frightened.'

Startled, Ulyss looked at Julia, and she stood back from him, smiling apologetically. 'I wasn't going to tell you — probably it didn't mean anything —— '

'What was it?' Ulyss demanded.

'Just that on our way to the station a man rode by and leaned down to look into the carriage, and in a moment he came back on the other side and did it again. I wasn't really frightened, very much. It — it seemed a little strange, but probably he was hunting for somebody — that's what it looked like —— '

Fear touched Ulyss, coldly, slightly but unmistakably. The man at the hotel could have meant nothing: there were always likely to be strange people in public places. But he became sinister when he was joined by the prying horseman. A lady and a child in a private carriage might be stared at once by accident, but twice? It was possible that neither incident had any significance, yet Julia was not easily disturbed. There was unrest in the city, caused chiefly by the continuous impromptu celebration which kept men from their work and disrupted ordinary life, which at once fostered and veiled the violence and lawlessness that lie in the stagnant bottoms of men's hearts. Ulyss could not tell exactly what he feared. Julia and Jesse — what plan, however mad and criminal, would encompass them? But he believed, more than he would admit to Julia, that they were somehow threatened, and he sat in tense watchfulness for the few moments before the train pulled out.

He relaxed as the car lurched and ground protestingly forward, then settled into its stiff-kneed swaying. He had been careless in allowing his family to stay in Washington in its present state, but they were safely away now. A few wan street lamps floated past; one or two crossings were rattled over; then there was nothing more to be seen from the windows. The blackness of the country night pressed close around the car and set apart the three people in it. Jesse, deprived of any interests outside, began climbing over the backs of the seats, with only casual protests from his mother. Julia was too tired to enforce discipline, and shortly took off her hat, folded her hands in her lap and began to nod. Ulyss took out the papers he had brought with him and tried to concentrate on just what supplies should be bought for Sherman, but the figures bobbled hazily before him. He looked up in exasperation at the overhead lamp, which had a badly smoked chimney and gave very little light. Fortunately there were other lamps in the car, and one, the farthest forward, was reasonably bright.

'What is it?' Julia woke instantly when Ulyss rose.

'I'm just going to sit under a better light. Go on back to sleep — we've got a long way to go yet.'

The light was indeed better, and Ulyss did not mind the front wall of the car cramping his feet. He sat down next to the window and began to work in earnest. There was a sound at the door, but he did not notice it, and Julia was asleep. Jesse, sitting astride the back of his seat, turned and saw a man peering into the car. There was little the man could see. A long, dimly lighted car, empty save for a sleeping woman and a small boy with his finger in his mouth. The man made a motion as if to come in, but the brakeman appeared behind him and in a moment both went away from the door. Jesse went on staring, hoping for something else of interest, but there was nothing more, and in a moment he slid down to the seat and went to sleep.

'You can't come in, I tell you!' The brakeman's voice, high and angry, could be heard clearly in the car when it stopped at Philadelphia. The Grants, putting on their wraps for the trip across the city to the next train, stopped to listen. 'I've thrown one man off this train already, and I'm not going to let you on to annoy the General ——'

'What's that all about?' Ulyss muttered. He stepped into the vestibule, and a man standing on the platform rushed up to him.

'General Grant — it's a message from Secretary Stanton — it's highly important ——' Ulyss took the telegram and stepped back into the car to read it.

He looked at it once, and then again. Lincoln and Seward assassinated, and probably Vice-President Johnson. Return at once. His mind tried not to believe, to go back to that time, only a few seconds past yet lost forever, when he had not seen the words. Lincoln dead. His mind persisted that it was not true, could not be true; the warm, full life he had touched that morning could not have disappeared tonight. Yet he knew it was true. 'This time I could almost see the shore — it must be a big victory.' Defeat for Lincoln's plans and beliefs and determination, but victory for Lincoln the man, who had lost the joy of the battle long ago, and had fought on with the grimness of the condemned.

'Ulyss, what is it? Is it very bad?'

He became conscious at last of Julia's frantic questioning. 'It's bad,' he said. 'It's the worst possible, for us.' He handed her the telegram.

'Oh, Ulyss!' Her face was twisted in horror. 'Ulyss — if you had been there ——'

'I might have stopped it.'

'No — you'd have been killed too —— Those men ——'
She shuddered, and began crying, standing upright and apart
from him, the noiseless tears running down her cheeks unchecked, as if she were not conscious of them.

'I don't know, dear. We can't tell.' He said words in a
soothing tone, with little thought for their meaning. Probably
the men who had frightened Julia had been looking for him.
It seemed likely, since the President, Vice-President, and Secretary of State had been killed, that the head of the army had
been marked too. He felt no relief that he had escaped, nor did
he feel guilt that he had not been at the President's side. Thus
it had been ordained, and he felt himself caught in a current
that had carried him into slack water while others had spun
forward to be wrecked, that was now sweeping him on into
a dark channel thick with peril, and still he had no choice.

On the way back to Washington he thought scarcely at all
of what was now to be done. The future was too formless and
stormy to be considered, but he thought over and over again
of the President as he had known him for thirteen months.
So many men had inhabited that rangy body: the genial citizen
who had recognized Grant in the reception crowd, who had
good-humoredly upheld Grant's authority against Stanton's
raging; the inverted humorist who read joke books to his
cabinet, whom Stanton called a baboon; the grave statesman
who had determined to rebuild the country with the tools of
his choice. Dead, all of them. Ulyss had known each one,
and had loved and respected the composite, but to his horror
he felt already an immense distance between himself and the
man he had known. Lincoln dead, Lincoln assassinated, shadowed and colored the living Lincoln. Even his words and beliefs and hopes, the legacy of other great men, had been erased
with him, for surely if his death had any meaning at all it
proved that his people were not what he had thought they were.

Ulyss shivered, with the chill death lays upon the living.

In the capital truth slowly overtook the rumors. Seward, who had been bedridden for some days, had been wounded, but would live. Vice-President Johnson was safe. Lincoln's body was not yet dead, but struggled all night long against the finality of the bullet in the brain. The small room where he lay was too crowded, and the doctors, having no more useful function, tried to clear it, but there were too many people whom office and relationship entitled to a part in the scene. Mrs. Lincoln alternated between hysterics and pleas that the boy Toddie should be brought to see the meaningless remnant of what had been his father. Robert Lincoln stood at the head of his father's bed, and wept in the arms of Senator Sumner, almost the only man who had reached the brink of his father's patience. In and out of the room were the cabinet members and government officers who had fought for Lincoln or against him or changed sides by the day, all of them now aghast and helpless.

Only Stanton was active. That night there was none to deny him the authority he had always believed was his. Dana was with him, and he dictated telegrams and gave orders till all the country was roused to horror and vigilance. But by three o'clock even that work was done and Dana dismissed. There was no more sound in the room but sobbing, and the whispered consultations of the doctors on what course to take when none led anywhere, and the rasping breathing from the bed.

Morning slunk over the city, gray and damp and unlovely, and cast its raw light on the marks the night had worn in men's faces. Soon after it came, Dana, who had gone home to bed, was waked by a tapping on his window. 'Mr. Dana,' said the messenger, 'the President is dead, and Mr. Stanton directs you to arrest Jacob Thompson."

CHAPTER SIXTEEN

LINCOLN is dead. The news stormed across the country
and made wreckage of much that men had believed, and almost all that they had hoped. For a few electric days the
North awaited the renewed uprising for which Booth's act
must have been the signal; and the South waited helplessly for
the punitive raids it was certain were coming; but no armies
moved. Nothing happened, and in a little while it was clear
that Booth and his group had struck in the course of a fantasy
that touched only in that tragic instant on reality. The fear
of immediate conflict passed then, but the emotional vacuum
that followed Appomattox had been filled by suspicion and

uneasiness and cold fear, and the peace had become an armi-
stice. While the funeral train crept westward there was quiet,
but no one expected it to last, and some were eager for its
end. These were the men who knew that though the Union
had been preserved it was not the same Union: new men with
new methods and new standards, reaching for power in a new
world. Lincoln was dead.

The law was clear. When the President dies, the Vice-President succeeds to his office. When life gasped its way from
Lincoln's body, Andrew Johnson was President. But the law
could not govern the inheritance of a President's power, and
that bright prize was left dangling. No one knew what Johnson
was. A Democrat, elected on a Republican ticket. A Tennes-
sean, who had fought at the hourly risk of his life to bring his
state back into the Union. A man almost illiterate until maturity, with a passion for the Constitution and the intricacies
of its meaning. A friend of Lincoln's, with a bitter hatred of
slaveholders, not because they had held black men in bondage
but because by so doing they had held white workers to precarious lives. These facts were known of Johnson, but they
said nothing of what he would do as President, with the meaning of that office enlarged by the war and threatened by the
peace.

It was a question that troubled Johnson also. On that rainy
April morning when he repeated after Chief Justice Chase the
words that made him President, he knew what his problems
were but had no certainty about their solution. He had been
chosen as a loyal Democrat to strengthen Lincoln's ticket, and
it had been no part of his work to consider what should be done
with the country. Now leadership was his, on terms that made
it a dangerously heated sceptre.

He had advisers in plenty. There was Senator Sumner, the
straight-lipped New Englander of endless erudition and one
absorbing passion: absolute equality for the negro. A free

man, said Sumner, has no genuine freedom at all unless he
has the right to vote. Suffrage is a matter for the states,
Johnson answered, but he listened. Zachary Chandler and
Thaddeus Stevens, Radical leaders with aims of more immediate practicality than Sumner's, came to the new President
and talked of the South, of the necessity of firm control and
the dangers of sentimentality. 'Treason must be made infa-
mous,' Johnson said, 'and traitors must be impoverished.'
Seward came, many times. The Secretary of State believed
firmly that he should have been President in Lincoln's stead,
not because he had disagreed with Lincoln but because he had
felt that he could do the same work better. He was a proud
man, and self-assured, but he was also loyal, and now he talked
to Johnson of Lincoln and Lincoln's plans.

Thus through those April days Johnson considered the hands
that strove to draw him forward. He could fall in with Sumner's
rigid mysticism, that scorned to take account of mere possibilities. He could join with Stevens, Chandler, Wade, Butler, and
the other Radicals, and consider the South a conquered province. He could cleave to Lincoln's plans, which had already
encountered ominous opposition. Or he could do as was generally expected, call Congress into special session, turn over to
it the whole responsibility, and hold his office in peaceful inertia.

This last possibility seemed the only one that Johnson never
considered. All the factions could draw equal comfort and uneasiness from him, none despaired of converting him. He
retained the whole of Lincoln's cabinet, a group in itself representative of most of the opposing divisions; and for some time
he was on fairly good terms with all its members. Many men
insisted that they had definite commitments from the President, but their claims could not be traced to a solid, immovable basis. Yet there was something solid and immovable in
Johnson, a fundamental stubbornness that would never weaken
once he had decided in which direction he wanted to face, and

had taken his stand. All over Washington, and circling out over the country, men maneuvered and watched each other, waiting for the wind.

And through the wet spring fields of Virginia the assassin dragged his shattered leg, trying to escape a pursuit that surprised and horrified him. He kept a diary while he crawled across the earth, a muddy paper mirror of his heart, filled with confusion, cloudy glory, and terror; acknowledging God's view of his guilt but looking for the gratitude of men; loathing himself as a murderer, but alight with pride because he had had the courage to do a deed that others were not brave enough even to take advantage of. He was found in a barn and shot, and took a long and very painful time to die. It did not matter, except to the people of the country, who were still mourning the dead President. At the capital it almost seemed that Lincoln had belonged to another era.

Ulyss was only half aware of the silent tensions of that spring. He had come back to Washington the night of Lincoln's death prepared to meet a new uprising. He knew the South had nothing to rise with, but he could believe that impossibility more readily than he could believe that Lincoln had been shot for no reason at all. Stanton had sent orders to all commanders to be in readiness, and men so firmly expected an outbreak that the first shot seemed already fired. But when a week passed and the only response from the South was a doubled anxiety for its future, Ulyss concentrated again on the weary paper work of his office, not troubling to wonder what the non-military effects of the assassination might be. They were not his affair. He liked Johnson well enough, save for the man's bitter tone toward the Southern leaders. There was talk of hanging, confiscation, treason trials — measures which Ulyss felt had little to do with the soft-spoken, upright officers he had sometimes encountered as prisoners; nothing at all to do with the grave, heartsick man who had met him at Appomattox. Even

Rawlins, who had doubted the wisdom of Lincoln's lenience, felt that Johnson's projected severity went beyond the bounds of justice. Aside from that, however, the new President seemed pleasant, and Ulyss liked him when he thought about it.

General Grant had no lack of friends, and he was finding that Washington was not altogether unpleasant. His office overflowed with admiring callers, and social engagements filled every hour he would consent to give them. Genial people, all these friends who sprang up so suddenly. Many held office; some had no official place but were dimly connected with the government. One, Jay Cooke, was credited with having created a new method of financing in order to float the enormous government loans the war had made necessary, yet he seemed as simple and friendly a man as though he were poor. Another, Zachary Chandler, Ulyss had known long ago in Detroit, and had quarreled with him about an icy sidewalk, but now Chandler remembered the affair as a joke, even seemed proud to have such a link with Grant. Ulyss was touched and a little surprised that these men, mighty figures in finance and government, should be so eager for his friendship. He liked them. They enjoyed playing poker all night long when the cards were running well, and they knew that a drink of whiskey can be a pleasant thing, not necessarily material for newspaper editorials all over the country.

Late in April Johnston surrendered to Sherman. It had been known that he must, and there was more satisfaction than rejoicing in the news, until the proposed terms were delivered in Washington, and then there was outrage. Ulyss was summoned to a cabinet meeting, and found the group in grim consultation.

'The man's a fool,' Stanton snorted. 'He can't be trusted — did you authorize these terms, General?'

'I authorized Sherman to propose the same terms I gave Lee,' said Ulyss cautiously. He had first been startled by the dispatch, then alarmed for his friend. Johnston's army to return

to its state capitals, and there deposit its arms in the state
arsenals. Existing state governments to be recognized, on their
officers taking an oath of allegiance. All political rights guaran-
teed. A general amnesty. It was no surrender, but a treaty.

'He's gone considerably beyond that,' said President Johnson
sharply.

'The man's a traitor,' said Stanton. There was a murmur,
not altogether in confirmation, but not in marked dissent.

'Sherman heard what President Lincoln said to the peace
commissioners last winter,' said Ulyss. There was no passion
in his voice, but his hands were cold with anger. 'Lincoln told
them that if they would preserve the Union and abolish slavery
he'd let them write the rest of the terms. Sherman thought he
was following the will of the President.'

'There's a new President now,' Stanton interrupted.

Ulyss glanced once at him, and looked away. 'As for him
being a traitor,' he continued, with only a slight edge in the
words, 'these terms are conditional on acceptance by this government. None of these things has happened, nor will happen
until you give the word. A man can't be blamed for seeing how
badly this country needs peace, real peace.' Ulyss closed his
mouth in a hard line, and looked slowly around the table at
the ring of dark faces.

'Do you approve of these terms, General Grant?' Johnson
demanded.

'I think they're beyond the province of the military forces,'
said Ulyss. 'That's why they had to be made conditional.'

'I want you to go down there and take command yourself,
and settle this business. As you say, the reconstruction of the
state governments is not the affair of the army.'

'Congress can look after that all right without any upstart
interference,' said Stanton. There was an instant when his
eyes and Johnson's met, but their common anger over Sherman's terms held them firmly together. Ulyss withdrew, for he

had no wish to hear anything further. He himself disapproved of the terms, as inexpedient if not actually improper, but it enraged him to hear Sherman criticized in such fashion. He made haste on his journey to North Carolina, to set the thing right as quickly as possible, for already there were rumors in Washington that Sherman had been bought by Confederate officers.

'But what in hell's the matter with the terms?' Sherman demanded. Grant had come to his friend's headquarters almost in secrecy, unwilling that his presence be widely known. He had said simply that the terms could not be approved, without saying how violently they were disapproved, but even so Sherman was angry in his turn. 'I thought them over carefully,' he said. 'They fix things up just the way they used to be, except for slavery and the secesh nonsense, and that's all we fought the war about.'

'It's felt,' said Ulyss slowly, 'that those things can't be properly arranged between two generals. It's a matter for the civil government.'

'Poppycock,' said Sherman. 'It's the terms themselves. If this isn't the way things are going to be settled — what is going to be done?' He stopped striding up and down the room and looked keenly at Ulyss.

'Well — I don't know. I don't think anybody knows.' Grant hurried on, before Sherman could say what he thought about that. 'Nobody even agrees about whether it's the responsibility of Congress or the President.'

'But what's the main thing? What do people aim to do? Bring things back the way they were, or make something new out of the country?'

'I — don't know. There's so many different ideas, and everybody is so sure he's right. But I don't think things will ever be the way they were, Sherman. The war changed too much, and changed it forever.'

'They needn't be as different as it looks like they're going to be. I don't like it, Sam.' Sherman pulled at his signal lock of hair, and rubbed his foot thoughtfully on the floor. 'I hear things — maybe they're scare stories, maybe they're not. Things like people wanting to give niggers the vote. What sort of nonsense is that? And a lot of other ideas about the South that aren't going to do anybody any good. I don't like it, I tell you.'

'Maybe it won't be so bad.' Ulyss wished he had given more attention to the endless talk that went on in Washington. He had been glad that it was no part of his work to enter into it, but his indifference weakened him now when he had to deal with Sherman's skepticism. Rawlins would have known what to say. Rawlins was well acquainted with the muddy stream of events, and seemed to know something of where it was flowing. 'Now that the country's united again,' Ulyss slowly answered Sherman's insistence, 'it will have a different future — better than it ever could have had before the war. Stronger, and — and more able to take advantage of its opportunities.'

'Sounds good,' said Sherman, renewing his march, 'but I don't think it means much. I don't think anybody in Washington knows what he's doing, or if he does it certainly isn't for the good of the country. I reckon you're right, Sam — things won't ever again be the way they were, but I sure God don't like what they will be. Sam ——' He paused in his tramp again and waved his arms in angry emphasis. 'I don't think we're honest any more. We say one thing and mean another, or take words that have meant the same thing ever since Bunker Hill and twist 'em around to mean the opposite. You can't trust people any more ——'

'Look here,' Ulyss protested, 'you're going mighty far with not much of a start. I know it's upsetting not to have your terms approved, but there were some good reasons ——'

'Oh, it's not the terms. They're better and wiser than anybody will admit, but you can't expect a bunch of government lunkheads to see that. It's the look of things in general that worries me, Sam — it's Washington. There's something bad about that town. It takes good men and makes fools or thieves of them. And now it's getting hold of things more and more ——'

This was a favorite theme, and Ulyss only half listened. Sherman felt himself wronged, and was not the man to accept injustice with bitter pride, as Meade would have, nor with a sense of fatality, as would Ulyss. He had very definite ideas even on matters which were not his direct concern, and was certain to orate for a while on the evils of the government that disagreed with him, but Ulyss knew that when he had talked long enough he would loyally carry out the orders that had been given him.

The surrender was duly concluded on the new terms. Ulyss had not taken too seriously the order to relieve Sherman, knowing the effect it would have had on the Army of the Tennessee to disgrace its commander at the high moment of victory. The renewed negotiations with Johnston were still in Sherman's charge, and Ulyss went back to Washington as quietly as he had come. Few people knew that he had been in North Carolina at all. The affair had been handled with the smooth ease of friendship.

Yet it was not finished. Ulyss found that the Washington authorities were not appeased by having reprimanded one of their most outstanding generals and forcing him to revise his terms. The President and the Secretary of War made public statements in extreme criticism of Sherman, the newspapers were full of condemnation, and there were even those who called him traitor. Ulyss was enraged, but under his great anger there was an even greater bewilderment. There was no reason whatever for this disproportionate tempest. However unwise the original terms may have been, they were entirely harmless, for they had been sent to Washington for approval and no action could have been taken on them without government concurrence. Perhaps Sherman had made a mistake, but this official vilification was not for that. It seemed closer to the persecution of a dissenter by convinced fanatics — or by those who would like to believe themselves convinced.

By late May, when the Grand Review was held in Washington, the popular feeling against Sherman had disappeared. Whatever the government leaders thought, the people had always been fond of him, and found it easy to forget the nebulous error he had committed. During the parade the crowd laughed and cheered at his men, and Sherman forgave it for its recent stupidity: he found it difficult to hate in bulk. But he held to his individual resentments, and would not take the hand that Stanton offered him on the reviewing stand.

In that small space where the heads of the nation sat together there was an electric discomfort. Stanton, who had brought himself to be magnanimous, was enraged by the rebuff to the centre of his touchy soul. Sherman's bearing, of cool, careful unawareness, was a continuing gall. President Johnson seemed absorbed in some dark difficulty of his own. Ulyss looked at all of them occasionally, wondering how, in this dawn of peace, they had become so embroiled with each other.

Each man in the group had his uncertainties, and resentments, and hopes; and each was conscious, under these things, of the rapid, changeless beat of the regiments marching past, marching away from the oriented existence of the last four years into a future none could see. For two days they marched: Meade's men, Sherman's men, the east and the west, the thousands upon thousands of individuals making up a whole that was about to disappear forever. The Army of the Potomac, lean and hard, its defeat of Lee lighting its way into legend. The Army of the Tennessee, that had cut through the heart of the South with the dull, haggling knife of pillage rather than the sharp sword of battle; some companies now driving before them donkeys laden with their goods, and surrounded by live ducks and chickens. The long lines swept from the Capitol down Pennsylvania Avenue, endlessly, a uniform stream with its progress marked by occasional bursts of louder cheers and shouts when some popular figure was recognized.

At the far end of the line of march the men fell out and wandered back over the city, exhausted and empty. Householders supplied them with bread, and they sat on the curbs and ate, staring at Washington. Many had never seen it before, and to them the name meant a place that was always being threatened just when they were making progress somewhere else. Many had seen portions of it through long, glaring hospital windows, and to them the name meant interminable months of waiting with hope dashed daily when some companion was taken away, his cheerful predictions silenced and his face covered. Now they looked at Washington the city, the capital of the country they had been fighting for. It was good to see. Twilight was hiding the unpaved streets and dew was laying the dust, and the buildings were dark, blocky shapes against a luminous purple sky.

This was the time that some thoughtful people had feared, the time when the mighty thing that was the army should be told to exist no longer. There had never been such a time before, never a period when the carefully balanced structure of the state had had to deal with such single, enormous force. It was a new thing, and some, looking back to old precedents, had been afraid. But the army melted. On that May night it was there, all over the city, but in the next few days it crowded by companies into the trains, cheering and singing, and sank back into the shops and farms and factories from tidy New England to the wide plains of Nebraska. And those who had been afraid sighed with relief, and talked of the American soldier, who fought only for causes he understood and championed, who could never be led into fighting for power itself. It was a matter for pride, and the fearful saw no reason to look farther into the shadows of that night, beyond the streets crowded with released soldiers, into drawing rooms and hotels; into the dark and echoing Capitol, dark with the unknowable years to come, echoing with battles in a war not yet begun. It did not occur to them that new tensions within the structure itself might be more dangerous to its balance than any exterior weight.

Slowly President Johnson determined on his course. Perhaps Seward's quiet, undemanding talk of Lincoln affected it, but the author of Johnson's policies was Johnson. He could hate with thoroughgoing emotion, but he was not malevolent; he was just, and he could be generous. Now, faced with issues wherein it was hard to distinguish between hatred and justice, he ignored his impulses, his friends' advice, the incompatible, shrieked demands of the press, and measured the problems against his own convictions. He thought secession was a crime. He abhorred slavery and slaveholders. He believed the Constitution was supreme and immutable law, not to be slighted for caprice or convenience. In these lights he considered the South, the chaotic territory with its society disrupted, its economy shattered, and among the ruins no man knew what emotions; and slowly his uncertainty disappeared.

The North Carolina Proclamation, the first public evidence of Johnson's policy, made clear that he had taken Lincoln's precarious line. The states to reconstitute themselves, no requirements as to the suffrage, few permanent disabilities laid on their citizens — the Radicals had perhaps feared it, but had not suspected that the President would proclaim a program so flatly opposed to the notions of their majority in Congress. There was an outcry from Sumner and those who intended that there should no longer be any difference between negro and white in the South; from Thaddeus Stevens and those who felt that the punishment of the defeated and the rewards of the victors could not be foregone. In letters and speeches and in some newspaper editorials the defrauded groaning was heard. Congress was not in session. It would convene in December, and the Radical majority began making plans for translating their protests into action.

At first it seemed that Johnson's proclamation of general amnesty was evidence of a sterner spirit, for it did not apply to those who possessed twenty thousand dollars or more. The small men of the pine barrens and upcountry hills, the few clerks and mechanics, the renters who had owned no slaves and therefore had been despised by slaves, were automatically pardoned. All others must make individual applications. It was objected to Johnson that crime cannot be measured by finances, and he agreed, but maintained that power can. This sounded like an echo of his earlier remark, 'Traitors must be impoverished,' but it lost all comfort for his opponents when he made clear that any man in the exempted class who wanted a pardon should receive a prompt and considerate hearing.

They came to Washington that summer by thousands. They bore themselves erect, with masked eyes; their voices were quiet, respectful and self-respecting, in the dead tradition. They had practically all been slaveholders, owners of wide plantations, rulers born and trained to rule, such men as the urchin Andrew Jackson had held horses for, and sometimes they had been kind to him, and sometimes not. The plantations had been laid waste, the slaves had spilled happily over their boundaries and gone somewhere, and now the rulers must make application for pardon, to Andrew Johnson.

What was he to do with them? They stood for a thing he hated, but the thing was gone now, and they were people. To imprison and execute them would be idiotic; to hound them for years with petty restrictions, senseless; to use their intelligence and abilities to help in restoring the wrecked portion of the country, reasonable. Hour after hour the President talked, while the White House baked under the sun and the military aide sweat at attention beside the pile of pardons. Johnson was not a diplomatic man, and he said what he thought without considering what effect it might have on those to whom he spoke, or on others to whom they might speak. The opposition is wrong and shortsighted; this is the time for the South to restore itself with wisdom and the long view. Be loyal, cooperative, wipe out all evidence of rebellion, even, perhaps, give the suffrage to those few negroes who have chanced on education and intelligence and character, and can appreciate it.

It was good advice. Sometimes it was enlivened with more detailed comments on the opposition, for Johnson did not like to be crossed. Often it was not understood. But it was good advice, and it had results of a kind. The men who had come to Washington in stiff humiliation went back thoughtfully, with a flicker of new hope.

Congress might make trouble, they said. Congress is full of sharpers, but Johnson's our friend, and he'll look out for us. We needn't be too much concerned about what Congress says.

That summer Ulyss spent in traveling. He had one excuse and another, and firmly believed in them, but at bottom he traveled because he liked to be moving forward, free of the room in Washington where he ruled over the garrisons scattered through the South, in the intervals between peremptory orders from Secretary Stanton; free of the unstable inertia that filled the capital while it waited for summer to end, for Congress to convene. And it was not unpleasant to see the crowds massed thick wherever his train stopped; to hear the deep roar that curved forward to meet him when he appeared; to feel the vast and insatiable interest of hundreds of people centred in himself. There had been a time when he had been grateful for the dogged championship of a few, for Julia, for Washburne, Rawlins, and Lincoln, those who had broken a path for him where he had seen only barriers. He had known their trust, but he had never known the half-laughing, half-mystic affection of a large group. He did not actually have it now. People drove long distances over the choking powder of country roads to see his train stop for water, and cheered him enormously when he said a few limp words they could not hear, but their feeling was somehow pride in themselves rather than love of him. It looked the same, however, and Ulyss liked it despite his embarrassment.

In Galena they had stretched a banner in front of the station, announcing, 'General, the Sidewalk is Built.' There was more than the sidewalk, there was a fine new house, where all the leading citizens came to dine and do him honor. But it was not his place. He felt it vaguely even while former acquaintances called themselves neighbors, and spoke of Galena's pride in her son. This town was inhabited by Cap Grant, who worked for his younger brothers, going his unmarked rounds in the old army overcoat that had no longer any meaning. He spoke of someday coming to live in his new house, as it was necessary for him to speak, but he could not imagine doing it.

It was different in St. Louis. True, it was the owner of Hardscrabble who lived there, carting his logs into town on frosty mornings, avoiding old army friends because he was too poorly dressed to go into their hotels, but Hardscrabble had been his own. And Julia was best content during their stay at White Haven, seeing her father's crotchety pride in her husband, watching her children run riot over her old home. That was a quiet period, a week or two to be spent as any family would spend its holiday. The long hot days fell into the same pattern: energetic mornings, still afternoons when no one did anything, thick black nights when the air that stirred from the fields was the breath of the fecund earth.

Once, in the hot hour after dinner, Jesse began shouting,

'Look, everybody, I'll show you how papa makes a speech!'
He stood beyond the family semicircle, looking impatiently at
them until he had their full attention, then made a bow.

'Papa doesn't bow,' Buck objected. 'Who ever saw a soldier
bow?'

'That wasn't papa, that was me. This is something like a
piece, so I have to bow before I start. Now I begin.' There
was a sudden change in the boy, a constriction, a certain rigid
slouch. 'Ladies and gentlemen,' he muttered, staring straight
before him, 'I am very glad to see you. I thank you very much
— good night.'

The group laughed, for Jesse's piece was a true echo of a
dozen incidents. Ulyss felt himself reddening, and could not
stop. He had a sense of injury even while he admired the
cleverness of his son. It was true that he could not make
speeches. As soon as people were silent to hear him he could
think of nothing at all, not even a graceful phrase, let alone
aspiring to the few words that would sow laughter in those
blankly receptive faces. But it seemed a hard thing to have
his family tease him for his shortcomings.

Julia somewhat abruptly changed the subject, and Ulyss was
mollified, but at once felt guilty, for Jesse seemed aggrieved to
have lost the stage so quickly. Ulyss called the child over to sit
on his knee. What difference did it make if he could give a
good speech or not? He was a soldier, and talking was not his
work. It belonged to that other world of policy and argument
and the mysterious ways of civil government, and had nothing
whatever to do with him. He bounced Jesse on his knee, careless of his seven-year-old dignity, well pleased with him, with
himself, and with all that the future seemed likely to bring.

CHAPTER SEVENTEEN

...'EACH officer and man will be allowed to return to their homes, not to be disturbed by United States authority so long as they observe their parole and the laws in force where they may reside.' Ulyss remembered the words very clearly. They came at the end of the terms he had written at Appomattox, a final detail automatically included. He had not wasted time to think about so obvious a provision then, and had not thought about it since until this uneasy autumn.

Now, with Lee's letter lying on his desk, the words took on a sudden personal importance. The commander of the Army of Northern Virginia was applying for his pardon, as required by law. He was also protesting against being tried for treason. Ulyss's lips tightened as he read. There had been absurdities enough in the backwash of the war, but this folly amounted to

indecency. To put Lee on trial — what for? Was this country
no better than those in Europe, that it must take its small-
minded revenge even on its own people? The thing troubled
his respect for his own side, but went deeper than that, and
struck at his personal pride. He had signed those terms. Any
persecution of any member of the Army of Northern Virginia,
from Lee down to the last conscripted private, was a violation
of his word of honor.

'I don't understand the President at all,' Ulyss told Rawlins.
'There's the North Carolina Proclamation, and all this palaver
with the pardon-seekers, and then he turns around and treats
a man like Lee as if he were a horsethief. It doesn't make
sense.'

'He's got a damned queer mind,' Rawlins agreed. 'He seems
to think some rebs are angels, and some a shade or two blacker
than the devil — and that he can do as he pleases about all
of them.'

'But Lee ——'

'Yes, it's too bad. It's a pity Johnson won't listen to anybody ——'

'He's going to listen to me. He can't do as he pleases about
my promises.'

There was, as usual, a crowd of people waiting to see the
President, standing in the anteroom, jostling up and down the
stairs, even filling the lower hall, but Ulyss was admitted immediately. Johnson was always ready to see him, and always
friendly. Usually Grant found the interviews pleasant enough,
but today he was too angry for any amenities. He dropped
Lee's letter and his own written endorsement of it on the desk,
and said flatly, 'You can't bring Lee to trial.'

'Why not?' Johnson asked slowly. He had a temper of his
own, but he throttled it. 'He was one of the first leaders of the
rebellion. He was a traitor, and treason must be stamped out.'
The necessity of punishing the outstanding leaders seemed as

clear to Johnson as the stupidity of persecuting the mass of followers. The small men of the South had already suffered too much for their fault; the bulk of the owner class had rendered an adequate price in the loss or destruction of almost all their property. But Jefferson Davis and Lee and the other figures who had been the centre and the strength of the secession movement — their lives would be a small enough payment for their attempt to take the nation's life.

'Lee's doing all he can to bring back good feeling in the South,' said Grant. 'Besides, he's covered by the terms at Appomattox. The whole Army of Northern Virginia is covered.'

'When can he be tried, then?'

'Never. Not until he breaks his parole, or the laws. I don't see him doing that.'

'I think you're mistaken in your views, General.'

'Lee can't be tried for treason,' Ulyss said stubbornly.

The matter stood there for a few days. Ulyss waited, content to say nothing more so long as no further steps were taken to bring the Confederate general to trial. In his office, however, the subject was constantly discussed. Rawlins said little beyond agreement with the others — in these days Rawlins said little about anything, as if all his strength were concentrated in listening and watching. But Porter and Badeau were as outraged as Grant, and Babcock expressed himself on the subject of honor with such vivid fluency that Ulyss was a little embarrassed, as he would have been on seeing a published poem celebrating his love of Julia.

In due time he received a letter from the Attorney General, respectfully and firmly differing from his interpretation of the law. Once more Grant called on the President.

'You see what he thinks,' Johnson said gently. 'I'd like to oblige you, General, but this is what the law is.'

'Are you going on with this trial?'

'I'm sorry — yes.'

'Then I resign my commission.'

'But General!' There was instant alarm in Johnson's eyes. 'This is in no way your fault. You've protested until the law was definitely established ——'

'I promised Lee he wouldn't be disturbed so long as he kept his parole and the law. I won't stay in the army if you won't keep my pledges.'

There was a dull red flush on Johnson's cheeks. He was angry, though not with the cold anger that, once it possessed him, could never be placated. He said nothing for a moment, nor did Ulyss. Then, with a somewhat labored laugh, Johnson remarked, 'You make a good friend. I'd like to have you for mine.'

'I scarcely know General Lee,' said Ulyss. 'I just don't think it's right to bother him.' He had heard no more than the primary significance of Johnson's words, but he felt that his point was won. He was right. Stanton expostulated with him and with Johnson, but not even the Secretary of War could prevail against Johnson's order that the proceedings be discontinued, and there was never another effort to bring Lee to trial.

Somehow none of the treason trials was coming to anything, not even those of rebels who were not in Grant's province. Everyone knew what the aftermath of rebellion was, and few had questioned that this one too would be concluded in a grim assizes. But the docket kept shrinking because of amnesties, paroles, other less tangible reasons, and most of all a lack of public insistence. A few legal gestures of great ferocity were made, the press and public speakers made much of the Southern menace and iniquity, but personalities tended to fade into unmolested obscurity. None of the Southern leaders suffered more than inconvenience, helplessness, and the general Southern poverty. The measures that were to be taken against a whole people, less reasonable, more damaging, half unconscious, were not controlled by established law, and were not planned and deliberate punishment so much as the results of new forces set free by the collapse of old structures.

Ulyss had assumed that such friendliness as he had had with the President would be cut short by their encounter over Lee. It did not matter. He would prefer to be on good terms with his superior, but not if they demanded the sacrifice of his personal convictions. He found, however, that Johnson was rather more cordial to him than before. The crowded White House office was as open to him as ever, and the President frequently walked over to army headquarters, even on trivial errands. At the receptions which the Grants frequently gave, now that they had so many friends, the President was almost always there. He talked of his policies quite often, which made Ulyss uncomfortable, for some of his other friends had explained to him that there was widespread disagreement with the President, and Ulyss was afraid of being drawn into the controversy. If he had been sure of what he believed he would not have been so troubled, but in those hostile and suspicious months before Congress opened it seemed to him that everyone who talked to him — and everyone made a point of talking to him — used only the most unassailable logic. The conclusions were bitterly opposed, but no one, so far as Ulyss could see, could find any weakness in the arguments.

If, said the Radical group, the South is left in Johnson's hands, it will vote back into power all its old leaders, and will dominate the country more than ever before, for all the slaves, freed but not allowed the suffrage, would now be counted for representation as whole human beings rather than fractions. Why was the war fought, if the country was to be bound forever to the treasonable Democrats? If, said Johnson, the South is turned over to the Radicals, they will bring down in ruins the whole structure of civil liberties, will make a revolting joke of the suffrage by disfranchising all those of any ability or training

and giving the vote to a mass of Congo savages, so that the
South would become a draining sore of corruption that would
infect all the rest of the country with political leprosy.

Both very convincing. Ulyss wished that he could attain
the peace of mind of wholehearted agreement with one side or
the other, or else that both sides would leave him alone. He
could not understand why they wouldn't. He was the head
of the army, his only part in the affair would be to carry out
the orders when Johnson and Congress at last made their
decision, but he was courted as though he were a prime factor.
Men who could not speak each other's names without an inflection of loathing were united in striving for intimacy with
General Grant, and in trying to draw from him an opinion.
Individuals who had once encountered his icy silence rarely
tried again, but there were always others to make the attempt.

'Every time I get out of bed,' he complained to Julia, 'somebody wants to know what I think about negro suffrage, or if the
President is going to start another civil war, or how the election
will go next fall. It's ridiculous.'

'It's because they admire you so much, dear,' Julia answered
placidly. 'After all, Ulyss, you won the war and you're lieutenant general and a friend of the President's, so people naturally
want to know what you think.'

'But none of this has anything to do with me.' He looked at
her and repeated, 'Nothing to do with me at all.'

'No, dear.' She smiled at him — in amusement? 'No, of
course not.'

'Well, it hasn't. I wish Congress would meet, and ratify
what Johnson's done or make whatever changes it's going to,
and let things settle down.'

The supporters of the President said that Congress was only
the Radicals, that that one group controlled it so firmly that its
decision had no general meaning. Ulyss did not think it was
true, or if it was true it meant that the will of the people sup-

ported the Radicals. However uncertain he was between the claims of Johnson and of the Stevens-Sumner group, he still had an unshaken faith that Congress did in truth represent the people, and Congress's word would be the people's word.

On a day in November Johnson touched on the subject in talking to Grant, as delicately as he could. 'The trouble is,' he said slowly, 'that there's so much nonsense being talked about the South that some of the — less intelligent members are likely to believe it. Of course I'll make a report, so Congress can deliberate on something more than rumor, and I want to make it as exact and clear as possible.' He leaned forward a little, his eyes fixed directly on Grant's. 'General, I want you to go down there for me and let me know exactly how things are.'

'I'm a soldier,' said Ulyss uncomfortably.

'That's why you're the very man. You're not a politician — you haven't any party ties, or any particular public you've got to please. After the way you handled Appomattox the Southern people trust you, and the North knows it can believe whatever you say. It would be a very great service to the country if you'd do it.'

'I'll think it over,' said Ulyss. He was tempted. It would be an interesting journey, and he would like to see the peaceful realities of the places he had known as points on a military map. But suppose there was some other significance in the thing? Ulyss did not altogether trust the President, Rawlins still regarded him with skepticism, there were rumors in plenty that he was entirely unscrupulous in gaining his way; and Ulyss dreaded being involved in anything he did not fully understand. Yet Johnson had but asked for a simple report, and his reasons for wanting it were obviously sound. Ulyss took his problem home with him.

'I think it's a nice idea,' said Julia. 'You do hear the silliest things, and nobody will know they're not true unless someone goes to see.'

'Go ahead,' said Rawlins. 'Not a bad thing to show yourself.'

South through Virginia and the Carolinas, back through
Georgia, all of it a panorama of desolation. This was the end
result of Grant's own policy: not cities, not factories, but
armies, and through the armies the people. Weeds were slinking up through the sour soil of farms whose masters were dead
at Shiloh, Vicksburg, the Wilderness, Five Forks, or had come
home mangled in body and nine-tenths dead in spirit. Charleston the proud and wayward was a fringe of smoke-black, crumbling walls beside the rotting wharves. Houses, city and country,
rich and modest, were empty and mutilated and sagging —
perverse, troubling caricatures of houses, worse when sometimes a head appeared around a corner and drew back with the
causeless, fierce timidity of the wild. For even the people were
wrecked. It was as if their spirits had been burned and shelled,
and those ruins too could be seen, in their eyes.

Ulyss had seen the trail of war before, in Mexico, but that
had been different. Horrible, yes, and marked with intolerable
tragedy, but not like this. That had been simply war, an unnatural catastrophe that killed thousands and despoiled cities,
but finished when it was finished; and the people had settled
again into their old pattern. There had been none of the human
disruption that began with the end of the Confederacy. Ulyss
did not understand it, but Rawlins could have told him, for
Rawlins knew that war's final horror comes when men fight
for their ways of thought rather than for what they possess.

For days Ulyss talked to those who came to see him as he
made his way across the South. There was always the shadow
in their eyes, but they talked quietly and with an odd trust in
this man who had defeated them. Much of the wreckage
sprawling in their fields was a result of his work, but they could
accept fairly the verdict of a fair fight, and his work was finished.
They talked now of their plans for the slow rebuilding, and

touched on the worst of their problems. Nearly all the negroes were convinced that freedom meant also free land, and they flocked to the camps of the Federal garrisons to sit down and wait for the distribution. They had no conception of working for wages on another man's farm, and if anyone tried to teach them there was always an agent of the Freedmen's Bureau to interfere. The negroes were a problem indeed, but, said the men with whom Grant spoke, the South could solve it if unhindered, for had she not the best knowledge of the race? The garrisons also were disliked. It was a bitter thing for the Southern states, on whose soil the first successful battles of the Revolution had been fought, who had supplied so many leaders for the gangling republic, and who now acknowledged the impossibility of separation from the whole, to be occupied by Northern troops as if they were foreign territory.

Thus men talked to Ulyss, without whining, without bravado, discussing on equal terms a common difficulty. Their clothes were worn, but neat to the last thread, their boots polished and their linen white, showing no signs of the desperate measures that had been taken at home to make them fit to appear to General Grant. Nor did the look of the people as a whole show the taut limit to which they had come, the darkness beyond, the ancient methods they might remember if they were pushed into that darkness. For the most part Ulyss talked to the old leaders, the men who were going back to build again the only way they could build, and must build, although all the foundations were gone and the earth had turned to quicksand. He did not see the smaller men, who had fought with tenacious bravery despite the logic of their position, and had returned to find that position worse than it had been before. He did not see the women, who were fighting still, with a bloodless bitterness that rankled as deeply as a physical wound. He saw little of individual negroes and almost nothing of the race, vast and mysterious, unpredictable now as a container half filled with quicksilver. He saw nothing at all of the men who were coming down from the North.

Looking and listening, he remembered what the country had been six years before, and felt much the same sickened horror as he had felt at field hospitals after a battle. Here there was no loud scream of a man's agony, but there was worse: the silent pain of a people. Ulyss wrote to Julia: 'People who talk of further retaliation and punishment, except of the political leaders, either do not conceive of the suffering endured already or they are heartless and unfeeling and wish to stay at home out of danger while the punishment is being inflicted. . . .' He could not use words of such heat in his report to the President, but the tenor was the same. The South was in deplorable condition, but it was the result of the war, not an evidence of bad faith. The negro problem was being dealt with fairly, by those who knew most about it. The people had suffered much, but were prepared to be loyal. He made no recommendation, for policy was no concern of an army officer's, yet in every word of his statement was an implicit plea for patience and generosity.

'Thank you very much, General,' said Johnson. 'I knew I'd get a fair view from you. To judge by our papers you'd think the woods were still full of bushwhackers down there.'

'There's no more rebellion,' said Ulyss. 'A lot of unrest, and for the next year, until they get things straightened out, there'll be a great deal of suffering, but the rebellion is over.'

'The new state governments are nearly all set up now,' said Johnson. 'Maybe they can straighten things out in less than a year.' He asked a few further questions, most of them turning on the negro, and Ulyss repeated what he had already said, that the problem was naturally troublesome, but was being solved.

There was another report on Johnson's desk, and he frowned at it when Ulyss had returned to army headquarters. It had

been submitted by Senator Carl Schurz at the President's
suggestion, but if Johnson had hoped that a personal inspection
of the South would modify Schurz's foreign intellectual convictions he had been badly disappointed. Grant had gone
with the prestige of his military position, which perversely gave
him a nonpartisan standing now that the war was over. But
Schurz, the German immigrant, the man with neatly formu-
lated and unyielding beliefs on democracy, freedom, and other
abstractions, had no standing with the Southern leaders and
wanted none. If Grant believed what he was told and made
no effort to examine the dark and dangerous things that were
not mentioned, Schurz believed what he saw and made no
effort to understand it in its setting of a shattered tradition and
a bewildered people. Grant saw an enormous bloc of beings
who had been slaves, given a freedom which they interpreted
as a complete absence of responsibility, clogging the economy
that had been based on their labor, and in their ignorance and
mass threatening whatever new structure could be built.
Schurz saw people who had been held in barbaric bondage,
grudgingly given a freedom without meaning, forbidden to be
on the streets after a certain hour, forbidden to be idle, terrorized on occasion, and entirely without hope of the suffrage,
as though they could not be accounted human beings.

The negro was not actually the chief problem of reconstruction. The adjustment of power in the reunited nation was
more truly important, but the figure of the freed slave was
dark with emotional implications, and in his shadow a mis-
cellany of groups could join forces without too inconveniently
clear a view of each other. Sumner and Schurz, with a genuine
concern for the future of the race; Chandler and Morton, playing for party power; Stevens, who belonged in both groups;
Butler, who pursued his devious ways beyond any group; the
men who saw opportunities for exploitation of the South, and
the larger men who were building an industrial empire — all

fought together in the name of the negro. Those who opposed
them, the President and the Democrats and a sprinkling of
conservative Republicans, were promptly labeled lovers of
slavery, and traitors to the Union dead.

Congress met in mid-December, and with appalling sudden-
ness the growling mutter of the past six months became violent
war. There had been tension and dislike between other exec-
utives and their Congresses, sniping and frustration and loud
criticism, but between Johnson and his Congress there was
hatred. His message, a grave summary of the situation in the
South and an outline of his methods of reconstruction, was
received with a howl of outrage. It did not insist on suffrage
for the Southern negro, who, said Sumner, was 'better fitted
to establish and maintain a republican government than the
whites.' It provided no adequate punishment for rebellion,
offered no possibility of recompense to the North, and gave no
assurance of continued power to the party of the Union, the
Republicans. Congress spent little time in arguing. It set up a
joint committee which excluded all the representatives from
Johnson's reconstituted states, heard Thaddeus Stevens give a
shrewd, biting speech asserting Congress's own plan of reconstruction, and settled down to destroy the presidential pre-
sumption.

To the accompaniment of turbulent applause from the galleries, with a hardened disregard of both parliamentary and
constitutional law, a series of bills of sweeping import were
acted upon that spring. The Freedmen's Bureau Bill was vetoed
by Johnson because, he said, the organization was notoriously
corrupt, and furthermore no members from Southern states
had been admitted to vote on it. The veto was upheld, nar-
rowly, and then came a legislative avalanche. The Civil Rights
Bill, making freedmen citizens, vetoed because it infringed on
the rights of the states: veto overridden. The Fourteenth
Amendment, removing from the Constitution the ban on the

negro vote — and incidentally freeing the rising business men from unamenable state interference. And in full circle, the Second Freedmen's Bureau Bill, vetoed again: veto overridden, thus canceling Johnson's one small victory.

There was little dignity and no reasonableness in Washington. The Radicals loudly proclaimed that Johnson was constantly drunk, and had adorned the White House with his mistress; Johnson, who had no tact, publicly called one of his opponents a dead duck. A torrent of dissension boiled through the session, rising and swelling until the old methods of government crashed before it, a thing nobody had planned and few realized. It was impossible for Sumner to pause in his daily holy war for the negro to search himself and his colleagues for unapparent motives; or even for a man with Schurz's convictions to restrain his angry enthusiasm long enough to consider what was happening to his ideal of government. The nation stumbled blindly forward into the paths the war had opened, pushed by passion and greed and high ideals and craft.

PART SIX

Retribution

VI. THE THRUST OF GREATNESS

CHAPTER EIGHTEEN

THE Radical Republicans were strong. Their party had been formed by the pressure of the landless and the liberal and the impatient business men, and hardened in a war that had much the character of a crusade. It was backed now by the surplus passion that the ending of a war leaves unconsumed. It had ensured, in dealing with the South, that there would be no resurrection of the Democratic vote.

Yet the Radical leaders were much concerned, in that session that lasted through the first half of 1866, over the preservation of their strength. The mid-term elections were coming in a few months, and in only two years the presidential election. No man could tell with certainty what the results would be. The South need not be considered, for Congress had not yet enacted its own program of reconstruction after stalemating Johnson's, but the coming of peace had made an incalculable factor in Northern politics. How many Democrats would now ignore the stigma of defeatism? How many conservative Republicans differed with the Radicals on the South, or even on the benignly protective tariff? How many objected to the new impotence of the executive?

One of the most difficult problems was General Grant. In all Washington, in all the country, there was no man so generally trusted nor so widely respected. In the North the casualty lists of the long struggle between the Wilderness and Appomattox had been forgotten, and it was remembered only that under Grant's leadership the war had at last been won. In the South nothing was forgotten, but the fairness of his terms was remembered, and his stubborn stand against the persecution of military men was appreciated. His was a unique standing in that year of irreparable divisions. In two years, when the people came to elect a President, they would elect Grant — and he did not know it. If he had any suspicion of it, any secret inkling, no one in Washington had his confidence. Some had tried to tell him, and their words had crumbled in his withering silence.

Worse, he would not indicate what his politics were. He would be President, whether as a Radical or conservative Republican, or even as a Democrat. And it was conceivable that, should he refuse to run himself and give his outspoken support to Johnson, the country would turn on Congress, and re-elect the man it had historically humiliated. It was utter anguish for the political leaders to contemplate so much power in the hands of a man who did not know he had it, or if he knew would give no indication whatever of what he intended to do with it.

Obviously the situation was equally clear to Johnson. The President nurtured his friendship with Grant with an assiduous patience phenomenal in an impatient man. There, however, the Radicals had an advantage, for though Grant would not talk freely to them he found some of them to be companions more to his taste than the President. Roscoe Conkling had an easygoing, unpretentious manner, and a talent for vivid presentation of issues; Zachary Chandler played a shrewd hand of poker, as shrewd as his politics. It was not hard to comment, while the cards fell whispering to the cluttered table. 'If that drunken tailor don't quit lallygagging with the rebs we'll have another rebellion on our hands, sure as death ...'

Perhaps Grant's only comment would be, 'It's your ante,' but he must have heard.

The night the Civil Rights Bill was passed, giving wide powers to Grant through the Federal garrisons in the South, the Radicals swarmed to a reception at Grant's house. The crowd was so great that passage through the surrounding streets was almost impossible. Ulyss and Julia stood together at the head of the stairs, looking down at the gathered heads of great men, men whose names were known from end to end of the country. Figures of all parties were present: Democrats, Copperheads, cabinet members, even a few of the more resilient Southerners, but in effect this evening belonged to the Radicals. Sumner was there, grave and impeccable; Schurz's spectacles glittered as he talked with his ineradicable, piquant accent to a group of ladies; Chandler walked about with the free bearing of an old friend. Secretary Stanton himself had come, an honor so great in his own eyes that it took on importance to others.

He stood a little apart, giving but a few words to the Radicals around him, given none too many by the other cabinet members present. Ulyss felt that his tongue was growing thick from too long repetition of pleasant inanities, and the carpeted floor on which he stood was more wearying than the saddles that had carried him over mountains and through the long monotony of forced marches. But it was pleasant to see his friends, many of them powerful and wealthy but still his friends, and even had it meant nothing to him there would have been joy in seeing Julia's radiance.

'The President of the United States.'

Other names had been announced without being clearly heard by anyone in those crowded rooms, but this phrase made a silence of its own. Then at once there was a burst of talk louder than ever, as some made openly outraged comments, and some talked quickly of the first indifferent subject that came to mind, as charitable people try to ignore a glaring *gaucherie*. Did the man not understand how utterly he had been defeated? After all his futile vetoes did he feel that he still had strength enough to make worth while a gesture of this impertinence? In most of the scattered groups there was resentment, in some there was an unwilling admiration of Johnson's boldness, in almost all there was real fear while they watched Johnson standing with the Grants, talking with easy informality, sometimes laughing.

In July Congress — with the delighted concurrence of the President — made Grant a full general. There had not been such a commission since Washington had held it, and Ulyss was pleased by the honor even though he had some uncertainties as to its significance.

'There's just one trouble,' said Julia. 'It ought to be a different title, marshal or something. You've been General for years now, and this sounds just the same.'

'What difference does it make?'

'I like to hear it,' she answered simply.

That was the important thing, he realized. It did not really matter if he were called Lieutenant General or General: he had more power than anyone else in the army anyway, and so long as Stanton was Secretary of War he would be summoned across the street to the Department when he was wanted whether his title were Second Lieutenant or Grand Cham of Tartary. Probably the advancement had been made as a token that Congress expected him to use as it had intended the powers it had given him. Nevertheless it was a great honor, Julia was happy in it, and that gave it meaning enough.

The next move was Johnson's. In late August he was to go to Chicago to visit the tomb of Stephen Douglas, and he planned to use the opportunity to talk to the people, to tell them his view of the issues before they went to the polls to construct a new Congress. He was taking Seward with him, and Welles, the stubbornly loyal Secretary of the Navy, and Farragut, as a popular naval hero. He wanted Grant and Rawlins to come. Grant found it difficult to refuse, but was very reluctant to accept, and delayed his answer as long as he could. Then, when Johnson pressed him, he went to talk it over with Rawlins.

That was plainly his intention, but for some time he said nothing, smoking his cigar with elaborate care and looking out of the window. Rawlins waited quietly. Not even he was sure how much his chief knew of what his future was likely to be. Grant was silent when he did not understand, silent also when he understood but had not made up his mind. It did not matter. It was not yet time for definite plans, when the future itself was so indefinite. Apparently in this last session Congress had asserted its power over the President, but Rawlins, wise in the puffy, veering winds of politics, was not certain. There was enough dissension in the press to make him doubt, and the fall elections might assert another and greater power beyond Congress. His problem for the present was not guiding Grant to a commitment, but helping him to avoid one.

'The President talked to me about his trip again last night,' Ulyss said suddenly. 'He makes such a point of it, it looks like we'll have to go along.'

'There's nothing much to hold us here right now.'

'No.'

Nothing was added to the single word, but there was no finality in the tone. Ulyss carefully put out his cigar, and lit another, frowning a little.

'It seems to me,' said Rawlins slowly, 'that it's the right thing to do. If for no other reason, he gave you your way on the army list, when he was damned unwilling to have some of those names put through. It's only fair to do as he asks about the trip. And you don't want to hurt your chances to re-organize the army the way you want it.'

'Yes.' Ulyss struggled once more with his dislike of asking advice, and won. Rawlins was at home in this involved world, and would make a better guide than his own uncertain instincts. 'The trouble is,' he said at last, 'I'm afraid there's more to it than just going along to keep him company. I'm afraid if I go with him I'll appear to agree with his policies, and I'm not sure I do.'

True, thought Rawlins, but if you don't go with him after he's urged you so much you'll be marked as a Radical, and it's too soon for that. 'You don't have to commit yourself,' said Rawlins. 'It's just proper subordination for you to go with him at his request. He's the President.'

Ulyss nodded with some relief, for the comment shifted the matter to a familiar plane. He settled back in his chair and said: 'I wish there weren't all this wrangling. I don't see why he doesn't give in and let the country settle down.'

'He'd have to give up his own policies altogether then,' Rawlins murmured. He was not so much defending Johnson

as wondering how much Grant had thought about the subject,
how much he had been influenced by the President's persistent
friendship, or by the Radicals' subtle siege.

'Well, he ought to,' said Ulyss. 'Some of them are all right,
but Congress doesn't agree with him. He shouldn't hold out
against Congress like this.'

No influence, thought Rawlins. After all these months of
discussion and persuasion, direct and indirect, Grant still believed what he had believed ever since Rawlins had known him:
that the United States was governed by the will of the people.
Rawlins believed it too, but not with Grant's uncomplicated
faith. How would it be with that faith when Grant knew for
himself the twisting strategy of party politics, the unstable
balance of varying aims, the real uncertainty of wisdom, the
ephemeral character of majorities? Rawlins put the thought
away from him. Not yet, not yet.

The President's route lay north to Buffalo, turning thence
west to Chicago, and down and back through the great cities
of the midwest. The trip was dubbed 'the swing around the
circle,' and the Radical newspapers were prompt to point out
the vulgarity of a President thus directly pleading his own case.
Trouble was expected in Philadelphia. Only a few days before,
a Radical convention had been held there, resounding with
tales of savage iniquity in the South being nursed and defended
by the President. And Pennsylvania was the home of Thaddeus
Stevens, the complicated old man who ruled Congress. But
Philadelphia received Johnson warmly, and cheered his speech
on the theme that he used in the halls of great cities and on the
rear platform of his train when it stopped at a crossroads: the
Union had been preserved, and the present task was to forget
old enmity and new vengeance alike, to go forward in justice
and honor. That stop was a triumph rather than a catastrophe,
and the President's party continued its journey with relieved
confidence.

At first Ulyss was uneasy. He had come as a matter of duty, but he could not forget his original misgivings. The cheers for himself and Farragut mingled with those for the President, and he was well aware that his presence on the platform with Johnson was a silent endorsement of Johnson's policies. Yet there was nothing really subversive in what the President said, nothing with which Ulyss did not fundamentally agree, and after Philadelphia was passed without trouble he began to enjoy the journey.

True, every day some member of the group made occasion to talk to him with elaborate offhandedness, of the President's struggle with the Radicals and how he merited the support of all who cared for the country's integrity or future. 'The Constitution... irresponsible adventurers... civil liberties... system of checks and balances... a humane policy of reconstruction...' Ulyss did what he could to avert the discussions, but the very purpose of the journey made it impossible to avoid them altogether, and even if he were not personally drawn in, general questions were asked that were intended for him. But he had an answer when one was demanded: he was for the Union, for the restoration of the Southern state governments as quickly as possible, and no persecution of the rebels. If there were complaints that all those points were open to interpretation, it was not his fault. It was what he believed.

Sometimes he was annoyed by these subtle and overt attempts to make him say he was the President's man, but he could always go back to the baggage car to lie on a trunk and smoke, and no one troubled him there. And it was not unpleasant to appear several times a day to be cheered and admired. There was as much warmth in the shouts of his name as there had been the summer before, perhaps more. When the President finished speaking, his hearers always surged up to talk to him and shake his hand, and to press around the military heroes who accompanied him. 'The girls always kiss me, the pretty ones,' Farragut boasted. 'They never come near you, Grant.'

'They're too shy,' Grant told him, 'and it wouldn't be proper. They only kiss old men.'

At a few places the Radical leaders had prevented the appointment of welcoming committees, and the President's party was received only by the crowds who came spontaneously to hear him. In New York, however, formal attentions and popular demonstrations were of equal warmth. There was a resplendent welcoming committee; workers were released at noon to see the President, and all through the crowded day he was summoned to the window again and again to be cheered. The whole city seemed to be of one mind, and in the midst of that enthusiasm the winter's conflict with Congress was an impossible memory. 'I feel from what I see,' Rawlins wrote his wife, 'that the chances are favorable to the Conservatives and Democrats in New York this fall. . . . I am now more than ever glad that the General concluded to accompany the President, for it will do Grant good, whatever may be his aspirations in the future.'

On up New York State, through West Point and Poughkeepsie and Albany on the way to Buffalo. The cheerfulness of the group began to fray as each morning they woke to more hours of turmoil and rush and noise. The journey was having better results than anyone had expected, but even triumph is fatiguing, and strain began to show itself around the mouths and eyes of the travelers, in suddenly irritable tempers, in Johnson's voice, lifted to speak to the people five, fifteen, twenty times a day. He would not omit a single stop, would not cut short a single talk. He had it, the thing he wanted, the attention and respect of the people whose representatives were tearing down their safeguards. Congress had thought itself master: Congress would find in a few weeks that it was after all servant, to be punished and cast forth.

Then, at Cleveland, a strange thing happened. There was a great crowd, as usual, and much cheering, but when Johnson began his speech there was a sudden spatter of catcalls from the rear of the crowd, and someone shouted, 'New Orleans!' There had been a particularly bloody riot in that unpeaceful city a few months before, with a clash of negroes and whites, but it had little to do with Johnson's subject that night in Cleveland. He tried to go on, but no one could hear him, for the crowd crept and heaved uneasily, and there were more shouts of 'New Orleans!'

'You let the negroes vote in Ohio,' Johnson cried angrily, 'before you talk about letting them vote in Louisiana!' The taunt was fair enough, but it delivered him up to the power of the beast. The one barrier, the crowd's sense of distance between itself and him, crumbled at the touch, and there was no longer any possibility of stopping the affair within the limits of decency. There was a further exchange between the trouble-makers and the President, and the President was defeated.

An accident, an unfortunate accident of no significance. The members of the President's party earnestly reassured each other, and thought with dread of the next stop. It did not always happen. Sometimes the reception they were given was as satisfactory as any before Cleveland, but it never seemed so, for each member of the group was taut with waiting for the first sign of disturbance. More and more often it came, until, as they started on the homeward arc, it seemed that the entire country was filled with an insane loathing of its President. Always now there were so many hecklers in the crowds that the President could not be heard, unless he was goaded into making a retort that would look badly in the papers next morning, and that was always heard clearly. If he were allowed to begin a coherent address, he was given but two or three words between shouts and cheers for Grant or Farragut. Johnson had handled turbulent crowds before. When he had gone into

Tennessee, lately wrung back from the Confederacy, to be its
new governor, he had faced mobs that would have regarded
his murder as high patriotism, and had on occasion spoken with
his pistols handy on the table before him. Courage he had in
plenty, and it kept him to his planned course, punctually
appearing to crowds that sometimes would not let him speak
at all. But courage and obstinacy and the conviction that he
was right were not enough. Crowds like these, thirsting not
for his life but for his dignity, could be handled only by a man
who could strike fire from other men, who could laugh and give
back a shrewder blow than had been given him, who could
make a brilliant opportunity from a moment's chance. Johnson
could not. He had only his temper in reserve, and that betrayed him.

The thing puzzled Ulyss, and however much he had disliked
being lumped perforce with Johnson's supporters, it outraged
and embarrassed him when the President's voice was drowned
by cries of 'Grant!' Once, when Johnson had been beaten
into silence, Ulyss stepped forward and spoke. 'I'm ashamed
of you,' he said. 'Go home and be ashamed of yourselves.'
Yet he did not rebound to a deep sympathy with Johnson.
He could not approve a man's policies simply because the man
was being persecuted, and he looked down and reddened when
the tired, harsh voice made itself heard in some phrase better
suited to a backwoods stump speaker. If the President had
submitted to the will of Congress there would not have been
this spectacle of the people humiliating the symbol of itself.

It was a strange thing, thought Rawlins. How much was
spontaneous, how much planned strategy of the Radicals? It
was impossible to tell, and Rawlins suspected that it made little
difference. Whether this was actually the way the country
felt about Johnson, or whether the political leaders were well
enough entrenched to make it appear so, the election results
would be the same. Johnson was a defeated man. There were

two years of his term yet to go, but they would be simply
a troublesome interlude required by the Constitution — unless,
indeed, a way were found to shorten it, and in this howling
progress across the nation Rawlins could even envision that.
However right or wrong he might be, Johnson was finished.
The fact sounded in the yells of the mobs, that were otherwise
pointless bad manners; it was written plainly if invisibly in
the newspaper articles that commented on the intemperate
behavior of the President, and said little of the provocation
the President had been given.

'We're pretty close to Covington,' Rawlins said to Grant.
'Your father still lives there, doesn't he?'

'Yes.' Ulyss was quick to understand the unvoiced suggestion, and grateful for it. He was particularly troubled that
day by a memory of the night before, when Johnson had gone
out on a balcony to speak to a crowd that had clamored for
him, and had ended by exchanging furious words with the
groups that yelled at him. It was not a pleasant memory, of
the President of the United States red-faced and shouting.
Ulyss was not over-fond of his father, nor of his father's
numberless schemes for making much money from the opportunities of Ulyss's official position, but a visit to him would be
an entirely valid excuse for breaking free. 'I think I'll go see
father,' Ulyss said with a nod, and added frankly, 'I can't stand
around watching a man dig his own grave.'

They went down to Covington, leaving the dogged group
of supporters who kept to the schedule of the journey because
to abandon it would be the one humiliation greater than those
they were suffering. Ulyss would have been glad to forget the
thing altogether, but he got no help from his father.

Old Jesse was a Radical by nature, had been one long before
the term had acquired so precise a meaning, and he exulted.
'That's fixed him for good and all,' he chuckled. 'They say
he was so drunk he had to be held up from behind, and not a

soul on God's green earth could understand what he was trying to say, his words were so mushed up.'

'That's not so,' said Ulyss abruptly. 'He was never drunk at all, on the whole trip.'

'No need to get so hot about it. He was full as a tick at his own inauguration, wasn't he? And it don't matter, anyway. He's through. If he knew what was good for him he'd resign.'

'I don't think he will.'

'I guess not, he's too bullheaded. Maybe old Thad will throw him out and put Wade in his place. Anyway, it's only two years till we get a real President.' The old man's eyes sparkled, and his smile was wide. 'I been waitin' a long time for that day, Hiram Ulysses Grant. There's some folks ain't going to be so quick to laugh at prophets then. The man felt your head and told me — 'long about there he felt it ——'

'You're going to be disappointed, father.' Ulyss knew that his face was as blankly unresponsive as it had been for others who had made that suggestion, but he was also aware that in his heart there was not the same easy withdrawal. It was as if a fear, a wonder, a growing uncertainty in himself had taken his father's form, to sit and grin at him half in malice, half in triumph.

'You'll see ... you can't go against what you're born with.'

Before he left Ulyss tried to talk for a while to his mother. It was a thing he ought to do; a man's mother had a right to know something of him if she chose, but his mother did not choose. She sat quietly in the parlor, blinds drawn against the hot September sun, eyes veiled against the intrusions of a world that did not interest her. She never seemed dissatisfied, nor unhappy, nor joyous. What she thought about no one knew, but whatever it was it occupied her time satisfactorily and she had no need of anything else. She listened politely to what her son found to say, kissed him good-bye gravely, and went back to her chair.

There were no messages from Grant's parents to his wife and children, save one from old Jesse to his namesake. 'Tell the young rip I'll send him a gold hunting-case watch as soon as he can write me a letter to ask for it.' The other children were of no interest to him, and Julia was a Dent, daughter of another old man whom Jesse disliked with stubborn relish.

Little Jesse wrote the letter promptly, outraged that at the age of nine his ability should be questioned. He did not like school, and neither Julia nor Ulyss would consider forcing him to attend, but he learned rapidly when he chose. He could write well enough, and while he waited for the answer he boasted to the small friends with whom he played on the steep lawn in front of army headquarters. He was to have a watch as big as a lemon, and solid gold, even the works.

In a few weeks the answer came. 'You are still too young to own so handsome a watch, Jesse, but as soon as I am convinced that you will not play quoits with it, you shall have it.' Jesse was at length soothed by inordinate amounts of candy and a ride along Rock Creek with his father, but Ulyss found the incident very hard to forget. He was touchy about small things in those days.

Apparently Johnson's experience on the swing around the circle left him unchanged. He was as friendly to Ulyss as ever, as persistent in advocating his views to those who would listen, and as freely abusive of those who would not. Washington was fairly quiet, but everywhere else the campaign was fought with invective and florid oratory. There was a fashion among the speakers that fall to identify the Democrats: 'Every man who murdered and stole and poisoned . . . every bounty jumper, deserter, sneak . . . every officer dismissed for cowardice . . .' The list could be long and varied, and touched with poetry. It was the invention of Indiana's Governor, Oliver Morton, and when he spoke, with his eyes burning in the pallor of his face,

the indictment seemed to gain more than emotional conviction.
Ben Butler and Roscoe Conkling concentrated rather on
Johnson than on the Democrats, and put the case for impeachment with vivid detail. Stevens and Sumner and Wendell
Phillips, the abolitionist, talked tirelessly to the groups where
they were most at home: to the workmen and mechanics; to
the thoughtful people of New England; to the men and women
with shining ideals or easy hysteria who had formed anti-
slavery organizations.

The Democrats gained a few seats, a very few, not enough
even to make a satisfactory token victory. The Republicans
lost a few, not enough to imperil the two-thirds majority that
was Congress's orb and sceptre. The only clear indication
in the results was that the people were not impressed by
Johnson's alarm for the Constitution, nor stirred to defend him
and his position; they were not sufficiently alarmed by the
Radicals' picture of the Southern menace to increase the number of Radical seats, nor sufficiently concerned over the Southern chaos to destroy the Radicals' majority and endorse another
policy. It was not the South nor the Constitution nor any of
the fine-drawn problems of governmental balance that concerned them, but the protection of their own interests from
governmental interference.

Life had blossomed with gaudy possibilities since the war,
but President Johnson might have endangered the fruit. It
might have been disastrous had the masses of the ignorant and
purblind, the troublemakers of factory towns and unprofitable
farms, drawn together under the leadership of a President with
no sound understanding of the nation's potentialities, and no
responsiveness to the arguments of wiser men. 'The war of
finance,' he had said, 'is the next war we have to fight. . . .'
An aristocracy based on nearly two billion and a half of national
securities has arisen in the Northern States to assume that
political control which the consolidation of great financial and

political interests formerly gave to the slave oligarchy.' There was satisfaction in the banks and offices of eastern cities when the peculiar events of the swing around the circle indicated that there would be little to fear from Johnson; and when the election established the fact there was rejoicing among business men, bankers who had learned their trade with government war loans, and owners of bantling industries born under the protection of a Congress in which the agricultural representation had dwindled to impotence.

After the elections Ulyss at last found certainty. Whatever doubts Johnson's persistent arguments may have given him were refuted as the votes came in, for plainly the people held with Congress. By Congress's will, then, the country was to be governed. Yet even now the President held to his own way, and slowly Ulyss began to wonder if the man were not only headstrong and unwise, but actually dangerous. There was trouble in the South, more and more trouble every week, riots and defiance and a strange new hatred. The spent quietude of the summer after the war had disappeared, and now the whole section was convulsive, like a man struggling against bonds that have been fastened on him in his sleep. The leaders with whom Ulyss had talked, who had planned an orderly progress to stability, had apparently failed, and now the only native Southern authority rode by night, armed and masked. It was horrible to Ulyss that now, a year and a half after Appomattox, there was less trust and good will between the sections than there had been in the first days of peace, that the wounds had not closed, but festered. The reason seemed to him simple. A people may accept the inevitable, but not if they do not recognize the inevitable. How should the people of the South know what they must do if Johnson first denounced them and proposed rigorous punishment for their leaders, then allowed them to set up state governments with no real supervision, then openly fought Congress's attempts at supervision, leading them to think they need not obey that body? Even after the election they would not submit — for Johnson did not submit.

Many things had happened since Grant had been in Washington that he disapproved, but he had clung to the fact that as General of the Armies it was his duty only to carry out the instructions of Congress, not to worry about problems that had nothing to do with the army. Yet, as he read the ugly stories from the South in that raw November, Ulyss began to feel that he did have a certain responsibility in the matter, an obscure one, but compelling. At his command the South had surrendered — was the reconstruction of the South then no concern of his? He had friends there who might listen if he spoke, who might have influence if they listened. And he had learned enough of the ways of politics to believe that the South could get better terms now than at any time since Lincoln's death, if it would accept them, and quickly. Congress had returned unshaken, and capitulation from the South now would give it a national triumph. It would insist on the South accepting the Thirteenth and Fourteenth Amendments and the restrictions on the white vote, but Grant believed that would be necessary however long the South waited, and if it waited too long there would be other and even more humiliating terms.

Certainly it did not concern the General of the Armies, but Ulyss was inclined to believe it did concern that General Grant who had talked to Lee at Appomattox, that Ulysses Grant who wanted to see the united country he had fought for really united. Perhaps there was little he could do, but that little he must do. He talked to all the Southerners he met, and all Southerners who came to Washington came to him. He spoke to delegations, forgetting in his earnestness how much he disliked speaking. He wrote letters, among them one to a brother-in-law of Jefferson Davis.

' . . . The day after you left here the President sent for me, as I expected he would after my conversation with the Attorney

General. I told him my views candidly about the course I thought he should take, in view of the verdict of the late elections. It elicited nothing satisfactory from him, but did not bring out the strong opposition he sometimes shows to views not agreeing with his own.... Since then I have talked with several members of Congress who are classed with the Radicals; Schenck and Bidwell for instance. They express the most generous views as to what would be done if the constitutional amendments proposed by Congress were adopted by the Southern States.... Even the disqualifications to hold office imposed on certain classes by one article of the amendment would, no doubt, be removed at once, except it might be in the cases of the very highest offenders, such, for instance, as those who went abroad to aid in the Rebellion, those who left seats in Congress, etc. All or very nearly all would soon be restored, and so far as security to property and liberty is concerned, all would be restored at once. I would like exceedingly to see one Southern State, excluded State, ratify the amendments to enable us to see the exact course that would be pursued. I believe it would much modify the demands that may be made if there is delay.'

'Do you think it will have any effect?' Ulyss asked Rawlins abruptly as he signed the letter.

'God knows. You've done what you could, anyway.'

'Yes.' Ulyss sighed and set his lips. He had done what he could. He had talked, with all the force of which he was capable, and seen the listening faces polite and unconvinced. He had written, and been answered with very courteous and quite meaningless phrases. He had done what he could, and knew in his heart that it was not enough.

The Flag of the Secretary of War

CHAPTER NINETEEN

Break the President, break the Supreme Court, let there
be no impediment to the rule of the country by men who understand what the country has become. The old conception of
triple authority had done well enough when the nation was
young and weak, but now that it was surging forward to wealth
and greatness it had outgrown such cautious swaddlings, and
had need of bold leadership unaffected by the whining objections of the contrary-minded. Gleefully Congress set itself to
the task, bent on reducing executive and judiciary to the harmless state of the Congressional minority, lost in the shadow of
Stevens's 'fatal two-thirds.'

Very early in the session the House appointed a committee to
consider whether Johnson could be impeached. It was an excellent opportunity to rehearse all his sins of arrogance and ob-

struction and stubbornness, but it ended there, for none of these could be defined as the necessary high crimes and misdemeanors. As Ulyss had noticed long ago, Congress was full of lawyers. There were still a few timid spirits who felt that plausibility was important in a bill of indictment, and to satisfy them it was necessary to wait until the lawmaking body made an appropriate law. A few months one way or the other did not matter, for the end was certain.

The President had some supporters, men who believed as he did so firmly that they could blind themselves to the hopelessness of such beliefs, and a few rare spirits who disagreed with him but looked beyond the personal elements to the principles of political theory. It was not easy to be a friend to Johnson. The Radicals who referred to the President as the dead dog in the White House were not subject to sudden attacks of delicacy in speaking of the President's associates; a certain political blackmail was used against those who could be reached by it; and sometimes Johnson's own unadroitness alienated those who had a love of dignity. From time to time the constant battering found some weakness in a dissenter, and he fell away from the President to stand with the other spectators, uneasy, regretful, helpless.

Not even in the cabinet was there unshaken loyalty. Most of the members stood with Johnson for what they remembered as Lincoln's policies, but some wavered and counseled conciliation though no conciliation was possible unless it were capitulation; and Stanton, who had sometimes fought Lincoln, was fighting still. No one was sure how much he did. He had firm ties with the Radical leaders, but kept them fairly secret lest he lose his usefulness as Johnson's officer, and on occasion the Radical press yowled that he was defiled by Johnson's pitch. Treachery was a simple word to describe his methods, but it lost some of its force in the light of his immovable conviction that he was right. He did what he decided was best, as careless as God of where the blame fell. Johnson had been much criticized for being pointlessly vindictive in allowing the woman who had been implicated in Lincoln's assassination to be hanged, despite a recommendation of clemency from her judges. Johnson had never seen that document: produced by a military court, it had been sent through the War Department — and had not reached the White House. Authority, to Stanton, was not a matter of cooperation, and right as he saw it overshadowed smaller considerations of loyalty and straightforward conduct.

By this time Johnson no longer tried to make a personal friend of Grant. If the swing around the circle had made clear to Ulyss that the President did not represent the country, it had made equally clear to Johnson that the General would never support him with a whole heart. But Grant was not yet fully committed to the other side, and his position in the eyes of the people made him valuable to the President even if their relationship could never be more than lukewarm. Johnson saw him frequently, and sometimes invited him to cabinet meetings, hoping that he might be affected by personal knowledge of the difficulties of government by Congressional caprice.

Sometimes still the President's men made an effort to draw Ulyss into a definite statement. They tried it at a cabinet meeting which considered a bill for negro suffrage in the District of Columbia, a Radical measure of shining political beauty, for it proved to the South that the black vote was not merely a horrendous threat, yet did not risk offending the similar prejudices in Northern states. 'What do you think of it, General?'

What did he think? Once he had been sure, had looked with impatient disgust on those who wanted to give the vote at once to the thousands of ex-slaves who could not read nor write nor reason. But now it seemed to be wise, as it is wise in war to take a risk in order to win the campaign. 'No loyal man is safe,' Sheridan had said of Louisiana. No loyal man would be safe, Ulyss was beginning to see, until the Southern vote was adequately weighted by the negroes who knew they owed their freedom to the Republicans. He was beginning to see, and yet —— Ulyss ended the pause by a firm statement of the one thing he was sure of: 'It seems pretty contemptible for men to vote it for the District but not for their home states.'

There was a look of exasperation in Stanton's face, but some satisfaction in the others'. If Grant could criticize the Radicals, even so slightly, he might yet be of use to the President's cause.

In February Congress passed two bills, to settle the most obvious issues which had preoccupied it since the war. One at last mapped the road the South must follow to return to the Union. The fragmentary governments that had been formed under the North Carolina Proclamation and had been struggling for admission ever since were obliterated, and the region was divided into military districts under the command of army generals. In the bill as Stevens wrote it and the House passed it there was no provision for the end of that status, but the Senate would not pass it in that form. The upper house, under Sumner's leadership, insisted on negro suffrage, and in order for the negroes to vote they must have a state to vote in. For the sake of the negroes, then, it was provided that each rebel state might return to the Union when it called a convention without regard to race or color, accepted the Fourteenth Amendment, and set up a satisfactory state government.

The other measure was a legal straitjacket for the executive, called the Tenure of Office Bill. Henceforth the President could not remove any civil officer without the consent of the Senate; if Congress were not in session he might suspend an officer, but the suspension would not stand unless the Senate upheld it at the next session. Further, every removal, appointment, acceptance or exercise of office contrary to the proposed act was declared a high misdemeanor. Given Johnson's temper-

ament, Tenure of Office seemed likely to satisfy the requirements of even the most scrupulous Congressional lawyers.

Both bills were vetoed, as automatically as the veto would be
overridden. Johnson knew that his messages would mean
only a slight delay before the two-thirds vote was counted, but
he was as careful to see that they were clearly written and
soundly reasoned as though someone would hear them. The
dreary discussion of the veto for the Tenure of Office Bill did
have unexpected comedy, for Stanton, who was the bill's
primary object for protection, said he favored the veto. It was
his first concurrence in a long time, and no one understood what
he meant by it, but Stanton frequently acted for obscure reasons that would not have occurred to anyone else.

'Then we stand agreed,' said Johnson. 'Will you write the
message, Mr. Stanton?'

'I'm very busy,' said Stanton, a little too hastily. 'The
affairs of my office ———'

Smiling only enough to show that he had scored, Johnson
turned to Seward. 'You prepare the message, then,' he said,
'with, of course, Secretary Stanton's assistance.' Seward
thoroughly understood his commission, and fastened on Stanton
with so bland an assumption of cooperation that the Secretary
of War was as helpless as he was annoyed. In the end Stanton
did write the veto message. He was angered by the incident,
though neither humiliated nor greatly troubled, but it was of
some satisfaction to the President.

On the night of the first of March Johnson was restless. He
walked for some time up and down the long hall on the second
floor of the White House, sensing without thought how strange
it was to see it darkened and empty. All day long his visitors
crowded there; all evening his family walked through it on
cheerful errands from room to room; and that night what
trusted friends he had had come to him there, for in the morning
Congress was to hear his vetoes. Hear them, and override

them. Johnson was at least spared the torment of a faint hope.
Yet he could not go to bed and sleep in resignation. He was
driven to this restless walking, not in concern for tomorrow's
battle, which he knew would be a defeat, but in painful speculation on the whole campaign.

The hall seemed inimical in its shadowy desertion. It was no
longer simply a channel of walls and floor for the day's business,
but a place in itself, a part of the President's house, sharing
with all that building the residue of old conflicts, hopes, de-
spairs. To Johnson's weary and troubled mind it appeared that
the house too scorned him. The accidental President. The man
without party backing, without influence, without significance,
for however wisely he planned, however sincerely he spoke,
there was none to listen. Jackson had walked here, a strong
man, a successful man. Lincoln had walked here, fighting
every battle, political, military, ethical, in his own spirit, and
winning. Lincoln — could he have fought these other battles,
would he have won them too?

Johnson turned into the library and went to the great curved
window. There was little to see outside. Few stars, a bare
branch or two within reach of the lamplight. It was such a
night as comes in late winter, not very cold, not warm at all.
He stood and thought deliberately about Lincoln. It was hard
to do: the very name stood now for the martyred President, a
symbol for passion, a standard changing shape and size according to the invocation. But Johnson had known him, had talked
to the living man, touched the warm, bony hand. It was
Lincoln's place that Johnson had taken, Lincoln's work that
Johnson had tried to do. He had not done it. He knew it, and
could admit it in that lonely hour. Somewhere he had failed,
not because he had not fought with good will, but because he
lacked a quality which he could neither name nor recognize.
Lincoln had had it. It would have been necessary for Lincoln to
struggle too, and perhaps he might not have won a complete

victory, but he could not have been defeated as Johnson was defeated.

Tomorrow the old America would disappear. Indefinite military rule would supersede the proud state governments in the South, and with that precedent how could the North count itself safe? The suffrage, that had been the token of a free and discriminating manhood, was now to be a political trick that seemed to Johnson as dishonest as a butcher's thumb in the scales. His control over his own officers was taken from him, leaving him bound and ridiculous until Congress should be pleased to impeach him.

What the future would be he did not know, but he believed that the great days of the country had come to an end. By nature he never saw more than two alternatives, and now, with the safeguards of the Constitution a wreckage, he saw the country helpless, waiting to be looted. The looters were also plain to him: well dressed, big-bellied men who lived in banks; slick-haired and shifty-eyed agents of the Freedmen's Bureau; power-drunk army officers; and eventually the over-long fingers of foreigners. The picture did not seem at all exaggerated as he stared through the dim panes of the library window. All that he believed in was being shattered: what reason had he to think that his enemies had any worthy belief, that any new structure might rise by their labor to replace the one in which he had grown up and which embodied all his notions of integrity?

In a few hours the vote would be taken, and the bills would become acts, laws that must be obeyed unless some court upset them, years after their work was done. A few futile protests, and the nation would set off blindfold down a stony path. Yet it would not be entirely unguided. Perhaps it did not want him, perhaps he was sneered at and laughed at and genuinely hated, certainly Congress had every intention of impeaching him, but until the day that happened he was President. He did not intend to cower in the White House until he was dragged out. He could fight still, not with much hope of winning, but at least giving an opportunity for unexpected chance to bring him help. It was not a decision, simply a recognition of a personal necessity, but it warmed him, and he went to bed.

In the South that spring people sang, but not in public. Only negroes sang where others could hear them, combining the plain names of Chase and Sumner and Stevens with the Biblical imagery that was their only language for wealth and power and the ecstatic possibilities of their new world. The whites, who had been swept into poverty and helplessness by the same wave that had lifted their slaves to fantastic privilege, said as little as possible when they went outdoors, and tried to close their eyes to what they could not bear to see. But indoors, in their parlors set with scarred and meagre furniture, in the mean rooms they struggled daily to pay for, they sang.

> Three hundred thousand Yankees is dead in Southern dust,
> We got three hundred thousand before they conquered us;
> They died of Southern fever, of Southern steel and shot —
> I wish they was three million instead of what we got.
>
> I hate the Constitution, this great republic, too;
> I hate the nasty eagle, and the uniform so blue;
> I hate their glorious banner, and all their flags and fuss.
> Those lying, thieving Yankees, I hate 'em wuss and wuss....
>
> I can't take up my musket and fight them now no mo',
> But I'm not goin' to love 'em, and that is certain sho';
> And I don't want no pardon for what I was or am.
> I won't be reconstructed, and I don't give a damn.

It was such a song as an angry and unhappy child might sing, but it helped a little. It was not safe now to make a joke, even a less bitter one, where a soldier might hear, and the soldiers were everywhere. Some of them, perhaps, would have been friendly or even sympathetic, but the laws that were made in Washington left little play for sympathy, and the blue uniform was as damning a mark as a black skin. To the Southerners they were all alike scoundrels and invaders, just as to a good part of them the Southerners were an unreasonable and sullen people, somehow not quite American.

Trouble was everywhere, but it appeared most often in New Orleans. The mixture of the white races there had resulted in a charming and highly unstable compound; the blacks had the savagery of the canefields for background; the city was rich even in the present chaos, and drew many of the least inhibited Northern adventurers; and there was in the region's history a long tradition of violence, and a certain indifference toward government. Even when there was not actually fighting in the New Orleans streets there was such tension that conflict was a continuing possibility.

Sheridan had been set in command over Louisiana. It was said of him that at the battle of Five Forks one of his men had cried out on being shot, and Sheridan had assured him that he was not hurt at all. The General's certainty was so compelling that the man charged forward twenty feet before he realized he had been killed. Sheridan enjoyed the story. He was the type of military man who becomes the centre of legends: dashing, eager for a fight, gloriously untroubled by doubts of anything whatever. The command of Louisiana was perhaps not so exciting as a war, but Sheridan found a great interest in it nevertheless. As he read the Reconstruction Act the military commanders had wide powers, and what were they there for if not to be used? He used them, faithfully. Decisions of civil courts favorable to troublesome rebel elements were overruled, civil officers who proved uncooperative were removed with all speed, and the army was used freely as an argument to uphold Sheridan's views.

'It is just the thing,' Grant wrote him, 'and merits the universal approbation of the loyal people at least.... I only write this to let you know that I at least approve what you have done.' There were some who disapproved, Ulyss knew. Johnson and his friends were outraged by Sheridan's methods, and Stanton said that the cabinet had already discussed relieving the high-handed General from his command. Johnson and his friends seemed always outraged by anything that would protect the cause of loyalty in the South, by any reasonable sternness toward the persistent rebels. Another war was what the President wanted, the Radicals insisted. Was he not from Tennessee, had he not been a Democrat, did he not rush to succor any traitorous Southerner who refused to recognize the sovereignty of Congress? It might be true. Ulyss was not sure, but he believed the charge enough to be watchful, to keep careful guard lest the President influence the army, and to write to Sheridan with grim preparedness. 'Every loyal man in the country admires your course in civil affairs as they did your military career.... You have acted boldly and with good judgment, and will be sustained by public opinion as well as your own conscience, no matter what the result.'

In midsummer, almost as soon as Congress adjourned, Johnson summoned Grant to his office. 'General,' he began abruptly, 'I am removing Secretary Stanton and General Sheridan from office.' He paused, but not long enough for Grant to answer, then added, 'I want you to take Stanton's place ad interim.'

'I can't.' Ulyss was not surprised, but he was troubled. Stanton, the only wholehearted Radical in the cabinet, and Sheridan, whose firm hand might undo the harm that Johnson's slackness had done. Sheridan was still under the ultimate authority of the President, but Congress had taken thought for Stanton —— 'The Secretary can't be removed,' said Grant. 'Not unless he wants to go.'

'I can suspend him,' Johnson answered quietly, 'until Congress reconvenes in December.'

'Congress was still in session less than two weeks ago. Why

didn't you remove him then, when there could be an immediate decision?'

'I have a right to choose my time.'

'The Tenure of Office Act was meant to keep Stanton in office,' Ulyss said flatly. 'Maybe you can get around it by twisting the words, but the meaning is clear, and everybody knows it. And Sheridan —— Everybody in the North trusts him, and the rebels are scared of him ——'

'He's been too hasty and gone too far.'

'He's had a harder job than any other district commander. Since the day he was appointed the papers have been saying he didn't have the confidence of the administration and was going to be relieved. No wonder he's had so much trouble, with the people down there thinking they needn't bother to obey him. Mr. President' — Ulyss leaned forward, so earnest in his appeal that he lost his reserve — 'we all want to see peace in this country. We'll never have it so long as nobody knows where he stands, so long as you say one thing and Congress says another.'

Johnson's face looked tired, but his eyes were level and his lips smiled a little. 'I suppose you don't think,' he said, 'that Congress might sing my tune for a while?'

Ulyss drew back and set his lips. Apparently there was no point in expecting the President to give the least consideration to the people's Congress. He sat still while Johnson spoke on and on of the excuses he had contrived for his headstrong plan. Sometimes it was necessary for Ulyss to speak, and then he repeated without change his original position: Stanton, by the will of Congress, could not be removed, and Sheridan for the sake of the country ought not be. When at last Johnson gave up for the day Grant went back to his office and wrote a letter saying it all over again. It was a difficult letter to write, for its tone had to be decently subordinate, although its matter came close to expostulation. Ulyss cast it as much as he could in the proper form, but nevertheless it sounded like a protest on behalf of all loyal men.

For a week Johnson argued, and Ulyss revolved wearily between him and the Radical leaders. Their response to the threat somewhat surprised Ulyss: 'Go ahead, take it. If you don't he'll give it to somebody who'll wreck everything we've done. The best help you can give us is to take the place and keep a watch on him.'

'But it's a civil office. It's work I know little about.'

'It doesn't matter. The country needs you in that place.'

The proposal was logical enough, but Ulyss dreaded the weary business of cabinet meetings with the odds always against him in discussion, and a constant pressure on him to nullify Congress's intentions for the South.

'Maybe,' he said hopefully to Stanton, 'the President will see after all that he can't remove you. Congress would never uphold your suspension — he must know that.'

'He'll do it, never fear,' said Stanton. 'A mere law wouldn't stand in the way of our exalted President.' The leaden anger in his voice came close to pain. 'So you'll come in — you'll have to.'

'I don't want to take your place ——'

'It isn't a question of what you want. With you as Secretary ad interim there'll still be some check on him.' The words were an imperative order, yet Stanton spoke as if by decision rather than conviction.

'He wants me to take the office, all right,' Grant told Rawlins, 'but he acts like he thought I was playing Johnson's game by doing it.'

'It's a very hard position for him,' said Rawlins, with a malice so faint that Ulyss did not sense it. There was no great sorrow at army headquarters over Stanton's downfall. Politically it was deplored, but in the small matters of everyday procedure it would be a relief to have a Secretary of War with-

out Stanton's sweeping notions of authority. Rawlins was more
thoughtful than ever, listening to the conferences between
Grant and Stanton, to Grant's reports of his talks with the
President, to the faint murmurs of the rising political wind.

As soon as Ulyss was convinced that the removals were to be
made however much he objected, and that if he objected much
longer he would not be offered Stanton's place, he abandoned his
opposition and accepted the President's proposal. It was a
sultry August Sunday, and after the interview with Johnson
Ulyss went to Stanton's house to tell him that the thing had
been done. He walked slowly in the heat, wishing the coming
five months were over. Congress would reinstate Stanton,
there was no doubt of that, and the affair would end simply as
another of Johnson's thwarted attempts, but meanwhile his
own position would be equivocal and uneasy. He wondered if
government were always a matter of clashing wills, of ruthless
domination or ill-adjusted compromise. It seemed strange that
the country had survived at all with such lack of unity in its
leaders, and in his present depression he wondered if it would
survive much longer.

It was dusk when he reached Stanton's house, but the Secretary could be seen sitting in the wide hall with Edwards
Pierrepont. Grant greeted him, and said abruptly to Stanton,
'I'd like to speak to you for a minute.' They went into the
library, and Ulyss said at once, 'I told him today. I said I'd
take the office ad interim.' Stanton was bending over the lamp
and said nothing, but the light drew black lines between his
heavy cheeks and strangely small mouth. 'Like we decided,'
Grant ended lamely.

'Yes.' Stanton raised his head and said suddenly, 'You'll be
Secretary of War now, won't you?'

'Ad interim ——'

'It's all the same.' He drew breath sharply, and his hands
were clenched on the table, then relaxed slowly. 'You'll do all

right,' he said, looking over Grant's shoulder. 'The great thing
is to keep an eye on him — he's sharp.'

Their talk was soon over, and Grant took his leave, hurriedly,
for he was puzzled and a little angered by what he thought he
had seen in Stanton's eyes. Stanton returned to Pierrepont and
told him briefly of the decision that had been taken.

'So that's the end of it,' he said. His voice was steady, but
he made constant small motions with his hands and feet. 'You
can't argue with him, you can't fix him with a law — there's
nothing for it but to impeach him.'

'Isn't that what's intended?' Pierrepont's voice was soothing. '"A high misdemeanor," the act says ——'

'Yes, it's what we'll do. It's what Stevens and Sumner and
the rest were planning when they told me to hold on, when he
first tried to get rid of me. You told me not to.' Stanton rose
and went to the door, back to his guest, eyes on the darkness in
the street. 'You told me not to stay where I wasn't wanted,
and Mrs. Stanton said the same. I wish I'd listened to you.'
He struck the door frame, softly, and dropped his hand to his
side. 'I wish I had,' he said.

CHAPTER TWENTY

AFTER all the decisions were made on both sides the dismissal of Stanton was performed publicly, with nice attention to timing and the details of procedure. The elements of the affair were real enough — Johnson's determination to use his office, while he had it, as he saw fit; the division in Stanton's heart between his conception of himself and his fidelity to his party; the compulsion Grant felt to accept an office he did not want to further a cause he believed in with reluctance — but all these had their play before any action was taken. The conflict that the public saw was governed by the requirements of law and the dictation of politics, and its meaning had to do with impeachment, the constitutionality of the Tenure of Office Act, and the coming presidential election rather than with three men and their clashing conceptions of truth.

The first move was made by Johnson, requesting Stanton's resignation, which was promptly refused. Public considerations of a high character, said the Secretary, made it necessary for him to keep his office until Congress met again. Thus the issue was defined for the newspapers as a problem is stated on a blackboard. Then the President wrote an order in strict and literal conformation with the Tenure of Office Act, suspending Stanton and appointing Grant to the office until the Senate should decide if the executive had a right to dismiss an avowed enemy.

This was Grant's entrance cue, and he too wrote to Stanton. The opening paragraph was simple enough, transmitting the President's order, but Ulyss felt that his part in the matter should be clarified by a few more lines, and these were difficult. He wrote: 'In notifying you of my acceptance of the duties thus imposed on me I cannot let the opportunity pass without expressing to you my appreciation of the zeal, patriotism, firmness and ability with which you have ever discharged the duty of Secretary of War and also the regret I now feel at seeing you withdraw from them.' He read the letter over before giving it to Badeau to copy, and hesitated. He and Stanton were fighting now together, but it seemed to him that his purpose would be served as well without the words that savored more of subordination than of alliance. He struck out the reference to the duties 'imposed' on him, and his regret at Stanton's withdrawal. Appreciation was surely enough.

If he was not altogether pleased with his own letter, Stanton's answer pleased him less. It began, as expected, with an inclusive denial of the President's right to suspend Stanton, appoint Grant, or take from Stanton's custody any of the records of the Secretary of War. It continued: 'But inasmuch as the President has assumed to suspend me from the office as Secretary of War, and you have notified me of your acceptance of the appointment of Secretary of War *ad interim*, I have no alternative but to submit, under protest, to the superior force of the President. You will please accept my acknowledgment of the kind terms in which you have notified me. . . .' Behind the words Ulyss thought he could hear Stanton's acid 'You'll be Secretary of War now, won't you?' Of course Stanton must object to the thing as illegal, in order to strengthen the case for Congress, but it seemed to Ulyss that the tone had a certain resentment of him personally. He knew all the reasons for it, given the situation and Stanton's temperament; nevertheless he was annoyed. But the game was turned over to him now, however ungraciously, and he would play it as he thought best.

There was also a puzzling fury in the Radical newspapers' reaction to Grant's appointment. He had assumed that they would understand, as Stanton and Rawlins and the Radical high command understood, that he had taken the place in trust, to keep it from being given to someone who might not fully acknowledge Congress's power in the matter, but apparently the newspapers neither understood nor believed the strategy. Traitor they called Grant, lickspittle, fool and rascal won to Johnson's side for a price, probably for the price of a joint military dictatorship. It was a bewildering attack from sheets that Ulyss had considered friendly to him.

There were difficulties enough in his position aside from Stanton's peculiarities and the journalistic clamor. He could not save Sheridan: a week after he took office that dashing general was relieved and a new commander was given to the District of Louisiana. In other matters he was more successful, for the Military Act had given great power to the Secretary of War and the General of the Armies, and now Grant was both, yet occasionally he was forced into a dangerous lenience by Johnson's insistence. Even the routine of his work was troublesome, for he was careful to remember that he held two offices, rather than that two offices had been merged in one official. Sometimes in his mornings at the War Department he wrote an order for army headquarters, to be received by himself in the afternoon. The process amused his staff, but he did it gravely and without any sense of comedy.

'It isn't as if I were really Secretary,' he explained to Badeau, who had smiled at a document awaiting his double signature. 'Stanton is Secretary of War, or will be as soon as Congress meets again. I'm just substituting for him till then.'

'But maybe the Senate will uphold the suspension.'

'Time enough to change things if they do, but they won't.' It was all the explanation he gave for his gingerly tenure, and all he admitted to himself, yet there was more in his feeling than a scruple for Stanton's vested interest. Ulyss was at ease in the army world, with its rigidly simple organization and clear lines of responsibility. But the Secretaryship of War was a civil office, its holder accountable not only to his superiors but to the faceless shadow that was the people, and it was Stanton who had the backing of the party, the instrument of the people, while Grant had only its sufferance. Ulyss was restless in the Secretary's chair, and used what he knew of Stanton's beliefs as a standard for his own acts.

Cabinet meetings were, as he had expected, the worst of his difficulties. Always the talk was of the network of laws that had been thrown around the President, and of the possibilities of finding a hole in them. Always Ulyss was conscious that some of the talk was not of policy but of principles, an argument to convince someone — to convince him. He sat silent. He was doing as he thought best in a situation with no really good solution, and he would make no concessions.

Once he made an effort to be excused from the meetings: 'I'm an army officer, really,' he said to the President. 'I'm only Secretary until Congress passes on Mr. Stanton's suspension and restores him or confirms a successor. It isn't part of my work to make policy.'

'You're one of my cabinet officers,' said Johnson steadily, 'and you have all the rights and duties of your office.' He paused, then added with a mildness unusual in him, 'And I want you to come anyway, General. I want you to feel that you're one of my advisers, that you can give me your views of things ——' If they coincide with yours, thought Ulyss. The President had stopped again, looking down at his desk in indecision. Then he raised his head and asked openly, 'Why won't you?'

It was not fair. The question was sincere, and demanded a sincere answer, but Ulyss knew that if he stated his position frankly Johnson would promptly forget his contemplative mood, and lose himself in the haze of sardonic invective that opposition always raised in him. It had become impossible to discuss his quarrel with Congress in any calm. And what could Ulyss say? I don't agree with your policies. I wouldn't be so quick to pardon every rebel who blusters that the South will be entirely loyal as soon as the Federal troops are gone. I wouldn't be so anxious to take back states with Black Codes that only a Philadelphia lawyer could tell apart from slavery. Johnson would forget the suggestions, in his memory that Ulyss had once also favored mild measures. It would be impossible to show him, a Democrat, the peril in abandoning the loyal Southern Republicans; impossible to make him see that Southerners had turned out to be a vindictive and bitter people, with rebellion still just beneath the surface of their resentful submission.

'I'm not really Secretary,' Ulyss said at last, taking refuge in the one dogged belief that stood firm in the controversial bog of that autumn. 'I'm just holding Stanton's place ——'

'Yes, I know that's what you think. But why? I've suspended Stanton and chosen you — nobody can work with Stanton, as I think you know, General.' Ulyss could not avoid a slight answering smile. 'It's too bad he had to go the way he did, but he wouldn't resign and there wasn't any other way. And I won't have him back.'

'Congress ——'

'Laws have been contested before, and I'm certain this one is unconstitutional ——' It was as Ulyss had expected. The softness in Johnson's tone disappeared, and he began talking of Stevens and other Radicals in a manner that would have repelled Ulyss even in a man who was not President. Ulyss excused himself, wondering why he had ever thought that his request might get a reasonable hearing. Apparently there was no way short of insubordination to avoid attending the cabinet meetings, and thereafter he went regularly. But he too was a stubborn man, and he made a habit of presenting all the affairs of his office, waiting for the discussion of them, then leaving before any other business was considered.

September, October — surely the months were longer than usual this year. The period seemed poised, with Johnson and the Radicals, Stanton and Grant, rising new industries and the collapsing South, impeachment and the coming election, all suspended together until Congress should meet and set their unstable forces in motion again. Ulyss was no longer deeply concerned about the result of his own part in events, only about the speed with which it would come. His secretaryship ad interim was proving even more disturbing than he had expected, for he was troubled not only by the misconception of it in the Radical press, but by a growing, grudging appreciation of Johnson's side of this particular quarrel. It was true that Stanton was almost impossible to work with, and in Grant's military code it seemed fantastic that any man should try to hold to his place when his superior wanted to be rid of him. But whatever happened, whether Stanton resigned and Johnson appointed someone Congress would accept, or Congress forced Stanton back on the stiffnecked President, Ulyss would have none of it. He withheld his own resignation only because he had promised both Johnson and the Radical leaders to hold the office until Congress met.

There was no one to whom he could talk with full freedom, although there were those in plenty who talked to him. Julia, naturally, followed his lead rather than advised him, and he could not trouble her serene happiness with a discussion of his perplexities. Rawlins shared his indignation over Johnson's blind obstinacy, but seemed preoccupied. Sherman was in town on army business, and Ulyss took pleasure in rehearsing with him the men and methods and incidents of the war, but he avoided talking with him of politics. Sherman made valiant efforts to be tactful, but Ulyss felt that his friend had not followed the political path he himself had taken. Day by day a shell of silence hardened over the doubts in Ulyss's heart — perhaps, he thought hopefully, it would hide them even from himself before he had to make the decisions that were lying in wait for him in the year to come.

Shortly before Christmas Ulyss bought Jesse a watch. He had not forgotten the incident of the letter to his father the year before, nor had young Jesse, who had suggested recently that he write again. Ulyss had put a stop to that plan, but Jesse was too young to take pleasure in mere safeguarded pride, and Ulyss did not intend to leave him disappointed. He bought the handsomest watch he could find, and took it home to show to Julia and Nellie.

'It's for Jesse's Christmas,' he said. 'Don't tell him. I want to surprise him.' He smiled in anticipation of the boy's delight.

'It's beautiful, Ulyss,' said Julia slowly, 'but isn't it almost too beautiful? He's so young to have a watch like this ——'

'He's a little boy,' Nellie agreed, her pretty face filled with thirteen-year-old prudence. 'He'll break it right away.'

'He wants it,' Ulyss answered. 'If he knows enough about it to want it he knows enough to take care of it.' Apparently they did not understand about wanting things.

At dinner that night Jesse chattered of the wagon that had got stuck in the mud in front of army headquarters, and Ulyss watched the play of excitement and fun across his face. All his children were very dear to Ulyss — Fred, now almost a man, planning to follow him into the army; Buck, so wise about so many things; Nellie, growing into an astonishing beauty and mature grace. But Jesse, spoiled, graceless, with all the quick sympathies and cruelties of childhood, had a special place. The boy finished his story, or abandoned it, and went to work with dangerous haste on an apple pie. Ulyss pulled the watch out of his pocket and laid it in front of his son. 'It's yours,' he grunted.

Jesse shouted until the pendants in the chandelier faintly answered him, and Nellie sighed, but Julia smiled at Ulyss. 'I thought it was for Christmas?' she said. She did not whisper, for an ordinary tone was made confidential by the boy's jubilance.

'He didn't want to wait,' Ulyss chuckled, 'and neither did I.' He felt for no good reason as if he had evened a score, and the honest noise his son was making was a pleasant thing to hear after the muted uncertainties with which his days were filled.

There was business enough before Congress when it convened. The railroads webbing across the country were forever clamoring for land, or for an adjustment of their debt to the government, or about some other aspect of the affairs that kept their lobbies active and their entertainment accounts enormous. The opposing pressures of English and Pennsylvanian iron were raising a tariff wall as a mountain range is heaved out of the shrinking earth. Seven of the Southern states had been readmitted after fulfilling Congress's requirements, but they were represented by adventurers, by the Northern-born, or by men with pasts so dubious that no label could be attached to them, and there was no peace anywhere in the South. Little attention was paid to any of these things: Congress had assembled for the final defeat of Johnson.

'The Senate will decide on Stanton's suspension in a day or two,' Sherman said to Grant on a Saturday in January. 'Do you think there's any chance it will be upheld?'

'Not a chance in the world.'

'Then what are you going to do?'

'Turn the office over to Stanton. It's his.'

'Does the President know that's what you intend?'

'He ought to by this time.' Grant struck his knee impatiently. 'Nobody can be sure what he knows. He just wants his own way, and I think sometimes he won't look at anything that might show him he can't have it.'

'It seems to me,' said Sherman, 'that you ought to tell him straight out, now, so he can appoint somebody else if he wants to before Congress acts.'

Ulyss hesitated, but at length agreed to go. He was weary of the whole affair, of the meetings and discussions, the senseless obstinacy on both sides, but he wanted to be as fair as he could, and perhaps Johnson really did not understand his determination. He was received at once, and he told the President bluntly that he would vacate his office immediately should the Senate reinstate Stanton.

'Wait a minute, General,' said Johnson. His voice had a rather grating overtone, and there was an air of excitement about him. Ulyss had seen him look so in the wretched days of the swing around the circle. 'The Tenure of Office Act is unconstitutional. No court will uphold it, but the thing can't ever be settled until a case is made of it ——'

'The act says,' Grant interrupted, 'that holding office contrary to it is a high misdemeanor. It provides fines and prison sentences ——'

'You'd be doing it under my orders. And I tell you the act isn't constitutional. I'll guarantee to serve for you every day of a sentence and pay every dollar of a fine that any court in this country would impose on you under that act.'

'If Congress decides you couldn't remove Stanton I'll leave the office immediately,' Grant said with literal distinctness. 'If that isn't the way you want it you can appoint somebody else before Congress decides.'

'But I want you to work with me on this. If we make an issue of it ——'

'I leave when Congress acts.'

'Think it over. We'll talk about it again — Monday, perhaps?'

Ulyss said nothing, for he had already made his decision clear and there seemed no point in saying it again and again to a man who would not listen, and he left while the President still spoke of another meeting. He had done what he could: it was not his fault if Johnson could not recognize an opponent when he saw one.

At the moment he wondered why he should concern himself with any sort of compromise. In his annoyance it seemed only just that Johnson should be saddled with Stanton, that the two difficult beings should infuriate each other for what remained of the term. But as the hours of that week-end passed without action Ulyss could not avoid concern.

'He must want Stanton after all,' he said gloomily to Sherman. 'He's losing his last chance every minute he waits.'

'Maybe he can't think of a substitute for you,' Sherman suggested. 'Evidently he thought until yesterday that you were going to stay on, and it isn't so easy to get somebody else overnight.'

'I don't believe he's trying,' Ulyss grunted. 'There must be dozens if he'd give in enough to consider them.'

'Not so many, if you think about it. Remember, it would have to be a man to suit him and Congress too. Sheridan he wouldn't have, and Congress wouldn't have Hancock ——'

'How about you?'

'Me work in Washington? I'd go to hell first.' Sherman

waved his arms in discourteous horror. 'Anyway, I'm not
sure it's a good idea for an army man to be Secretary. You see
it isn't easy to choose somebody. But there's Cox — he did
well in the war, and he's been governor of Ohio ——'

'He's a Republican, too.'

'Yes, but conservative enough to work with Johnson. Cox
would be a good man. Why don't you suggest him?'

'I' — Ulyss reddened, but said flatly, 'I don't want to go
near him again till the thing's settled. I'm tired of being argued
at. You talk to him, Sherman. He might shut up long enough
to listen to you.'

'All right. It looks to me as if we ought to try whatever we
can. This isn't any kind of government, Sam — this everlasting pully-hauly while the country goes to pot.'

Sherman stopped, not sure just where Grant stood in the
matter, but Ulyss nodded, for he was not entirely sure himself.
Sometimes he agreed with his Radical friends that Johnson
must be defeated even at the cost of permanently crippling the
executive branch; sometimes it seemed absurd to be so concerned about him, with an election for a new President only
ten months off.

Early on Monday Sherman went to the White House to propose Cox's appointment. Johnson heard him through, but
made no comment, and all that day took no action. Late in
the afternoon, however, the Senate did act. The reasons for
Stanton's suspension were found insufficient, and he was automatically reinstated as Secretary of War.

In the morning Ulyss went to the War Department and
bolted the Secretary's office. He gave the keys to the Adjutant
General, saying, 'I'll be in my office, at army headquarters.'
Then he wrote to the President, telling him what had been
done.

The results were immediate and characteristic. Stanton
summoned the General of the Armies across the street to say

that the Secretary of War had returned to his rightful place. Ulyss was surprised to find how angry it made him. It was not only the cavalier disregard of his rank, nor the curt announcement of facts he had good reason to know already, facts such as he had himself announced by private call and formal letter when the situation had been reversed the summer before. These were annoyances, but he had long known that Stanton was annoying. The thing that angered him now was an almost indefinable change in Stanton himself. Hitherto Ulyss had felt that Stanton worked for the public good, perhaps mistakenly, perhaps with a confusion between the good of the country and what seemed good to Stanton, but certainly with a larger motive behind his self-conceit and domineering methods. Now, as Ulyss stood watching his eyes and the corners of his mouth, he wondered if in his months of exile Stanton had lost his direction, if his reinstatement were not essentially a personal triumph. There was the arrogance of the impregnable in his voice, and he talked of little except the certainty of Johnson's impeachment.

An hour after Ulyss was dismissed from Stanton's presence he was summoned to a cabinet meeting. He went, for he had often attended the meetings when he did not have cabinet status, and he saw no reason to refuse now. Johnson gave him a long look as he entered, and said distinctly, 'Good morning, Mr. Secretary.'

The words surprised Ulyss much more than they should have. He had been so sure that the affair was at last finished that this sudden reopening of it bewildered him. 'I'm not Secretary,' he said. He spoke quickly, too quickly for dignity. A smile tinged the lips of some of the men, and Ulyss felt himself flush. 'I wrote you about it,' he hastened on. 'I told you that after the Senate acted I wouldn't stay.'

'That was not according to our understanding,' said Johnson. He was angry, and he showed it. Grant had often seen him

enraged at someone else, but never before had he seen that
towering temper directed at himself. 'You were to hold the
office until I appointed a successor, or if you decided you
couldn't you were going to tell me. Why didn't you come
yesterday?'

'It seemed useless' — Ulyss fumbled. He had been taken
off balance, and could not steady himself while he was confronted by the ring of curious, faintly contemptuous faces, and
Johnson's blazing eyes. He had not said definitely that he
would not return — had his silence implied that he would?
The President seemed so sure — 'I wasn't sure the Senate
would act so soon ——' This was not right, it was not what
he wanted to say, but there was an obscure, hostile pressure in
the room that would not let him think. 'I was busy,' he murmured.

Some were smiling outright now. Johnson did not smile.
He stared levelly at Grant and said, 'You promised.'

'I did not promise.' The words were automatic, an instant
reflex by what he knew of his own intentions, but they rang
on the air like drawn steel. The two statements had been
made and could not be reconciled, and as Grant's tight lips
faced Johnson's set jaw it was clear that neither would be withdrawn.

Other things were said, but could not clothe those naked
words. Ulyss went back to his office shaken, still too startled
by the direct contradiction of his word to be fully conscious of
his own rage. He was accustomed to abuse: during the war he
had been called drunkard, butcher, coward, and fool; since then
the newspapers had on occasion called him many things. But
no one yet had given him the lie. The thing was so incomprehensible to him that he believed it an error, a misunderstanding
not unnatural with a man of the President's temperament.
Johnson might have persuaded himself that Grant would in the
end do as he asked. Surely he did not really believe that

Grant had broken a promise to him. Ulyss wrote a letter, explaining more fully than he could trust himself to do in direct conversation, denying altogether that he had ever promised to reconsider his decision, or to call again.

The reply from Johnson was uncompromising. If the General did not remember that he had promised, why had he made excuses in the presence of the cabinet for failing to keep his word? Everyone there had heard him, and could bear witness.

Then at last Ulyss was angry. He had been troubled about Johnson before, had doubted his wisdom and methods, had even suspected his loyalty and thought he might ruin the country, but he had never hated him. Now he did, with a total loathing he had never felt for anyone, that clawed at him for action but could not even be put into words. The letter he wrote in answer to Johnson was absurdly inadequate, and Rawlins took it from his hand.

'It won't do,' he said, 'it's not enough.'

Surprised, Ulyss looked up at the white face of his chief of staff. For a long time Rawlins had seemed somewhat withdrawn, saying nothing while the others argued, saying little even in these last days of indignation, and now his action had the greater force. It was as if he had been waiting for the moment. He took the letter and made a few changes. There were only a few, deftly shifting the issue to a personal basis, and accusing Johnson of an attempt to involve Grant in lawbreaking and to blacken his reputation in the country.

'That's what I meant,' said Ulyss. 'That's good.'

His staff murmured around him, and Badeau, who had been a newspaperman before he was a soldier, looked at Rawlins. There was triumph in the sunken dark eyes, and the white cheeks were marked with a red that rarely appeared there now. It was not the challenge to Johnson that mattered to Rawlins; Badeau knew that. The quarrel in itself was of little significance to him, for he seldom troubled himself about people. His was a mind that dealt in larger things, in ideals of thought and methods of action, and he would not fail to see the uses of a break between Grant and the President. For a moment Badeau saw the vista that stretched before Rawlins: the little sheets of paper that were the letters of two angry men; the newspapers that would print and discuss the letters; and the people who would read them, remember them a little, and remember what was said about them more. It was an interesting picture, in election year.

The general effect of the letter did not occur to Ulyss when he sent it, and if he noticed it later it had no importance to him. His quarrel with Johnson was an absorbing passion, and beside it all else lost meaning. But the people of the country read that Grant, the victor of the war, the tireless laborer for harmony between sections and between parties, had been grossly accused by the President, who no doubt was trying by this craven method to rid himself of the General's opposition to his diabolic schemes. Therefore Grant, who had been beyond party, had joined the Radicals, who were the only group in the country with the courage and foresight to fight the President while there was yet time. The Radicals were proudly grateful for his leadership, and would not fail to present him to his country at the nominating conventions in the spring.

It was true enough. Ulyss had associated himself with the Radicals, for their partisan attacks on the President had almost as much fervor as his personal hatred, and had a better chance of results. It was not possible to strike the face of the President of the United States: it was possible to impeach him, and to that effort Ulyss gave his whole heart. He was aware that the Radical newspapers were speaking of his election to the presidency as an assured fact, and that probably it was an assured fact, but just then it did not interest him. It was a thing to be accepted without joy or pride or aversion, not to be fought for and not to be avoided, and not to be thought about until he had finished with Johnson.

In February Johnson discharged Stanton again, and when the Senate duly voted that he could not, he appointed Lorenzo Thomas Secretary ad interim. The situation was apparently just as it would have been had Grant agreed to hold to his place, but there was a vital difference: Stanton was now in physical possession of the Secretary's office, and he barricaded himself there, shouting defiance. The scene was absurd, but it was quickly forgotten, for at the Capitol the House had at last found its bill of indictment.

Eleven articles of impeachment were drawn up, all those of importance resting on the Tenure of Office Act. It was unfortunate that so narrow a base must be used, but it was difficult to make high misdemeanors out of a man's indiscretions of speech and behavior, and the Act would be enough. A two-thirds vote of the Senate was required for impeachment, and had it not been shown, over and over again, that a two-thirds vote in either house was an automatic process? Thad Stevens led the House Committee to inform the Senate. He was old and very ill, so ill that his body seemed almost dead save for his blazing eyes and remorseless, lashing voice, but he made of these and of his cross-grained will a vitality that would sustain him long enough for his final triumph.

Thirty-four votes for conviction were certain — the voters had said so. Twelve would vote for acquittal. That left eight men in doubt, and pressure was brought on them. There were letters and telegrams and calls from their constituents, it was said that money was offered to them, there were threats and promises to their women. Ulyss called on one of them, Senator Frelinghuysen, and came away with the happy knowledge that that vote could be counted for conviction. He made other calls, not with such clear success, but undiscouraged. Ben Wade, who would fall heir to the presidency on impeachment, was already pondering his cabinet, and Washington was thronged with seekers of office for the ten remaining months of the term.

At the opening of the trial no one doubted that the verdict would be conviction. Those who were in power hated Johnson, the mass of the people were indifferent to him, his friends were few and without comparable influence. The doubtful votes were slow to declare themselves, but the Radical leadership had grown expert at persuasion, and had produced a two-thirds vote on many measures of far deeper importance than the impeachment of a President whose term was nearly over, and who was in any case helpless. The result seemed certain by every test of logic and experience and the political probabilities.

But as the trial drew to its close in early May, a cold uncertainty filtered into the Radicals. In the doubtful eight, Frelinghuysen's capture was offset by the loss of Fessenden and Grimes to the Democrats, and there were rumors that others were going too. It was impossible to find the exact reason for the shift, and thus impossible to counteract it. Perhaps the sober exhortations in the press to consider the solemnity of the decision actually had an effect on some of the men who were to make it. Perhaps the long obsession of the country's mortal danger, and the feverish response to leaders who claimed that they could spy out the danger and avert it, had at last run its course, and men were beginning to see the shrunken, dull proportions of reality. Or perhaps the reason was at once more simple and more subtle: an intangible element in the concept of the President, so faint that men would not hesitate to revile the holder of the title and make mock of his authority, yet so strong that they faltered and fell back rather than assault holder and title together.

Whatever the reason, the more realistic among the Radicals admitted to themselves that they could not be certain. Acquittal was not sure, did not seem even possible in memory of

the way the trial began, but the betting odds slipped relent-
lessly to even money by the time the first vote was taken. The
vote was on the three most telling counts, and it resulted in
thirty-five for conviction and nineteen against. One short of
two-thirds. One vote, but all nineteen formed a welded unit
that it would be impossible to shatter. The other counts never
came to a roll call. The Senate adjourned sine die, and the one
issue on which Andrew Johnson defeated his Congress was his
own impeachment.

There was neither horror nor rejoicing in the nation, for
though some had hated Johnson none had loved him. With
surprising speed the trial was forgotten, a tacit truce was declared, and the politicians turned to concentrate on the election.
But in Washington there were two who did not readjust so
easily. Stanton had been given a mortal blow, for it was his
own conduct that had stood trial as Johnson's guilt, and it had
been condemned. There was no comfort for him in his knowledge of all the other elements that had been involved. Stanton
had been judged wrong; he had known in an unacknowledged
depth of his spirit that he was wrong; and to him that knowledge was utterly insupportable. It took from him the chief
factor of his life.

The result of the trial was also a shock to Grant, and could
not be easily dismissed. He had believed in cause for impeachment, and still believed in it. The trial had not been a political
performance in his eyes, but a sober effort to remove a dangerous man, and failure of that effort was tragedy. He had not
the easy resilience of those accustomed to the fantasies of
politics, and came close to horror as he watched some of the
men who had been most violent go to call on the President, as
though all their thundering warnings had been stage effects.
Ulyss was shocked, and he was uneasy.

Four days after the trial Grant received a call from Stanton.
It was the first time the Secretary of War had left his office to

call on the man he considered his subordinate, and it would be
the last, for Stanton was resigning now that there was no dignity
or satisfaction for him whether he went or stayed. He came
quickly up the stairs, often looking over his shoulder as if he
feared to see someone racing after him, and he was quite
breathless as he cried, 'General — you've been nominated
——' He stopped, and began again with proper respect for
the occasion. 'General, I have come to tell you that you have
been nominated by the Republican Party for President of the
United States.' Then he looked again over his shoulder, and
said, 'I'm the first, a'n't I?'

'Yes — I hadn't heard. Thank you.' Ulyss shook hands
with him, and suddenly the whole group about him — Rawlins
breathing fast with excitement, Babcock with a shimmering
smile, Porter and Badeau slapping each other on the back —
seemed alien because it was joyous. Later, when he told the
news to Julia and the children, he would realize the honor that
had come to him and take due pride in it, but he could not now,
for he was being welcomed to the ship of state by a drowned
man. Everything about Stanton, the strained, dry look of his
eyes, the too-eager clasp of his hand, his very eagerness to bear
the news, told of the inner wreck to which civil authority with
its complex tensions can bring a man. Ulyss let his hand be
pumped up and down and nodded to the young men whose
faces glowed with joy for his sake, and hid in silence a terror
such as he had not known since he had marched uphill against
the rebel Harris, long ago in a war that he had understood.

PART SEVEN

Galena Celebrates

The City of Washington

VII. CROWN OF VICTORY

CHAPTER TWENTY-ONE

IT WAS hot that summer in Galena, and strangely quiet after the stormy excitements of Washington and the east, but Grant went there and stayed, for that was his place. Office must not be actively sought. Speeches and pamphlets were written by the hundreds, Badeau wrote a campaign biography,

Rawlins stayed in Washington all summer to watch the machine he had set in motion, but all this, felt Ulyss, had nothing to do with him. The hours when he had any personal pleasure in the thought of his election were rare, for he had seen Lincoln and Johnson driven and desperate in the office, yet he had a sense of obligation. He believed in the people, and if they wanted him he had no right to hold back. Meanwhile he would make no move, for if he talked himself how could he hear the people's voice?

The Republican leaders were not pleased. They believed they could elect Grant, but not so firmly that they were willing for him to isolate himself, without speaking, without appearing before the voters, without even answering letters. The men who guided the party groaned over the necessity of working with a balky soldier rather than a man bred in political methods and aware of political objectives, but they had no choice. Much could be done by partisanship — local officials elected, even revolutionary bills carried, but in that year of 1868 the people would not elect to the presidency an immoderate man. There was bitterness in them, and fear, and greed, and the cruelty of ignorance, but beneath these things was something else, an instinct for peace and rebuilding. Democrats would not have voted for a candidate who had been disloyal; Republicans would not have voted for a candidate who had taken active part in the fight for power. Grant's letters to Johnson had made him a Republican, but his three years' struggle to hold the balance gave him a neutral background, and his war record of firmness and sound sense drew to him those who were troubled by the chaos and doubtful honesty in the nation's affairs. The leaders had been forced to nominate him and work for him, but they could not make him work for himself. Their worst threat would be the loss of the election, and plainly that would trouble them more than it would him.

The campaign was fought chiefly on the issues of negro

suffrage and of coin payment on five-twenty government
bonds. The first was clear enough: the Republicans stated in
their platform that negro suffrage should be required of all the
states that had been in rebellion, but that loyal states should
be allowed to decide for themselves, and the Democrats howled
in unified outrage. But the money issue divided the partisans
of both sides in so many ways that it almost canceled itself.
Many Republicans insisted that payment should be made in
greenbacks — the bonds had been bought with greenbacks,
and the law made no promise of payment in coin. But Jay
Cooke, who had floated the bonds, had advertised that interest
and principal would be so paid.

'My word is as binding to me as any law,' Cooke had said
to Ulyss, who visited him at Ogontz. 'It's a hard thing when a
man is forced to break his faith.'

'Mm,' said Grant sympathetically. He knew little about the
bonds, but he did know how sensitive a man's honor is.

Yet Cooke financed the Republican campaign; and the
Democrats, who would normally have given loud support to
the greenback side, called for payment in coin. That year the
party was largely directed from New York, for most of the old
Southern leaders were discredited or disfranchised. The candidate was Horatio Seymour. It was hard to say what his chances
were, or would have been — had the South been allowed to use
its Democratic strength, had the party called for greenback
payment, had Grant not been the Republican candidate . . .

On a day in November Ulyss went to the polls and voted the
Republican ticket for all the offices but president, which he
left blank. Four years ago he had not voted, for Illinois had
not made arrangements for her soldiers to vote in the field.
(City Point, at the beginning of that stagnant and anxious
winter before Lee surrendered . . .) And eight years ago he
had not voted, for he had not lived in Galena long enough to
establish residence. There had been a great many candidates

then, he remembered. Lincoln and Douglas and Breckinridge
and — and Bell, that was it. He had been still afraid that one
day Julia might reproach him, describe in exact and brutal
words the life she was living for his sake, and what would he
do then? She never had. She had met him every evening at
the top of the steps, smiling, her dear uneven eyes bright.
Ulyss remembered, while he made his methodical crosses down
the length of the sheet, and before he turned away he paused
for a moment with his fingers on the empty space at the top.

At Washburne's house he and a few friends gathered to hear
the returns. A telegraph instrument had been installed, and
for hours the others snatched at the successive bulletins and
argued loudly over their meaning. Ulyss sat quietly in his
place, smoking and listening to what they told him, without
much sense of reality. He was waiting to hear if he had been
elected president. He tried to think of that, to realize the
solemn hour before it had passed into history, but his mind was
clouded by little things: the odd resemblance between the
chatter of the machine and the chatter of his friends; a vague
memory of a stranger's fingers passing over his head; a prophecy
that had not seemed so strange on that summer day in his boy-
hood as it did now that it was being fulfilled. Perhaps he did
not really remember it, perhaps his was only a reflected memory
from hearing his father talk about it so much. This was the
great moment of his life. This was his entry into that estate
that is dreamed of for American little boys, that fewer than
twenty in a century claim. He ought to feel proud and awed,
but he felt nothing. He had known joy at Vicksburg and
desperate resolve on the second night of the Wilderness, he had
even been aware of history at Appomattox, but now he felt
none of these things, and sat waiting with as much patience
and as little excitement as he would have waited for an evening
newspaper.

A little before two in the morning the indications became

certainties, and Ulyss was congratulated on his election. He
rose to go home, and found outside the house another group,
not of close friends but of acquaintances and strangers, a fragment of the electorate come to see the completion of its work.
There were not many of them, for Galena kept early hours even
on election night, but there were between fifty and a hundred
who had been keeping vigil, and they followed him home. Then,
in the November night of a chill that his overcoat could not
altogether shut out and a darkness that the torches could not
really dispel, with the sound of feet all around, unordered, all
going in the same direction but with no resemblance to the
clear rhythm of a march, Ulyss began to realize what had come
to him. He was President. He belonged to these people and
they to him, and they trusted him. They waited outside his
house for him to speak, and he turned to face them. He could
not see them: it was too dark and there were too many of them;
but they could see him, standing alone in the flickering glare
from the torches.

He said a few words in appreciation of their confidence. There
was something more he wanted to give them, an assurance, a
pledge, but it was hard to find words for it. 'The responsibilities
of the position I feel, but accept them without fear,' he said at
last, knowing it was not altogether what he meant, but trusting
it would be understood. He used the phrase again in his inaugural address, and wise men frowned. His would be such
responsibilities as required humility. But that night in Galena,
speaking directly to his fellow citizens and receiving their direct
answer, Ulyss felt that he had a standard so simple that it made
all else simple: the will of the people expressed through him, the
choice of the people. With that to guide him he had in truth
nothing to fear.

The President-Elect went to Washington and set to work.
There was much to be done, but the amount of his work

troubled him less than the number of people eager to help him. Political leaders were anxious to tell him of the balances that must be preserved, of the sections and men of influence and local problems that must enter into his strategy. Washburne and Rawlins wistfully waited hour by hour for him to ask advice of them. These were concerned by his problems in general, but beyond them was a multitude of men with specific suggestions, from office seekers high and low to Corbin, the fiancé of Grant's sister, who presented him with an entire inaugural address.

Badeau opened the thick manuscript, and began reading, 'Fellow citizens, I appear before you at this time ——'

'Seal that,' said Ulyss abruptly. 'Put it away, right now, and make sure that nobody touches it till after the fourth of March.'

Letters asking for office he would not read at all. It was a definite order, but Badeau, who was in charge of the correspondence, occasionally broke it to mention some particularly important figure who was willing to enter the new administration. Grant listened without reproof but without comment, and those letters also went unanswered. No one was in his confidence, not because there were not many whom he trusted, but because all these matters were his responsibility, not theirs. As a general he had never called councils of war; as President he did not intend to let his authority be blown about by the puffy breezes of advice. He would make his decisions with his own mind, the mind the people had chosen.

Even Julia was shut out from his preparations. She had no wish to advise him, but she was curious about his plans, and she was really concerned about the inaugural address.

'Mr. Washburne has had such long experience, and Mr. Conkling, he's a wonderful orator. They'd both be so glad to help ——'

'They'd write me a fine speech all right, but it wouldn't be mine.'

'But Ulyss — you know ——' Julia stopped, too afraid of hurting him to persist, too afraid for the appearance he would make to avoid the subject.

'Yes, I know I'm not much of a speaker. But I'll pull through all right, and if I don't I can always get Jesse to help out.' Laughter put a stop to that attempt of Julia's, and she made no more. If Ulyss were so sure of himself he might make the speech safely after all, and she was too absorbed in her deep happiness to worry very much about anything.

As February began to dwindle the wonder and irritation over Grant's silence became alarm. It was chiefly the cabinet that troubled the repose of his friends. Some were concerned for the quality of the choices, some for the political wisdom of the entire composition, and some were afraid that they themselves had not been given a place. Ulyss said nothing, sometimes not even to the men he had chosen. His silence piqued or enraged many people, but to Rawlins it was insupportable. The chief of staff was becoming a bitter man. He had come to Grant at Cairo when he was one among dozens of brigadiers, and had gone with him through all the military victories that had twisted so quickly into personal humiliations, through the long struggle with purblind authority, through the bloody campaigns that had made him the country's hero. It was Rawlins who had first seen what the outline of Grant's life was to be, Rawlins who had done most to give it the necessary shadings and emphasis, and now Rawlins waited while the months slipped off to finality for a word that was not given him.

'I should think Arizona would suit you well,' Grant said at last. 'I always did think an active command was the thing for you, if we could only have spared you from the staff, and the climate would be good for your trouble ——' Rawlins's white face silenced him. Without a word the chief of staff left the room, and a few minutes later Ulyss learned that he had gone home, that he was feeling ill.

'He's not getting any better,' Porter lamented. 'I thought when he didn't have to live in camp any more he might throw it off, but it seems to me that lately it's been even worse.' Ulyss said nothing. He knew how ill Rawlins was. He too had seen the thin white cheeks marked with unearthly red, and heard the cough that now racked even those who listened to it. But he knew that Rawlins had not taken to his bed that day because of his consumptive fever. Ulyss waited for his chief of staff to come back, knowing that he could not bear to stay away.

In a few days he came, directly to Ulyss. 'I won't go to Arizona,' he said.

'Of course not, if you don't want to,' said Ulyss gently. 'But I want you to take some sort of place, Rawlins. You've been a good friend to me, and I'd like you to work with me now.'

'I ought to be Secretary of War,' said Rawlins. He leaned a little on the desk, and his face was entirely white now. 'God-damn it, you know it, but you don't want ——'

'I'd be glad if you'd take the place. I'd thought of you for it, but I didn't like to ask because ——'

'I can do it. You shouldn't have hesitated.' Rawlins did not smile, and gave Ulyss a level look as if to say that he would not render thanks for his due, yet Ulyss was touched with sudden pity. Rawlins knew well enough the tormenting strain of the office he had chosen, and must know how quickly it would consume the strength he so desperately needed. What could he find in it that would be worth so great a price? Power, position, title? He knew their nature too well. It was something else, an aura of office that drew alike the naïve and the wise, the unscrupulous, the upright, the men of no distinction and the great of the land. A nonexistent thing for which some men sacrificed dignity, and Rawlins would give life itself.

It was Rawlins who rode with Grant to the Capitol on Inauguration Day. Ulyss had refused to ride with Johnson, and therefore the retiring President did not attend the ceremony at all. He was almost the only one who stood aside. It seemed to the nation that Grant's inauguration marked the end of a struggle as clearly as had Appomattox, for he stood without real commitments to any party or group. The entire country, North and South, farmers and miners of the west, merchants and men of industry of the east, could unite behind him, and he had shown in the war that he knew how to use overwhelming strength. He would know how to use this greater strength that was now given him, not for the tragic necessity of subduing half the nation, but to make real the peace he had enforced. The country believed in him, even those who had not voted for him joined in glowing assurances of his success, and the packed crowds sped him down Pennsylvania Avenue in one long shout.

Grant gave his promise in his address, the address he had so rigorously kept a secret to insure that no one would find in it any voice but his own. 'I have taken this oath without mental reservation and with the determination to do to the best of my ability all that is required of me. . . . The office has come to me unsought; I commence its duties untrammeled. I bring to it a conscious desire and determination to fill it to the best of my ability to the satisfaction of the people.'

So many there to hear him, and his words could reach so few. But they stood still, the soldiers and the plain people and the marching clubs and the negroes and the office-seekers, a dense, unfeatured mass attentive to what only the handful in front could hear. Those far back, on the fringe of the crowd, could scarcely even see the new President, only a tiny figure that sometimes chopped at the air, but they stood still too.

'On all leading questions agitating the public mind I will always express my views to Congress and urge them according to my judgment, and when I think it advisable will exercise the constitutional privilege of interposing a veto to defeat measures which I oppose; but all laws will be faithfully executed, whether they meet my approval or not. I shall on all subjects have a policy to recommend, but none to enforce against the will of the people.'

Behind him Julia and the children. He knew how she looked, serene and unruffled. The wife of a President makes no show of her emotions in public. Was she remembering Hardscrabble and Galena? Probably not — she never stored memories, except of family trivia to make her smile and shake her head. His memories were as black gulfs in his mind, that sometimes opened under him.

'In conclusion I ask patient forbearance one toward another throughout the land, and a determined effort on the part of every citizen to do his share toward cementing a happy union. . . .'

His voice had dropped so low that almost no one beyond himself could hear it.

At dinner that night, at the White House, the Grants became conscious of rhythmic footsteps outside the door. Before he actually heard the sound Ulyss had a sudden picture of his cabin at City Point, with the same unobtrusive beat, beat, beat, the continuous background for the maps he studied. Napkin in hand, he went to the door and spoke to the sentry he discovered.

'How many of you are there?'

The young man's heels clicked as he came to salute. 'Two more on the main floor, sir, and several at the doors.'

'How long has it been the custom to have sentries in the White House?'

'Since the beginning of the war, sir. For President Lincoln and President Johnson.'

'Go tell your commanding officer that I don't want sentries, and to have the others recalled too.'

'Yes, sir.' The sentry saluted again and walked off, his

quick, precise steps fading into silence down the corridor.
Ulyss smiled as he went back to his seat. It was a little thing,
certainly, but even a little thing can be a symbol, and he
believed in symbols.

Two days after the inauguration the list of cabinet appointments was sent to the Senate, and released to the press. It was
received eagerly, and searched for the new, austere principle
Grant must have used as he evolved it in isolation. Washburne
for State; A. T. Stewart of New York for Treasury; Rawlins
for War; Rockwood Hoar of Massachusetts for Attorney
General; Creswell of Maryland for Postmaster General; Borie
of Pennsylvania for Navy; Cox of Ohio for Interior. Some very
good men, some good enough, some indifferent — where was
the guiding principle? There was an effort to find it in the
wide variation in the politics of the nominees: Grant is choosing
the best men where he finds them, Grant is bound by no claims
of party. But men who were unhampered by the will to believe
that Grant would straightway lead the country to peace and
reason, saw that there was no underlying cohesion in the new
cabinet, no pattern of policy, not even a nonpartisan unity.
It was not a group with seven members, but simply seven men.
And as the people talked, commending the wide range, approving this member or another, there was a silent undercurrent of
disappointment, too vague to be fastened on any one fact, but
real nevertheless. Something that the country had expected,
that it had not itself defined, had not been given it.

'Look at these papers,' Grant said to Babcock, half in complaint, half in bewilderment. 'There's not a single nomination
that somebody doesn't object to, or wonder why I didn't name
somebody else I hardly know at all.'

'It's always that way,' Babcock answered easily. 'People
are never satisfied with a cabinet.'

'Nobody tried to choose my staff when I was a general,'

said Ulyss moodily. 'A man's got to work his own way, not the way some fool paper thinks.'

In the Senate, however, there was more noteworthy opposition. The political leaders were aghast to see the cabinet posts, the principalities of the new conquest, assigned with no sense of empire whatever. Did this Grant think he had been elected in a vacuum? Some of the nominations were an injury to party interests, and all of them were an injury to party feelings. Yet confirmation was a necessity. Rawlins, Cox, and Creswell could not be questioned. Nobody knew anything about Borie. It was discovered that he was a wealthy citizen of Philadelphia, a philanthropist in poor health who played a good game of cards, a friend of Grant's; and he had not known of his nomination as Secretary of the Navy until he read of it in his morning paper. He did not want it; he knew nothing of the navy nor of official life, and did not wish to learn, but he saw that Grant had meant to do him a favor, and returned it by allowing himself to be appointed until he could tactfully resign.

There was some opposition to Hoar, deep-felt though helpless. He was a Massachusetts man, with a mind as luminous as New England autumns, a wit as sharp and bracing as New England winds, and a sense of rectitude as unyielding as New England granite. He was certain to prove troublesome in some delicate matters concerning the Department of Justice, but there was no reason against a unanimous confirmation. The silent dissenters submitted, and trusted to the political event.

No one was surprised that Washburne had been given an office, for even Grant, with his horror of buying and selling obligations, would remember the man who had stood by him in the first precarious years of the war and had kept guard on his political career. It had been generally expected that Washburne would be Secretary of the Treasury, for his work in the House had made him a financial reputation. But State —— He had never had the least interest in foreign affairs. He had

never even stirred beyond the boundaries of the country. And
in the last ten years, in which the United States had been occupied entirely by its own struggle, foreign problems had banked
up around it in a miasmic fog. There were disagreements with
Denmark and with Canada, and a slowly increasing tension
with Spain. Most serious of all, there were claims against
England based on the damage done by the Confederate cruiser
Alabama, claims that all thought must be settled by a large
price, and some felt could be satisfied only by the cession of
Canada. The State Department was murmurous with coming
storms, and there was wide uncertainty of the wisdom of
putting Washburne at its head.

'That's all right,' Ulyss explained. 'Washburne's going to
be Minister to France, really.'

'But this nomination ——'

'It's only for a few days. Washburne feels the French would
think he amounted to more if he'd been Secretary of State and
not just a representative from Illinois.'

Thus the matter was arranged, and Grant had to find another
man for the State Department. He had originally chosen Wilson
of Iowa to succeed Washburne's token tenure, but now Wilson
declined. He could not afford it, he said. Perhaps too after a
week of reflection he was reluctant to enter a cabinet chiefly
remarkable for the number of objections to it. Grant had also
considered Motley the historian, a friend of Sumner's, and
certainly a man learned in the ways of foreigners, but had
decided against it after an interview. 'He parts his hair in the
middle and wears a monocle,' Grant told Badeau. 'I might as
well get the Earl of Clarendon to run the State Department.'
Motley he would not ask, and Wilson would not accept, and he
turned to Hamilton Fish of New York, who was well traveled,
steady, widely respected, but uninterested in office. Grant
asked him and Fish refused, but before the refusal came his
name was sent to the Senate. Then Ulyss wrote again, asking

him to accept if only for a little while, and sent the letter by Babcock. Babcock could persuade anybody to anything, and he came back with Fish's temporary agreement.

All these nominations had to be confirmed. Misgivings on the use of Federal departments as compliments to friends or stimulants to prestige were not adequate grounds for refusal, nor was dislike of the unyielding quality in such a man as Hoar, But A. T. Stewart for the Treasury — there was a mistake, an impossibility, and the Senate fell on it with righteous delight.

It had seemed to Ulyss that Stewart was a particularly good choice. He was supposed to be the richest man in the country, and his great store in New York was a model of consistent profit and success. What better qualifications could there be for a Secretary of the Treasury? He had been an immigrant, and public office would have a special meaning for him, a fulfillment that his riches could not give. The appointment seemed a rare combination of public good and private friendship. Stewart was indeed confirmed by unanimous vote, but almost immediately it was discovered that he was legally ineligible. No person 'concerned in trade or commerce' might be Secretary of the Treasury.

It was an old law, almost forgotten, but it served the party leaders. Grant requested that it be set aside, and some of the weaker spirits in the Senate, men who thought their struggle against Johnson had been a personal thing, would have consented, but Sumner and others had the suggestion sent to committee. Stewart offered to put his business in the hands of trustees while he held office, with the profits to go to charity, but he too was refused. It was not really a question of Stewart. For four years the Senate had been winning in the ancient struggle between it and the President, and it had no wish to lose ground in that struggle simply because the President was now another man. Grant, who had been forced on the party by popular prejudice, had shown a disconcerting indifference to party interests. He should be instructed as soon as possible in his own interests.

The nomination was perforce withdrawn. Grant did it reluctantly, but it was clear that he could not win over the Senate, and he was a little frightened by its sudden opposition. He had seen Johnson thwarted and tormented, and had been sure that he himself could have avoided that futile struggle, as an onlooker at a chess game is sure he would not have made the losing move. But now, with the inauguration ceremonies scarcely finished, he too found himself opposed to Congress. He was not sure how it had happened — surely it was only an accident, a misunderstanding he could soon put right. He did not insist on Stewart, and when the party leaders came to talk over other possibilities for the Treasury Ulyss did not listen to them blankly and retire to make his own uninfluenced choice.

'There's Boutwell of the Internal Revenue Bureau,' they said. 'He's a good man, and he'd add strength ——'

'Are you sure he'd be acceptable to the Senate?' With Borie holding office only temporarily, and the general muddle over the Secretaryship of State, Ulyss dared not make another nomination that he was not certain would be confirmed.

'Oh, sure, not a doubt of it.'

'All right. If you think so ...'

The Bureau of Internal Revenue had an unlovely reputation, but no one had ever suggested that Boutwell was not personally honest. He had been a member of the Joint Committee of Fifteen on reconstruction, and had been one of the leaders in Johnson's impeachment. He held to the protectionist creed of the Radicals, a belief that might not have been shared by Stewart, who had grown rich in the importing trade. But the beauty of Boutwell's appointment lay in his Massachusetts origin, for Attorney General Hoar was also from that state, which was too small to justify two out of seven places. Thus Boutwell represented at once a victory and a reserve force, and Grant sat down to preside over his first cabinet meeting wiser in the ways of his new world.

John Aaron Rawlins, 1831–1869

CHAPTER TWENTY-TWO

APPOINTMENTS — Grant's days were crammed with them, and they overflowed into his uneasy dreams at night. He had known that for the first few months of his administration he would be bayed by the pack of office-seekers. Civil war had not abashed them in Lincoln's time, the national grief at Lincoln's death had not kept them from descending upon Johnson, and in this peaceful year there would certainly be nothing to restrain them. But for all his observation Ulyss had not realized how difficult the thing would be. He had wanted to make his own decisions, to choose men he thought fitted to their places. Necessarily then most of his early appointments were of men he knew personally, friends and relatives and their friends, and the newspapers promptly cried nepotism. 'No president,' said the Washington wits, 'was ever got in the family way so soon after inauguration.' Even his personal staff was not uncriticized, for many of his aides came with him from army headquarters. Rawlins, of course, had a new eminence of his own, and moved across the street to the War Department, but Porter and Babcock came to serve the President as secretaries, and Badeau lived at the White House while he completed a military biography of Grant. These men were Ulyss's friends, but the papers found something sinister in them too. The White House is full of uniforms. Are we to be ruled by a military junto?

Appointments and uncertainties, appointments and criticism, appointments and utter weariness. With hundreds of places to be filled and thousands of men eager to fill them, with a troubling hostility in the Senate, and in himself a growing awareness that nothing was as simple as he had believed it would be, Ulyss grew ready to take help. Sumner and Schurz, men who had led the party through the war and the following convulsions, were ready to give it, expected to give it, but Ulyss distrusted them. Sumner was alien to him, a fanatic intellectual with enormous erudition and no humor, who considered everything in the light of ideas which were sometimes good and sometimes bad but never to be questioned, since they were Sumner's. Schurz was also a man of theories, even more suspicious to Ulyss because of their foreign origin. Grant turned to another group among the party leaders, to men who were already his friends: Conkling, a superbly handsome man and a rousing orator, with a minute knowledge of the party structure in New York; Cameron, the political emperor of Pennsylvania now that Thad Stevens was dead; Morton, who spun with the Washington wind and carried the votes of Indiana with him; Chandler, a good companion who held Michigan in fee. During the war Grant had chosen to work with men who knew war as their business, who made their marches and fought their battles without stopping for speeches; and now that he was concerned with politics he was going to work with men who knew politics as their business, who concerned themselves with elections and not with some rigorous unattainable ideal.

Affairs went more smoothly then. Offices were filled with
men suggested by state leaders, men who had deserved well of
state organizations or who were of definite use to the national
organization, and there was no such outcry over the appointment of assistant secretaries and chief clerks and collectors of
revenue as there had been over the cabinet. True, some unfriendly papers said they were disappointed in the character
of the new office-holders, and there were still occasional objections to the number of uniforms around the White House, but
there was no word of disapproval from Congress, and that was
the important thing.

A few months after the inauguration Grant received General
Lee. The Confederate leader was in Washington on business,
and came to call on the new President with a punctilio at once
gallant and awkward. Grant was glad to see him: he had admired him personally ever since their meeting, and he was
always eager for any sign that the old enmities were fading.
But as Lee entered, Appomattox rose up between them, not
deliberately on either side, not with bitterness, but as a memory
ineradicable from either mind, a brief hour that would hold
them distant from each other all their lives, and bind them together for the whole of history. Grant looked at a man who
was grayer though no less erect, with a face that spoke of
suffering in its very stillness. Lee looked at a man a little
heavier, a little older, with a mouth still set in obstinacy, but a
new uncertainty around the eyes. Both men saw figures of four
years before, uniformed and intent, with a sheet of paper between them.

'What brings you to Washington?' Grant asked.

'Some gentlemen of my acquaintance have been interested
in the construction of a railroad, and I came to see about a
franchise.'

'I see. You and I have had more to do with destroying railroads than with building them.'

There was no answer. Lee paused just long enough to indicate that he had heard the remark, and then spoke of the new constitution for Virginia, which was soon to be ratified. Grant was glad when the ordained ten minutes were over and Lee took his formal leave.

Slowly Ulyss came to know the issues that were to be his work, came to recognize them with weary patience as they recurred in the round of cabinet meetings. Reconstruction, of course, he had always with him in one form or another, from Lee's quiet, hopeful mention of the Virginia constitution to Boutwell's horror of the same constitution.

'It's madness!' cried Boutwell. 'Why have we worked four years to protect loyal men if we're going to let this stand?' He thumped indignantly a report on the composition of the new legislature, which would be dominated by a coalition of Democrats and conservative Republicans.

'Those men are loyal,' Cox observed, 'and they're some of the best-known figures in the state. Do you think men like that will permit excesses — on either side?'

'We're talking about Virginia,' said Boutwell bitterly. 'Virginia made the rebellion — it wouldn't have lasted a month if it hadn't been for her. I doubt if there's ten loyal men in the whole state. Mr. President' — he turned on Grant — 'are you going to let this stand? Is Virginia going to get off scot free?'

'I don't think I'll interfere,' said Ulyss slowly. The Virginian leaders had been writing to him and coming to talk to him for weeks, and he had come to believe in their sincerity. 'The men are loyal, and I think they'll keep the state loyal.'

There was a brief comfort for Boutwell and the other Radical leaders when the general commanding Virginia announced that all members of the legislature must take the test oath, but that resource was at once destroyed by Attorney General Hoar, who overruled the soldier. Virginia was lost. The Radicals

fell back to guard the other states, wondering if the unpredictable President would let them too slip from his party's grasp.

The problems of reconstruction, however, no longer blotted
out the rest of the world. The *Alabama* claims against England
were growing to include half the cost of the war, on the theory
that the war would not have lasted half so long without
England's help to the Confederates. Cuba was in revolt against
her Spanish mismanagers, a periodic effort that always aroused
American sympathy, and usually kept that sympathy heated
close to the point of intervention. And San Domingo wanted
to be annexed to the United States. That was one version;
another was that a group of questionable men had options on
most of the island, and wanted annexation in order to exploit
it at leisure. Whatever the truth was, the Caribbean islands
were on the agenda at almost every cabinet meeting, and
Ulyss came to think of them as hazy facts entirely surrounded
by controversy.

Usually it was Rawlins and Fish who disagreed on foreign
affairs. Fish, who had proved to be an able man, prudent, un-
excitable but stern on occasion, spoke of international law;
of the inchoate character of the Cuban rebellion; of the uncertain wisdom in accepting San Domingo's offer, and the impossibility of judging its motives. Rawlins was in favor of
action, so passionately in favor of it that it sometimes seemed
to the other members of the cabinet that it was a real flame
burning in his eyes, that it was not so much disease as his own
fervor that was consuming him. The mighty nation on which
he had kept his eyes while its citizens were dying on the battlefield could now be a reality, and hesitation seemed to him a
treachery to the dead, North and South alike.

'You can't deny,' he insisted, 'that those God-forsaken
Cubans have been treated like we'd hang a man for treating a
dog.'

'No, that's true,' Fish admitted. 'The Spanish don't make

good colonists. But Cuba belongs to them, and we've no right to interfere —— '

'Suppose,' asked Grant above Rawlins's profane rejoinder, 'we recognize the Cuban belligerents, like Spain recognized the rebs in our own war?'

'The Confederates had a president, and a congress, and a capital. The Cubans haven't anything. It looks a little ridiculous to recognize a government that's running through the jungle about ten feet ahead of its pursuers.'

'It looks Goddamn brutal,' shouted Rawlins, 'to let 'em be tortured and burned till they give in while we look up what the law says! What do we mean when we talk about freedom, anyway?'

He was quieted after a while, not by the arguments against him but by the exhaustion that flooded over him and made it impossible to talk any longer. But he never failed to return to battle when the subject of Cuba was considered again, or when the annexation of San Domingo was discussed. 'Why should we hesitate?' he demanded, with sparkling eyes. 'The Dominicans themselves want us to take them over. We're a progressive nation — they want to join us. Why should we hold back?'

'I wonder,' said Fish slowly, 'if the Dominicans really do want us. Their leaders say so, but it's hard to be sure with men like that. Most of them can be bribed, and this group of our own citizens that's so interested in the idea might not stop at that —— '

'Why not find out more about it?' Ulyss inquired. 'We haven't much to go on now, but we could send somebody down there to make a report, and then we'd know.' Fish had no objection to that, and Ulyss gave the mission to Babcock. Ulyss was drawn by the idea of San Domingo, but was more willing than Rawlins to wait for the accumulation of facts that would be their own argument.

These were the things that Ulyss found to be the body of his work, these questions rising from Spain, from the Caribbean, from England, from Virginia across the river. To him they had no relationship beyond their common difficulty and the passion with which they were argued, for he had no clear realization of the mood that was making itself felt in the nation. The war had ended many lives and many traditions, but it had been most significant in bringing to an end the old America. In its chaotic aftermath new beliefs appeared, new values were accepted, new ambitions began to stir, and old limits lost their meaning. It was as if the nation, having slipped close to death and clawed its way back, now looked at the world with the crystal, depthless perception of a convalescent, and with a convalescent's sense of unsuspected power. Let England make amends for having been on the wrong side, then ineptly hedging, by turning over to the newly strong America the whole expanse of Canada. Let Spain be wary of trying American patience, for America knew the right and had proved herself able to enforce it. Let no restraint be set upon American business, freed now of mercantile patterns and colonial attitudes, finding in the growth of industry the exaltation and dizzy confidence that allows a man to forget that he is mortal. Let the South stop striving after the old order and turn to the bright opportunities of a limitless world, or, if it would not, let it submit to authority and leave unhampered the men with the new vision.

No one expressed it. Almost everyone, like Grant, saw individual events in individual terms: the *Alabama* claims as Sumner's fantastic egoism, or as proper grievances against a half-hostile country; the South as a controversy so entangled with justice, fear, expediency, and sincere uncertainty that it was impossible to solve; and the new relationships of business and policy were not seen at all. The temper of a time cannot easily be defined and analyzed by the men of the time, but it can be felt. This was the new America, strong, ambitious, vulgar. It filled Henry Adams, that man of frigid brilliance,

with distaste and even despair. It filled with nameless excitement and tragic impatience Rawlins, who was objective only
so far as he chose to be. Grant was not affected in either of
these ways, not being given to contemplation, but he too felt
the electric air, and had a sense of being surrounded by unseen
immensities that sometimes elated and sometimes depressed
him, and sometimes only made him restless.

'You see' — Jay Gould's dark eyes and precise tone helped
to give his argument impeccable clarity — 'it's the price in
London that really counts. If they say wheat goes up, it goes
up in New York too, and we haven't any say at all. We can't
affect the price they give — but we can do something about the
price our farmers get. Gold is at a premium of a little over
thirty cents to the dollar. If it was raised about ten cents,
say if every gold dollar was worth a dollar and forty-five cents,
then it would be worth while for our farmers to ship every
grain of wheat they could. I've had it all gone into ——'
Apparently it was not necessary for Ulyss to say anything
yet, though he was sure that soon the smooth logic would be
interrupted for a contribution from him. Gould and Fisk had
been so anxious that he should make his journey to Boston as a
guest on their boat, and had been so quick to introduce this
unlikely subject, that it seemed clear they wanted some reaction from the President. Ulyss sat in silence while Gould
painted his enormous panorama of the grain ripe and golden
in the western fields, and crawling in innumerable freight cars
to take ship at New York. There were three hundred other
ships also in the picture, sailing out of the Danube with wheat
for England that ought to be supplied by America. The picture
was very clear, but Ulyss was uneasy, for there was something
in this talk that he did not fully understand. He looked around
him, at Fisk, florid and glistening in an admiral's uniform that
looked overly splendid for a coastal steamer; at Corbin, Grant's

new brother-in-law and apparently an old friend of Gould's; at Julia, who was eating her dinner with quiet enjoyment, untroubled by the vast affairs the gentlemen chose to discuss.

Corbin and Fisk, Ulyss was sure, were waiting for Gould to finish his exposition and give the President an opportunity to express an opinion. Opinion of what? The theory, or plan, seemed to Ulyss to have nothing to do with his office. It hinged on the price of gold, and that was the affair of business men such as these, not of the President. Perhaps it was really Boutwell's policy that concerned them. The Secretary of the Treasury had one very firm idea: the reduction of the national debt. Taxation stayed heavy and tariffs stayed high, government expenses were low, and the mountain of debt the war had thrown up was being quarried away. Grant could not see, however, that the government debt had any real connection with this discussion of wheat, not enough to bring Corbin's eyes dabbing quickly at his, as though it were a thing the man had determined not to do and could not help. Fisk did not trouble to pretend, but sprawled in his chair, his gross belly making horizontal creases in his uniform, staring at the President.

The time had come. Gould ended with a glowing vision of the farmer finding a reward for his labor that he thoroughly deserved and rarely received, and thereby giving impetus to the nation's prosperity, which was already great but could be much greater. Now he waited for Ulyss to speak. Ulyss said nothing, and the silence grew so tangible that Julia noticed it and looked up.

Fisk was neither confused nor intimidated. 'What's your view?' he demanded.

'I think,' said Ulyss slowly, 'that our prosperity is fictitious to a certain extent. The bubble might as well be tapped in one way as another.' Other men of business believed that, he knew. They talked of the unsteady foundation the greenbacks made for any true progress, and some spoke of having to get worse before one can get better. They were eminent men, and better friends of Grant's than Gould and Fisk, who had so suddenly discovered their admiration of him. Ulyss's words were indefinite, they were as vague as the question so vaguely put to him, but he knew they would have a discouraging effect. He was glad to be discouraging; he resented feeling that Gould was trying to get something out of him without letting him know what it was. Fisk blew out his cheeks and sighed with an open disappointment that was disarming, and tried to catch Corbin's eye, but Corbin was talking about something else with great speed, as if each word were a milestone between him and a dangerous corner.

Nothing more was said about wheat on that journey, nor when Grant returned to New York. Gould and Fisk entertained him there, as if to show that his rebuff had not cooled their friendship. Ulyss did not like them — not as well as he liked Jay Cooke, for example, who could take a drink and play a game of cards with an enjoyment as simple as though he were not possessed of millions of dollars and lord of the Northern Pacific. Ulyss was proud to call Jay Cooke friend, but he was uncomfortable with Gould, despite the financier's munificent courtesy and subtle deference; and Fisk's profane gusto was no more reassuring. Nevertheless, both were famous for their financial feats, and Ulyss knew poverty too well to regard wealth lightly. He accepted their attentions, and forgot his uncomfortable, indefinite suspicions of them.

After Grant returned to Washington Corbin held conference with Gould. 'There's no need to give it up,' Grant's brother-in-law insisted. 'I know he sounded discouraging, but he often does. It's his way when he isn't sure. As soon as he sees the advantage for the farmers he'll pass the word to Boutwell to hold the government gold, and we're fixed up.'

'Who's going to make him see?' Gould's tone was neither

irritated nor eager, as though he had asked merely for one more figure to use in making his enormous, impersonal calculation.

'I can do it.' Corbin leaned forward and tapped Gould's arm, as if to emphasize their comradeship, but the uncertain, half-frightened look in his eyes made that emphasis offensive. 'I've a good deal of influence with him. He knows he can trust my judgment, and he'll listen to me.'

'Mm.' Gould would not commit himself despite Corbin's urging, but after several more talks he did begin to buy gold. Not very much at first, but he made sure that part of it was in Corbin's name. The man's influence with the President might be questioned, but his relationship was certain.

Much of that summer Grant spent in travel, to West Point, to Boston, to Saratoga. The country remembered Lincoln, who had gone to the Soldiers' Home in Washington when he felt the need of cooler air in which to work; and Johnson, who had left his labors only to go forth and campaign for his beliefs. Many saw in this President's freedom a happy sign of slackening tension, while some saw a lazy disregard of the executive's responsibilities. But Ulyss was not entirely free. His problems rode with him on his travels, and often called him back to the capital for discussion with the clashing opinions in his cabinet. San Domingo could be forgotten until Babcock's return, and the *Alabama* claims had little urgency when Congress was not in session, but there was always Cuba.

The American minister had been sent to Spain with the suggestion that Cuba be allowed to buy its freedom with money borrowed from the United States. The proposal was to be withdrawn at the end of September, but Spain delayed decision and used Cuba as a factor in her own internal politics. Meanwhile American ships, American citizens, the American flag were suffering indignities verging on outrage from the Cuban authorities, who seemed to have all the Spanish arrogance and disposition to cruelty with none of the Spanish grace. And tales of the savage reprisals on the rebels were adding the impulsive power of indignation to American pride. The subject was considered yet again at a cabinet meeting in August. Recognize the rebels as belligerents, Rawlins insisted. Why waste time waiting for Spain to make a decision, when clearly she would never relinquish her rotten grasp on the island until she was forced? Why waste time — the question obsessed Rawlins that summer. He was in a hurry, to see Cuba freed and under America's protection, to see San Domingo annexed, to see his whole glorious vision of America's future fulfilled, at once, at once.

The answer from Secretary Fish was always the same. It was too soon for recognition, it was against the ancient principles of international law. The objections seemed pale and timid as against Rawlins's driving urgency, but they held, for a little while at least. It was a precarious line that Fish had taken: the cause of intervention was much more clearly seen and more easily defended to the emotions than the nation's need of peace; but he had chosen his policy and he meant to hold to it. If after every cabinet meeting, every discussion with the President, he could be sure only that his course would be upheld for a little time, he was well enough pleased, for the little times, the doubtful days and grudging weeks, may become salvaged years, and merge at last into that eternity where passions cool and a man may find what wisdom is.

Early in September Ulyss passed through New York again on his way to Saratoga, and stayed at Corbin's house. His brother-in-law was prompt to bring up the subject of the wheat crop, and this time the plan seemed to Grant to be more simple and acceptable. There was a shadowy depth in Gould that troubled Ulyss, but Corbin's enthusiasm seemed to have no overtones.

'It's such a simple thing,' he explained, 'and there's not a soul

in the country who wouldn't benefit. The farmers first, and
then the merchants, and the railroads ——'

'Yes, I see that.'

'If only the Treasury don't sell any gold while the crops are
moving. Every time it does it keeps the price from going up,
and there's no point in selling wheat to England unless gold's
at a hundred and forty-five . . .' In the quiet afternoon Corbin's
voice went on and on, and at last Ulyss sat down and wrote to
Boutwell. Probably his officer had been so intent on the government debt that he had never considered the wheat problem
at all. Ulyss pointed out to him the relationship of the price of
gold to the wheat market, and the importance of not allowing
the price to sag so that the farmer's profits would drop to
nothing. Corbin promised to mail the letter, and seemed much
impressed at his glimpse of the wide interests of the government.

The price of gold, which had been around 132, began to
waver upward. Gould bought occasionally, and sold occasionally, but his agents bought steadily. It was a slow rise at first,
but point by point the price went up, and other men began to
take interest. They bought too, selling out with a gain of a
point or two, and then watching the quotation steadily climb
far beyond the level they had fixed as reasonable. Something
very strange was happening in gold, but not even the traders
in the Gold Room, buying and selling and buying again, were
certain of what it was.

Interest began to stir outside the exchange, but Ulyss knew
nothing of it. A few days after his talk with Corbin he received
a message in Saratoga that abruptly wiped out of his mind all
the concerns and satisfactions of his office, and made his self
of eight years before more tangible than the President. Rawlins
was dying. Ulyss was not really surprised by the news: there
had been death in Rawlins's eyes that summer, and it was
knowledge of death that had made him try so hard to spur
forward the progress of events, that slow, measured parade that

will not turn aside for the helpless in its path, nor change its pace to suit the eagerness or fatigue of its marchers. So much that Rawlins had believed in, so much that he had wanted to see, to help create — and now he was dying in this summer of 1869, having held to life just long enough to see the beginning of a new nation. Hemorrhage, they said. How Rawlins would hate that, to see his life, scarlet and tangible, pouring from him.

The last train of the day had gone, and Ulyss had twenty-four hours to wait before he could begin his journey. Every hour that he waited, and that he spent on the long trip back to Washington, he saw Rawlins: in the bare, cluttered office at Cairo; in that bleak hour at Fort Donelson when Grant's new-born career all but died; at Vicksburg, loyal, vigilant, almost a part of his chief; through the Wilderness campaign and the strained months before Petersburg, not so close then but still holding a unique place; and then the time under Johnson, when Ulyss could not so much remember Rawlins as sense him, the friend with clear eyes who weighed each word and every action and molded them into a logical and inescapable chain. Rawlins... At their last cabinet meeting his plea for Cuba had so exhausted him that he had sunk to his chair in near collapse.

'I have been your adjutant,' he had cried to Grant, 'and I think you will excuse me for being earnest.'

'Certainly,' Grant had answered quickly, 'and you are still my adjutant.' It was as though in those few words Rawlins had already told him the thing that this urgent telegram could only confirm. Your adjutant, he had said. Since then he had been chief of staff, a title in which he took more pride, and General, and Secretary of War, but he had said, your adjutant.

Grief rode southward with Grant. He had never given his full self to anyone: not to Rawlins; not to such young men as Babcock, for whom he had much affection and entire trust; not to any of the political and business friends who came to spend comfortably masculine evenings with him. Each had some part of him: cabinet members sometimes knew his intentions when Julia did not; other politicians might know some points of his policy when cabinet members did not; his young secretaries knew a Ulysses Grant never shown to others. Julia, of course, had all of him, but that was the merging of love rather than the mutual complement of friendship. Yet Rawlins, who had sometimes seemed more alien to Grant than any of his other intimates, was bound to him as none of them were bound. Their first years together had marked each with the other, forever.

Mrs. Rawlins met Ulyss at the foot of the stairs. 'He's gone,' she said. 'Not an hour ago.' Grant looked at her, remembering the Miss Hurlbut Rawlins had undertaken to protect at Vicksburg just six years before. She had changed, but not only with the alterations of marriage and motherhood. She was thinner and her face was white, but even in her sorrow there was that bright, dangerous red along her cheekbones, and when she pressed her handkerchief to her lips she glanced at it automatically, in hopeless habit. Rawlins had passed to her the legacy he had received from his first wife, a bequest that would bring her to him soon. Ulyss touched her hand, but suddenly he could not speak.

He went upstairs alone. Rawlins lay long and still beneath the sheet, black hair and beard startling against the linen. The utter stillness of the room shouted that he was dead, but to Ulyss the shattering truth of it was made clear by his face, quiet at last, with his eyes, that had blazed and darkened with his mood, hooded and blind. Ulyss felt tears on his face, a taunt to the dead as they caressed his own warm flesh. He wished that his friend had had time to say good-bye. But perhaps he had said it, more adequately than he could have had he waited:

'I have been your adjutant, and I think you will excuse me for being earnest.'

Beautiful to Annex

CHAPTER TWENTY-THREE

FALL had already come to these Pennsylvania hills, even in mid-September. The trees had not yet entirely turned, but the woods had lost their summer look. The air was pointed with crystal, and fallen leaves flew across the croquet ground and in and out of the wickets, as if in derision of the balls that moved so heavily and so often in the wrong direction. Ulyss was not at all sure that he could beat Porter, and he worked hard at it. It was pleasant to overcome the mallet's tendency to hit to the right, to calculate the absurd angles between wickets, to wring a groan from Porter by sending his ball into the sumac bushes down the hill; and to forget the swarm of problems, regrets, and uncertainties that were forever buzzing at him.

A servant came out from the house and spoke to Porter, who nodded and turned back to the game. It was his turn, and Ulyss waited for him with a smug smile. Porter's ball was in an impossible position, and Ulyss hit the stake resoundingly while the young man was still struggling back up the hill.

'That's two for you,' he protested. 'I'm not even good competition any more. Will you excuse me a moment? There's someone waiting to see me.'

Ulyss followed him in idly, a little resentful that even a Sunday in this far-off place must be interrupted. Porter turned and handed him a letter. 'It's from Mr. Corbin,' he said. 'Mine is just a note asking me to make sure that you get it.'

Ulyss frowned a little and took the letter outside. He was beginning to discover that he was not really fond of his brother-in-law. There was no reason that he could find in the letter for writing it at all, for it was only a repetition of all the arguments against releasing the government gold. Ulyss put it into his pocket and went back to the house to see if Porter wanted another game.

The messenger was still standing where he had been left, tapping his foot impatiently. 'Is it all right?' he asked as soon as he saw the President.

'All right,' Ulyss answered, and looked at him with some surprise when he caught up his cap and left the house half running.

'Queer sort of chap,' said Porter as he entered.

'Yes. Didn't seem as well trained as most of the post-office men.'

'Oh, he wasn't. He was a special messenger.' Ulyss stared at him, and Porter elaborated, 'He said something about coming all the way from New York with the letter.'

Pulling the envelope out of his pocket, Ulyss found proof. It was unstamped, and marked 'By Bearer.' What was there in the rambling, essentially pointless message to make it important enough to be borne several hundred miles by hand? Ulyss could not tell, and tried to forget it, but it troubled him.

The messenger had hurried to the nearest telegraph station.

It hadn't been as easy a job as he'd expected, what with the miles of dust he'd had to walk, and the long time he'd had to wait for the reply, but he was just about through now. He woke up the drowsy operator and gave him the message, 'All right.' It was addressed to Mr. James Fisk, New York City.

All the rest of the day Ulyss thought about the letter. He talked it over with Porter, and told him of the paltry contents.

'I couldn't say about the letter,' Porter answered, 'but probably it has something to do with this gold business.'

'Gold?'

'Yes — the price has been going up fast lately, you know.'

'Yes, on account of the wheat.'

'That's it. And there seems to be some speculation on it, too. I got a letter the other day saying that five hundred thousand dollars of it was being held in my name. I refused it of course, but just the same ——'

Then Ulyss was sure he understood. Corbin was speculating on the rising market, careless of involving the President's name, or perhaps eager to involve it. Ulyss set his jaw and went to Julia.

'I want you to write a letter to Jennie,' he said. 'Tell her to make her fool of a husband get out of the market — he's got no right to mix up in a thing like that.'

'Yes, dear. Now?'

'Please.' Julia put aside her sewing and went to the desk, and Ulyss watched her in satisfaction. She could handle it all right. Women could make such things very clear, without the awkwardness of an official letter.

My husband, wrote Julia, is annoyed by your husband's speculations. 'You must close them as quick as you can.' The letter was a bitter blow to Corbin. Only a few days before there had been the telegram, at last the definite word of understanding and agreement, and now this. It seemed outright malice, but however difficult it was to make sure what the

President thought there was no doubt that what he ordered must be obeyed.

Corbin went to Gould and asked him to buy his interest in the pool. 'I've got to tell Grant I'm out of the market,' he said ruefully, 'and I expect I'd better tell him the truth.'

For a moment Gould said nothing, but surveyed this man who had not enough courage to make his imagination useful. It was Corbin who had been most enthusiastic about the scheme, Corbin who had boasted of his influence with the President and, through the President, with the government, and now it was Corbin who cringed and whined and had no thought but to come to heel. Gould made out a check for a hundred thousand dollars and pushed it across the desk.

'You won't talk about Mrs. Grant's letter?'

'No — no, certainly not.' Corbin put the check in his wallet and straightened his shoulders, but all real dignity had been stripped from him, and he could not pretend to it under Gould's aloof and mocking eyes.

Everyone knew now what was happening to gold. Fisk was appearing daily in the Gold Room, roaring his bids and boasting of his powers. Importers and others who had need of gold, the metal, were crowding in, frantic to secure it before the price shot up to impossibility, and were imploring Washington for help. Gould was selling, as only his brokers knew, but not to Fisk, and from time to time he bought a little in order not to advertise his knowledge.

On Friday Boutwell came by the White House to see Grant, who had come back from Pennsylvania. 'I think,' said the Secretary of the Treasury, 'that the government had better sell some gold. There's an awful howl in New York about the way it's going up, and talk of a corner on it. That wouldn't do.'

'No, of course not,' Ulyss agreed. 'How much do you think you ought to let go?'

'Three million would break the combination, I'm sure.'

'Better make it five.' Three million seemed an absurdly small twig to shake at this runaway bull, but Boutwell seemed to think five unnecessary. They settled on four, and the Secretary went back to his office to give the order.

In New York the quotation passed 145 that morning, and then began to skyrocket as the available supply was captured. The fractional rises that had seemed so alarming a few days before were forgotten as gold went to 150, 155, 160; and Fisk was shouting that he would put it to 200. The sweating, half-mad men around him were sure he would. The tumult in the room was intolerable, as men screamed and swore, and some laughed in helpless, tragic abandon, and others wept.

The ticker tapped out a message: the Treasury wished to sell four million dollars of gold. It was a small thing: the amount did not even cover the bid that Fisk was making at the moment; but this was real gold. At its solid touch the hollow tower of speculation collapsed, at once and completely, in utter chaos. In fifteen minutes the price of gold was 132, and Black Friday was over.

Brokers failed, their respected firms and honored names swept away in the hurricane Gould had ridden. Speculators were presented with losses as fantastic as the profits they had imagined, and many of them canceled the bill with suicide. Fisk himself was ruined for a little while, but that amiable buccaneer shifted many of his losses to other people, and maintained his alliance with Gould, who had emerged from the wreckage with another fortune. The economy of the nation trembled, but did not crumble. It was pounding forward in the prosperity of the new railroads that were opening up the northern wilderness and the empty plains, with all their treasures of lumber and metal and the land itself. Black Friday was a catastrophe, but when it proved limited in scope people tended to set it down as a dreadful thing of which they disapproved, and to turn their thoughts back to the opportunities with which their prosperous world was filled.

A few men, a very few, wondered at the irresponsibility that had made the affair possible, and wondered if it were widespread among the group that had gathered so much power without anyone's knowing very clearly how it had happened. It was a useless question. Since the war the nation and its affairs had grown as some youths grow, into a rangy, uncoordinated, raw-boned figure, given to jerky gestures and of an awkward bearing, with no disciplined control. Government, business, labor fought for their own interests, made blunders and won their individual victories with little reference to each other and no check from any source. If Black Friday had resulted from a carelessness of the public interest that came close to crime, there was none to punish it. The government could investigate, but found nothing to prosecute, and the people were too busy to be angry.

There was little public outcry over Black Friday, further than the usual howls that the eastern bankers were sucking the country's blood, but many people felt a certain uneasiness over the odd connection of the President and his family with the affair. The Congressional investigation made clear that he had been in no way implicated in the conspiracy. He had made no promises, nor implied any agreement, nor cooperated in any way with the men who had tried to corner gold. No one did believe him guilty, but — somehow the vision they had had on his inauguration day seemed a little childish.

Babcock returned from San Domingo full of enthusiasm and laden with samples of the island's products. The members of the cabinet, gathering for a meeting, found him in the cabinet room with the samples on display, and eager to lecture them on the beauties of annexation. The trifling cost; the yearning of the people; the great number of fertile, unused acres; the wealth of ore waiting for enterprise to mine it; the strategic importance of Samana Bay as a naval base and a guard for a possible isthmian canal —— He was at his most persuasive, and Babcock could be very persuasive, but he was listened to with only the interest demanded by courtesy. When he left the room the cabinet sat down around the table, the members glancing at each other but saying nothing.

That afternoon Grant abandoned his usual routine of calling on his officers in set order for their reports. 'As you see, Babcock has returned,' he said at once. 'He's brought a treaty of annexation with him. I suppose it can't be formal, since he didn't have diplomatic powers, but we can cure that. We'll send it back to the consul for his signature, and since he's an officer of the State Department that will make it all right.'

The cabinet sat in astounded silence. Babcock had been sent to make a report, to gather fuller information than that given by the little group that was so much in favor of the plan. Grant waited, looking from one face to the next, his mouth set. He had made his suggestion. He would not weaken it by persuasion or explanation until someone answered him.

It was Cox who broke the silence that was increasing in awkwardness by the square of each passing minute. 'Mr. President,' he asked, 'has it been settled, then, that we want to annex San Domingo?'

Grant glanced at Fish, in whose department the matter lay, and at Boutwell, who had been chosen for the cabinet by the party leaders. Neither made any comment, and Ulyss passed on to the rest of the agenda.

He had not expected this. He had known they might not be enthusiastic at once, not having talked to Babcock, but this determined silence — Ulyss was surprised, and angry. There had been no objection to Seward's purchase of Alaska, an acquisition of acres of snowdrifts and a menagerie of polar bears. Why this skittishness over San Domingo? All navy men

coveted Samana Bay, and Babcock said that business men
would find the island a paradise of opportunity. 'It's unbe-
lievable,' the young man had insisted. 'There's mines there
that would make Golconda look cheap, and the soil's so rich
things grow while you look at them.' He had talked of nothing
but San Domingo since he had returned, and his enthusiasm
had made of Grant's original interest a solid determination.

The island had become Ulyss's chief preoccupation, and he
saw that it could be the answer to some of his other problems.
The South, for instance, was in a constant fever that occasionally mounted into spasms, because she could not assimilate
the freed slaves. Those awkward citizens could be settled by
the thousands on San Domingo, where they could form a state
of their own with all their rights protected and their freedom
assured, yet with their pressure removed from the social structure of the existing states. But the cabinet members seemed
filled with uneasiness at the mention of the island's name.
Ulyss did not argue with them, he was not accustomed to
cajoling his officers, but he made sure that Fish left with
Babcock's treaty in his hand.

There was no desire for San Domingo in Fish. A tropic island
with a foreign background seemed to him of little value to the
United States, and he saw, as Ulyss either did not or would not
see, the difficulties of getting the Senate to accept the proposal.
It had already put aside a treaty for the purchase of one of the
Danish West Indies, careless of offending that friendly little
nation. Refusal to annex San Domingo would offend no one
of importance except the President, and in the last few years
much of the Senate had come to regard flouting the President
as a duty and a virtue. But there was another factor that led
Fish to take up the treaty with good grace. The American
offer to help Cuba buy herself free would expire at the end of
September, in only a few days. There was not the slightest
chance that Spain would accept it, and her refusal would be

fuel to the flaming hearts of the interventionists. Recognition of belligerency would be inevitable, and after that, given Spain's temper, war — war for a few thousand half-savage men who had been brutally abused, but who were equally brutal when they had the chance; war for the holders of Cuban bonds that the junta of exiles had sown among statesmen, editors, business men, and others whose influence might be helpful. Fish had all but given up his hope for peace, and then the mighty weapon of San Domingo dropped into his hands. If President and Senate were fully occupied by Dominican problems, which were many and thorny, they would have little leisure to beat the drum for Cuba. They would not even have time to make any further oratorical complications in the tangle of the *Alabama* claims. San Domingo would be worth its price as a political will-o'-the-wisp, and Fish prepared with some satisfaction the treaty that Babcock was to take back for more formal negotiation.

There were two new members of the cabinet that fall. Borie resigned, and was replaced by Robeson of New Jersey. Very little was known of him except that he was a lawyer and a Radical Republican, and there seemed small reason for him to head the navy, but then Grant rarely gave his reasons for appointments. Rawlins's place in the War Department was given to General Belknap, a large, kindly man with a routine army career behind him, and a wife who tended to dominate him.

'I'm not quite sure,' Ulyss had said to Babcock before he made the appointment, 'whether to make it Belknap or Porter . . .'

'If I were you,' Babcock answered, 'I'd put in Belknap.' Babcock was always ready to discuss Ulyss's problems, not simply as a passive listener but with ready, friendly suggestions that Ulyss thought most helpful. The President found the young man a valuable assistant: Ulyss made him a cherished friend. 'Belknap's background is good,' Babcock continued, 'and he'd be a fine man for the job. With Mississippi and Texas still under the Department you don't want to take any chances —— Of course you wouldn't with Porter either, but Belknap seems to me to fit best.' That was the view, Ulyss found, of Chandler and Morton and his other friends among the party leaders. He appointed Belknap, to Mrs. Belknap's joy.

At one cabinet meeting, after the agenda was finished small Jesse appeared, shy, but determined. 'Gentlemen,' said Grant gravely, 'Jesse has a matter which he wishes to bring before you.'

Seven heads turned courteously to the boy, who flushed and shifted his feet in embarrassment, but began his tale with hurried earnestness. 'It's about some stamps,' he said. 'I ordered them a long time ago, a month anyway, and I sent the money. Almost three dollars, it was. I've waited and waited, and I think they've stolen it. They mustn't steal from the President's family, can they?' He was encouraged by a unanimous growl of agreement, and straightened in confidence. 'I didn't know, but I thought maybe the Secretary of War or the Secretary of State, or maybe Kelly, ought to do something about it. I didn't know, but I thought I'd ask.'

'It's a matter for the State Department,' said Fish with emphasis.

'I disagree, sir,' Belknap cried. 'As Secretary of War, I cannot allow you to infringe on my department's affairs. I'll act at once. A company, or perhaps a regiment ——'

'Gentlemen!' Attorney General Hoar's voice was all reasonableness, but cold with determination. 'You forget that Kelly is a police officer and has guarded the White House for many years. His constitutional powers are enormous — greater, I may say, than either of you possess — and his influence is beyond compare. It would plainly be a contravention of all precedent and established law to confide action to anyone but Kelly.'

The debate was prompt and bitter, until Grant called for a vote. Fish and Belknap voted for themselves, glaring at each other, but all the others for Kelly.

'The sense of this meeting,' Grant announced to his son, 'is that Kelly shall write a letter to the stamp company pointing out that their delay is alarming in view of their having already received full payment. Affirmative, five; dissenting, two.'

'Thank you,' said Jesse, and went in search of Kelly, who apparently had even greater attributes than the admiring Jesse had suspected.

In December Grant sent to the Senate two nominations for the Supreme Court. One was of Stanton, who had once greatly desired the place, but it was difficult to know what he desired now. He had shut himself away since Johnson's acquittal, out of the political world where he had played so stormy a part, into a silent solitude where he could face his self, that self he had so fully trusted, that had led him to defeat. It was only eighteen months since his catastrophe, but he seemed to belong to another age. The name 'Stanton' was linked to 'impeachment,' 'tenure of office,' dead and dusty terms already. Grant nominated him hoping to please him, remembering now the spiny virtues of the man and hoping to give them effect in this new period. The Senate confirmed him at once, but no one ever knew what he had planned to do with his new office. Four days after his confirmation he died.

The other nominee was Rockwood Hoar, who was too plainly fitted for a place on the Court to be kept in the cabinet. The Senate tabled the nomination. It was an amazing affront to the President's officer, a man of unquestioned ability, but the Senate had felt itself affronted by him. Several months ago he had appointed judges in some of the reconstructed states in complete disregard of what the Senators from those states had suggested, and he had not been discreet in expressing his opinion of the Senators' calibre. Hoar was a witty man, and independent. Ulyss, amazed and deeply troubled, would have withdrawn the nomination, but Hoar preferred to let it stand and force open action, and Cox and Fish angrily seconded him. In due time the Senate flatly rejected it.

With this clear warning of disharmony in the party, Ulyss took careful thought for San Domingo. Shortly before Christmas Babcock had come back with the formal treaty of annexation, and it would be submitted to the Senate in a few weeks. There was still an irritating lack of enthusiasm for it in the cabinet, but Ulyss was not disheartened. When the people learned of his plan their approval would sweep their representatives forward, and when it was explained to the representatives they would need no urging. Ulyss was going to be very careful. The Senate's treatment of Hoar was evidence that presidential support was no warrant of success, but if he could assure himself of Sumner's support the treaty could hardly fail. He did not like Sumner, but for San Domingo he could be diplomatic.

On the second day of the year Grant walked across Lafayette Square to see the Senator, who made him welcome with wine and cigars. There were other people present, two journalists come to listen to Sumner's encyclopaedic conversation, but Ulyss came straight to his errand.

'It's about the San Domingo treaty,' he said. 'I wanted to talk to you, as head of the Judiciary Committee ——'

'I'm head of the Foreign Relations Committee,' Sumner interrupted.

'Of course, that's what I mean.' Ulyss knew what committee Sumner headed, but often made the slip — perhaps because the man bore himself with such an air of assured omniscience. 'I wanted to talk to you about annexation. The treaty will go to the Senate in about a week ——'

'Mr. President, I haven't seen the treaty.' Sumner's tone
was of patient and respectful reproof. 'This is the first I've
heard of it.'

'I know.' Ulyss pulled various sheets of paper from his
pockets and shook his head at them. 'I thought I had it or a
memorandum with me, but I must have left it behind. No
matter — I'll send Babcock to you with copies in the morning.
And by the way, there's been about a hundred and fifty thousand dollars spent on it from the Secret Service fund for the
West Indies. If there's any question about that I hope your
Judic — your Foreign Relations Committee will back it up ——'

Grant settled down into an exposition of how necessary it
had been to spend that sum, and how paltry it was by comparison with the riches San Domingo would bring, while Sumner
waited with growing restlessness. The Senator rarely spent
much time in listening to other people talk, and this endless
praise of a hot West Indian island, without even any documents
to give a definite basis for discussion, was making him impatient. Annexation — it was impossible to say yet, but Sumner
felt he was going to disapprove. Canada, of course, really belonged to the United States by any standard of true justice,
and would be possessed as soon as the administration stopped
its faint-hearted sparring with England, but the value of San
Domingo was doubtful. Spain had acquired it not long ago,
and had been glad to relinquish it after four years of jungle
war. Yet the President talked on and on about it, while Sumner
waited to bring up a matter of interest to himself.

When Ulyss paused for an answer the Senator drew out a
letter and cleared his throat. 'Mr. President,' he said, 'I have
here something I think will interest you. Ashley was unjustly
removed, I am certain, and it seems to me that he should be
restored to office. He says here ——'

The letter was long and angry, and as he listened Ulyss grew
angry also. This Ashley had been an abolitionist, and as such

had Sumner's unwavering friendship, but he had said unforgivable things of Grant and his policies, and surely had no right
to object when Grant removed him from the governorship of
the territory of Montana. Did he expect a President to work
with an insubordinate officer? 'He's a worthless fellow,' said
Grant succinctly, careless of Sumner's veiled eyes and grim
mouth. He disposed of Ashley at some length and without
mercy, then returned to San Domingo and the secret service
money that Babcock had spent. He was still talking of it when
he took his leave and Sumner went with him to the door.

'Mr. President,' said the Senator stiffly, 'I am an administration man, and whatever you do will always find in me the most
careful and candid consideration.'

Walking home through the shadowy winter nakedness of the
Square, Grant was well pleased with himself. Sumner had given
his promise, and the Senate flocked after Sumner in foreign
affairs. San Domingo was safe. There had been some things
in his administration that Grant regretted, things such as
Black Friday, the confusion over his cabinet appointments, his
uneasy relations with the Senate, that had not fitted into the
pattern he had hoped to make. But San Domingo would make
it right again, San Domingo would show that the people's
President understood his work and served them well. Even the
fanatics who were forever yapping about the tariff or civil
service or monetary reform would be quieted by this achievement of constructive statesmanship.

The treaty went to the Senate on the tenth of January, and
was at once referred to the Foreign Relations Committee.
Ulyss expected an immediate report, but it did not come. He
was inclined to be impatient, but reminded himself that Sumner
had said he was an administration man, and undoubtedly he
would give a favorable report in good time. Perhaps he was
waiting for the popular interest to make a better showing.
It was true that the people had not shown the excitement over

the proposal that Ulyss had expected. Many of the newspapers put all their emphasis on the island's alien population and unhealthful climate, and seemed indifferent to its potential advantages. Others supported the treaty as wholeheartedly as did Grant, but in general the tone of the press was disappointing. People need time, Ulyss assured himself. The thing's too big to be understood all at once, but in a few weeks it will be, and then Sumner will make his report. We have until the end of March.

There was a multitude of other things to occupy the President's attention in that time. Every few days there was news of some outrageous event in the South, where the citizens were fighting each other with fierce hatred, and the governors of the reconstituted states so often appealed for troops to uphold their piebald authority that there seemed little difference between statehood and the old military dominion. There was a growing number of complaints from the Indian reservations. There were complaints everywhere, and if measures were taken to satisfy them there were complaints from the other side. The Supreme Court handed down a decision that the greenbacks were not legal tender for debts contracted before their issue, and the country howled that the poor man was being thrown to the greedy fangs of his creditors. On the day of the decision Grant made two new nominations to the Court, both of men known to consider greenbacks as legal tender for all debts, and the country howled that the sacred Supreme Court was being corrupted by political demagogues. The voice of the people, Ulyss was learning, was never without dissonance.

Senator Schurz, too, found matter for complaint in the appointment of one McDonald as Supervisor of Internal Revenue for Missouri. McDonald, said Schurz, was a rascal, and would disgrace the government service.

'I don't think you need pay any attention to that,' said Babcock. 'Why, I know McDonald well, and he's a fine chap.'

'Schurz seems pretty positive,' said Ulyss.

'I tell you McDonald's a friend of mine. I'd know if he wasn't straight, wouldn't I? And you know how Schurz is. He thinks everybody who draws a cent from the government ought to have a doctorate in political economy.'

'Yes, I know,' Ulyss chuckled. Schurz was a leader of the group of civil service reformers who joyed in questioning the integrity of their own government. Ulyss had no love of critics, and he let McDonald's appointment stand.

The San Domingo treaty was at last reported out in the middle of March — unfavorably. Ulyss found it almost impossible to believe. Had not Sumner promised his support? Ulyss was sure he had. In all those troubling weeks of delay he had taken comfort in the knowledge that Sumner, though obsessed with his own viewpoints and difficult to deal with, would not go back on his pledged word. Now he had not only led his committee in making an unfavorable report on Grant's cherished project, but was defending that report in oratory that was ranked with his speeches before the war, when he had stood before the Senate as a prophet of God.

If a man does not keep his pledge he has no right to expect that his dishonor be kept secret. Ulyss said what he thought of Sumner. All that he had disliked in him, the intellectual pomposity, the humorless self-assurance, his fanaticism on his chosen subjects, Ulyss remembered and expressed. And the Senator, with what seemed to Ulyss brassy dishonesty, denied that he had ever given his pledge at all. Sumner had once been attacked and caned on the floor of the Senate, an event that had not only shattered his health and given him a useful aura of martyrdom, but had left a certain savagery in his spirit. He had promised, he said, only to consider the administration measures, not to support them, but the President's misunderstanding was perhaps natural. The President had been drunk, as was proved by his intemperate abuse of the mistreated

Ashley. Sumner struck at Grant because Grant had struck at him; neither saw that their blows were but thrusting them apart, and that into the gulf between them the prestige of the administration was toppling.

Ulyss fought for his treaty. He went to the Capitol and wrought with individual senators, he summoned batches of them to the White House, he even talked to Schurz about it, but changed the subject abruptly when he was confronted by a blank wall of methodical objections. There was never any profit in arguing with Schurz, for he discussed everything with reference to a set of principles as binding as revealed religion. Ulyss argued with almost everyone else, however, yet nothing was done by the end of March. The time allowed for ratification lapsed then. Grant got an extension from the Dominican government, and prepared for the decisive campaign. San Domingo had been close to his heart; now it was his heart, and he meant to fight for it with every means he knew or could learn.

Perhaps, said Fish, the treaty would be accepted in an altered form. Fish had never had any enthusiasm for the project it was his duty to defend, and his friendship with Sumner was suffering because he did defend it. Nevertheless, San Domingo was overshadowing Cuba as he had hoped, and he preferred a battle in the Senate to a war with Spain. Ulyss accepted his suggestion, and drew up a few changes relating to the purchase price, which was to be applied to the island's public debt, and assuring that the United States would have no further liability.

It was not what Fish had meant. His own ideas would have provided for a retrocession of the island, should circumstances make it wise, and looked to an independent confederation in the West Indies under American protection. Ulyss refused to consider them. Some alteration of the terms he could accept, but not such changes as these, which would compromise his whole intention. San Domingo ought to belong to the United

States. This was what he believed, this was what he was fighting for, not a temporary relationship, a reaching-out of one
hand with the fingers crossed on the other.

There was a lull in the battle during April and May, when it
was necessary for the government to concern itself with the
South. It had been thought that when the states were readmitted, with representatives hand-picked for loyalty to the
new order of things, the Southern question would be answered.
But somehow the renewed states did not seem satisfied. Legislatures busied themselves in throwing out one or another bloc
of members, governors called for help against their populations,
and the only law observed was a matter of uniforms: blue of
Federal troops by day; glimmering white of ghostly riders by
night. Congress considered how the negro voters, newly edu-
cated to their rights and interests, were in danger of being
persuaded to vote on the wrong side or not at all, and passed a
bill making it a penal offense to interfere with elections, and
providing army supervision of the polls. There was some objection from theorists, but there seemed only a technical difference between using the army to put down electoral rebellion
and using it to meet a military one.

On the same day that the bill was passed Ulyss reopened the
Dominican question, sending to Congress his proposed changes
in the treaty, and informing it that the time for ratification
had been extended.

'I feel an unusual anxiety for the ratification of this treaty,
because I believe it will redound greatly to the glory of the two
countries interested, to civilization, and to the extirpation of
the institution of slavery.... The people of San Domingo are
not capable of maintaining themselves in their present condition, and must look for outside support. They yearn for the
protection of our free institutions and laws, our progress and
civilization. Shall we refuse them?... The acquisition of San
Domingo... is, in fine, a rapid stride toward that greatness

which the intelligence, industry, and enterprise of the citizens of the United States entitle this country to assume among nations.'

Surely now Senate and country alike would see the myopic stupidity of opposition. Point by point the argument was unassailable, and not even Sumner's turncoat violence would prevail against it. Grant waited with the confidence of a man who knows without question that he is right.

Then, like a tidal wave heaving without warning from the depths of political processes, came a series of new objections. In the spring American warships had been sent to guard San Domingo in a dispute with Haiti. Was that not essentially waging war without Congress's consent? The Senate made much of that, eager as always to discover executive pretensions, and then it found an even greater grievance. There were accusations against Babcock from a man who had lived in San Domingo for some years. The President's secretary had let him, an American citizen, molder in a Dominican jail because it was known that if he were free he would oppose the treaty, and Babcock had personal reasons to work for the treaty's success. He was associated with the promoters of Dominican mines; he had been dined and flattered, and probably bribed, by the Dominican authorities who were trying to hoodwink the United States.

The Senate appointed a committee to investigate the charges. Babcock was exonerated, but a minority led by Schurz maintained that he was guilty. 'Babcock's name,' shouted Sumner, 'should be struck from the roll of honorable men.' Was the august Senate to truckle to presidential megalomania in order to enrich presidential parasites?

'You see how it is,' Ulyss said grimly to Julia. 'First me, and then my friends. That man won't stop at anything to pull me down.'

'Poor Colonel Babcock,' Julia lamented. 'It seems so hard

that he should be attacked just because he stands by you.'

'Babcock knows what loyalty means — that's more than
Sumner does. When I think that I went to that man — !
He's the only person I was ever anything but myself to — that
was my mistake, he's been trying to ruin me ever since. Of
course, if a man is his friend it's all right. There's nothing at
all wrong in Motley taking his instructions from the Senator
instead of the State Department, nobody could say that was
dishonorable ——'

'Will this have an effect on the treaty?' Julia asked hastily.
It was alarming to see Ulyss so enraged, and even the subject
of San Domingo seemed less disturbing than the man Ulyss
had come to hate.

'Sumner thinks it will. He thinks he has me beaten, but he
forgets I'm President. There's still one or two things I can do
without getting his permission first.' Ulyss reckoned up his
resources as he had once reckoned the number of men he could
throw against the rebel lines. Persuasion, influence, patronage.
Those who had been honestly in doubt and open to persuasion
were nearly all aligned now. Influence held firm the Radicals,
Morton, Chandler, Conkling, Cameron, who were Ulyss's
friends: it was a negative force on the Schurzes and Sumners
who were struggling to humiliate the man the people had chosen
to lead them. The estimates of the vote were sometimes a little
up, sometimes a little down, always considerably below two-
thirds. The patronage. Ulyss used it: here a foreign post,
there a word to the Treasury to install someone in a customs
house —— These might not be the best men available for
the work they were to do, but Ulyss was beginning to see, as
his friends insisted, that degrees of excellence do not always
show a proportionate variation in practice, and an appointment
may serve a greater end than the actual work involved.

For a while he considered a suggestion that he appoint
Sumner as Minister to England in Motley's place. The thought

of having Sumner out of the Senate and across the ocean, orating to the English, was deeply tempting, but Ulyss knew in his heart that the Senator would not go, and would make the offer appear as an attempt to buy him off. Furthermore, the worst objection to Motley was that he was Sumner's man, and at first had obeyed the instructions of the chairman of the Committee on Foreign Relations before he considered those of the Secretary of State. Should Sumner himself hold the post he would work with no regard for the State Department at all. Had there been any possibility of helping the San Domingo project Ulyss would have tried it, but there was none, and he supposed it was as well to have the man in the Senate, where his colleagues could remind him that he could not constitutionally wage war entirely by himself.

By mid-June the most optimistic estimate of the vote still left the treaty short of two-thirds. Ulyss had hours when he wondered if it would in truth fail, but shook free of them with a sense that he was betraying his own cause. It could not fail. He had worked so hard for its success, risked on it the unity of his party, the reality of his leadership, the record of his administration. It could not fail. Yet the estimates could not be dragged upward, and Ulyss was sometimes chilled as he looked at them.

Then a group of senators from the reconstructed states came to see the President. They were not such men as had once represented the South, in the tradition of Randolph and Calhoun. They hardly seemed Southern at all, but they had been duly elected under the new state constitutions, and they had full votes.

'We've been thinking over San Domingo,' they said. 'It's hard to say about these things, but we notice Senator Morton's in favor of it, and Senator Chandler, and the rest.'

'Yes, they are,' said Ulyss eagerly. The Radicals were supporting him almost to a man. The Radicals were responsible

for the election of these men who had come to him now, and
Ulyss wondered if the creed of party loyalty they had preached
would hold firm beyond the limits of the black vote. 'They're
good men,' said Ulyss, 'and don't drop their party just as soon
as it looks like they can't get their way.'

'Fine men,' the callers agreed, 'and good friends to the
South. We wouldn't want to criticize, Mr. President, but we
do sometimes wish you had more friends of the South in your
official family. Attorney General Hoar, for instance ——'

'Highhanded Yankee,' muttered one before he could be
hushed by his suaver companions.

'The nominations he made for Southern circuit judges last
fall ——'

'What was wrong with them?' asked Ulyss. 'The Senate
confirmed them.'

'Oh, there was nothing really wrong with them, unless maybe
they didn't understand conditions very well, or know about
just the right methods. But those were judges in our states,
and it seems to us we might have been consulted.'

'Mr. President,' said one bluntly, 'do you think it's fair for
Massachusetts to have two places in the cabinet, while the
whole South hasn't got one?'

It was very plain. Remove Hoar, and there would be an
additional group of votes for San Domingo. Grant liked Hoar,
but it was true that having two cabinet officers from one state
was poor policy, and Hoar himself had offered to resign when
Boutwell came in. It was an unfortunate thing, but in the complex political balance it seemed impossible to gain anything
without losing something else, and San Domingo stood for so
much more than any one office . . . Grant wrote the Attorney
General that he was under the necessity of asking him for his
resignation.

The letter was inexplicable to Hoar. There had been no
word of disagreement, no suggestion of a strained friendship,

no reason whatever for such an abrupt demand. Yet the demand had been made, and its lack of reason could not affect the necessary answer. Hoar promptly returned his resignation, to take effect as soon as his successor was appointed and qualified. He said no more, scorning to ask for explanations where none had been offered. Some members of the cabinet were enraged for Hoar's sake, and some of the press was enraged at him, for a member of the White House staff made a mistake and issued Hoar's letter alone to the public. A resignation without warning or reason, in the midst of a struggle for which the administration needed all its strength, filled those who had approved of Hoar with indignant surprise. Hoar could not explain his own action without criticizing Grant's, and he said nothing. Nor did Ulyss explain the matter — he could not be forever defending himself. He had been elected President, and must be allowed to make his own decisions, to advance his policies by the methods that seemed best to him, without trying to balance every move against all the complaints and suggestions and demands of those who had not been chosen.

Late in June an effort was made to recognize Cuban belligerency, but the Senate, absorbed by the battle over San Domingo, defeated the measure. A few days later the San Domingo treaty came to a vote, and it also was defeated. Twenty-eight were for it and twenty-eight opposed, and sixteen votes were not counted for one reason or another. Not even a clear majority. Ulyss felt a blankness rather than any actual emotion. Defeat in itself did not astound him, for the agitation over one man in jail and Babcock's alleged friendships had given a dangerous emotional thrust to the opposition. But when he had allowed himself to know that he might be beaten he had seen it as a close decision, swayed at last by men who were his personal enemies. He had never thought of a failure so complete that it could come only from a public indifference to the project, and made his championship ridiculous.

His leadership of the nation had been mocked, his office made meaningless, and his friends maligned, to no purpose, and he was denied even the comfort of hot indignation for a defrauded people. Perhaps the people had been defrauded, but plainly that was what they wanted. All that was left to Ulyss was his personal emotions.

'I want Motley removed,' he told Fish. 'I won't have him running around London representing Sumner.'

'But he hasn't done anything wrong lately,' the Secretary of State objected.

'How about last summer, and the way he went dead against your orders so as to obey Sumner's?'

'That was a year ago. If he's removed now it will look like retaliation to Sumner for San Domingo.'

'I want Motley removed,' said Ulyss with satisfaction, and Fish obeyed unhappily.

That summer of 1870 the administration that had been so promising two years before, that had been credited with firmness, magnanimity, and quiet strength, seemed lost in a morass of futility. The record of Congress was gray with disappointments. Nothing new and constructive had been done; there was no measure stamped with the fresh outlook of an administration founded on good will and wide support. The only two events of importance had been the passage of the Enforcement Act directed against the Ku Klux Klan, in itself an admission that the Union had not truly been restored; and the defeat of the San Domingo treaty, something which few people cared about but which pointed to the lack of any unity in the government.

'Congress is soon to adjourn,' Grant wrote a friend. 'The reflection is almost a compensation for the suffering endured during its session. If it were not for the feeling of loyalty of the people, and the almost certainty that a Democratic success would be repudiation and surrender to old Southern leaders, there is little doubt but that the Republican Party would lose control of the country at the next election. Lack of attention to material interests, wrangling among themselves, dividing and allowing the few Democrats to be the balance to fix amendments to every important measure (and voting against the whole bill when brought to a vote), attacking each other and the administration when any individual's views were not conformed to, has put the party in a very bad light.' He ended with a hope that in two years, when it must face the presidential election, the party would have learned to discipline itself.

The hope was not a result of ignorance, nor of overblown optimism. Ulyss had been accustomed to learning from his battles, from victories and defeats alike, and from the catastrophe of San Domingo he had learned who his friends were in the party, whom he could trust to back him. Chandler, Conkling, Morton, Cameron, the practical men, each with a state organization behind him, had stood together and worked for the treaty with a will. It was Sumner and the theorists who had defeated him, who apparently believed that since they had been leaders for so long they had acquired squatters' rights to Republican power.

Sumner's victory over San Domingo could be the introduction to the defeat of Sumner and all his associates. Ulyss knew from his friends that it was so, that a strong element in the party was eager to be rid of the ponderous, unamenable influence of such men as Schurz and Sumner. All that was needed was the cooperation of the party's head, and Ulyss was eager to give that. Sometimes, when he was very tired, he was nagged by the memory of a phrase, 'I commence its duties untrammeled...' He was not greatly troubled by it. No man is untrammeled, he has only a choice of loyalties.

PART EIGHT

The Alabama Claims

The White House Was a Happy Home

VIII. WEIGHT OF THE CROWN

CHAPTER TWENTY-FOUR

THE Grant family was happy in the White House. The howling winds and twisting currents of politics had little effect on their family group, but they were absorbed by the cheerful, disordered social tumult. Society in the capital had come to new life after the long, dark hiatus of the war. Entertainments had a new magnificence, receptions were thronged, and elaborate gowns and jewels were brilliantly set against the black broadcloth of legislators. Ulyss was at first ill at ease, but he learned to tolerate the code, and then to enjoy it. It was pleasant to be told that under the Grants there was again such a thing as Washington society, and it was true. Some objected that it was not the same society, that its tone was more of the cornet than of the flute, that where the old families had reigned in the name of good taste the new leaders were frequently lobbyists with a tin sceptre of something for nothing. The Grants ignored the carpers, as Ulyss ignored the indignant murmur that rose from somewhere whatever he did.

It was young Nellie Grant who took the greatest delight in the fantastic world that had closed around her family. At fifteen the beauty that had lurked in her childish face was suddenly clear, a manifestation that startled her parents. They had thought of her comfortably as bordering upon girlhood, and now suddenly she was a woman, very young, radiant, and in endless demand. Her brother Jesse was drafted as her escort for the functions that crowded her days, a duty he loathed but doggedly performed, for he knew that a girl so young must be chaperoned by the gentlemen of her family. Nellie had critics enough already, hissing behind decorous hands of her late hours and forward behavior, and of the number of serious admirers she had collected in one season, even at her age. Ulyss and Julia had some doubt of their own wisdom in the matter, but could not bring themselves to put a curb on her, and she went her way, trampling hearts she was too young to notice had fallen in her path.

Julia entered her place as the wife of the President with uncomplicated pleasure. There were difficulties at first, as with the steward they had appointed, an army man whose notion of a menu for a formal dinner was turkey, and for a state dinner a bigger turkey.

'Don't you think,' Julia had asked, 'that we might have a change of menu? Something a little more — more fancy, perhaps?'

'Madam,' the steward told her gently, 'we are living at the absolute pinnacle now.' Julia waited until Ulyss's reluctance to discharge the man was overcome by the danger of being made ridiculous, then replaced him by a chef with imposing foreign experience. She waited with all her problems until she could see clearly what method would give her her own way yet offend as few outsiders as possible. Her name would never be counted on the roll of great ladies, but she was well liked, and she was very happy.

Only once did she consider making a notable adaptation to the public view of what she should be. It seemed to her that the cast in her eye, hitherto unimportant, was a drawback to the wife of the President, and she made arrangements to have it corrected. But a few days before the operation Ulyss flatly forbade it.

'I won't have it,' he declared indignantly. 'Your eyes — that's the way I know them, it's the way I love them. I won't have them changed.'

'Yes, dear,' said Julia.

One enlivening factor in life at the White House was the feud between Ulyss's father and Julia's. 'Allow me to give you my seat, sir,' Dent insisted each time old Jesse entered the room. 'You will be so much more comfortable. Do you feel a draft? Shall I close the window?' He hovered over Jesse with a solicitude that shouted in every syllable that Ulyss's father was old, very old, so near death that the comforts of this world must be offered to him as hospitality is pressed upon a departing guest. Jesse always curtly refused Dent's cushioned place before the fire, and sat bitterly erect on the hardest chair in the room.

They never had very much to say to each other when they

sat together, but their hostility was a bond between them. It
was not only that their backgrounds were so widely different,
with Jesse formed by the raw Ohio country, where calculation
had been a virtue and the graces of living faintly suspect; and
Dent coming from a Missouri plantation, so far north that its
pattern of life seemed imitative rather than logical, but therefore all the more conscious of the tradition. It was not only
that they embodied two feelings about the war so extreme as
to be academic: Jesse had delighted in infuriating his neighbors
by forecasting its coming and its results; while Dent mourned
the old South daily in graceful if somewhat ungrammatical
periods, and could give a mint julep the emotional tang of a
libation to the heroic dead. These things made them inimical,
but the real bitterness of their relationship, and its zest, lay in
their age. Jesse's hearing was no longer acute, an infirmity not
amounting to deafness, but making it necessary for him to give
close attention when he wished to hear. Dent unfailingly
shouted at him, and then talked about him in ordinary tones.

'Daughter, you should take better care of that old gentleman.
At his age, and deaf as a post, he never ought to go out without
an attendant, but you let him roam around all over Washington
by himself. It isn't safe ——'

Behind a shielding newspaper Jesse poked a finger into his
small namesake's ribs. 'D'ye hear him, Jesse? D'ye hear
him? I hope I'll never live to be as feeble as your poor Grandfather Dent ——'

Both men were proud of Ulyss's office, and delighted by the
opportunities it gave them. Both had homes of their own, and
Jesse was postmaster of Covington by President Johnson's
appointment, but they spent a good part of their time in
Washington, Dent at the White House and Jesse at a hotel.
'The House,' said Jesse, 'is too damn full of Dents and their
ninety-eighth cousins. Buzzards.' Dent occupied his days in
genial talk, sometimes of the glories of the South and sometimes

of his son-in-law the President, and a chat with the old gentleman was an unfailing custom of Ulyss's friends. Jesse was not
interested in petty satisfactions. He went among the office-
seekers, and made his recommendations to his son. Ulyss
sometimes took them, as he sometimes accepted Julia's pleas
for an aspirant who had sought her sympathy, and Jesse chuckled at old Dent's senile contentment with mere blow and brag.

These things made Grant's happiness. His hours in his office
were often unpleasant; he was never free of a faint sense that
somehow things had not developed as he had planned, that he
had lost something nameless, shapeless but vital to him; and he
had days of black misery. Yet when he sat in the evening with
Julia, while Jesse and Nellie quarreled affectionately in a corner
and the two grandfathers stabbed at each other with sly enjoyment, the realities of his work lost their sting. They would
be waiting for him in the morning, they might even intrude
here if some caller came and wandered into discussion, but
they could not really hurt him while this older reality held him
warm and safe.

The midterm elections in that fall of 1870 confirmed the
summer's indications that the public was not pleased by the
administration it had so hopefully welcomed. Disappointment
and dissatisfaction showed itself in the addition of four Democrats to the Senate and thirty-two to the House, but the most
disturbing thing was the shameless advertisement of the Republican schism. It appeared even in the cabinet. Secretary
Cox of the Interior resigned because, he said, the President's
friends were allowing him no control over the personnel of his
own department, and he timed the step to have the greatest
possible influence on the elections. He was replaced by Colum-
bus Delano, a man of no brilliance and no cantankerous sense
of his own authority. Ulyss was tired of contending with officers
who were forever referring his wishes to their own views and

striking a dubious balance, and he was well enough pleased by the change, but much of the press added Cox's name to Hoar's in a mournful list of worthy men who could not stomach the administration.

The height of apostasy was reached in Missouri, where Carl Schurz led his adherents into a coalition with the Democrats to rewrite the state constitution and return the franchise to former rebels. Schurz was beginning to notice that the restrictive measures he had so passionately championed were not leading to that just and perfect democracy of which he had dreamed. He was seeing very clearly now that a large section of the country had no voice in the formation of policy — and that the policies it would have favored were those that were close to his own heart. Monetary reform and lower tariffs were needed by the midwest and the South, but their registration lists were of necessity practically limited to Republicans, and Republicans were bound to Boutwell's deflationary policy and the high protection demanded by eastern business men. It was very plain to Schurz, and he came to the White House to explain it, for he was always eager to explain his views, but Grant would not see him. Ulyss had always felt a certain distrust of the man, and no amount of talk about a citizen's sacred right to the franchise, and the necessity that all the interests of the people should be represented, could blur the fact that Schurz had turned traitor and lost Missouri to the party for two years. Did he think he could wander in and out of the party as he chose and still keep the confidence of the party's leaders?

Punishment would come to the disloyal, to Cox and Schurz and all the others. Ulyss was sure of it, and was willing to wait for it with indefinite patience, for an immediate reckoning was being presented to Sumner. When the Republican caucus met in March to organize the new Senate there was a strong movement to separate Sumner from the Committee on Foreign Relations. It was not only Grant's Radical supporters who

furthered the measure, for the Senator's razor tongue and overweening manners had alienated others who had not been
troubled by his attitude on San Domingo. He had attacked
the President in a speech of such distilled, essential bitterness
that even those who had no love of Grant were shocked. And
he had promised to see that every treaty supported by the
Grant administration was defeated.

This was one of the chief elements in the pressure for his
removal. Fish was Sumner's friend, and had defended him from
the new, restless party members who had resented his control.
Fish was now inclined to believe that the Senator was not quite
sane, that perhaps his mind had been affected by the caning
he had received so long ago, or perhaps was cracking as the
weight of age was laid on his unresilient temperament. But
whether he was to be pitied or to be feared, he must not be
allowed to block the treaties, for Fish was at last making
progress on the *Alabama* claims.

The claims were not the only friction between England and
America. There were controversies over Canadian fisheries,
Fenian troubles originating in the United States, boundaries,
and a number of smaller issues that would ordinarily have been
settled by routine negotiations, but had piled up around the
Alabama claims as around the key log in a jam. It was Fish's
hope to settle them all at once, and put both nations on a
ground of unshaken understanding. The project would not be
easy: Grant frequently changed his mind on foreign affairs, and
the Senate grew balky at the first mention of any treaty, but
Fish was a determined man, and had progressed so far that a
British commission had come to Washington to discuss methods
of settlement.

No treaty supported by the Grant administration. If Sumner
were reappointed now he would hold office for two years. The
labors of the commission would be entirely useless, and the
Alabama claims would remain to stalemate the work of the

Department of State for years to come. Fish supported the effort to oust his friend. Grant waited eagerly day by day to hear from Chandler or Conkling or Cameron of the progress of retribution.

It was not done without a struggle. Sumner spoke in his own defense, defied the insurgents to criticize his record, refused the easy compromise of the chairmanship of another committee. He fought hard, but he lost. Cameron was elected in his stead, and Sumner became simply the Senator from Massachusetts. He could not fight against his time. Like Stanton and Stevens, he had done his work in the war years, when a President of mild voice and wise eyes had known how to deal with their great capabilities and barbed spirits. They had built a party then as men build a house, intent on hundreds of bricks and piles of boards, on the relation of roof to foundation, window to floor. Now the tenants had moved in with their own furniture and their own way of life, ignorant of the structure in which they lived, indifferent to the builders' idea of what it had been for, and annoyed by the builders' presence.

Eighteen months until the presidential election. Many grave problems were to be considered in that time, the settlement of the *Alabama* claims, the tariff, the greenbacks, the everlasting Southern question, the pressure for civil service reform, and all of them were increased in weight and difficulty by the necessity of winning votes with the solutions. The Democrats were battening on the public restlessness, and Schurz had sunk so far in treason that he had set up a separate organization and christened the bastard Liberal Republicanism.

Some members of the new group had a national prestige of real danger: Sumner; Cox; the great newspaper figures, Samuel Bowles and Horace Greeley; and men of such intellectual eminence as Charles Francis Adams and William Cullen Bryant. When they spoke they had a respectful audience, and

they began speaking often. Federal offices were being cynically
used as a unit of exchange. The tariff had become a towering
wall of special interests, cemented with a total disregard of the
people's welfare. The South, staggering under the double
burden of the untutored negro vote and the unscrupulous
Northern adventurer, was going to drag the whole country
into the abyss.

'It's a bad business,' said Morton, shaking his great white
head. 'That's just the kind of talk that gets people all stirred
up, and our side is likely to come in suckin' the hind tit.'

'Not a chance of it,' said Ulyss. 'It's just a lot of noise.'

'But a good many people would let those men pull 'em
around by the nose and think it was an honor.'

'Listen,' said Ulyss. 'When I was in Mexico I went hunting
with a friend one night. We got out on the prairie, and when
the moon began to come up the coyotes started howling, thousands of 'em. My friend asked me how many I thought there
were.' Ulyss stroked his beard and smiled, remembering that
night long ago, with the high, white beauty of the moon and the
unearthly howls ringing from horizon to horizon.

'Now, I knew he was from Texas and knew about such things,
and would expect me to shoot way beyond the mark. But I
wasn't going to show how green I was, so I took the lowest
number there could possibly be and cut it in half. I said, "Oh,
about twenty," not much interested, like I knew all about
coyotes. He smiled a little but didn't say anything, and pretty
soon we topped a rise and saw the beasts.' Ulyss stopped to
chuckle. 'There were just two of them. Looked like mangy
dogs, sitting back on their haunches with their heads together,
and making all that racket.'

Then he looked at Morton and nodded quietly. 'That's all
this business is. Just a few disappointed politicians who've
walked out on their associates, and sound like the whole country till they're counted.' Ulyss refused to fear the activities of

disloyalty, and his stubborn calm was comforting to his more excitable friends.

Most of the Radical leaders shared Grant's faith in the disproportionate noise of coyotes, knowing the historic lack of stamina in reform movements, but they took measures to dampen the insurgents' powder. Troops were sent into Southern states at the least indication of disorder. The Liberal Republicans cried that this was military tyranny, but they could be answered that loyal men and insufficiently subservient negroes were being terrorized, and could not be abandoned simply because protection of them was also protection of the Radical vote. The tariff was lowered, not very much and by an arbitrary reduction that took little account of the different requirements of different goods, but it was lowered. Many good friends of the party in the east were alarmed by that measure, and had to be soothed by repeal of the income tax. They had tolerated the tax for the sake of the war, but now in peace they had been complaining of the stupid injustice of a tax on a man's ambition and industry. The repeal was very popular with men of considerable importance. A bill appeared in Congress to create a commission to draw up rules for civil service examinations. Ulyss promptly supported it, and thus at several points the sting was taken from the Liberal Republicans' outcry without really damaging party policy or alienating party friends.

All these things were helpful, but the best assistance to the embattled party came from Fish's work on the *Alabama* claims. The commission he had summoned to Washington had arranged for the claims to be submitted to a commission of arbitration, and the other controversies to go to individual arbiters. One by one the decisions were made, sometimes not giving the United States all she wished, but never intolerable and on the whole very satisfactory; and the claims themselves were being settled by full discussion between dignified and able men. The nagging problem was not only being solved, but solved with such evidence of diplomatic intelligence that the nation had a new pride, and the solution gave some illogical prestige to the administration even in domestic affairs.

As soon as the arbitrations were under way Fish turned in his resignation. 'I've done what I wanted to do,' he said. 'I don't like official life, and there's nothing to keep me here now.'

'Stay for a little while,' Ulyss pleaded. 'Stay until after the election anyway.' He did not want to lose Fish, for he was fond of him and relied on him, and it was said that the Secretary of State was the only man of true stature remaining in the cabinet. In these months before the election the steady mutter of criticism of Grant and his policies and his friends had grown to vituperative thunder, and Ulyss wondered sometimes if it were real. Was it true that this was not simply a political trick, that the people who had once trusted him and chosen him to lead them now believed him a villain or a fool? The election would tell him, and before then he did not want to risk yet another cry that worthy men would not work with him. Fish stayed, surrendering to Grant's urgent request, and to the importunities of almost all the newspapers and more than half the Senate.

The Liberal Republicans would not be able to break through the Radical defenses. The Democrats were not yet so clear of the disloyal taint that they could carry the election. But Liberal Republicans and Democrats together might have a chance. This was the possibility that alarmed the Radical leaders. They could take measures to stalemate the Liberals' criticisms, but it was impossible to placate the Southern Democrats, or revise their opinion of Grant. Once they had in a measure trusted him, remembering that as a general he had been a remorseless fighter but a forbearing victor, and hoping that in his new office he might see an opportunity to extend to all the South the magnanimity he had shown the Southern armies. For four years they had waited, seeing all the states readmitted, but most of them with governments that were running state debts to staggering levels, proscribing whole classes of the population, and clinging to power with the bayonets of the Federal army. Perhaps, thought some Democrats, Grant did not really know the true state of the South: perhaps he heard only of murder and terror at midnight from friends who had reasons of their own to keep the region as it was; and he did not stop to think of a better way to put an end to violence than more violence. Some believed that he too had an interest in the complex tissue of corruption that netted the South, knowing the ease with which he accepted gifts and the delight he took in them; and those who believed him personally honest condemned his choice of friends. Whatever the reason, the South had nothing to hope for from Grant, and must try to elect some other, and it was likely to combine with the rebel Republicans if it could.

In May of election year the Liberal Republicans held their convention, and nominated Horace Greeley. No one quite knew why. Only a few of the leaders of the new party were wise in the ways of politics; there was not enough disciplined guidance to mold the various groups of discontents into a malleable mass; it was inevitable that there should be cross-purposes, misunderstanding, shortsighted dealing, and an opportunity for manipulation by men who had no wish to see a strong candidate nominated. However it was, the party that sprang in part from the desire for low tariffs nominated a high protectionist. The men who were already branded turncoat chose to lead them a man who was notorious for his wavering course during the war. The group that wanted the cooperation of the Democrats, who were largely Southern or had Southern sympathies, invited support for a man who at one time had seemed to think Southerners were animate beings lacking even the better instincts of animals. There were great abilities in Greeley, but his record made his nomination suicidal, and his personal eccentricities, which might have been overlooked in a really suitable candidate, were a gift of the political gods to the cheerful savages who drew cartoons.

There was a note of horror even in the jubilation among the regular Republicans, for to some of them such a blunder was as painful as is the spoiling of good material to a sound workman; and others, whose views of Greeley were somewhat prejudiced, felt that the nomination showed the decay of the people's conception of the presidency, and remembered how proud Romans had appointed a horse to the consulship. 'The work has been done,' Grant wrote privately, 'and no one is satisfied but Greeley himself and a few Tammany Republicans. . . . I predict that Greeley will not even be a candidate when the election comes off. The Democracy are not going to take him, and his following in the Republican ranks is not sufficient to make up an electoral ticket, nor is it composed of respectability enough to put on such a ticket. His nomination has had a good effect, however. It has apparently harmonized the party by getting out of it the "soreheads" and knaves who made all the trouble because they could not control. . . .' Ulyss was quietly happy. This absurd nomination marked the dissenters' adventure as a farce, proved that it was no mass of the people that condemned him, but only a few frustrated exiles.

The Democrats did nominate Greeley. They did it unhappily, knowing there was hardly a chance of electing him, but knowing also there was no chance at all of defeating Grant unless the dissatisfied groups clung all together to one candidate. Any chance of defeating Grant, however small, must be taken. The Democrats took Greeley, and tried hard to believe that they had not simply chosen between two impossibilities.

The campaign was hard fought. Ulyss took no personal part in it, relying on Conkling, who confidently answered to him for New York; on Cameron for Pennsylvania; on Morton for

Indiana; on Chandler, the chairman of the Republican National Committee, for the nation as a whole. Ulyss held still to the belief that he must not work to advance himself, not even in this year when it was his own honor and intelligence that was attacked, and he sat waiting. His friends could defend him, and he left to them the enormous complexity of a presidential campaign. It was the result that interested him, not the procedure.

Greeley wanted the presidency with uncritical fervor, and spoke well and frequently for his own cause. His great desire magnified the crowds who came to hear him, and the cheers they gave him, while it blinded him to the larger crowds, to the vast multitude of voters staying home, reading the papers, sensing the currents of loyalty and prejudice and ridicule that creep through an election year. Grant — a little highhanded, maybe, in small things, and he hadn't seemed to do as much as had been expected in large things, but he might improve in a second term; and his party had safe men in it, not a lot of new people with ideas that might work and might not. Greeley — it was hard to think of him as President; the pictures of a fussy old man in a white hat and a linen duster seemed to say all there was to say about him.

In September the arbitration of the *Alabama* claims was concluded, and Radical last-minute orators seized on it as a fine solid achievement with just the right connection with the flag of a reunited nation. In October a few early state elections gave a clear forecast. In November it was sweepingly confirmed, and Grant was returned to office by a larger majority than he had had in 1868.

So much for criticism, thought Ulyss. For four years every action had been condemned by someone, and occasionally it had seemed to be everyone, yet at the first opportunity for the people to speak for themselves they had spoken in approval. The critics had been given the lie, had been discredited as they had tried to discredit him. The people still trusted and believed in Grant, and in his party as it had been altered under his leadership, and Ulyss joyed in the knowledge.

This was what he wanted to say when he spoke at his second inauguration. Great things had been planned for that occasion, pageantry that would make its triumph visible, but the dawn was a line of steel in a frozen sky. Snow fell all day, not in the thick beauty of a driving storm but by grudging flakes that blew unmelted along the icy ruts in the streets; and the wind howled mercilessly from the west. Flags were ripped from their places; the music began bravely but came to an abrupt end in squawks and gaspings as breath froze in the instruments. It was all but intolerable torment simply to stand still, yet when Ulyss took his oath and stepped forward to speak he faced as large a crowd as he had before, too large to have any hope of hearing him, but enduring that merciless wind and murderous cold simply to look at him.

He spoke with requisite pride of his first term, touched on negro suffrage, and lightly indicated the other horn of the Southern dilemma. 'The States lately at war with the General Government are now happily rehabilitated, and no Executive control is exercised in any one of them that would not be exercised in any other State under like circumstances.' San Domingo was mentioned, and the currency and the civil service. Then Ulyss drew breath for the most important part.

'I acknowledge before this assemblage, representing, as it does, every section of our country, the obligation I am under to my countrymen for the great honor they have conferred on me by returning me to the highest office within their gift, and the further obligation resting on me to render to them the best services within my power. This I promise, looking forward with the greatest anxiety to the day when I shall be released from responsibilities that at times are almost overwhelming, and from which I have scarcely had a respite since the eventful firing upon Fort Sumter, in April, 1861, to the present day.... I did not ask for place or position, and was entirely without influence or the acquaintance of persons of influence, but was resolved to perform my part in a struggle threatening the very existence of the nation. I performed a conscientious duty, without asking promotion or command, and without a revengeful feeling toward any section or individual. Notwithstanding this, throughout the war, and from my candidacy for my present office in 1868 to the close of the last presidential campaign, I have been the subject of abuse and slander scarcely ever equaled in political history, which today I feel that I can disregard in view of your verdict, which I gratefully accept as my vindication.'

He knew as he spoke that it was useless. It was not only that the wind tossed his words out as pointless syllables to those who could hear them at all, but this was not really what he wanted to say. As he looked down at the pavement of faces turned up to him, pinched and blank with cold, he saw them suddenly not as friends come to rejoice with him, not as a symbol to which he could defend himself and which could give him absolution, but as a vast indifferent watchfulness, observing him now and in every hour of the four years he was yet to serve it, knowing no friendship, no expediency, no human heritage of error, weighing him day by day and pronouncing a result that would endure through his lifetime and as long as his name was remembered. He would have liked to cry out, to make them hear, but not the speech he had written in warm, unthinking pride. He would have liked them to hear and remember the verse he had kissed in the Bible when he took his oath. He had seen it when he raised his face: ' ... and he shall not judge after the sight of his eyes, neither reprove after the hearing of his ears.'

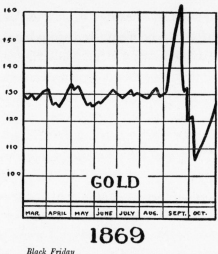

GOLD

1869

Black Friday

CHAPTER TWENTY–FIVE

THAT summer was the tenth anniversary of the siege of
Vicksburg. Ulyss thought of it sometimes as he drove up and
down the roads around Long Branch, or sat on the wide porches
of his cottage and looked out to sea. He remembered the things
that had troubled him then: controlling McClernand's cocksure,
dangerous gallantry; keeping the men patient while they had
little to do but sit in the hot sun and wait; making sure that
Johnston was held so far off that he could be of no help to the
besieged city; quarreling with Rawlins over that trip to New
Orleans. McClernand had disappeared from public notice before the siege had ended, and now probably not one newspaper
reader in ten thousand would know his name. Johnston was
trying to rebuild his life without any of the military simplicities

to help him. Rawlins was dead. No one knew where the armies that had fought the siege were. Individual members could be easily found at Grand Army rallies, but the great mass had been swallowed up in the humming bustle of the post-war nation. And Ulysses Grant was beginning his second term as President of the United States.

It startled Ulyss to realize how long ago that period seemed. His memory of Vicksburg, his first resounding victory and the basis for all the success that later came to him, was very clear even to details of people's appearance and how it felt to sit on the levee and watch the rain, but the memory as a whole had a slightly fictitious quality, as if another Ulyss were telling this one of an experience they did not really share. Perhaps it was because no one wanted to remember the war, the actual war. Reference to it was expected and appropriate in patriotic speeches, it figured still in politics and smoldered as a half-proud, half-resentful tradition in the South, but these were matters of word and legend rather than the reality that still lay encysted in the minds of the men who made it. Ten years could be a long time. They could make somewhat calculating business men out of eager youths; dry, meaningless terms out of issues that men had died for; a vigorous, expanding nation out of one on the edge of dissolution.

Rawlins had died too soon. Had he lived only a few years longer he would have seen the greatness he had envisioned for his country, a greatness that had seemed irrelevant and doubtful to Ulyss while they were fighting for it, but had become reality now. New railways opening up new land; new industries and new men; new ideas and a new courage to carry them out — Rawlins had seen them coming, and most of Ulyss's grief for his friend lay in the fact that he had not seen their arrival. The country was sweeping forward on a tide of prosperity that had drowned out the critics and the timid men, that need have no ebb. What was there to draw it back? There was land in

plenty for the growing population and for the thousands pouring
in from Europe too. There was no longer the solid opposition of
the South to such measures as the tariff, that protected the
young industrial growths. There were no jealous neighbors to
be feared and fought. The United States would be first among
nations, and Ulyss felt that now he knew better how to be its
leader. He knew the men who could best advise him and who
would help him avoid the mistakes he had made in his first term;
all that he need do was conduct the affairs of his office quietly;
and when the four years ended there would be none of that
slander which had pained him more than he liked to admit. In
the last ten years America had risen from the blackest hours of
a civil war to a prosperous unity: the achievements of the next
ten years would be even more miraculous.

In September Ulyss put young Jesse into a school in Philadelphia. He and Julia made periodic efforts to give their
youngest son a formal education, but though Julia sometimes
withstood the boy's homesick pleas Ulyss never could. This
time they hoped that since Jesse was older his exile would not
be so painful, and they tried again. Ulyss entered him and
gave him more money than he ought to have, then went to
spend the night at Ogontz, feeling himself a traitor. Cooke
made him welcome, and gave him comfort by drawing him into
talk of the children. 'Jesse's so smart,' Ulyss confided. 'Learns
like lightning when he wants to, so he doesn't see much sense in
going to school every day. Doesn't like being away from us,
either.'

There was no reason for shyness with Cooke. They were good
friends, and Ulyss was entirely at ease with him even in the
splendors of Ogontz. He spoke of Buck, who had finished Harvard and gone into the banking business — 'That boy's got
real brains, Cooke. I never could make much of business myself'; of Fred, who was on duty with Sheridan, having scraped
through West Point largely by virtue of his amiable disposition

and broad smile; of Nellie. 'We sent her abroad with the
Bories. She's so young yet, hardly through playing dolls, but
she's been getting offers —— We thought it better to get her
out of harm's way.'

'She's beautiful,' said Cooke. 'One of the loveliest girls I ever
saw, Miss Nellie.' His interest was plainly sincere, without any
tinge of the perfunctory, even though several times he excused
himself to go and meet some messenger who waited in the hall.
He always came back with a comment on the subject that had
been interrupted, and he listened with pleasure until Ulyss
talked himself out of his depression and proposed a game of
poker.

In the morning there were many more messengers for Cooke,
but he bade them stand aside while he said good-bye to the
President. Ulyss went back to Washington impressed once
more by the multitude of the man's affairs, and the simple
friendliness he showed although his name was a power in the
dark mysteries of the financial world. Ulyss was always a little
puzzled by great financiers. He knew many of them now, some
of them intimately, but he had never yet identified the difference that had made them lords of telegraph lines and railroads
and steel companies at an age when he had been failing to make
a profitable farm out of Hardscrabble. He too was a success
now, he had proved his worth in the army and in the political
world, and there was no longer any bitterness in his interest in
business, but the interest he still had. Perhaps if his father had
not sent him off to West Point he too might have achieved
wealth and its peculiar power. He would never know, now, but
his sons would. Fred would have an army career uncomplicated
by any of the difficulties that had beset his father's, and Buck
would make a name in business as bright as Cooke's.

The news reached the Stock Exchange in New York at noon
that day, and Ulyss heard it a few minutes later. 'Messrs. Jay
Cooke and Company have announced their suspension in con-

sequence of large advances made to sustain their Philadelphia house and a heavy draft upon their own deposits. It is hoped the suspension will be only temporary.'

It can't be so, thought Ulyss. Jay Cooke and Company isn't a firm that would have the troubles other businesses have, that might run into difficulties and fail. Cooke controls the Northern Pacific, with all that rich land on the Canadian border, and a connection in a few years with the China trade. He found money for the government during the war when other rich men hung back, thinking maybe secession would succeed, and afraid to risk anything to see that it wouldn't. If Cooke has really failed it's the biggest news, and the worst, that we've had in years. He can't have failed. I saw him just last night, and he didn't say anything ——

All those messengers. Every time Cooke had left the room he must have been given further tidings of disaster, and had come back with a smile to say, 'Now, while your Fred was at West Point ——' Ulyss felt his scalp prickle.

At the Stock Exchange there was no disbelief, but there was even greater horror. Trouble had not been entirely unexpected, as for some weeks there had been a number of reasons for uneasiness, none fatal in itself, but confirming an ugly total. There seemed to be hard times in Europe, perhaps as a result of the recent war between France and Prussia, perhaps for other reasons, but some men in New York believed that even the United States' prosperity might be threatened. There were causes for alarm within the borders of the country too. In the South some people were making much money, but not on a basis that seemed either sound or permanent, and the reconstruction policies were apparently resulting in race riots instead of reconciliation. In the midwest the farmers were pouring by hundreds into something they called the Grange, an organization with high-flown classical titles for its officers and with the single, unswerving purpose of fighting the railroads. Most of the members were farming railroad grants, all of them were shipping their produce on the railroads, but they seemed to have no sense either of gratitude or of the necessities of finance, and sat about in schoolhouses clamoring for lower rates and public control of the roads. Worse, they swarmed to elections and put men who shared their ideas into office. There was not really anything to be feared: Europe was very far away, the South need not be a major factor in the new economy of the country, the Grangers were effectively blocked by the Constitution and the eastern majority against them. Yet all these factors troubled the smooth waters business had sailed in since the close of Johnson's administration, and the stock market had shown a fitful caprice all summer. A few banks had failed, even one or two big firms had suspended, but it was insisted that a prosperous country could survive a sprinkling of unimportant disasters.

Some men of gloom had said that there might be trouble in the fall, money might be tighter, times might be harder. It had never occurred to anybody that Jay Cooke and Company might fail. The traders turned to hear the announcement — and when they turned back they found there was no prosperity in the country, none. At a touch the confidence that had been their golden asset turned to dust, the values they had never thought of questioning vanished. The progress of business, that had been so clearly based on the undeniable necessities of the country, was shown to be founded on speculation and reckless, indefensible expansion. The people could not trust the banks, and came all at once to get their money. The banks called in the loans they had made in such number and uncritical optimism. Business saw its markets disappear and its debts become intolerable all in the same instant. And business, banks, and people were engulfed in terror.

The day after the catastrophe was Friday, a blacker Friday for more people than had been the day of Gould's raid on gold. It rained with dismal, clammy persistence, and the excitement

around the Exchange had no warmth in it. Men watched the
quotations shooting downward as though they watched the
approach of death. They moved restlessly through the building,
and up and down the streets outside, but there was no escape.
The thing had happened, the impossible, the thing that had
been supposed never to happen again, and they were as bewildered as though it were the physical world that had crumbled
in their hands.

There were some suicides that day, of men who had identified
themselves with their ruined businesses so entirely that a con-
tinuation of their own lives seemed irrelevant. A very few men,
such as Jay Gould, who occupied themselves in finance as a business and had none of the graces of faith in the future, grew rich
as the collapsing quotations fulfilled the forecasts they had
made in selling short. The majority were heartsick at first, then
filled with anger because they had been cheated of their future,
then eager to find some specific cause of the trouble and force
someone to remedy it. There were several different theories,
but the favorite was that there was not enough money. Boutwell's policy of steady contraction, the gradual withdrawal of
the greenbacks from circulation, the whole deflationary policy
of the government, had naturally had this result, and it was the
government's duty to repair the damage it had done.

This was the cry that Ulyss heard when on Sunday he came
to New York with Oliver P. Morton and Richardson, who had
been Secretary of the Treasury since Boutwell had resigned to
become a senator. The President's suite was crammed with
men, more stood clustered in the corridors until there should be
room for them, and more still waited in crowds in the lobby.
The air of the room was thick gray with smoke, and the noise
mounted steadily to chaos as each man shouted to make himself
heard over the shouts of the man next to him.

'We've got to have more money!' they cried. 'Mr. President,
right this minute a dollar bill is worth more than a certified

check — we can't get cash to meet our payrolls, even though our books show we've made the money three times over. Reissue the greenbacks, the people can't stand this long ——'

'That's true,' said Morton heavily, remembering the needs of his people in Indiana and how quickly indifference to them would wreck a political organization. 'They've got to have more money just to live on.'

'Reissuing the greenbacks,' said a few, 'would be inflation and nothing else. It would make this temporary difficulty an irreparable disaster.' These men were far outnumbered, but their steady insistence gave them a certain strength. They were grave and composed, and looked at the red-faced, frantic majority with a pitying distaste, as priests disposed to martyrdom might look at congregations getting out of hand.

'Perhaps just a few ——' Richardson suggested timidly. His appointment had been opposed by some of these men on the same issue, because he had released a few greenbacks when he was Assistant Secretary.

'Yes, a few anyway,' came the instant clamor. 'If the payrolls aren't met the workmen can't buy food for their families — if there isn't any cash every value in the country will go to pot ——'

'Values will be reduced, but they won't disappear. And they have to be reduced before we can have specie resumption. That's a pledge of the Republican Party, Mr. President ——'

'The country can't stand resumption now. We've already had all we can take ——'

'The country will have to stand it, or it will be ruined for good ——'

'Mr. President, Mr. President —— '

Specie resumption, inflation, contraction, were to Ulyss neutral terms that glowed or darkened with the speaker who used them, without illuminating the hearer. He made no definite promises, and went back to Washington to think it over. There was no unity in his advisers, either, for Morton, Logan, and Chandler were for some inflation, but Conkling was against it; most of the members of the cabinet were for it, but Fish and Creswell were determinedly opposed. It was hard even to find broad lines to define the adversaries, but it might be said that the farmers and small business men were set against the large industries; the west against the east; the party leaders who supplied the votes against the party supporters who supplied the money. Ulyss listened to those who came to talk to him about it, and there were hundreds, and to those who talked about it to each other in his presence, but he said little, for when occasionally he did make some comment the newspapers attacked him with varying degrees of malice, indignation, and sorrow. Fortunately he need not make his decision until Congress considered all the suggestions that were so heatedly advanced, and presented him with a bill.

There was misery both of mind and body that winter. The Stock Exchange, which had been forced to close a day or two after Cooke's failure, reopened in less than a fortnight, but reopened to a changed world. The panic was over, and a worse thing had come — the leaden weight of hard times, so much more difficult to bear because it called not for spectacular courage to meet a spectacular thing, but simply for day by day endurance of the ugly and the uncomfortable. The railroads had been the driving force of the prosperous era, and now they led the reversal. Cooke failed because he had put all his faith and too much money into the Northern Pacific. Kenyon, Cox and Company was pulled down by the Canada Southern. Then the equipment companies closed their factories, and their workers walked the streets in company with the workers of the raw material industries that had been supplying them. Unemployment rose in an icy drift, and froze shut many firms that had thought themselves safe from the original trouble.

There were at first voices that said, 'Business is good, this is only a minor storm on the Exchange'; and then, when even the most hopeful pragmatism could not suck comfort from the events of that winter, they said, 'The fundamental wealth of the country is untouched.' But in the cities soup kitchens opened, and men stood in line under the cold sky, pushing their feet forward a few inches at a time, keeping their hands clenched in their pockets and their eyes fixed on the heels of the men before them.

Even another Cuban outrage did little to distract the people from their own misery. Early in November an American ship, the *Virginius*, was captured on the high seas and taken to Havana, where many of her crew were killed with an indifference to law and ethics that came close to savagery. It was a valid cause for war, and a few years before it would certainly have started war, but now the United States was too occupied with itself to enforce its resentment on another country. People were interested in the *Virginius*, even excited about her, but willing enough to be reminded that her claim to the American flag was doubtful, and that the members of her crew who had been put to barbarous death were known as filibusters in the cause of the Cuban rebels. None of this was a real excuse for the affair, but made it possible for Fish to reach a speedy settlement with the Spanish government without being pushed into conflict by an outraged people. It was his last great service in the field of foreign affairs, last for the same reason that it was successful: the nation had neither the energy nor the ambition to assert itself abroad.

All that winter the battle over the currency was fought in newspapers and angry speeches, and as soon as Congress opened the conflict absorbed it. In his message Ulyss referred to the matter somewhat unwillingly, for he had still not decided exactly what his policy would be, but he pointed out that in the past year there had been in truth an actual contraction, both in direct withdrawal of currency and in the changed proportion as the population rose. He made no positive recommendation, but promised hearty support to whatever measures Congress proposed to take. The finance committees were promptly smothered with bills, and struggled to consider them carefully despite the bitter division of opinion in the committees, in both houses of Congress, and from end to end of the country.

It seemed to Ulyss that the clear, uncomplicated view of the future he had held the summer before was an impossibility, that he could never seriously have trusted it. He had thought then that he had learned how to meet all his problems, how to balance his personal inclinations and the party requirements to reach the best result, how to choose men to give him advice and other men to carry out the advice, how to stand aside and let things work themselves out. Now, only a few months later, he was waiting to be presented with a question to which he did not know the answer, and he had no certainty that anyone else knew it. The problems of his first administration seemed simple and far away, and his worry over them a type of innocence.

Even his family was being altered, slipping out of the old pattern. Nellie had come back from her trip to Europe, which had turned out to be an imposing tour by the daughter of a reigning family, with a secret that shouted itself to the most casual observers. She told her parents about it at once, but it was hardly necessary, for her face was too young and un-hardened to hide her happiness.

'It's really my fault,' Julia sighed, with a lurking smile that amazed Ulyss. 'I should have known better than to send her abroad to get her away from admirers. They say everybody falls in love on a ship.'

'I think,' Ulyss told her flatly, 'that you're almost pleased.'

'Oh, Ulyss, how can you say that? Our little daughter, scarcely more than a child, wanting to marry a man we've never seen ——'

'You think it's romantic.'

'I don't——' His eyes were on her, half-hurt and half-laughing, and she smiled. 'Well it is, in a way. She's so much in love, and he sounds so pleasant, and he's English——'

'Too bad he hasn't got a title,' he grumbled. 'That would be really stylish, marrying a child to the Crown Prince Thingum-bob.'

She ignored the sneer and adopted his bluntness. 'That isn't what's really worrying you, Ulyss, his being foreign, or her being so young. You just don't want to let her go.'

'I——' This time it was her eyes that forbade evasion, and he flushed slowly. 'I just can't get used to the idea,' he admitted. 'Maybe I've never really noticed that she isn't a baby any more, and the idea of her being anybody's wife just isn't possible.'

'What did you think would happen to her, dear?'

'I don't know. I'd never thought, really, but just had a sort of picture of all of us at White Haven, maybe, the way it used to be, only with everything all right.'

'She'd go sometime.' Julia's voice was gentle, and her hand on his was comfort for a sorrow unnamed and unrecognized. 'The girls always marry, and the boys go off too. But there'll still be us, Victor. We can be together, and nothing will change that.' He held her fast, knowing that what she said was true, the only important truth, and content in it.

Nevertheless, there was no delight in his welcome of Nellie's lover when the young man came to make his formal avowal. His name was Sartoris, he was a nephew of Fanny Kemble's, he was very handsome and a good singer, and there was a radiance on Nellie's face when she looked at him that cast a shadow in Ulyss's eyes. All through dinner the young man conducted himself with painstaking propriety, with occasional glances at Ulyss which Ulyss interpreted as terror of Nellie's father, but which Julia suspected were awe of President Grant. Probably this young man with a foreign background saw the American eagle roosting in dreadful majesty on her husband's shoulder.

After dinner Ulyss conducted Sartoris to the billiard room and prepared to listen to him, with some confusion as to which was to sit down and which was to be allowed the manly stimulant of walking the floor. Ulyss offered the young man a cigar, but made no other effort to smooth his path, and sat silent, watching shyness, apprehension, and uncertainty contend in that handsome face. For once Ulyss felt no sympathy with someone who was having difficulty in opening his mouth.

The young man looked desperately at him several times, and at the door once, then almost stood to attention before him and said all in a breath, 'Mr. President, I want to marry your daughter.'

'Mm,' said Grant. Now that it was his turn to speak he was almost as much at a loss as Sartoris had been. He already knew the necessary things about the young man's background, and there was no need to question him. He was not going to consign Nellie to him in words that were as appropriate to a deal in horses, nor was he to be dragooned into a congratulatory pleasure he did not feel. 'Nellie wants it,' he said. 'Mostly I give Nellie what she wants — I hope you will too.'

Marriage, then, for his daughter, but death for his father. Old Jesse had come to the second inauguration, filled with peppery, wry pride and indifferent to the atrocious weather. Probably the cold would not have hurt him, for his was the type of constitution that is invulnerable out of simple stubbornness, but he slipped on the icy steps after the ceremony and his aged body rebelled at last against his tyranny. He would not admit it at first, and went home to Covington insisting that he was quite well and only needed a little rest from his labors in the capital — grossly unappreciated yet freely rendered because he was both wise and patriotic — but in a few months the desperate, unadmitted battle came to a sudden defeat, and Jesse was dead before Ulyss could reach him.

It was not exactly grief that touched Ulyss as he looked at his father's face with its abrupt lines aggressive even in the final stillness, but a species of helplessness. He had never felt a warm affection for his father, had usually been annoyed with him for one reason or another, and had sometimes come close to hating him. Yet it was as impossible to be indifferent to Jesse dead as it had been to be indifferent to Jesse alive. There had been so much vitality in him, in his anger, his egotism, his love of combat, and there was pathetic irony in the fact that the things he really wanted had been withheld from him and given to the son whom he half admired and half despised. His life was almost in the pattern of the old tales in which the gods promise many great things and fulfill their pledges with a literal, perverted exactness that amounts to a divine jeer. I wish, thought Ulyss, it could have been different. He was not sure just what he regretted, but he felt dimly that perhaps if his father had been more satisfied he might have loved the old man more. As it was, he did not grieve for him, not really, but missed him to a surprising degree.

Old Colonel Dent missed him too. He sat now in triumph and mourned Jesse with elaborate pity, but there was no savor in it when Jesse was not there to be enraged. Dent had won their silent duel and remained alone in the field, but he knew that he himself was a simple target for their common enemy, and his victory was ashy to the taste.

Under the cold wind of hard times the pleasant mental habits of prosperity blackened and broke. The country developed a sudden taste for investigation, and began inquiring into matters that a few years before it had ignored or never thought of questioning. The Crédit Mobilier scandal put many members of Congress in a dubious light, and gave telling ammunition to those who were attacking the railroads' power. Several comparatively minor peccadilloes of the government were exposed, and then the investigators turned to the Treasury Department and discovered a major one. A man named Sanborn, a friend of Ben Butler's, had been given a contract to collect delinquent taxes, and had been paid on a percentage basis. A good part of the money he collected would have been paid in full to the government without any intervention, but the part of the affair that most interested the investigators was evidence of collusion between Sanborn and some officers of the Treasury itself, including the Secretary.

So far as Grant could see all this nosing out of facts in order to label them 'corruption' was simply an effort to annoy him. He had not thought, when he had accepted the presidency, that he would be thus everlastingly galled with criticism. The Crédit Mobilier had nothing to do with him, for its activities in Congress had been before his election, but the investigation during his administration identified it with him nevertheless; and the attack on Richardson, a man he had himself appointed, was intolerable impudence. There was even criticism of the President because he did not ask for the Secretary's resignation, criticism that particularly enraged Ulyss because it implied that he could desert a friend under fire. In these days, with the country restless and unreasonable, Congress apprehensive in memory of what other depressions had done to the election returns, and even his close friends divided in opinion, Grant had to cling fast to the elemental beliefs he had carried all his life. Friends were not to be made for policy nor deserted for policy. Richardson stayed on in the cabinet with the full confidence of his chief, while the investigating committee bayed on his trail.

In the midst of that affair Congress completed its monetary bill, after four months of struggle and discussion and vivisection by amendment. It was a work of art. It looked like inflation, for it authorized $400,000,000 in greenbacks and $400,000,000 in national bank notes. On consideration, however, it would have scarcely any inflationary effects, for all but a few million

of the authorized greenbacks were already in circulation, and
the issue of the bank notes was so cramped with requirements
of deposited collateral and other restrictions that it was likely
to have no effect at all. Yet over this innocuous bill the winds
of controversy howled with all the force that a solid obstruction
would have given them, and even the iniquities of the Sanborn
contracts seemed footling beside the yawning dangers that the
opposing sides discovered in it.

Almost everyone assumed that the President would sign it
without question. In his message to Congress he had mentioned
something much like it, and had promised support for whatever
measure was adopted. Ulyss himself expected to sign, but he
felt he owed the contractionists at least some delay. The vote
by which Congress had passed the bill showed an almost exact
geographical division. Ulyss dreaded them. When North and
South became not directions but an easy label for a hopeless
division of opinion, there had been civil war. He did not yet
fear war in seeing the west drawing together against the east,
but he did fear to increase the friction. If he vetoed the bill the
west would feel itself betrayed. If he passed it the east would
be angry, but since in general it was stronger it would have little
sectional resentment. Morton, Chandler, and Logan insisted
that Indiana, Michigan, and Illinois would be forever lost to
the party if the bill were vetoed, and pointed out that there
would be no actual inflation as an effect. Specie resumption
was an impossibility until business improved anyway. Ulyss
would approve the bill, but not too quickly.

The delay was an opportunity for hundreds of individuals
and delegations to call on him and argue with more or less tact.
The great majority of them wanted a veto, but that was because
Washington was in the east, where the contractionist faith
was strongest. The western supporters of the bill had not time
nor money for the long journey to make themselves heard.
Grant listened to both sides with considerable patience, but he

wondered sometimes why men troubled to vote other men into
the presidency, for apparently each one in the country considered himself best qualified to do the work.

Drexel of Philadelphia, a man of note comparable even to Jay
Cooke, discussed the bill all one evening, drawing horrifying
pictures of the value of money disappearing, faster and faster
as the presses strained to pour out more and more, until the
very laborer who now cried out for paper money would be burning it in his stove in lieu of the kindling wood it was too worthless to buy.

'But this is only a million or two,' Ulyss objected slowly.
'Lots of people think the effect of the bill might even be contraction.'

'I know.' Drexel's voice had little heat in it. He chose his
words carefully and enunciated them with a precision that indicated his pleasure in the mere sound of good English. Ulyss
thought irrelevantly that the man not only had a fabulous
amount of money himself, but his family had had it for years
before him. He made the circular upstairs library in the White
House look slightly middle-class. 'That is almost the chief
difficulty in the thing. The bill is not really inflationary, but it
appears to be so, and when it fails of the expected effect there
will be an immediate outcry for more inflation. The damage
will be done — after the first concession it is much harder to refuse another.' There was an impressive quality in his very lack
of passion, as though he did not feel it necessary to use vehemence as a cloak for ignorance or uncertainty. Having so much
money himself, he must surely know more about its mysteries
than other men. Ulyss thanked him, but gave him no assurances.

Most of the other callers were not so impressive. One group
from Boston infuriated Grant by inferring with crude directness
that Richardson's reissue of part of the greenback reserve to
meet current expenses was illegal, and they were dismissed

with withering chill. A delegation from New York argued with desperate clarity for a veto, with a convincing analysis of how New York's interests would suffer if the bill were passed. 'That may be so, gentlemen,' Ulyss told them, 'but there are other interests in the country besides New York's.' The delegation said nothing, shifted their feet a little, and soon took leave. It was too discouraging to argue with a man who had already made up his mind, and it was humiliating to argue in the smug presence of some of the Congressional inflationists, who had, accidentally, arrived just before them.

They left with the President the petition they had brought with them. There were two and a half thousand signatures on it, and Ulyss looked at them for some time. Many of the names were of men he knew personally, men who had come to wealth and power because they were shrewder than others. Many that he did not know were familiar to him in Chandler's talk, names of men who had given solid support to the party in the last election. It was an imposing petition. But it did not mention the west, the territory beyond the Appalachians, where the petitions were editorials in hundreds of newspapers; where Republican supporters, said Chandler and Morton, were going to be raging Democrats in the fall if they were not given satisfaction.

By the middle of April there was no further reason to delay action. The arguments on both sides had become only exasperated repetition, and more time would probably make them mere snarls. Ulyss sat down alone in the library one night to write his message. Ordinarily he made no comment when he approved a measure, but this time he felt it needed explanation — whatever he did about it would need explanation. Slowly he set down the reasons for his approval, picking his way gingerly through the esoteric, half-mystic concepts of money and its causes and its effects. A few years ago he had scarcely known the alphabet of this language, but now its study absorbed his days, fevered his nights, and made the actual bills and change in his pockets seem absurd, a childish irrelevance.

The greenbacks that had been withdrawn and only partially reissued. The harvest periods when there was too little money, even though at other times of the year there might be enough. The population that was increasing faster than the money supply. One by one, his reasons for signing the bill. He had thought them over so long, heard them questioned and disproved and reaffirmed on other grounds so many times, that they had become all but meaningless, as any single word will if it is repeated often enough.

The message finished, he read it over. He lit a cigar and read it again, frowning and concentrating word by word. The reasons were there, the line of argument was clear, but the thing did not satisfy him, and it seemed to him it would not satisfy anyone. It was as though he had grasped an object and found his hand closing futilely on itself. Perhaps it was because he was so weary of the discussion that his reasons seemed to have lost their validity . . . But these were not his reasons. He knew that suddenly. They were the reasons that he must give the public, that he had tried to give himself; they were even true enough, but they were not the truth. He was going to sign the bill because if he did not the party was likely to lose its strength in the midwest, and if he did the voters would think they had been given the measure they wanted although it would make almost no real change. Lies, then, to both sides. Lies to the west, to make it believe it had won and keep it quiet; lies to the east, to make it believe it had lost for the sake of the people of the west and not the party in the west.

Grant was a party man. He wanted the party to be strong, to keep the executive branch in its hands, to hold majorities in both houses of Congress, to flourish in all the states; he had come to distrust and dislike the Democrats not only because of their criticism of himself and accusations against his friends, but because they were a constant threat to his party. He had done much that once he would not have done, or would have done differently, because he wanted to serve the party interests. Yet this he could not do. This was not a question of policy or method, but of his own honor.

If he could not sign the bill, what should he do? He sat quietly, stroking his beard, thinking about the issue all over again in the light of his new perception, until his alternatives were clear to him. There were two: he could call for a real inflation instead of a legislative weasel; he could veto the bill on an uncompromising stand for hard money. Actually he had no choice. Nobody he knew really wanted inflation. Even Morton and Logan wanted only enough to keep the voters quiet, and a Republican Party with such a policy would surely ruin the country even more quickly than would the Democrats.

Ulyss sighed with the pleasure of a decision that no part of him questioned, and began to write rapidly. ' ... I must express my regret at not being able to give my assent to a measure which has received the sanction of a majority of the legislators chosen by the people to make laws for their guidance, and I have studiously sought to find sufficient arguments to justify such assent, but unsuccessfully ...'

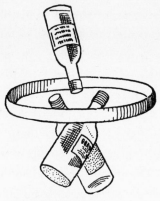

The Whiskey Ring

CHAPTER TWENTY-SIX

THERE is doubtful constitutionality in vetoing a bill with such popular backing...'

'The Republican Party is certain to lose the fall elections...'

Astounded and dismayed, most of Ulyss's close friends strove to make him reconsider, but they found themselves helpless. 'I am confident,' said Grant, 'that the final judgment of the country will approve my veto.' His uncertainties, his anxious willingness to listen to partisans of either side, had entirely disappeared, and he had acquired a rocky confidence. He was sorry that his close friends were so troubled, but was certain that he had after all saved the party, and their error would be made clear to them in the fall.

In the few weeks after the veto he discovered how pleasant it was to be praised, and realized how long it had been since any praise had been given him. From the eastern states, from the men of money all over the country, from nearly all the eastern newspapers, there was a steady chorus of commendation, and grateful references to the General who had once shown that he could attack the forces of dissolution, and had now shown that he could stand firm in defense against them. The letters that flooded in to him had a tone of gratitude that came close to piety, and he could not doubt that all the most valuable men of the country, the real leaders, supported him.

Yet the Republicans did lose the election. The Democrats took possession of the House and surged forward in the Senate, and captured many state governments, even New York's. There were many factors in that result. The indignation of those who were pinched and breathless in the grasp of hard times, and had looked to the inflation bill for deliverance, was important, but it was not everything. With a great mass of people set astir by the lash of poverty, there was a birth of new attitudes and a death of old prejudices. Ever since the war elections had been fought on one or another of the issues of the war, but now that hard times had come to the whole country the North had less leisure, interest, and passion to give to the South, and was more inclined to let that tumultuous region settle its own troubles. Northern business men deplored the economic waste of these nine years of half-smothered warfare. Northern liberals made room beside the image of the terrorized negro for the image of the terrorized white, and the demand for legal interference fell between them. The election of 1874 turned on new issues: hard money; rumors of government corruption; other rumors of a third term for Grant; all the angry suspicions and demands that rose out of the collapse of 1873. These were the questions that were fought over in the campaign, and the answers were written in the Democratic majorities appearing in places that had been regarded as inalienable Republican property.

It did not seem so to Ulyss. 'There's nothing definite about

it,' he said angrily to Chandler. 'Look at Butler's defeat —
he was running as a Republican, but he was in favor of inflation.
What does that prove?'

'Maybe nothing. But we lost New York too, hard money
and all.'

'Why did our man there have to blow off about a third term?
It has nothing to do with this year's election, and it's none of
his business anyway.'

'Do you want a third term?' Chandler asked suddenly.

'No, I don't think so.' Ulyss was quite sure of that, most
of the time, but he was entirely certain that he wanted to say
so himself, and he greatly resented a disclaimer of him in an
attempt to win the votes of the party he led. 'But that's got
nothing to do with it. He shouldn't have dragged it in, and if
he talks against his own party how can he expect to win? It
doesn't mean the party's lost strength.' Chandler said nothing
more, and Ulyss stubbornly believed that his friend was convinced. Individual men had won or lost on different issues; the
total had no real meaning. It could have nothing to do with
him; it was not he who had been standing for election. He had
been vindicated of all the malicious charges against him two
years before, and he saw no reason to question that verdict now
simply because other men had failed before the capricious
tribunal.

There were others who considered the results with more uneasiness, and some who considered them with thoughtful
interest. The old Republicans, the Sumners and Stantons who
had fought for a united nation and a free people, were dead,
and their times were history. Their party had been split over
San Domingo, and had fallen apart with the formation of the
Liberal Republicans; and now the pieces lay in three groups,
divided on almost everything, with only the negative unity of
not being Democrats. The Radicals, the Conklings and Mortons and Chandlers who had based the party's power on the

enormous, malleable black vote of the South, had succeeded the first leaders, but their tenure was limited by its very nature, and there seemed to be clear signs that its end was at hand. The Liberal Republicans, who had believed naïvely that power may be built with a lofty superstructure and no practical foundation, had made a political spectacle of themselves and were now wandering unhappily in the limbo of their own minds. Thus two of the inheriting groups had no usefulness for the future.

But the remaining group, the Blaines and Garfields, men who understood party solidarity and the mechanics of party supremacy, yet had not been fully identified with the party's Southern policy, saw both logic and promise in the election results, for men bold enough to read them. For fourteen years the country had been governed by the necessities of the war and the aftermath of the war. This year there had been no such compulsion on the electorate, and it had turned promptly to the opposing party. What the Republicans needed was a new point of reference, no bloody shirt, worn to rhetorical rags now, but a policy based on the trends of the modern nation. The policy was there, ready-made, and it was Grant who had blindly created it. He had vetoed the inflation bill, and had thereby saved the good name of the Republican Party for business men.

The growth of business was the outstanding feature of the new America, and the favor of business would make a far better and more permanent basis of party power than the struggle for negro freedom. Certain changes would be made necessary by such a shift. Business required orderliness and predictability, and the government would have to be cleansed of some of its more obvious black marks. Grant was perhaps not responsible for them, but his chosen associates were the Radicals who were either responsible or complacent, and they would all have to go together. It was not a question of disloyalty as the aspiring leaders saw it, but of party preservation. Even as it was the next presidential election would be close, for the pendulum, having started to swing, might go so far that the Democrats could catch it, and two years was a short time in which to seek out new Republican supporters and make sure that they saw where their advantages lay. There was some risk in the project, for nothing could be certain while Grant with his half-trustful, half-headstrong temperament was in the White House, but assurances could be given to some who were most grateful for the inflation veto that future safeguards would not be held so long in doubt. Grant and the Democrats and the Radicals — all were dangers, but the political entrepreneurs would be doubly armed against the dangers by their own standard of decorum, and by the support they knew how to bind fast.

There was already a popular pressure that succeeded in forcing the resignation of Secretary Richardson. Ulyss resented it, for he liked Richardson and was indignant at the criticism he had suffered, but accepted his resignation rather than have him humiliated by a vote of censure. Ulyss would have liked to appoint Washburne, a hard-money man from the west and therefore ideal, but Washburne was well suited in Paris and declined to come home to struggle with the financial problems the panic had left behind. There were several other suggestions of little interest to Ulyss, and then suddenly he chose Benjamin Bristow of Kentucky, who had been doing sound work as Solicitor General. The approval of the appointment was almost universal. A nation that had had economy forced upon it was gratified when the new Secretary of the Treasury discharged hundreds of employees who had been spending peacefully inactive lives in the overstaffed Department. The political figures who had put them there made a private outcry, and in public spoke with pathos of the war widows and old soldiers thus cast upon the streets, but Bristow made little answer and no surrender. Ulyss was well pleased with him, and pleased also with the chorus of public approval.

In October Grant took Julia and Babcock to St. Louis. It was a journey he liked to make. Some day he would return to St. Louis to live, when he reached the end of the responsibilities that had grown inevitably, fantastically, from the telegram Governor Yates had sent him when the war was scarcely more than a gesture. He would not go back to Galena, his memories of that place had too much bitterness; but though he had fought hard at Hardscrabble and failed, and had known silent humiliation as he walked the streets hoping that none of his old friends would see him, he had known happiness there too. He had not seen then where his downward road was taking him and how impossible it was to turn aside, and he and Julia had still believed in the future. Whenever he came to the city now he was showing that young pair that their belief had been justified, more fully, more brilliantly than they had dreamed even when they had told each other fairy stories to keep their hearts warm. Only when that other Ulyss, growing stooped and afraid at Hardscrabble, looked up at him did Grant know what it really meant to be President. Most of the time now he forgot that it meant anything beyond a list of responsibilities and a number of vexations that did not fall to other men; but when he met his own eyes out of his past he knew that the presidency is no better described by its tribulations in practice than it is by the constitutional phrases that set it forth in theory. It is the conceivable impossibility, the symbol of a national fluidity that makes its whole history out of fairy stories.

During their stay they were diligently entertained by McDonald, the Supervisor of Internal Revenue, who was a close friend of Babcock's, and who devoted himself to making the visit as pleasant as possible for all of them. Trinkets and flowers came to Julia every day; every night arrangements were made for Babcock, who was fond of gaiety; and McDonald's magnificent pair of horses was at Ulyss's command. The man was almost fulsome in his attentions. Grant entered a colt from White Haven in a livestock show, and McDonald, who was one of the judges, promptly awarded it the blue ribbon. The applause was as slight as courtesy to the President would allow, for even to untrained eyes the colt was outclassed by several other entries.

'That's disgusting,' Ulyss muttered to Babcock. He felt that McDonald had a right to give generous entertainment if he chose, but the bit of blue silk adorning the insignificant colt was in essence a lie, and compromised both of them. Ulyss ground out the butt of his cigar with obvious anger.

'Don't blame him too much,' said Babcock hastily. 'He just wants to show his admiration for you, and he doesn't know much about horses ——'

'But this sort of thing makes me look ridiculous.'

'Oh, I don't think so. It's quite ordinary, people rather expect it. And if you do anything about it it puts him in a bad spot ——' Ulyss allowed himself to be persuaded, for it did seem churlish to show public disapproval of a man who had only tried to please him. In a day or two he forgot the incident, and enjoyed driving McDonald's matched pair with no reminiscent awkwardness.

The rolling hills around White Haven were afire with October, and Ulyss and Julia delighted in standing on the porch of the old house to stare at the splendor that would surround their home.

'We'll build out a wing here, so as to get that view ——'

'Yes, and that will give us a good lawn.'

'We've got to have a good lawn.' Ulyss chuckled softly. 'A place for Jesse to make speeches.'

'Oh, do you remember that?'

'Of course I remember it. Young rascal — I should have licked him for it.' They laughed together, because it was funny to think of either of them being severe with Jesse, because the Indian summer beauty of the day was a temptation to laugh

without cause, because they were happy. They laid their plans
as eagerly as though they had come to good fortune straight
from Hardscrabble, and Babcock and McDonald stood aside,
talking quietly of something else.

Back in Washington, Grant was so promptly engulfed in
trouble that the Indian summer interlude seemed entirely
unreal. As always, the election set the South seething once
more. Ulyss thought sometimes that his whole presidency had
been spent in finding compromises to induce the Southern
factions to put away their arms and stop rioting in the streets,
only to have his laborious equilibria regularly overturned as
the elections came around again. It was not as bad now as it
had been in the beginning. A few states had evolved responsible
governments which were functioning with the confidence of
their people and no need of intervention by the Federal authority; a few others were on the threshold of that achievement.
But the remaining ones, and particularly Louisiana, erupted
regularly in riot, outrages, furious accusations and frantic
counter-accusations, with soldiers clearing out the legislatures
and citizens fomenting brawls that resulted in a score of deaths.
Louisiana had had nearly two centuries of practice. She had
been a troublesome possession for France, had defied her
Spanish masters, had refused to admit her American identity
fully until she grew interested in a battle fought on her door-
step, had remained stubbornly Confederate in sympathy even
though she was early recaptured by the Union and subjected
to Ben Butler's rule-of-thumb persuasions; and now she was
the most serious aspect of the Southern problem.

That fall the post-election riots punctually reappeared in the
South. In three states two factions claimed victory, and were
deadlocked until the Federal Government should put its weight
behind one or the other. In two of the states Grant refused
Federal aid, and thus one party lost its only strength and disappeared. The states were returned to their old leaders, and

gave fervent assurances of loyalty and peaceable behavior in
the future. Ulyss was not entirely certain of his course: he
remembered the fight in Congress to prevent the old leaders
from returning to their places and making fruitless the long
agony that had been suffered to remove them; he remembered
the long series of constitutional amendments and enforcement
acts based on doubt of the leaders' good faith. Yet the laws
had been accepted, the men seemed trustworthy, and plainly
if they were to be kept out of office their states would have to
be governed by the Federal army. The rival governments made
claims that were loud enough but easily disproved, and were
so discredited that support of them would be choice of a certain
evil as against a possible one. With much hesitation and many
misgivings, Grant released the states to their native governments, much as he would lower a boat of doubtful seaworthiness
into the water.

Louisiana he did not release. The Kellogg government there
had been certified elected by the returning board, and Grant
recognized it. He knew that the board's probing of intimidation and fraudulence at the polls had been designed entirely
to give Kellogg a majority he did not have on the face of the
returns, but he knew also that there had actually been intimidation and fraudulence.

'Maybe those returns are juggled some,' Morton said, snorting over the protests from Louisiana and the criticism of the
President's choice from other states. 'But they were juggled so
as to get at the truth. These holy Willies who froth at the
mouth because one big planter may have had his previous vote
thrown out, don't seem to care if a hundred niggers are kept so
scared they don't dare go near the polls.'

'Sheridan says the whole trouble's with the White League,'
Grant sighed. 'He says if he could stamp that out everything'd
be all right.'

'He's right, too,' said Morton. Sheridan always had a quick

certainty of the solution for any problem, and Ulyss and the Radicals agreed with him in this case, but his proposal was politically impossible. There was a new softness in the country that would forbid it, that was absurdly outraged even by the Kellogg government, insisting that Louisiana should be governed by the men of her own choice. Ulyss knew that it was not possible to come at the true will of the people of Louisiana without holding a new election, and even that possibility was more theoretic than actual. Between two dubious alternatives he might as well choose the most expedient one, and Kellogg was a Radical. Louisiana was a rich state with a large and busy port, and the Northern interests in her could not be charged off with a shrug.

In December Congress met again, the last assembling of the men who had been elected before the panic, in the remote, golden period when the nation was happily occupied in laughing at Horace Greeley and had little more serious to worry about. Now Greeley was dead, the second winter of hard times had begun, and in a few weeks this Congress must make way for another elected in a grimmer time. Then, with a Democratic House and a Republican Senate and President, nothing could be accomplished. Any action, no matter which party supported it, would be almost certain of defeat. Meanwhile, however, there was still a Republican majority, unstable, divided by sections and groups and individuals, rejected by the voters, but a majority, and free to act in its last hour without fear of the effect on elections.

Many issues would have jangled the group into useless dissonance, but on one it held reasonably true — the currency question. The Radicals had believed, before the fall elections, that the fortune of the party depended on yielding somewhat to the inflationary pressure. Now it was obvious that the President would not yield, and the wholehearted inflationists had joined forces with the Democrats. Thus the conservative

Republicans were dominant, with their dissenters either exiled or too dispirited to argue, and they introduced a bill for specie resumption. It was the best possible evidence of good faith in an alliance with business, and it could be passed now that the reckoning of the elections had already been paid. Morton and Logan, holding yet to party policy as they saw it, fought the measure, but found that their great influence was no longer enough. Conkling supported it, for though he was an outstanding Radical, in financial matters he reverted to the conservative gospel of his New York background.

In less than a month, well before the new Congress should convene, the bill was ready for signature. It was very simple: in four years, on January 1, 1879, all legal tender notes would be redeemable in gold. Ulyss signed it with pleasure. He could scarcely remember that he had ever been puzzled and uncertain about the money problem, for now he was instantly sure of his course whenever the question arose. The conservative theory seemed to him the only one with thorough honesty, and the opinion of Fish in his cabinet, of Childs and other sound men among his friends, confirmed him. The very ring of the phrase, hard money, was an argument in favor of it. He was glad that whatever the reason for the party's defeat at the polls it had been able to turn it to such good use.

Another currency bill extended the banking system and increased bank notes in the place of greenbacks. Morton and Conkling saw to it that Grant's policy in Louisiana was approved, and then the rest of the session passed in fruitless efforts to clarify the election law. The difficulties with the Southern returning boards were an alarming indication for the coming presidential election, when the new strength of the Democrats might confuse the result on a national scale. The Constitution established the general procedure for elections, but said nothing of methods for settling a dispute, and disputes were the possibility that troubled thoughtful men. The question was thoroughly discussed in Congress, in speeches that traced the whole history of electoral procedure and drew dark pictures of what might come in the future, but nothing was done before the session ended early in March.

The discussion was of little interest to Ulyss. He felt that the Democratic menace was being taken too seriously, an outgrowth of the unreasoning alarm over the previous autumn's coincidence of individual defeats, and in any case the coming presidential contest seemed to him a little remote, not in time but in relevance. He would not be a candidate himself. He did not really want to go on for another four years struggling with the Senate; exposed to all the spite and malice there might be in the heart of any newspaper reporter or cartoonist who happened to differ with him; eating and sleeping in the unlovely company of the Southern Question, the Cuban Question, the Civil Service Question, and his own uncertainties. But when a third term for him was mentioned in newspapers with frank apprehension he felt a certain perverse stubbornness.

The party, he had been assured, would not demand his active assistance. His friends agreed that he was entitled to a holiday after fifteen years of almost intolerable responsibility. The only dissenter was Julia. She was reluctant to see Ulyss withdraw, and although she did little overt arguing he was well aware of what she felt. Once, when he had called the cabinet to consider whether he should make a public announcement of his intentions, she remained in the room and he found it hard to speak before her. She rarely witnessed cabinet meetings, but did it often enough so that this time he could not be sure if she knew the purpose of the meeting or had come by accident. He spoke vaguely of subjects unrelated to each other or to the one in his mind, until she gathered up her sewing equipment and rose.

'If there isn't going to be anything exciting,' she said, 'I think I'll go along.' She looked at her husband as the gentlemen came to their feet, her glance half-reproachful, half-amused, but she made no more direct appeal.

Remembering the incident, he did not show her the letter making public his decision when the time came to write it, months later. There had been a constant stream of complaints that it was fear of a third term for Grant that was stripping supporters from the Republican Party, and though he felt that the talk was not only impudent but disloyal there were so many signs of genuine party weakness that it seemed necessary for him to do what he could. He wrote to a Pennsylvania convention that he had not wanted his first term, but had taken it because he had thought that thereby he could serve his country. The second, his vindication, he had appreciated, but a third he wanted as little as he had the first. 'I would not write nor utter a word to change the will of the people in expressing and having their choice.' But unless circumstances made it a duty to accept he would not be a candidate for renomination, and he thought it unlikely that there would be such circumstances.

The newspaper report was the first Julia saw of the letter, or knew of Ulyss's intention to write it. He had been wrong to do it, she was positive. She knew that there was no longer the wide admiration and trust for Grant that there had been, but he seemed much more certain of himself and his policies now, and surely if he had more time he would regain the confidence that had been withdrawn from him. And it would not be easy to leave the White House, where Nellie had been married and Jesse had grown from a boy to the gangling verge of manhood; it would be hard to construct a life without the pattern of either the army or the government to go by. There was much more to the question of a third term, thought Julia, than Ulyss and his friends seemed to realize, but she said little about it to him. If he had been so afraid to hurt her that he had kept his letter a secret from her, a reproach would be crushing however lightly it was given, and she began in silence to detach herself from the ground of association wherein she was rooted.

Slowly the wave of reform, set in motion by the Congressional investigations, gathered and lifted until it crashed over Ulyss with what seemed to him bewildering malignance. He held firm, buffeted from every side, never allowed to draw breath between one crisis and the next, and he was angry. His friends were being forced out of the posts he had given them, were pursued without mercy through all their intimate affairs, and held up to public scorn — because they were his friends.

Attorney General Williams was forced out by the uproar over his confusion of his private accounts with those of the Department of Justice. Richardson had resigned to avoid a vote of censure. Delano, after a long feud with Bristow, was made to withdraw because of his connection with some land frauds in the west. To each of them Ulyss wrote a regretful letter of acceptance, and he found other places for them if he could. Perhaps there would have been less criticism of himself if he had put on the reforming coat, had turned stern and chill to his friends when they were so unfortunate as to be accused, and had condemned them, as the others did, without sympathy. Perhaps then his own name would have suffered less, but he knew certainly that then his respect for himself would be utterly destroyed. He would not abandon his friends to curry favor; he would not acquiesce in their persecution even indirectly.

No one ever considered, thought Ulyss, that the culprit might not have meant to do wrong, might have been more unwise than guilty, or might have had reasons important to himself for what he had done. Always he was drawn as a gross creature scheming against the public good, and by implication, sometimes by outright statement, Grant was a complacent accomplice. That was the real intent of all this righteous vigor,

Ulyss was certain. He was to be discredited, his judgment, his intelligence, and if possible his honor to be condemned. He did not understand it. He had wanted to do well, and surely by a just standard he had not done badly, though he had been unfortunate in many things. Yet he thought sometimes that he was hated, that no one really wanted to see him do a creditable thing, or to understand any of the complexities that sometimes left the discreditable as the only possibility.

Only a few of the scandals seemed to Ulyss to have a more important base than a few peccadilloes blown up to look like crimes against the state and evidence of his own incompetence, but one discovery of Bristow's appeared to be really serious. The Secretary of the Treasury had heard rumors, as had nearly everyone, of frauds in the collection of internal revenue, but the whispered stories always vanished into nothingness when an investigation was made. He was a methodical man, however, with very general suspicions, and he worked slowly, taking but one man in the Department into his confidence. It was some time before he was ready, and when at last he struck his success was appalling.

The root of the matter was in the evasion of taxes by some of the whiskey distilleries in the midwest, particularly in St. Louis and Milwaukee, with the assistance of the government collectors. But after the primary evidence had been seized and the investigation began there seemed to be no end to the branches of corruption. Other distilleries had been ingeniously blackmailed into complicity. Newspapers had been hired and silenced. Workers in the Treasury Department in Washington had served as scouts to discover any threat by the authorities. And a large part of the money had been used to influence elections. Ulyss was deeply shocked by the thing, and his horror was undiluted by personal resentment. He knew some of the men involved, but thought that they were innocent of the plot rather than that the plot was being given undue importance.

'There's McDonald,' he told Bristow. 'I expect you'll find he had nothing to do with it.'

'Perhaps — but it looks as if hardly anybody in St. Louis had nothing to do with it. With so many people involved it's a wonder it didn't come to light before this.' Bristow paused, then added, without looking at Ulyss, 'Is McDonald a friend of yours?'

'I wouldn't say that,' Ulyss answered. 'He's been very attentive to me and Julia, and Babcock knows him well.'

'I see.' Bristow moved a little uneasily, and his lips tightened. He may have been afraid of Grant's implacable loyalty, but when McDonald was indicted and it was shown that he was not only implicated but had created the ring, Ulyss had only disgust for the conspirator. He did feel sorry for Babcock, knowing the pain of seeing a friend accused, and he understood Babcock's dislike of the investigation.

'It's a fine thing for Bristow,' said Grant's secretary, his teeth flashing under his curled lip. 'He thinks he can walk straight into the White House over the bodies of the big bad robbers he's laid out. Serve him right if the Democrats lick him.'

'I don't think he'll run,' said Ulyss in surprise. 'I don't think he could be nominated — surely not.' He did not like the idea. Long ago Rawlins had insisted that presidential prospects in the cabinet were an executive's worst stupidity, and Ulyss himself remembered the trouble Lincoln had endured with his cabinet, composed almost entirely of disappointed aspirants. He would not endure an officer who was observing everything he did as an object lesson for campaign speeches on how to do it better, who would inevitably use his office itself as an instrument for his own purposes rather than those of Grant. But Bristow had not mentioned it, and seemed absorbed in the exposure of the whiskey ring for the sake of justice alone. Ulyss put Babcock's remark down to a natural anger over his friend's trouble.

All that summer the disclosures of the ring were a cumulative sensation. Several times people came to Grant indignant and alarmed —— It's persecution, not a trial. Bristow will stop at nothing to advance himself. There's no attempt at a fair hearing —— Each time the Secretary proved to Ulyss that justice was being scrupulously observed, and sometimes he could prove that the objector had reason to fear justice of any kind. Thus assured, Ulyss made no attempt to interfere. He was sickened as bit by bit it was made clear that the whiskey ring's activities had been known to many of the party workers, and that its funds had been regarded as an indispensable weapon in the election battles of that unstable section in an unstable period. It hurt him to know that the party used such methods, and hurt him again to hear the fact cried aloud in public. There seemed almost nothing left beyond his immediate circle that was not touched somewhere by corruption, or at least the suspicion of it.

Then even that circle was touched. A letter came to Long Branch, confused in phrase and purpose, but for all its cloudiness making a point that touched Ulyss's heart like an icy fingertip. The investigation was going too far, said the letter. Of course some action had to be taken, but the government counsel seemed bent on tearing the party to pieces. If they were not stopped soon they were going to get hold of Babcock. There was more, with an offensive assumption that Grant too was involved, but it was Babcock's name that hurt and frightened and angered Ulyss. It was nonsense, of course, a baseless, stupid lie like that old story of Babcock's dishonest motives in favoring San Domingo. Such things were revolting, but seemed to happen occasionally to anyone in public life. The letter deserved no more attention than that necessary to tear it up.

Ulyss could not move his hand. A number of small things were dragging at his consciousness, pointing in a direction where he did not want to look. 'I tell you he's my friend. If he weren't straight I'd know it, wouldn't I?' — 'If you do anything about it it puts him in a bad spot.' McDonald was guilty, there was no doubt of that. On Babcock's word McDonald had been appointed despite the protest from Schurz; whenever Grant had been impatient with McDonald, or would have lessened their intimacy, Babcock had been there to soothe and reassure the President. It was friendship, of course; any man may be mistaken in his friends —— Ulyss groaned aloud.

Memories, like the ants of the tropics that swarm into a wound and make it mortal. One of the assistant collectors in St. Louis had been a business agent for Grant, and had once asked, 'General, I suppose you know what we're doing in St. Louis, and it's all right?' Ulyss could still see his face, with its rigidly casual look around the anxious eyes. What his answer had been he could not remember — he would not have remembered the question had it not seemed so absurdly meaningless. The man had shot himself a few months before Bristow had dragged the ring into the public view, at about the time the members of the ring would know their game was growing dangerous. Had he been so sure the President was involved because he knew that the President's beloved confidential secretary was?

'General, I suppose you know . . .'

'If he weren't straight I'd know it, wouldn't I?'

He must not judge. He had no right to believe his friend had betrayed him because one dishonest man implied that he had. But neither, in the light of his own racking uncertainty, had he the right to destroy the letter. He sent it to Bristow, having written across the back of it: 'Let no guilty man escape if it can be avoided. Be especially vigilant — or instruct those engaged in the prosecution of fraud to be — against all who insinuate that they have high influence to protect — or to protect them. No personal consideration should stand in the way of performing a public duty.'

Very soon Ulyss regretted that endorsement. He had written it in a moment when the mere fact that he could doubt his friend was blinding agony, throwing him back on his fundamental instinct for action forthright and unmistakable, action without consideration of the subtle complexities of any situation. He had not realized that in some circumstances a stern call for justice may be the beginning of unforgivable injustice.

Bristow wanted to publish it. 'It's a great challenge,' he said. 'It leaves no doubt that the thing will be pushed through without any regard for politics or party favoritism, and it will put a stop to any rumor ——'

'I don't need to defend myself,' Ulyss said stiffly. 'I meant it confidentially, just for your guidance.' It seemed to him that Bristow was being unnecessarily ruthless of the party's reputation. There was no need to trumpet aloud, before it was made clear by the grand jury, that attempts had been made to involve even the party leaders in the plot — unless the disclosure would make useful campaign material for an aspirant to the presidency. That was one aspect of the matter that Ulyss had forgotten, but he was remembering it now more and more often. The work Bristow was doing was painfully necessary, but was he more pleased than distressed by his examination of the corrupt fungus that had flourished under Grant's administration? It was disquieting to see how intimate the Secretary was with Garfield, a leader of the group of Republicans most inimical to Grant...

The endorsement was published, and for a time the newspapers had a kindlier tone for Grant. But by then Ulyss had another reason, more heartfelt and more personal, for wishing the lines had never been written. He had tried not to let Babcock see that he had questioned his loyalty even for a moment; but his shaken faith changed him despite himself, made him less warm, less open, set his lips in a harder line, turned his eyes away.

Babcock sensed it at once, and was as quick to ask for an explanation. 'What's the matter? What is it that's made you angry with me?'

'I'm not angry.' Ulyss had meant to add something about the depressing weather, to make some comment that they could both pretend to believe, but he could not. He sat staring at the paper knife in his fingers, dropping it point first on the blotter, rubbing his thumb over the carved hilt.

'Then something's happened.' Babcock's handsome face was dark with trouble. 'It seems to me you ought to tell me. We've been together a long time, ever since the Wilderness — I've never felt before that there was something you held against me.' Suddenly he leaned forward. 'Is it the whiskey ring? That letter you sent on to Bristow? Did you really believe I was mixed up in that?'

Ulyss said nothing. He could not lie outright and protest that the suspicion had never occurred to him. And it was impossible to believe now that Babcock might have been a traitor, seeing him with his eyes reproachful and his mouth a little twisted because he had been hurt.

'I did think,' said Babcock slowly, 'that you'd trust me before you'd believe a lot of dirty hints from somebody you hardly know. Or, if you couldn't trust me, that you'd at least talk to me about it before you made up your mind.'

'I didn't make up my mind!' Ulyss cried. 'I did wonder for a little while, and I know now I shouldn't even have done that. But I just didn't know — so many things have gone wrong ——' He stopped, realizing ever more keenly how tragically at fault he had been. The treachery of which he had suspected Babcock could not approach his own treachery in questioning him for an instant.

'I know.' Babcock's voice was gentle, and his hand moved

as though he would have liked to put it on Grant's. 'Nobody could blame you for suspecting your own grandmother, the way Bristow noses around for ways to put you in the wrong and set himself up as a little tin saint. But maybe he'd ease off a little if I cleared out. If you got all new people around you he'd have to lie low for a while — there isn't time enough before the election to cook up something really juicy to catch them in. You might even take his advice on some new appointments, and then he'd be hogtied.'

'No!' The syllable was almost shouted. 'I make my appointments to suit myself, not anybody who comes along thinking he can run things better than I can. You know that. And I'm not making any new appointments. I'm satisfied with my staff, and I'm not going to change it.'

'But this thing will come up again. They know I was a friend of McDonald's, and as your secretary I'm fair game. They might even indict me on some sort of charge. If I wasn't at the White House any more it would look better for you ——'

'I don't care how it looks. I want you with me. Even if they fix it to bring you up for trial, you can tend to it on leave of absence. Unless you'd rather not stay?'

'There's no need to ask me that. I wouldn't know what to do with myself if you sent me off — but if you thought it would suit you better that way I'd go like a shot.'

Babcock could say such things, which might make other men feel so awkward that they sounded insincere, with a simple sureness that combined a man's comradeship with a woman's romantic loyalty. To Ulyss his words were a shining token of a staunch spirit, and he remembered them again and again in the difficult months to come.

The affair did not stop with private hints, as Babcock had foreseen. A few weeks after that troubling, obscure letter Bristow and Pierrepont, the new Attorney General, came to Grant with a peculiar discovery. Telegrams apparently in code had been sent to St. Louis before one of the Treasury's early unsuccessful raids, and the original messages on file in Washington were in Babcock's handwriting.

'They had nothing to do with the ring,' said Babcock, looking with a slight smile at the grave cabinet officers. 'Of course you know that some of the men were friends of mine, and I telegraphed them about some of my private affairs. How could I have warned them about the raid, when I'd never heard of the ring?'

Ulyss believed him — not again would he put his first faith in the word of his friend's enemies — but Bristow and Pierrepont were courteously doubtful.

'The ring was warned,' they insisted when Babcock left the room, 'and every evidence would show that it was warned by these messages. They must be submitted to the grand jury, even though ——' They broke off, looking at each other rather than at Grant.

'I see that,' said Ulyss smoothly, rejoicing that he could speak with no terror of his own words. 'If Babcock were guilty nobody would want it proven more than I would. That would be traitorism to me I couldn't forgive.' There was no point in trying to avoid a trial: it would be a vindication more complete than any private discussion could establish.

In November Babcock was indicted, and his trial set for early in the new year. His trial and, Ulyss felt, the trial of himself and his party. The prosecution was recklessly allowing the implication that the whole of the Republican organization was corrupt, and seemed indifferent to the presidential election that would come before the trials could fade in the public mind and a balanced judgment be reached. One of the government counsel, in an indignant speech to the jury, even openly attacked the President and his acts. The man was removed, but his breach was only one indication of the prosecution's delight in besmearing the administration. Bristow the pure and

stainless was not to be swerved from his Roman justice by any
ties of loyalty or demands of prudence. Of course, as Babcock
pointed out, if a nation with its puritan traits aroused should
wish to make Bristow president as a reward, his Roman sense
of duty would not allow him to refuse. It was becoming more
difficult week by week for Ulyss to suffer the man.

Soon after the beginning of the trial Babcock's counsel asked
the President to bear witness to the character of the accused.
Ulyss would have set out at once for St. Louis, but nearly all
his cabinet were horrified by the project. They talked heatedly
of the proprieties surrounding the position of the President, and
of the impossibility that the head of the government should
appear in person to defend a man the government was prose-
cuting, and Ulyss could not withstand them. Their reasons
seemed to him flimsy formalism compared with a man's right
to help a friend, but since his officers felt so strongly that a
personal appearance would compromise the government's dignity he did not insist on going. The government's dignity had
been compromised enough by the prosecution. There was
another way in which he could help, and the cabinet agreed
that he might properly give a deposition. He was interviewed
in the White House, and swore that never in all his association
with Babcock had he seen any evidence of connection with the
whiskey ring, and that if there had been a connection it could
not have been hidden.

The trial will prove that the charges are baseless. It did not
happen at once, as Ulyss had expected. Surely soon the trial
will prove —— It was hard to be patient, he must remember
that the law moves slowly. Day by day the trial moved forward, toward acquittal, for if Babcock were now found guilty of
fraud it would be necessary to find the President guilty either of
fraud or of blind stupidity. Yet the line it took was not the one
Ulyss had expected. He admitted to himself that he was disappointed, and then stood helpless while a worse thing than

disappointment knocked at his heart. Could the trial prove that the charges were baseless?

Slowly, as witnesses were questioned and points were made, Ulyss began to see a different Babcock from the handsome man who had been at his side for ten years, who had known so well how to lighten the weary routine. Here was a Babcock who had met the ring members many times, who had — perhaps? — sent them messages with no clear meaning unless it was what Babcock said they did not mean; who had — perhaps? — received money from them . . . There was nothing really definite. There was no proved point of which Ulyss could say, Herein he lied to me. But there was an atmosphere of futility in the proceedings, as though both sides knew the facts and could not, or would not, set them forth clear of the elaborate traceries of the law. Even Babcock's defense had not the air of fearless vigor that Ulyss had expected. You saw the money put into the envelope, but are you sure the envelope was addressed to Colonel Babcock? Did you see it mailed? What reason have you to think that Colonel Babcock actually received it? Thus pleads a clever lawyer — but not for an innocent man.

'That would be traitorism to me I couldn't forgive.' Ulyss did not say the words again, did not even think them when he was conscious of what he thought, but sometimes he found them in his mind when he had thought it safely filled with other things. This time he had not the cold sickness that he had felt when he had first doubted his friend, but only a numb weariness. He could not again endure the suffering over a betrayed trust, the joy and abasement of reassurance, the slow, painful return of misgivings, like the return of a cancer. He could not go on answering with the same fresh passion to every attack, feeling the same deep pain at every wound. There had been too many wounds, too many that strangers had dealt him in misunderstanding him, too many his friends had dealt him in not holding as scrupulously true to him as he did to them, too many that he had dealt himself in his groping progress. Perhaps Babcock had betrayed him. He could never be sure: the secretary was acquitted, because there was no legal proof against him, because Grant had protected him with all the weight of exalted office. If he were a traitor he was the closest, but he was not the first.

When Babcock returned he went again to his desk outside Ulyss's door, but none of the President's papers were on it. For a day or two he sat there, receiving congratulations from some of the callers and giving them his flashing smile; being elaborately ignored by others, and watching them with a grave, respectful face enlivened by the impalpable mockery in his eyes. Then one afternoon Ulyss asked him into his own office, and they sat facing each other alone.

It was hard to speak: Ulyss knew what he wanted to say, did not want to say it abruptly and could think of no subtle opening; Babcock had realized on his return that their intimacy as comrades facing a joint threat was gone, and he would say nothing until he knew what his standing was. At length Ulyss made a comment on the trial, and they talked of that, saying little, but with so many pauses that it took a long time.

Then Ulyss said, looking at Babcock but seeing little of him: 'I think maybe it would be better if you devoted your time to the Office of Public Works. Buck's been taking your place, and Mrs. Grant and I felt that we'd like to keep all the family together for the last few months we're here . . .'

'All right.' Babcock did not shrug his shoulders, but there was a shrug in his tone. 'Do you want me to go right off?'

'I think so,' said Ulyss, dropping his eyes, not in shame but because he was tired of looking at the indifferent, acquiescent face across from him. He heard Babcock leave the room, and thought he could hear the rattle of papers and a small sound as the outer desk was locked. Then there was silence.

This was how it happened, this was the way you put a friendship to death, choking it with a handful of stale words having nothing to do with the issue. There seemed to be no pain involved, only a feeling of pointlessness that spilled from the present into the past, making all the emotions that had once been clear and genuine, the hot anger, the steadfast loyalty, the love and the sympathy and the easy merriment between him and his friend, seem absurd and somehow cheap. Ulyss went to the door to see if any callers were still waiting to see him, dragging his feet a little, like an old man.

White House, Farewell!

CHAPTER TWENTY-SEVEN

THE chilly early morning sunlight fell through the window behind Belknap, and Ulyss kept his eyes lowered, to shield them from the light and to spare his officer discomfort. It could not be easy to say what Belknap was saying with some-one looking directly at you.

'She fixed it up before she passed on — I didn't know any-thing about it until after it was arranged, and it seemed a small thing to do for her. She loved pretty things so ——' Belknap choked, and Ulyss winced.

As usual, no one would understand any of the realities be-hind the thing. People would see only that Indian trading posts had been sold illegally, and that the Secretary of War, the Secretary's dead first wife, and his beautiful second wife had profited thereby for many years. No one would think of a woman who had an endearing way of touching her cheek to the fine silk of her gown, nor of a man who loved her.

'It will all come out now — they've been after me for weeks.' Belknap spoke so fast, and in so low a tone, that his words were a blur of terror. 'They're coming to you today, and to the House — impeachment — my God, my God —— ' He rocked forward, his face in his hands. 'Two women who bear my name — to be disgraced. In the grave, and at home —— '

'Give me your resignation,' said Ulyss.

'That's impossible, Mr. President.' Belknap sat still, and his voice was clear. 'They'll say you let me escape — you'll be politically ruined.'

'I'm not running for re-election,' said Ulyss. 'I demand your resignation, and I'll immediately accept it.'

The slip of paper was in his hand, and Belknap had gone, when the accusers came to the White House in full cry. They stood aghast when Ulyss told them what he had done, but he gave them no opportunity for comments, and they retired helplessly. An effort to impeach the erring Secretary would yet be made, but it must turn now on whether the Senate had jurisdiction over a man who no longer held office, a point in much doubt, rather than on whether the man was guilty, of which there was no doubt at all.

'I couldn't do less,' Ulyss told Julia that night. 'The papers will start howling all over again, but I only wish I could have done more.'

'The poor things,' Julia sighed. 'It does seem so sad. I'm sure you did exactly right, Victor. You've been criticized before and it hasn't hurt you, not really.'

Grant thought of the criticisms, year after year of them, with a Babcock scarcely torn from him before a Belknap was pulled down. The critics had not hurt Julia's Ulyss, but he could not tell yet how much they had hurt the rest of him.

'It hasn't been the way we planned, has it?' he said suddenly. 'I mean being President.'

'I think it's been nice,' she said, smiling at him warmly. 'You've done really wonderful things, and the bad things haven't been your fault. You couldn't help the panic, and the

way the Klan carries on.' He shook his head, and she rose to
put her arm around him, alarmed by his depression. 'You're
just tired, and that makes you see things the wrong way.
You ought to get right away from everything.' She felt him
stir, only a little.

There were some things which she knew he did not discuss
with her, some parts of his mind which were not closed to her
but beyond her understanding, yet she realized much in him
that he thought hidden from her. For some time she had
sensed his growing aversion to the plans they had made for the
future, his reluctance to settle in St. Louis again now that the
city was identified for him with the whiskey ring and Babcock's
trial. She paused, choosing words that would not even by inference touch on his bruises, adjusting her tone to the right note of
persuasion without letting it seem more than casual.

'It seems to me we might take a trip some place. You love
to travel, and I haven't ever been anywhere, really.'

He moved again, stiffened, but she was sure it was more in
surprise than in objection. 'What about White Haven?' he asked.

'Oh, we could lease it, I'm sure. Then when we came back we
could make up our minds what we wanted to do. Sometimes I
think I'd like to live in the east — I'm sort of used to it now.
But wouldn't you want to make a nice long tour somewhere?'

'I don't know.' His words were indifferent, but she heard
under them an eagerness there had not been in his voice for
months. 'We can think about it, anyway. There's no hurry.
It's a whole year till we can leave Washington.' She was content that the suggestion had been made, and let the subject
drop, but a quarter of an hour later he said, almost to himself,
'We might go to Europe,' and she all but laughed aloud.

That spring Congress investigated. It pried busily into the
affairs of departments and individuals, and showed equal glee
over glaring, cynical abuses or mere mistakes in judgment

that could be made to look like crimes. The committees had such arrogant disregard for courtesy and usage that even Grant's schismatic cabinet was at least united in fury. Many unpleasant and scandalous things were discovered in this wholesale inquisition, but plainly its motive was not so much righteousness as the necessities of the coming election. The newspapers had evolved the word Grantism for stupidity and corruption in office, and new instances of it were regularly supplied until the public appetite grew listless, and the public interest fastened on the choice of the next President, not on the shortcomings of the present one.

The Republican field was wide and uninspiring. The party had been shaken to the point of disintegration, had repudiated its leader and all his associates; and now aspirants by the dozen were sprouting in all the dissonant groups, contending bitterly with each other and distrusted by the party strategists, who knew that their candidate must have wide backing if there was to be any chance at all of defeating the resurrected and hungry Democrats. Bristow was often mentioned, and was popular with the reforming groups, but they disliked his courtship of the other elements, which would have nothing to do with him because the reformers liked him. Blaine perhaps had the greatest strength, but the inquisitorial House snuffed down the trail of his association with a railroad given to buying up votes. The results were inconclusive, but the investigation was a blight on Blaine's candidacy in a reforming year. Morton and Conkling were ambitious almost to the point of pathos, for their identification with the Indiana and New York machines made them impossibilities. A rabble of favorite sons completed the list, and the party managers found little comfort in it. Grant would have liked to see Fish get the nomination, and would have given him all his support, but the Secretary of State had had a microscopic view of the presidency for eight years, and did not find it tempting.

The June convention gave Blaine a long lead on the first ballot, and placed Morton and Bristow second and third with far less than half of Blaine's votes. On later ballots Blaine and Bristow gained a little, Morton's backing crumbled, and the only real strength was shown by Hayes of Ohio. He was not identified with any of the warring groups, though he was closely allied to the one in which Blaine and Garfield figured. He was Governor of Ohio, with a respectable record, and his wife was an earnest advocate of temperance. As the states completed their gestures to their sons they tended to assign their votes to Hayes, and his mounting strength became the conclusive argument for him. He was nominated as soon as it was apparent that Blaine had picked up all the votes he was going to get and still had not enough for victory. On the whole the party was well pleased. Its candidate might have no aura of greatness, but he was unimpeachable in all senses, and since the factions had contrived to nominate him without first quarreling until they were impotent from exhaustion, there was a good chance that they might hold together long enough to get him elected.

Four days after the convention Grant, coming down the White House steps to his carriage, encountered Bristow at the bottom. The Secretary of the Treasury bowed formally and in silence gave an envelope to the President. Ulyss took it and got into his carriage, also in silence. Bristow's resignation — for an absurd moment Ulyss wished that the man had never come into office, that the whiskey ring had gone undiscovered, that Babcock was still in his place, gay and handsome and trusted. For a moment: then he let even the wish slip from him. He was too tired for resentment; but there was a certain satisfaction on his straight mouth when he looked at the envelope in his hand.

The Democrats nominated Tilden of New York with terrifying speed and assurance. They were no longer the desperate party that had suffered a Horace Greeley for the sake of Liberal Republican votes. In the last four years of hard times and successive governmental scandals, while the passions of the war guttered out and the nation's usual restlessness under a second term set in, the Democrats had become a respect-worthy party again, a strong opposition with a sound chance of capturing the administration. Tilden was a Northerner, for the party could not yet risk a candidate from the South, al-though men were now in Congress whose voices had last been publicly raised in giving orders to rebel regiments. He was a conservative, for neither party would openly support the financial heresies that were beloved by great blocks of the voters. His record was not entirely clear on some controversies, but this was rather an advantage than a drawback, for he was to head a party which had tended to split its interests during its exile, with the Northern wing following the old pattern of party politics, while the Southern was concerned first of all with the redemption of the states still under carpetbag rule.

Neither Hayes nor Tilden roused any enthusiasm in Ulyss, but he sometimes felt more kindly toward Tilden, who was a Democrat and thus had a hallowed right to attack Republicans. Hayes had no such excuse, but he appeared to be basing his campaign on a repudiation of his own party's record. His speech of acceptance sounded the keynote: his enthusiasm for civil service reform was boundless — also sudden, thought Ulyss; he was going to run the government with unswerving purity and justice; he would not be a candidate for a second term. He was right on that point, Ulyss knew. Any such indifference to the patronage as he proposed would be political suicide for himself, and murder of his party. Ulyss remembered his own notions of appointments, his determination to put the best possible man in every place. He had learned quickly that the very volume of appointments made considered selection impossible; and that the needs of the party, the tactics of policy, the thousands of interlocking compromises which are the process of government, are necessarily the basis for the use of the patronage. The memory touched Ulyss with nostalgia, but gave him no sympathy for Hayes. He himself had been naïve, but his innocence had been genuine, not tin armor put on to dazzle the voters. He had stood apart in decent dignity from the process of getting himself elected, not run up and down constantly assuring the public that if it chose him he would certainly dissociate himself from all that his party had done.

True, Hayes did apologize to Grant for the acceptance speech, explaining that he had felt it necessary in order to draw together the Republican factions. Ulyss was not soothed by the implication that an attack on him was the best method of unifying his party, and he saw no change in Hayes's methods. If Tilden had not been a Democrat Ulyss would have preferred him wholeheartedly, but as it was he maintained a weary neutrality.

He had enough to do in the pre-election fever without concerning himself in its result. Once more two desperate sides in the South sought voters, and rumors of violence, threats of violence, and appeals for help against violence poured in to the President. There were now only three states that had not been reconquered by the Democrats: South Carolina, Florida, and that perennial political riddle, Louisiana, but they were turbulent enough to keep Grant in constant uncertainty as to whether he should intervene. For eight years he had been shifting the army around the South in an effort to establish a second party there, and had seen state after state by one means or another settle down under exclusively Democratic rule — and refuse to settle down until Democratic rule was allowed. He was tired of trying to change the political habits of a people by military force, and the rest of the nation was also tired of it. Business men wanted a South sufficiently tranquil to trade in, and were filled with sympathetic horror at the mushrooming figures of Southern state debts. Reformers were bursting with instances of Southern degradation under the carpetbaggers. And the mass of the Northern people were simply impatient at a problem that had outlasted their interest in it.

Yet the reconstruction governors and state leaders appealed desperately for Federal intervention, and a majority of the cabinet, seeing how close the election was going to be, urged the President to send in troops, with pathetic uneasiness. Zachary Chandler was angry and terrified at the prospect of his only three possibilities in the South being allowed to fall to the Democrats. Friendship and policy and habit combined on the side of action, and the arguments that were used had seemed sound to Ulyss many times before. But he delayed and hesitated, and used troops only where there was actual danger. In states that were not in truth so close to murderous riot as their governors insisted, he would do nothing.

It was hard to say why he was now so reluctant to interfere when he had formerly been quick to use his power at his friends' request. He had tried to work with the organization that set the frame for his office, always taking its wishes and needs into account, and never deciding against them unless they were in flat opposition to convictions of his own. Now, despite his service, the organization had turned from him, and was making his very name a reproach in an effort to prolong its power. Even the men who were his friends were following that diverging line: Chandler was managing Hayes's campaign; Morton and Conkling were giving all their great powers of oratory to the support of a man they half-despised. Ulyss did not hold it against them. Politics was their profession, as the army had been his, and it was necessary for them to battle under Hayes's banner — but he was not thus conscripted.

If he had been disowned he had also in a measure been given back to himself. He stood once more in a clear relationship to the people, unobscured by the party mechanism, such as he had not known since he had stood on the portico of the Capitol to speak to them eight years ago. There was a difference. They had looked toward him then, acknowledged a bond between themselves and him, expected much of him. Now they had turned away in disappointment, but the bond was still there, even though they had renounced it, even though it would be broken in a few months. He was free to do as he thought best, with no consideration of party policy or anything else except the people, who had forgotten he was leading them.

As a matter of courtesy he did do a few things for Hayes's campaign, chiefly in the patronage, but on the South he stood firm. By another summer he would be out of office, in Europe perhaps, and his connection with the South would be ended. It had lasted for a long time, ever since he had been a colonel, and had tried to see that his unruly men committed no depredations on unfriendly civilians further than those allowed by the usage of war. President Grant, on a summer day in 1876, chuckled suddenly as he remembered a regiment that had been unjustly fined for stealing honey, and had groaned at him: 'Who stole the honey? General Grant's bodyguard. Who ate it? General Grant's staff. Who paid for it? The Twenty-Second Illinois . . .' That had been on the way to Fort Henry. He could remember the clean, brown, frosty look of the empty fields in the light of a January morning, and the toothless, determined mouth of the woman who had complained so bitterly about the stolen honey.

Southern faces — he could remember thousands of them, in no way different from Northern faces except for the strangeness cast over them by the consciousness of enmity, yet that intangible thing making even the face of a small boy staring at the Union troops forever memorable. The anxious, resentful faces of the citizens of Oxford, when Grant had first discovered that he could supply his army from the countryside. Half-amused curiosity in the eyes of the Confederate sentries who had turned out the guard for him at Chattanooga. A whole procession of prisoners' faces, defiant at first but growing spiritless as the long torment drew to a close. Lee's grave, steady eyes bent on the terms he must accept. Then the faces of peace, of the men who had come to talk to Grant when he had gone South at Johnson's request, in that autumn when the future had seemed difficult but hopeful. Fewer and fewer faces as the South descended into chaos and Southerners came to think of Washington as the capital of a foreign oppressor; and then for a time Ulyss had felt that the South had no face at all, only the white mask of the night riders. Now at last, after ten years of bitter unarmed struggle, the war was nearly finished, and the cast of enmity was no longer to set a Southern face apart from one of the north or east or west.

The South was the only continuing line that Ulyss could see in his life, the only concern that had touched the General and the President alike. In a little while now it would be taken out of his hands, but he had marked it, and it had marked him. He would like to bring his part to an end according to his own basic inclinations, unaffected by political passions and necessities or the impulses of a day. He had never hated the people he had defeated, as he had never fundamentally feared them. They had had a right to rebel. He believed that as firmly as he believed that the rest of the country had had a right to suppress the rebellion if it could, and, having suppressed it, to impose its will on the defeated. He had hoped that when the last battle was fought and the question settled there would be enough tolerance on both sides to forget the catastrophe and turn to the future in unity.

Something had prevented that result — just what, he did not know. Perhaps it was the shock of Lincoln's death, or Johnson's stubborn, involved temperament, or the result of forces he had never understood, or perhaps all three. Whatever the reason, Grant, who had wanted a settlement involving the least possible humiliation, had advocated two constitutional amendments to be forced on an unwilling people, and had used the army to interfere in their civil affairs. Grant, who had regarded the negro as still too ignorant and primitive for the full privileges of citizenship, had approved the wholesale enfranchisement of the race, and used all his power in an effort to keep it from being meaningless. He felt now that he had not been wise, nor had any of his associates, but as he went back over the complex events that had thrust him forward he could not find a point where he might have turned aside. It was as if history had made itself, with a cynical disregard of the faith of its characters. Now eight of the Confederate states were quiet and well ordered again, and in the other three the Democrats were joyfully confident that the fall elections would put them into power and pry loose the last tentacles of Northern domination. It was what they wanted, and they could never be persuaded to want anything else. The peace was ten years late, and Ulyss had no intention of delaying it still longer in order to make sure of Hayes's election.

No one had any certainty of the result. Both sides forecast easy victory on the platform, but in the offices where the campaign managers sat calculations were anxiously made again and again, and never showed a conclusive answer. The Liberal Republicans, lamed by their independent experiment in practical politics, had chosen no ticket of their own. Some of the more uncompromising were supporting Tilden, but Schurz and his close associates found impeccably logical reasons for returning to party regularity, and aligned themselves with Hayes. Neither Schurz nor Hayes was thereby more endeared to Ulyss.

The parties began the campaign evenly balanced, with the strength given to the Republicans by sixteen years of power offset by the popular reaction that gave new vigor to the Democrats. Evenly balanced they came to Election Day, and then the verdict scarcely tipped the scale. Out of more than eight million votes cast, Tilden had a majority of half a million. He had 184 electoral votes. He needed 185. Hayes had 172. The votes from Oregon, South Carolina, Florida, and Louisiana were disputed. Oregon had chosen an elector who was a Federal officeholder; the votes from the three Southern states still under Republican governments were innately open to challenge from both sides. No decision — the country was quiet in sheer surprise at first, but in its quiet could be heard the faint rumble of anger and determination, and there was a hot constriction in the air.

The day after the election Ulyss was given the first evidence of the intolerably difficult task that would be his. He visited Childs in Philadelphia, and that evening the house was filled with jubilant guests.

'Hayes will get in now, not a doubt of it ——'

'I scarcely dare believe it. You know, when I went to bed last night I was perfectly sure we'd lost ——'

'Did you hear about Chandler? He'd gone to bed too, and they had to wake him up to tell him there was a chance in the South ——'

'It was a near thing. Too close for comfort — next time, when hard times are over, and people aren't blaming their troubles on anybody who holds office ——'

A steady hum of joy. These men had learned quickly that they could trust their interests and their point of view to the Republicans, and their rescue from a Democratic victory almost seemed divine intervention. Ulyss watched them quietly until he was sure that they were sincere, that they were not simply trying to comfort themselves. Then he remarked, 'Gentlemen, it appears to me that Tilden has been elected.'

As always, his tone was low, but it silenced the others more effectively than a shout. They turned to him, aghast, torn between due deference and a desire to assume that he was joking.

'He's failed to get a majority,' someone pointed out.

'He needs just one vote,' said Ulyss dryly. 'Do you think Governor Hayes will get every single one of those outstanding?'

'Oregon's safe,' said Childs, 'and the other three ——' He fumbled, began again, 'The three Southern states ——' and stopped.

'I should think Louisiana, for instance, is likely to have at least one Democratic elector.' Ulyss spoke as calmly as though he did not know that he was horrifying his listeners, as though he did not hear their silent cry — That can be arranged. Aren't you going to arrange it? His tone was coolly objective, and it gave them their answer — No, I won't.

Wait, be patient, hold firm, the word ran through the country. Time enough to act when we know the decision has gone against us. There were no outbreaks, and few open threats, but it could not be felt that the country was calm. It was waiting for the reports of the Southern returning boards, and after that it would wait to see what action would be taken on the reports. It was impossible to say what would happen then, it was impossible even to be sure that anything would happen, but in the autumn of that centennial year Americans' mouths were angry and their eyes were filled with sidelong fear of each other.

Grant knew that there was very little he could do. The solution must be found by others, by the party managers, the party leaders, the men who still carried the authority and responsibility to which he himself had only a titular right. Whoever the country had chosen to lead it and deal with its problems, it was not he. Yet ultimately he did have a responsibility, not so obvious as the others', but of even greater importance. It might be that no decision could be made, no facts established without any tinge of doubt, no compromise arranged acceptable to more than a few groups. And then? No one knew, but everyone remembered that not very long ago armies had sprung up to settle a question that statesmen had been unable to solve. It was Ulyss's responsibility, as head of the nation and steward of its destiny, to prevent a repetition of that tragedy, to prevent any development that might make men think they had no other choice.

This was the charge that possessed his mind by day and woke him in the darkest of the night hours to lie restless and aghast. There was no hysteric fantasy in his fear. The months after Lincoln's election in 1860 had been no more tense, and at that time civil war had seemed much more impossible than it did now, when a precedent had been set. If there was a nightmare unreality in the thought of defending the line of the Hudson, or of subduing Indiana, which was a Tilden state, by simultaneous attacks based on Illinois and Ohio, which had voted for Hayes, it was no more unreal than the river port of Vicksburg being known as the scene of a great siege, or the insignificant Bull Run flooding into history in a bloody torrent. Ulyss knew. He had seen forests and farming country become battlefields. He had seen the latent violence in a peaceful people transform mechanics and clerks and farmers into soldiers. Perhaps the horror of the war that had already been experienced and the torment of recovery from it had sobered the people. Perhaps it had only weakened their resistance to it, and made them forget the methods of peace. No one could be sure.

There was no positive action he could take to combat his fear. He could only hold steadily to his course, favoring neither side, and see to it that neither the strength nor the justice of the government could be questioned. It was hard enough to do. The pressure for intervention in the three contested states was continual, and was growing harder and harder to resist as the moderates in his party began to feel the tension and to cry out in terror. He would not interfere by sending in troops to make sure that Republican electors were chosen, nor could he interfere by identifying himself with any compromise plan. There

were dozens of them. Even Longstreet, the Confederate general
who had stood so long with Lee, who had long ago been best
man at Grant's wedding, wrote to Ulyss proposing that Hayes
accept the Republican votes from Louisiana in exchange for a
promise to recognize the Democratic government that state
had chosen. Grant could not answer. In these perilous months
he was the President of the whole people, and he must not take
sides even in an effort to reconcile them.

Congress met in December, a month after the election, while
the struggle over the returning boards still continued. It
would be the last session under Grant's administration. Eight
years must be accounted for in his message, the last report he
would ever have an opportunity to make, his final chance to
speak for himself to the people. He thought sometimes that
there had been a slight change in their recent opinion of him.
Since the end of the autumn campaigns they had not been
speaking so much of Grantism, and perhaps a majority of them
approved his course in the present crisis. Yet he knew there
would be little regret when he drove away from the White
House, whether Tilden or Hayes were at his side. He did not
believe he had failed in his trust. There had been mistakes, but
he had been savagely punished for them, and no one had
troubled to find out first if it were he who was primarily at
fault. He wanted to say so, to admit that his presidency had
somehow failed to fulfill his intention, but to defend himself
against the critics who had so delighted in tearing all that
had been done by himself or his friends into disreputable tat-
ters.

'It was my fortune, or my misfortune,' he began, 'to be
called to the office of Chief Executive without any previous
political training. . . .' As he wrote he wondered how it had
happened, what it was that had snatched him from the army,
which he understood, and set him at eight years of labor on
tasks of which he knew nothing, for a many-headed master

with inconsistent demands. There was no single reason that he could remember clearly, only a confusion of Rawlins's burning eyes, Johnson's exasperating methods, Stanton's unpredictability, and a steady barrage of whispered hints and suggestions and statements, until he could not be sure which of his thoughts came from his own mind. 'Under such circumstances it is but reasonable to suppose that errors of judgment must have occurred. Even had they not, differences of opinion between the Executive, bound by an oath to the strict performance of his duties, and writers and debaters must have arisen. It is not necessarily evidence of blunder on the part of the Executive because there are these differences of views.' If the people had wanted to be governed by the Springfield *Republican* they could have elected Samuel Bowles. They had seen in Greeley what sort of leader an editor makes.

'Mistakes have been made, as all can see and I admit, but it seems to me oftener in the selections made of the assistants appointed to aid in carrying out the various duties of administering the Government — in nearly every case selected without a personal acquaintance with the appointee, but upon recommendations of the representatives chosen directly by the people....' Remember that. Remember it, you who say my name with a sneer, as standing for corruption and dishonor. The hardest pressure has always come from Congress, from men insisting that this consulship, that post in the custom-house, must go to their candidate, for the sake of the party. For every Babcock that I trusted there have been half a dozen Tom Murphys that you urged upon me. The responsibility is mine, I know it, my name will carry it long after I am dead, but you who have been my friends and associates are not blameless. No one else will remember that — remember it yourselves. 'But I leave comparisons to history, claiming only that I have acted in every instance from a conscientious desire to do what was right, constitutional, within the law, and for the very best interests of the whole people. Failures have been errors of judgment, not of intent.'

The rest of the message recounted the story of his eight years — it looked strange, set down in the dry terms of an official document, with no tinge of the anxiety and triumph and silent disappointment that had marked the events themselves. There was but one brief glimpse, in a reference to San Domingo: ' . . . if my views had been concurred in the country would be in a more prosperous condition today, both politically and financially. . . . I do not present these views now as a recommendation for a renewal of the subject of annexation, but I do refer to it to vindicate my previous action in regard to it.' Then a brief farewell: 'With the present term of Congress my official life terminates. . . .'

Ulyss could not tell, as he looked at that statement, if he was glad to write it or not. Perhaps he would have been regretful had this recital of events been the full history of his administration. A war avoided, a nation's credit restored, these were good things to remember. But he had necessarily omitted other things, the months of palsying uncertainty while he groped toward decisions, building a road of knowledge and policy through unknown territory; the pain of finding that good intent may result in abysmal error; the sick weeks of watching Babcock appear as a complacent opportunist rather than a loyal friend; the growing fear that this centennial year of the nation might be its last. No — as he pushed the papers from him Ulyss was well enough pleased that he had finished, and in a few months could sink all his regrets for things done and undone into the broad ocean that he and Julia were to cross together.

Little attention was paid to the message, not enough to discover the few sentences of genuine meaning in the heavy matrix. No one was interested in the end of Grant's administration nor in what he thought of it, so long as no one knew who would head the next one. The returning boards, exclusively Republi-

can in membership, had certified slim Republican majorities
in all three contested Southern states. The Democrats submitted the returns as originally reported on Election Day, with
Democratic majorities not so slim, but not so overwhelming as
to make a conclusive case. Thus the problem had been presented to Congress, and Congress was entirely occupied by a
controversy over the election law.

The Constitution had a deceptive clarity: the President of
the Senate shall open the votes in the presence of both houses,
and the votes shall then be counted. But nothing was said of
choosing between two sets of votes from the same state, an
omission which gave vital importance to the question of who
should count the votes. Republicans found it clearly indicated
that the President of the Senate, who must open the votes,
must also count them. Democrats were positive that the count
was the duty of the House of Representatives, which was the
final arbiter in a drawn election. The one absolute certainty
was that neither side would agree with the other, and while
they contended the winter days were fast dwindling toward
March.

It was after the middle of January before a bill to effect a
compromise was worked out and brought before Congress. It
provided that a commission be set up to decide on conflicting
returns, to be composed of five members of the House, five of
the Senate, and five of the Supreme Court. All controversies
would be referred to the commission, and its decisions could be
overruled only by concurring vote of both houses. This formal
structure was at once translated as meaning seven Democrats
and seven Republicans, chosen by amiable arrangement between House and Senate, with the odd man from the Supreme
Court an independent. The House was thus well satisfied, and
passed the bill promptly, but the Senate balked.

Then at last there was action for Grant. He asked Conkling
to come to him, and said flatly, 'I think this commission ought

to be appointed. The country can't stand around and wait forever just because the Senate's afraid the count will go to Tilden.'

'It's Morton,' said Conkling with equal frankness. His mouth twisted, half in sardonic amusement, half in sympathy. 'Maybe he's unhappy because his own Hoosiers went and voted for Tilden right under his nose, but whatever it is, he won't give an inch.'

'He'll have to,' said Ulyss slowly. 'Somebody has to give in, or there won't be any country left for any President.'

'You think it's that serious?'

'I don't know, but I think the Senate has no right to risk it.'

'Well, I'll see what I can do. If I can't see you in this office I'd as leave have Tilden as Hayes, sniveling about the civil service all the time. He's soured — maybe it's all that water Mrs. Hayes makes him swill.' Conkling laughed, with the ringing, golden tone that made him such an effective speaker, and gave Ulyss an impulse to smile that he had not felt in weeks. 'Edmunds and Frelinghuysen are trying hard enough. I'll get out and push with them. I always get along so well with reformers.'

He lingered for a few moments, saying disrespectful things of various staid figures, until Ulyss forgot for a while the black foreboding that weighed on him, and talked of the bill as if it were an ordinary measure. He was not entirely disowned. Conkling still stood firmly at his side, and through Conkling and men like him he might yet have an influence on events.

By a close vote the Senate approved the bill, and Congress promptly met under its provisions to settle the election at last. The conviction that the commission's decisions would be one-sidedly Democratic was promptly disproved, for the independent justice who was to have been chosen resigned from the Court to take a seat in the Senate, and his place was taken by a man who insured that the decisions were one-sidedly Republican. The first disputes which the group considered concerned its own policy. It determined that it could not go back of the returns presented to it, and must confine itself to the electoral votes, without reference to the popular vote, the character of the returning boards, or anything else. All this was settled by a vote of 8 to 7. Florida, South Carolina, Louisiana, and Oregon then came up for individual rulings, and in each case the commission found, 8 to 7, that the legal electoral vote was Republican. The decisions were returned to the joint session of Congress, and the House repudiated them, but since the Senate upheld them they stood, and before dawn on the second of March Hayes was declared victorious, by an electoral vote of 185 to 184.

It had been generally agreed that the moment of such a verdict would be the most perilous time of all those months of peril. That day and the next men waited from hour to hour for the outbreak of civil war. Nothing happened. There were rumors in plenty of secret caches of weapons, of plans to inaugurate Tilden regardless of the ceremony for Hayes, of armed groups waiting for the signal to rise — but there was not so much as a riot to give the rumors body. There was angry talk in newspapers, but no real advocation of violence; Northern Democrats planned a filibuster, but the Southern leaders, with unearthly selflessness, dissuaded them.

And one rumor, little heard among the fascinating whispers of imminent revolution, was that a bargain had been made, that Southern freedom, alike from Northern control and from strict interpretation of the reconstruction laws, was the price Hayes had given to become the nineteenth President of the United States. There were other names for it than Southern freedom. Abandonment of the negro was one; betrayal of the Northern Democrats another. It was only a rumor, one among many, but it did have at least an appearance of truth as loud noises of outrage came from the Northern Democratic press, with only weak echoes in the South, and nothing more than noise anywhere.

If Ulyss heard the whisper he did not believe it. He knew that a compromise, an adjustment between two sides of such nearly equal strength, was necessary, but a bargain involving the negation of difficult years of policy and pledges spoken and implied was unthinkable to him. He believed soberly that there was very real danger of insurrection, or of a renewed, long-drawn legal controversy that would cripple governmental authority so badly that it might never regain its strength. For months business and industry had been functioning only enough to avoid a complete standstill, unwilling to put the slightest faith in a future so darkly uncertain. They could not withstand that tension indefinitely prolonged, and Ulyss prepared to see that the decision was enforced with such firm swiftness that rebellion would have no fuel of uncertainty to feed on.

The decision did seem a little strange to him. Florida and South Carolina, so far as could be seen in the cloud of violence and chicane that hung over them, did seem to have chosen Republican electors, and the contest in Oregon was essentially over a technical point. But he had thought that Louisiana had been fairly won by the Democrats, and he had been prepared to see that Tilden was duly inaugurated. Now Hayes was chosen. Ulyss was somewhat surprised, but it was not his duty to enforce his own opinion. The commission had been chosen by Congress, which had been chosen by the people. If its eight-to-seven decisions had plainly been partisan, still it had acted as representative of the people, and since it had chosen Hayes he must act on its opinion as firmly as if it had been his own.

That year the fourth of March fell on Sunday. Ulyss dared not delay the inauguration, according to custom, until Monday, for Tilden was being urged to take the oath on the traditional day and make his case on the hiatus in authority. Hayes was asked if he would take the oath privately on Sunday, and he answered that in no circumstances could the President-Elect commit such a profanation. It was impossible to persuade him to change his stand, whether by arguments based on the national interest or by an appeal to his sense of proportion or to his sense of humor, if he had one. It was at length decided that he would dine at the White House with the Chief Justice on Saturday, March 3, and take the oath then.

Nearly thirty guests assembled for that dinner, some suggested by Hayes at Grant's request, some that Ulyss himself had chosen to meet the new Executive. They talked with as much animation and pleasant laughter as though none was conscious that the nation was distraught, and that its fear and disappointment and anger centred over the house where they had gathered. Each was aware of it, but the awareness showed only in their avoidance of the subject, with a determination that was half courage, half cowardice. Apparently none noticed when the host and the most important guest disappeared shortly before dinner. No word was said of it, and the glances that were exchanged, speculative, grave, excited, were secret.

In the Red Room Hayes stood before Chief Justice Waite, his hand on the opened Bible. Ulyss stood at one side with Fish. 'I do solemnly swear . . .' Hayes's voice was deep, with a feeling for the simple, solemn words that gave him dignity, despite the limitations that Ulyss sensed in him, despite the humiliating setting for this high moment. Grant listened attentively, but his own thoughts whirled in dizzy confusion around a core of still perception. He had always liked this room, with its warm, rich coloring and wide view of the grounds from the curved window . . . Fish looks solemn and dignified. He's a good man . . . It is all safe now. Whatever happens, Hayes is President of the United States, properly inaugurated in the presence of witnesses . . .

This is the end of the story begun eight years ago, standing

in the sunlight while the people cheered, with Rawlins's somber
eyes for once alight in pleasure, with great work to be done and
the serene consciousness of strength great enough to do it.
Be forgotten now, Rawlins; San Domingo the golden island;
Babcock whom I loved; all that I meant to be and to do; be
forgotten. With these words being spoken by a stranger you
are finished. This is the end, here in the shadows, doing the
thing that must be done with an ear always ready for the angry
cries of a people that has not cheered for a long time, not daring
to think too clearly of what it is we do. ' . . . and will to the
best of my ability, preserve, protect, and defend the Constitution of the United States.'

It was over. Ulyss shook hands with President Hayes and
left the room as quickly as he could. He had a sudden great
need to see Julia and to touch her hand, that was always warm
and firm in his whether he caught it up in triumph or clutched
at it, as now, when he was sick at heart.

PART NINE

A Hospitable Europe

Europe-Bound to Know More of the World

IX. THE MAN NAMED GRANT

CHAPTER TWENTY-EIGHT

SMALL boys shouted 'Old Eight-to-Seven' at the President of the United States. There was a sudden exodus from Louisiana of men of Northern origin and dubious occupation, after President Hayes recognized the Democratic government there. Many Americans were puzzled and resentful, feeling that somehow they had been cheated, but they had not a clear enough understanding of how and why to be dangerously united in their anger. Slowly the nation quieted, lost its sense of historic crisis, grew indifferent, so slowly that there was never a moment when men sighed with relief and said, All danger is past; but after some time they realized that there was no more danger, and perhaps there never had been.

The events of the new administration seemed remote to Ulyss. He had forgotten how flavorless a newspaper article may be to a reader who does not know the skirmishes and maneuvers and pitched battles that occasioned it, and he felt resentfully that Hayes was making sure the former President would be thus excluded.

'I put him into office,' Ulyss said grimly to Julia. 'If I hadn't stuck by what the commission said, and persuaded the Senate to let the commission be appointed in the first place, Tilden would be President, or else we'd be having a war. And I was in the White House for eight years. But his nibs would go to Jeff Davis for advice before he'd come to me.'

'Senator Conkling says he's perfectly horrid,' Julia agreed placidly. 'His appointments ——'

'Appointments!' Ulyss rose and walked restlessly up and down. 'Didn't he put Schurz in the Interior, one of the men who's done everything in his power to injure me? Anybody who was ever an enemy of mine can have whatever he wants from Hayes. He isn't even honest. He couldn't recognize the Democratic governor in Louisiana and still keep the Republican electors. If he thinks Louisiana voted Democratic the only honorable thing he can do is to resign.' Ulyss went on talking, not to convince Julia, who never disagreed with him on such subjects, but to deny a flat depression in himself. He was annoyed by Hayes's slights, but he had not liked the man as a candidate and had never expected to like him as President. But it seemed to him that already he had been forgotten by the people, blotted out by even so puny a figure as Hayes. It was disconcerting and unpleasant, and it added a spur to his original eagerness to go away. It did not much matter where, nor for how long. He had a reasonably large amount of money, and he was going as far and as long as it would take him.

The morning of his departure from Philadelphia he was given the first evidence that he had not after all fallen into unhonored obscurity. There were editorials wishing him godspeed in all the morning newspapers, not only those that had been friendly to his administration, but those that only a few months ago had implied that he was either feeble-minded or criminal. Their good will was sincere, with the cheerful inconsistency of political partisanship when its object is dead or defeated. Even the ship he was to take lay in the river with so many flags spread to the May breeze that it looked more like a carnival float than a sober oceangoing steamer.

There was a great farewell breakfast, and he was toasted in champagne. Many of the guests were his close friends, an oddly assorted group, as if to typify the confusion of his intimacies. There was Childs, the banker; and Cameron, the Radical who dominated Pennsylvania; and Hamilton Fish, still an intimate even now that his caution and clear-eyed obstinacy were not of hourly importance. Sherman had come, with the warm, resilient friendship for Sam Grant that had endured through years of differing opinions. Sherman, so far as he thought about politics at all, would have approved a milder policy in the South, and he disliked many of Grant's political associates. He held heatedly to his opinions, Grant held coldly to his own, and it might have seemed inevitable that their friendship would crack, but it had remained untouched. It was rooted in things of greater importance to each of them, in memories of the war years when a man's friendship must withstand mutilation of the body and chaos of the spirit, so that a mere political difference was entirely meaningless.

As they crowded around Ulyss to say good-bye he was conscious of them as a composite of the world he had lived in for seventeen years, the only world that was truly his, for the period before he had entered it was meaningless and half-forgotten to him now, and he could not envision the world to which he would return at the end of his journey. Sherman, Fish, Cameron, and Childs: soldier, two varieties of politician, and man of business. These were his friends, who wrung his hand and laughed and were sorry to see him go. They shrank and grew indistinguishable among the hundreds of strangers on the shore as the ship gave herself to the tide and slipped downriver, but they stayed large and warm in Ulyss's thoughts. They were not men to be frightened by the word Grantism, or by the acid bite of newspaper cartoons, that did no more than break the skin but left a festering soreness in that small wound.

Perhaps he had more friends than he had thought, perhaps he was not wholly disdained. 'Take your time,' Cameron had murmured when he said good-bye. 'Give this milksop long enough to make a fool of himself. There may be something doing when you get back.' Perhaps, thought Ulyss, beneath the surface storms and whirlpools of opinion there was a quiet respect for him, as beneath the endless circular waves he stared at was the deep, mysterious quiet of the sea. He dared not believe it, unwilling to risk the pain of disillusionment, but the unadmitted thought warmed his heart and lightened his spirit.

England, a real country, not just a word connected with the *Alabama* claims. Ulyss and Julia and Jesse were met by Badeau, who had been the American consul in London under Grant's administration, and was now wondering uneasily about Hayes. The former aide found offensive the arrogant deference with which some of the ruling groups received his chief. He was acutely conscious of each minute that Grant was kept waiting by some titled notable, each slight inflection that might imply

a haughty comparison of backgrounds, each social delicacy
whereby the reigning prince of a pipsqueak European princi-
pality was given precedence over the man who had been elected
to head the United States. Ulyss was not aware of any of these
things. He found many of the English stiffly dull, and thought
no more about them, not having Badeau's democratic touchi-
ness. The thing that really interested him in England was the
great mass of the factory workers. He saw them by the thousands, for almost every city he came to declared a holiday in
his honor, and the laboring men left their looms and mills and
furnaces to come and look at him.

They did not come because he was Grant, he knew, nor
because he had been President. Many of them were scarcely
aware that he had held civil office. They came because his
name was bound up with the war, that distant war fought on
issues of no immediate importance to them, in which they had
taken so passionate an interest. It had affected them. They
had gone hungry because no cotton had crossed the sea to
give them work; yet it had been their enormous, unconsulted
weight that had balanced the scales against the Southern sympathies of their rulers, and held their country neutral. Now
they came to see Grant because he had ended in victory the
war against slavery. The war had been over a long time, all the
issues that had seemed so clear had clouded and wavered and
grown confused, and much that had been done since was the
sorry result of impulse and haste rather than of wise reasoning
from principles of justice. They did not care. Their own lives
were hard and often bitter; they had never seen a slave; but
the bondsman was a dark symbol of something that was important to them, so important that it overshadowed political
realities and made the figure of General Grant another symbol,
of an obscure victory of their own. He spoke to them, over
and over, in ugly industrial cities and in the small towns that
were growing ugly, and he spoke with an ease he had never

known before, for he sensed that they found point and satisfaction in whatever he said.

Other things were memorable in his English stay. There were small incidents of annoyance or pleasure, and an epic of Jesse defying the Queen, threatening to return to London from Windsor rather than dine apart from his parents with the servants — the titled men and women who formed the royal household. He overcame Victoria of England as he had all his life overcome his mother and father. Julia found a self-contained, innocent pleasure in the tidy English countryside, and in the famous fashionable circles that of necessity opened to the Grants. Ulyss too enjoyed these things, but in time his memory of them dimmed and lost shape under a mass of other impressions. He never forgot the workmen of the English cities.

All over Europe he found that there was, beyond the honors paid him as the former head of the American state, a special interest in him as the victor of the American civil war. Leopold of Belgium showed him a quick, warm friendliness that delighted Badeau by comparison with the stiff English neck. Bismarck talked with interest of the character of American armies. The French were very hospitable, and Ulyss had to time his recurring visits to Paris with some care lest he involve himself by implication in their current political crises. He had engagements to be kept in Copenhagen, Berlin, and Rome, as he had once kept engagements at army headquarters, the White House, and the home of a friend.

Early in his journey he began receiving letters from home that hinted, stated, or demanded the same thing: stay away, make it a long tour. Conkling wrote him thus, and Cameron, and Logan. It was the steady refrain of all the men who had stayed his friends in the last difficult years of his presidency, who had not begun to shout reform when that cry was popular, who had been called the priests and prophets of Grantism. He knew why they wanted him to remain abroad: they had shown him clearly enough that they considered the tour an excellent prelude to a third-term campaign. He did not want another term. He still felt bruised and sickened when he remembered what his title had meant, but he was grateful to his friends for their unwavering loyalty, and he understood their restlessness under Hayes's leadership.

Had their plan involved any positive action, any statement, or even the groundwork of an organization, he would have put a stop to it. All they wanted him to do, however, was to keep on traveling up and down in foreign lands, meeting the foreign great on a level of scrupulous equality; and all they were doing was making sure that American newspapers, and the American people, were fully informed of the honors shown him. With the nominating conventions three years off, it would be pointless cowardice for him to cut short his travels in fear that the Bristows and the Schurzes might accuse him of ambitions that he did not have; and meanwhile he had no objection to the publicity at home following his progress abroad, remembering the kind of publicity that had haunted him the year before. Time enough in six months or a year, when he was tired of wandering, to give his loyal friends a definite refusal. They would still have a long period in which to choose some candidate more willing than he.

Jesse grew bored with the grand tour in less than six months, and went home to enter Harvard. His parents felt that he could wait another year without damage to his education, but he had made up his mind, and they would not keep him. Julia grew very quiet in the few days before he sailed, and Ulyss also felt a depression that had not touched him in a long time.

'Do you want to go too?' he asked her suddenly one evening, as they drove through the bright streets of Paris. He had been bringing himself to say the words for the last quarter of an hour, and he was glad that the shifting lights would prevent him from seeing too clearly the joy that the question might bring to her face. He was afraid to see it, afraid to see plain evidence that she was traveling thus because she knew he wanted to, while all her own wishes set sail with their son for home. Yet he would understand. A woman, he knew, is rarely happy away from her home, and if, like Julia, she has no settled place, nothing seems so important to her as immediate construction of some safe and untroubled setting. He had no right to expect anything else of Julia, and no right to refuse her if that was in truth what she wanted.

'Go where, dear?' she asked placidly.

'Home, with Jesse.'

'Oh — I don't think so.' She spoke as though she had not considered it before, and certainly there was no regret in her tone. 'It would be silly, wouldn't it, to go back when there's still so much we haven't seen?'

'I'm not anxious to, but I thought maybe you — with Jesse going —— '

'Goodness, Jesse's big enough now not to need his mother tagging after him every minute. And Ulyss, I haven't ever had you with me so much. It's like starting out all over again.' She smiled, and if there was a knowing twist at the corner of her mouth that was not quite so artless as her words, he did not see it. But she saw his shoulders relax almost imperceptibly, and heard his sigh of relief. They were both well satisfied.

Italy — full of paintings, to which Badeau reverently conducted them. Julia admired whole galleries, properly if a little nervously, but Ulyss said nothing. He was vaguely suspicious of those who absorbed themselves in miles of bedaubed canvas and plaster, and gave scarcely a glance to the dark, flashing-eyed people who swarmed in the narrow streets. When he could take time from official functions Ulyss enjoyed going into the streets himself, listening to the strange syllables of an alien tongue, watching the faces, which were startling both in their undeniable, indefinable foreignness, and in their similarity to faces he had known in Galena and Washington and the blue ranks of his army.

This contemplative wandering with no goal was his favorite diversion, and he did it at every opportunity. Sometimes he got lost, and groped his way back to his hotel through the double mysteries of a strange city and a strange language. Once, in a town in Scandinavia, he lost his bearings altogether, and it was necessary to ask for help unless he was to let Julia begin to worry over his absence. He stopped the first man who approached him, and said distinctly, feeling himself redden, 'General Grant.' The man conducted him straight to his hotel, and took leave with wordless, beaming courtesy.

In Switzerland the mountains, lifting skyward in rocky grandeur, touched Ulyss with the awe and exaltation of beauty that he could never find in the paintings and statues he was so earnestly told were masterpieces. He felt it again in Egypt, when he walked in the shadow of massive pillars reared by men centuries dead. These were the things that impressed him, the enormous mass of a mountain, the colossal temples that still stood dark with meaning under the desert sun. The intricate conception of Milan cathedral had no interest for him. His was not a spirit to be stirred by delicacies of ornament or the esoteric values of art. He responded to the things that dwarfed a man by simple size and timeless quality; or to such new beauties of an engineering age as the bridges and fantastically difficult mountain highways, which stood witness to man's mental stature.

Still the letters from home urged him to prolong his stay; still a running account of his royal progress was featured in American newspapers. America was forgetting its picture of Grant and drawing another, a picture of itself, its unity, its unassuming solid character, being acclaimed by the peoples of the earth. Stay, said the letters from Grant's friends; each day's story is having a good effect, opinion is changing fast.

And Ulyss stayed, not because the plan for a third term had more than an abstract interest for him, but because he wanted to. He had thought that he would return in the spring, then that he would delay until fall. But it was early in 1879 before he left Europe, almost two years after he had come, and even then he did not turn homeward.

'I've been thinking,' he told Julia, 'that we might as well go back by heading east.'

'East?' There was in the word a note of alarm that she had not been quick enough to repress, but he was too interested in his plan to hear it.

'Yes — China, and those places. Likely we'll never do this again, and we might as well see them while we're here. Buck's been doing so well with the money that we can afford it all right.'

'He has been doing wonders, hasn't he?' she said eagerly. 'I'm sure I don't know where he gets his head for figures ——' She cut herself short, not daring to let her thoughts fasten on her sons. 'I suppose we could go east just as well, Victor. The world is round, they always told me.' She had a very clear picture of it at that moment, with only the Atlantic in one direction, and in the other the largest of the continents, the widest of the seas.

India and China and Japan. The Grants thought they had realized in Europe the pomp and ceremony surrounding rulers, but here they found the Oriental custom, that made something a little more than human out of its central figure. They had been surprised by the number of people in Europe, where every acre of ground seemed fully occupied, but here it seemed that every rod was crowded. All Asia was a solid mass of human beings, and apparently all the human beings had the one object of jostling for a glimpse of General Grant. The American war had no meaning here; to these vast masses whose way of life was one of fantastic material poverty, the condition of a few million

black men in the southern United States had no possible significance. Thus the last personal element in Grant's reception
disappeared, and he became simply an American emperor,
representative of a fabulous land. He found everywhere ex-
quisite, intuitive courtesy in the governors, and an enormous
enthusiasm in the people that was puzzling but very pleasant.

China seemed to him more like an imagined country than a
real place, but he was shown by the Americans there the opportunities it held for American capital, as incredible as the country
itself. And Japan, that miniature, mannered nation, had a
wholesale enthusiasm for Americans and American ways. He
had never given much thought to the Orient. Foreign affairs,
foreign policy, had for him been matters of Cuban eruptions;
dignified, stately haggling over the *Alabama* claims; occasional
tempests in South America. The whole of the Far East had
almost never been mentioned to him. Now he wondered if it
might not provide an opportunity for a peaceful commercial
expansion which would at last put an end to the economic
drowsiness that had fastened on the United States since the
panic. A Far Eastern policy, constructive, based on first-hand
knowledge, would have a significance far beyond foreign affairs.
He would further such a policy if he were President.

If he were — could he be — did he want to be —— Each
time Ulyss reached that point ordered thinking became impossible, and he was lost in a tangle of reluctance, desire, dread,
eagerness, that grew up and barred any path he chose. Surely
he did not want another term — yet when he considered giving
his refusal he drew back. What could he do with his days when
he returned? What place was there for an army man who was
now a civilian, for a President who had no office? He would
make a better executive now than he had before. He knew more
of the world, he was more sure of himself. The Democratic
and independent press would never believe it: their friendliness
would be at once forgotten if he became a serious candidate.

Julia would be very happy if he took office again. She had
loved the White House — so had he. Or had he hated it?
Why should he go back to that long torment of misconstruc-
tion? Why, if the place were offered him by the people in token
of renewed loyalty and faith, should he refuse it?

He had somehow forgotten his original decision to put a stop
to the plan when he returned. Insensibly the thing had grown
too large to be so simply disposed of, and his friends had invested in it too much of their thought and their own desires.
Once he had believed that the end of his journey must be the
end of his friends' kindly activities, but he saw now that it
must be the beginning of activity of his own, whether he fell
in with their intention or tried to dissuade them. He clung
uneasily to his months of freedom. There was much of the
world yet to be seen, and as his time in Japan drew to a close
he began to think of the Philippines, and the savagely beautiful
islands of the South Seas.

But then at last Julia's weariness asserted itself. 'I want to
go home,' she said, without defiance or coaxing, simply as a
statement that would make its own plea.

'Of course.' Ulyss was as direct as she. If he felt a slight
pang for the blue islands they would not see, its sting was
drawn by the opportunity to give her pleasure. For well over
two years she had followed his will, uncomplaining, delighting
in the things that delighted him, and now that her own wishes
had grown too strong for her to ignore, he was happy to meet
them. And he found there was no sacrifice after all in turning
homeward. He might have traveled a little longer, but as they
came eastward across the Pacific he too was eager to make port
in their own country. Uncertain as the future was, some of its
possibilities were bright, and there was an exaltation in the
thought of putting them to the test.

The Grants landed in San Francisco in September, 1879, two

years and four months after they sailed from Philadelphia;
eight months before the nominating conventions for the presidential campaign. The nation rose to meet them. For two
years it had been reading of the honors paid to Grant, to the
United States in Grant's person, and now the time had come
to show its appreciation and its pride. All across the country
cheering crowds gathered in railroad stations to see General
Grant come through, and to make sure that if his foreign tour
had been a royal progress his journey across America should
be an imperial triumph. They came to shout and wave banners,
and stayed to listen to him speak, which he did with a new ease
and understanding of how to make them laugh, and how to
touch on their national fervor. Ulyss was pleased by this
nation-wide welcome. His friends had been telling him the
truth, not inventing comfort for him in a chilly world. The
popular feeling had indeed changed; the distrust of him that had
still been strong when he went away had now utterly disappeared.

'You see how it is,' Conkling and the others insisted. 'We've
watched the feeling grow, knowing you didn't want your administration to be remembered forever the way the mud-slingers
had it. People see now what a mistake they made, and they
want to make it up to you ——'

'But I understand that,' said Ulyss slowly. 'I know they've
changed their minds, and I'm glad, and that settles it without
my trying for another term.'

'Well — it isn't quite as simple as that. They need you, too.
Look at the time we've had under Hayes — riots all over the
country, and nobody doing any business at all. People want
you to go back into the White House, but of course Blaine
and Schurz and the rest of their crew will fight like wildcats to
keep you out. It's a pretty big thing, General — you'll have
less trouble if you don't run, but this country will be mighty
disappointed ——'

'I'm not afraid of Schurz,' said Ulyss. He understood what they had too much delicacy to tell him: they believed he would be neglecting his duty if he refused them. Perhaps he agreed. If the people wanted him again he had no right to withdraw his trust from them, even though they had once withdrawn theirs from him. But he must be sure they wanted him.

'All that I want,' he wrote a friend, 'is that the government rule should remain in the hands of those who saved the Union until all the questions growing out of the war are forever settled. I would much rather any one of many I could mention should be President rather than that I should have it. . . . I shall not gratify my enemies by declining what has not been offered. I am not a candidate for anything. . . .'

I am not a candidate. It was one of his few certainties: if he were to run for the presidency again it must be only as the free choice of the people. No friend, no newspaper, no political prophet could tell him if he were, but he sometimes thought he heard the answer in the cheers echoing under the smoky roofs of railroad stations.

Eight months, his friends thought gloomily. The whim that had brought Grant home in September instead of the following April had set off their carefully prepared bonfires, letting them burn out with much noise and glare but no useful warmth, and had made a precarious venture out of what should have been a smooth, inevitable development. If the Republican convention had been held the month after his return it surely could not have nominated anyone else. There was no criticism of him then — there could not be in opposition to that vast shout of national pride; and unpleasant memories were blotted out by the figure of the modest hero returning from foreign lands, untouched by the adulation the whole round world had laid at his feet. But now the convention was eight months off, with a winter of doubt and a spring of consideration intervening. Only a few weeks after Grant's arrival some papers began to speak again of Grantism, and soon there was a general resurrection of the affairs of Babcock, Belknap, Williams, and the other tattered scandals that had been resting in decent burial since Hayes's election. The lull before the convention would be filled by a lively rattling of old skeletons.

These eight lost months hovered before Conkling and Washburne and the other Radicals, who were trying to break the chilly hold of the reformers on the party, as the easeful days of Eden must have hovered before Adam when he was cast forth to labor. But they were practical men, injured by the erratic twist of the instrument in their hands, but undiscouraged. They suggested to Grant that he add a knowledge of Cuba and Mexico to the rich store he had gathered in the other hemisphere. It was impossible, they knew, to rekindle the popular fires, but another journey would keep him satisfactorily occupied while they worked.

Obediently Ulyss and Julia set out again. In her excitement over the possibility of another term Julia had forgotten her weariness of travel, and this last jaunt was more enjoyable to her than any of the others, for she could occupy slack hours in thinking of the happiness to come. Ulyss had been interested in Mexico since he had fought against her thirty years ago, and now he thought he saw possibilities for American capital in this country too. A Chinese policy and a Mexican policy. Even so soon he would have these contributions to his work — if he were chosen. He had forgotten that he had ever been unsure of his desire — his only lack of certainty now was of whether it would be given him.

When he returned he went to Galena, for the little town held his political origins, and it seemed good policy to await the decision there. The states were beginning to instruct their convention delegates, and he was absorbed in counting over his votes, while he looked uneasily at those that strayed off to Blaine and the contingent of favorite sons. His number was large, but did not yet reach the three hundred and seventy-eight he needed. He conferred anxiously with Washburne and Conkling and Cameron, wondering if they could hold firm his present band of supporters, and if they were sure they could draw in stragglers from other companies. The people alone could tell him if they wanted him, but if he were not nominated they could not make him hear.

It was strange to his friends to see him so concerned. Badeau, who had come home on leave to participate in this new battle, was the most puzzled, for he remembered most clearly Grant's first campaign for the presidency, when he had refused even to answer letters, and had borne himself as if the election were of little more interest to him than to any other citizen. He still showed no sign of interest in public, but in private he could not disguise his racking anxiety.

Ulyss himself was not conscious of how far he had strayed from the aloofness which was his defense against fate. He knew only that re-election, and thus the nomination, had become more important to him than any office or honor he had ever held. His successive promotions in the army had pleased him, but they had been based on the requirements of military policy and had been a more or less expected recognition of good work done. His first election to the presidency had been a great honor, and he had been a little awed by it, but it was an honor paid to the victor of the war rather than to Ulysses Grant. His second election had humiliated his enemies, and he had been proud to take it as his vindication, but it had lost its value in the remorseless, envenomed attacks on him that marked his second term. Now he wanted to come before the people once again, that they might reconsider their verdict. That was the important thing to him. It was not that he was eager to have the power of office again. He wanted the score settled, the bitterness dispelled; he wanted to be freed of the festering, unreasonable sense of failure that lay heavy in his inmost heart.

So long as he had not hoped for anything he had maintained
a certain indifference to that pain, as a man can ignore the
steady pain of a disease he knows will kill him. But now that
hope had been thrust upon him he was torn between joy and the
terror of disappointment. If he could not succeed he did not
want to run: he was not gambling, but fighting for something of
so much importance to him that he would far rather not attempt
it than be defeated. He could not himself judge between his
heartfelt desire and his heartfelt fear, and he tried to find a
judgment in the results of the state conventions. There was no
certainty in them, and certainty was what he must have. It
was the lack of it that stripped him of the detachment that had
protected him since he had first entrusted himself to the caprice
of the people.

As the time drew near for the national convention, which
would make his commitment irrevocable, Ulyss felt that he
must have an impartial view from someone, but it was hard
to choose an arbiter. Julia was serene in her confidence of
victory. All his friends spoke with certainty of the result,
partly because they felt it necessary to cultivate that belief,
partly because they really were certain, with the unreasonable
assurance that develops in men who have put much effort into
an enterprise. At last Ulyss chose Washburne, who had insisted that Colonel Grant be made a brigadier, and had figured
in every campaign of his since then. Perhaps he would understand the meaning Ulyss felt in this last effort, where Conkling
and other new friends would see in it only a phase of the larger
political contest.

'Are you pretty sure about this?' Ulyss asked Washburne.
'Do you think I'll be nominated, and then elected?'

'Not a doubt of it.' Washburne's voice had a comforting
boom of optimism. 'You're as good as in right now.'

'I'm still way short of three hundred and seventy-eight.'

'You're sure of more votes than any other candidate, aren't

you? You'll lead the ballot, and on the second or third round Blaine and his outfit will have to give up, and you'll be nominated.' The old man glanced at Grant's thoughtful frown. 'You don't really think you might lose, do you?'

'No.' He didn't, not really. He couldn't. 'But I tell you, Washburne, if I did think so I'd withdraw my name.'

'You couldn't do that! Not at this stage of the game, when you've been in the race for months ——'

'Plenty of horses are scratched before they come to the post. If I thought I'd lose, I'd announce to the papers this morning that I'm not a candidate, and never will be a candidate.'

'There isn't a chance of your losing,' said Washburne hastily, soothing Ulyss and himself. 'Why, the people of this country want you, and they're going to get you no matter how loud Blaine hollers. You've never lost a fight yet, have you?'

No, he never had. There had been times when his defeat had been obvious to everyone but himself, but he had fought on in ignorance, and in the end had won. The fact was a talisman, and it gave him as much comfort as Washburne's bluff conviction.

A few days before the convention John Russell Young, the reporter who had accompanied the Grants on most of their travels, came to see the General at Galena. Ulyss and Julia were glad to see him, and to talk again of a journey that had already lost its inner perspective, and hung framed and apart in their memories. In the midst of their reminiscences the possibility of the nomination was mentioned, and Young frowned, saying a few colorless words that were pointed in their lack of enthusiasm. Julia frowned in her turn, and spoke determinedly of the climate in Bombay, and glanced with protective, resentful uneasiness at her husband. It was not fair that Ulyss should be troubled with other people's faint hearts now — he seemed to be uncertain anyway. Julia devoted herself to Young, and tried to avoid leaving the two men alone.

But Ulyss had also seen the implication in Young's attitude, and made occasion to go for a walk with him, away from Julia's steady vigilance. 'You don't approve of my candidacy, do you?' Ulyss demanded without preliminary.

'No, General, I don't.' Young spoke with deference, but bluntly. 'It's not so much a matter of approval — that's none of my business, but I don't think it's a wise move.'

'You mean you don't think I'll win.'

'That's it. I'd like nothing better than to see you in Washington again, but there's a lot of people in this country who don't feel that way. I think there's too many of them for your friends to buck.'

'Washburne don't think so. He thinks I'll be nominated on the second or third ballot, and elected without question.'

'Maybe he's right, but that's not the way I see it.' Young watched as he spoke for the blank chill on Grant's face that would tell him he had offended, but it did not come. There was only the straight line of the mouth that almost never softened, and the veiled eyes. The face had a heavy look that afternoon.

'If you're right,' said Ulyss slowly, 'I still can't withdraw now, without giving my friends a chance.'

'You could write them to withdraw your name if they have reason to agree with me.'

'Yes, I could do that — if you were right.'

Several times, whenever they could evade Julia, they talked the matter over again. Ulyss was certain that Young had not come of himself to urge a complete reversal on a man he had known but briefly, a man who plainly had enough advisers not to be in need of counsel. Someone had sent him, perhaps several people, perhaps many. Ulyss could not be sure who they were, but he was sure that they were his friends, that they were convinced of what they said with Young's lips; they knew what defeat would mean to Ulyss and were unwilling to see him suffer it. Whoever they were, their mere existence gave strength to their argument. Grant wrote the suggested letter, to Cameron. If he had made a mistake this was all he could do to mend it now. His Radical friends had had a long experience in diagnosing the political pulse, and they must know with some assurance what his chances were. Being his friends, they would publish his letter if they could not be certain of success.

The letter was not published. There were a few skirmishes in the organization of the convention which Conkling lost, evidence of the strength opposed to Grant, but as the floor was opened to nominations it seemed clear that no other candidate had Grant's following. He had all the Radical allegiance, while the conservative and liberal strength, though chiefly given to Blaine, had also enough other candidates to lose its effectiveness. That waste of power, thought Conkling, was inevitable when men burdened with theory engaged in politics. Some were squeamish about Blaine and the affair of the Mulligan letters; some supported John Sherman; others veered off to Edmunds. No man could trust their backing. Perhaps, even though the people had had eight months to remember what they disliked in Grant, the opposition could be shattered into as many pieces as it had intentions, when it encountered the solid force of the Radical group. They knew exactly what they wanted, had chosen Grant as the candidate most likely to win it for them, and worked for him with the discipline of clear purpose and long practice. Politics was to them a business, and they did not deplore its methods while they enjoyed its rewards.

A great advantage to the Radicals, next to their seasoned, solid organization, was Conkling's tongue. Other candidates were presented in routine panegyrics, but Grant's name was given to the convention shining with the fire of oratory and the steel of his great deeds. What Conkling said was of little importance, but his handsome golden head, thrown back in pride of his duty, and the compelling music of his voice gave every

syllable a meaning beyond definition; a meaning rooted in the
heart rather than the brain, fed by associations, memories, and
the uncontrollable response to phrases that carry in themselves
the color of a nation's history. It was impossible, while Conkling's voice rang through the hall, to weigh Grant's stubborn
will against Blaine's aptitude for public affairs, the whiskey
ring against the Mulligan letters. Grant was the silent, heroic
figure that had emerged from the battle clouds to recreate a
nation at Appomattox. Blaine did not exist. When at last
Conkling finished he had set off a demonstration that lasted
forty minutes, unreasoned, purposeless, an arrogant defiance
of the men who kept their seats and smiled with wan politeness
at the marchers.

The first ballot gave Grant 304 votes and Blaine twenty
fewer; the other candidates were so far behind that their in-
clusion seemed a technicality. Ulyss was well satisfied. He had
known he did not yet have a majority, but all the votes he had
counted on had been given him, and Blaine, he suspected, could
gain no more strength. There would be a few more ballots to
establish the position, as an army develops the enemy's line,
then the stray votes would begin to come to him, and would lift
his total to the nomination. He was sure of it, for his letter of
withdrawal had been ignored, and the demonstration after
Conkling's speech added positive proof to inference.

The second ballot showed no material change, nor did the
third, except that a man from Pennsylvania wearied of the
Blaine, Grant, or favorite son alternatives, and cast his vote
for Garfield of Ohio, who had not been a candidate. Then the
ballots succeeded each other all day until the convention adjourned, having voted twenty-eight times without result.
Twenty-eight. It seemed a large number to Ulyss, and he
remembered the fear that had not touched him since Conkling's
speech. He only remembered it, did not really feel it yet, but
he grew aware that it was waiting to fasten on him. In the

morning the twenty-ninth ballot was taken, and the thirtieth. Blaine's tally varied by half a dozen votes up or down; Grant's had varied by two or three, but had settled to an unwavering 306. The only one who showed any real change was Garfield, who had added one more to his Pennsylvanian on the first day, and in the morning began a slow climb, reaching 50 on the thirty-fifth ballot.

Then, abruptly, the break came. On the thirty-sixth ballot Grant had 306, Blaine 42, and Garfield 399. Garfield was nominated. Blaine had won the essential victory, though he had had to abandon a personal triumph; Grant was rejected by his party. The three hundred and six had held firm, untouched until they were handed over in a body in the usual motion to make the nomination unanimous, but the vote labeled them a minority, perhaps powerful but not to be considered as representative Republicans. Conkling shrugged — it had been a good try, but Grant's premature return had weakened it too much. At any rate, the Radical effort had shown so much strength that it had to be placated with a gift of the vice-presidency, which was assigned to Chester Arthur. The Radical leaders left the hall with the high bearing of defeated captains who had claimed the honors of war, and were now weighing new strategy to fit their new position.

None of this comforted Ulyss. He had not been running as a Radical, in his own mind not even as a Republican. To him his candidacy had been an issue between himself and the people, and the contemptuous answer had been given in that last ballot: three hundred and six had been loyal to him; but four hundred and forty-one had fallen away. A majority of his own party had so little faith in him that they would not even give him a chance to defend himself.

It would have been a relief to feel anger, to find warmth and vigor in such straightforward fury as Julia had. She was convinced that Ulyss had been betrayed, tricked by jealous men

who knew that the country would vote for him overwhelmingly
if it were given the opportunity. Her insistence touched Ulyss,
even amused him a little, but did not affect his own knowledge.
He knew the truth now. He should have known it at the beginning. It had been whispered to him in the silence of many of
his friends, it had been shouted at him in the newspapers, but
he had not allowed himself to hear. And when he might have
listened Washburne had stopped his ears. At the last point
where he could have turned from the disaster that lay in wait
for him, Washburne had urged him on.

Thus one more friendship was added to the heap of broken
and useless things accumulating in Ulyss's heart. The other
leaders who had persuaded him to be a candidate he did not
reproach, he was grateful to them for what they had tried to
do; but he never forgave Washburne. It was perhaps unfair;
he did not consider that Washburne might have been as confused between desire and probability as he himself, but he could
not help it. Never before had he ended a battle with his position
taken and his forces in flight, nor closed an elective contest in
awkward, unbearable condolences. In public he hid his pain,
said he was glad the burden of the presidency had not been
laid upon him, and believed it so long as he held rigidly to those
terms. But there was in him a black, silent fear of the future,
now that his fate had played him false. He broke with Washburne because he felt that he had been betrayed, and because
a man in terror of helplessness will sometimes strip himself of
what he has.

Ruined Fortune and Name

CHAPTER TWENTY-NINE

ULYSS, I believe you're going to get the appointment.'

'What appointment, father?'

'To West Point — I've applied for it.'

'But I won't go ——'

'I think you will.'

'I — guess so ...'

The words had been spoken over forty years before, when Ulyss was a stripling, but now they rang in his ears. Not since that distant hour, he felt, had he been faced with true uncertainty about his own future. Once he submitted to his

father's decree, his life was drawn forward by a motive power
not really under his control: through the rigid demands of the
army; through the years at Hardscrabble and Galena, under
the equally effective demands of poverty and a growing family;
back to the army, not by reasoned decision but because all
that his life had been made his return inevitable; up the
military scale, thrust by his victories, by the accidents of war
and temperament; and then through the last complex decade,
which had been an endless strain of making decisions for party,
government, nation, but never for himself. His personal affairs
had for years been governed by the demands of the historical
moment as strictly as they once had been by the crabbed,
affectionate ambition of his father. Nowhere in the whole
progress of his manhood could he have stopped to make a
choice, for there had never been a choice. When he became the
candidate of the Radical Republicans for the presidency, when
he moved to Galena to work for his younger brother, when he
marched south instead of north after the second day in the
Wilderness, he did so because circumstance would not permit
him to do otherwise.

Now he was free. His children were grown, he had enough
money not to be forced into anything, but not so much that it
made an occupation in itself. The army no longer needed him,
nor did the government. He campaigned for Garfield, loyal to
his party however disloyal it might have been to him, and supposed that his experience and opinions would be of value to the
new President. But Garfield listened to him politely, and made
clear in his actions that Grant's words were no more significant
than those of any other eminent outsider. Thus at last both
public and private demands were at an end, and Ulyss was left
without guide, to consider what he wished to do with the rest
of his life. He had little joy in the knowledge. He felt not so
much free as lost.

On his income he could live in the country in complete

leisure, but the prospect displeased him. He did not want to go to the St. Louis farm, with its heartache of the whiskey ring associations, nor to Galena, nor to strange and meaningless surroundings. Julia did not want to abandon the cities, but if he was to live in New York, as he too would prefer, he must have work, and what work was there that would suit both his abilities and his position? There were enough offers. The effects of the panic were at last dissipated, and all sorts of projects were appearing in the warm financial atmosphere, with the rootless luxuriance of tropical fungi. He did become an officer of the Mexican railway, and settled in New York, but he was not altogether satisfied. He felt that he stood on the outer edge, with a voice in politics that might be heard but would not be listened to, and a place in finance that could be seen but had no stature. His son Buck was doing great things in that field, and if Ulyss had not been so proud of him he might have been jealous.

Each of the children as they matured showed outstanding qualities — a scapegrace, generous charm in Fred, beauty and gentleness in Nellie, wit in Jesse; but all together agreed that Buck was the one who had a sense of business. He had not made a startling success as a banker, but he had started in the bad years, and while Grant was away on his travels Buck had entered into partnership with another young man, and was now making so much money that Ulyss believed the name of Grant would one day have much the same significance as Vanderbilt. The partner, a young man named Ferdinand Ward, sometimes came to call on the Grants, and when he talked Ulyss had visions of a fantastic world where half a million dollars might be acquired by half a dozen words spoken at the right time.

'It's all wrong,' said Ward, 'this idea that to keep your money safe you've got to lend it out for pins. The theory that high interest means high risk is exploded, but people just won't believe it.'

'Why should anybody pay high interest if there's no risk?' asked Ulyss. He had known other great men of finance, and remembered enough of their ways of thought to keep up a discussion.

'Because they need money quickly, to do big things, and most of the dodoes of bankers don't like to make up their minds on a loan till you're too old and feeble to need it. You see' — the young man leaned forward and struck his hand with a rather boyish gesture, and Ulyss felt the driving conviction that had made Ward a Wall Street power while he was still in his youth — 'there's no limit at all to what this country can do now that hard times are over. Railroads are starting construction again, the population's shooting up, our industries have scarcely got started ——'

The voice was different, the words were not the same, but Ulyss had heard the cry before. Something almost forgotten touched him with vague nostalgia, then came back to him with startling clarity. Rawlins at the campfire, a flush of excitement mounting in his thin cheeks, painting a picture of the American future on which he could keep his eyes, safe from the intolerable American present. He had not lived to see the reality of his dream, and Ulyss had thought that it had been only a dream, for there had been little sign of its coming in the strife and bitterness of the years since the war. But perhaps it was coming now. Perhaps the ringing confidence of such young men as Ward would finish the process that the stern sacrifice of such men as Rawlins had begun. Ulyss would like to believe it, and as he saw more of Buck's partner he found it easier to believe.

It was pleasant to hear always of the future instead of the old issues; pleasant never to be forced into the fruitless torment of rearguing past decisions. Ward might never have heard of the Southern question, or Grantism, or any of the other problems that had filled Grant's days, for all the awareness of them that his talk showed. Even the panic figured in his mind only as a factor that had temporarily held back the natural American development, and would give it the greater speed now that it was released, as an archer's hand draws back the bow. It was impossible to mistrust the future when the young man spoke of it. Ulyss knew that he was not alone in feeling that optimistic compulsion: men of affairs all over the city admired Ward, and were a little awed by the prodigies he performed; and some called him a financial Napoleon.

In that summer of 1881 President Garfield was shot, and after two agonized months he died. The country was shaken, not as it had been when Lincoln died, but with much the same horror it would have felt had the lurid warnings of a fanatic suddenly taken on flesh and reality. The assassin said he had fired because he had been cheated of a promised office: this, then, said the nation, is the logical result of the blatant office-hunting that has long disgraced us. No one speculated on the unbalance there must have been in the man's mind to make him alone a murderer, out of the thousands of disappointed office-seekers who had been characteristic inhabitants of the capital since the time of Jefferson. The President had been shot by the embodiment of the spoils system. The movement for civil service reform, which had come to puny birth under Grant's administration and had had an infancy neglected by all but theorists under Hayes, grew to swift maturity in the two months that Garfield lay dying.

Chester Arthur, the elegant bachelor who had figured conspicuously in the scandals of the New York customhouse, became President. He was a close friend of Conkling's, and had all Conkling's contempt for those who thought to run the government in separation from politics, but Garfield's martyrdom compelled him to follow a course that Garfield himself could hardly have taken. National politics as Conkling and Grant and Lincoln had known it, resting on officeholders up

and down the scale from fourth-class postmaster to United
States Senator, had come to an end. After Garfield's death the
structure was shifted to the foundation the conservative Republicans had already prepared: the business interests, which
could be more quietly dealt with and more fully satisfied than
the myriad officeholders who were now emblazoned civil
servants. The Logans, Mortons, Butlers, fell back into the
shadows of history to join the Sumners and Stantons.

The development troubled Ulyss. He had preceded his supporters into limbo, and thus had not enough intimacy with the
present leaders to understand the new policy. All that he could
perceive from the newspaper accounts, from Arthur's asking
his advice on appointments and then ignoring it, was that the
government had been wholly resigned to the reformers, to the
critics who had no sense of loyalty or friendship. It seemed to
him that nowadays almost no one appreciated those virtues,
nor troubled to remember transgressions against them.

He could remember. He encountered Bristow at a public
meeting, and the former Secretary of the Treasury approached
him smiling, with outstretched hand. At the sight of him
Ulyss was swept back to the time when his name was being
tarnished, his friendships undermined, in order to further this
man's designs on his office. He turned his back, slowly, so that
the movement had the effect of a calculated slap across the
cheek. He could remember, and he would.

Yet he did not feel as much pain at the final surrender of the
party as he would have once. It was over five years since he
had left office, and in that time some detachment had developed in him, partly because it had been forced upon him,
partly because his personal life was growing back into the space
left vacant by his public responsibilities. It was impossible to
be as disturbed by an event when he read about it in his Wall
Street office, or talked it over with Julia in the quiet of their
drawing-room, as when he experienced the direct blow at a

cabinet meeting, or felt it in terms of his immediate policies. Now, however exasperated he was by Arthur's absurdities, they could not be so important to him as his own projects.

He had shown so much interest in Ward's ideas that it had been suggested that a new firm be set up, with Grant and Buck contributing one half the capital, and Ward the other. The enterprise would have to do with finance, a sphere that had always filled Ulyss with uncomprehending fascination; and he found solid satisfaction in the thought that he could close his life with a business career to complement his generalship and the achievements of his presidency. It would be a fitting end, better than his meaningless place with the railway, better than the pointless leisure that made him restive. He had enough money to set forth on the adventure. A trust fund had been subscribed for him, and that he could not touch, but he could raise a hundred thousand dollars from his other resources. Buck had already invested that amount, and Ward agreed to put in two hundred thousand.

'I can't produce it in ready cash,' he said. 'I'm tied up in so many things' — his gesture indicated the extent of his interests, and Ulyss nodded — 'that I haven't that much coin in the bank, and I don't like to sell out of anything unless I have to. Money makes money, you know.'

'Yes, of course,' Ulyss agreed.

'A man shouldn't limit himself too much,' Buck added.

'I knew you'd both see it that way. You're business men, not hicks who won't take a dollar bill because they can't be sure it's not Confederate money. But just the same, this thing is my main interest.' His voice was vivid with conviction. 'The firm of Grant and Ward is going to be the biggest thing in this country, and you'd better believe I sit up nights making plans for it. Now, this is my idea.' He lifted his finger as he made each point, a gesture he frequently used, that underlined the direct simplicity of his thought. 'A firm's got to have working capital, and it's got to have a backlog. What you and Buck put in, General, is cash, and we can go right ahead with that, but we've got to have a backlog too. Why shouldn't I put in my share in securities? If it was cash we'd just have to go out on the market and buy the stuff, at a lot higher prices than I paid for it, you bet. This way it's much simpler, and the firm will be that much ahead.'

'It's a good plan,' said Ulyss, and Buck concurred. Ward showed them the securities, beautiful, crisp piles of them, gay with green and gold; slips of paper that stood for the financial blood of mines and factories and fleets of ships. There was a guarantee of good faith simply in their appearance, but neither Ulyss nor Buck had need of reassurance. The success Ward had already made was an earnest of his future; no man with his eagerness and daring could fail.

He had many ambitious plans for the new firm, most of them hinging on contract work, supplying services and materials to all who had need of them. Plainly it was a profitable field, and Ulyss had but one reservation.

'We must not handle government contracts,' he told Ward.

'You don't want to, General? There's a lot of money in them.'

'No, I don't want to touch them. It would be different if I hadn't held office.'

'Just as you want,' said Ward. 'There's lots of other pasture.'

Thus the firm of Grant & Ward was established, and promptly began to return quite startling profits. Money was freer than it had been in years, and the country was giddy with renewed confidence. There was no difficulty in finding investors for a firm headed by General Grant and including the magic abilities of young Ward, and those who ventured their money shortly received dividends for enormous amounts. The list included established merchants of New York; financial dabblers who heard of the wonders of the new enterprise and invested with the glee of shrewd discoverers; the family connections of the Grants, grown extensive now that all three sons had married; and swarms of veterans, men who had gone fresh-faced and lithe into the war, and were now paunchy, commonplace citizens looking to provision for their old age, which was no longer a distant abstraction. Their money was entrusted to their former general as their lives had been, with more consideration but also with greater confidence. These drafts Ulyss always turned over to Ward with a special request for care, and the young man gave assurances that were evidence of his sensitive understanding. Some of the old soldiers' investments were pathetically small, some were quite large, but all alike received frequent large dividends, and these returns were almost always reinvested. The patrons of Grant & Ward became forceful missionaries, spreading Ward's gospel of high interest and no risk with the exasperated zeal of converts.

The operations of the firm were left largely to Ward. Buck looked after some documents in the office, and Ulyss made daily appearances there, but the actual handling of affairs was in Ward's hands. Both Grants were content to have it so. Buck had a wholehearted, selfless admiration for Ward, and Ulyss in honesty had to admit not only that he himself had no such competence, but that even his son's great abilities were overshadowed by those of the Napoleon of Wall Street. It was Ward's talent that had set up the organization, and that ran it so that thousands of dollars a week were credited to the partners: it would be absurd to insist on meddling with the arrangements that he understood, and that produced such brilliant results.

Thus Ward carried the responsibilities of the business, while Ulyss sat in his office and received his friends, the friends of the head of Grant & Ward, the friends of President Grant, and those most dear, the friends of the General. If they came to

speak of business Ward could always be asked to step in and
make things clear; but the talk that Grant liked best turned on
matters twenty years old, and fought the old campaigns with
more excitement than Ulyss had felt when they were actually
in progress. There was color in those days, remembered now
without the shadow that had been cast over them by the
possibility of failure; and laughter, now that their tragedy
could be forgotten. Ulyss delighted in telling Sheridan, who
had almost as great a hatred of newspaper correspondents as
Sherman's, 'Now, we all know you couldn't possibly have
ridden around Lee in two weeks. You just went off with some
men from the *Herald* and helped them write up all those battles
out of their heads.' Sheridan could blush as vividly as though
the canard were true. And to Badeau: 'Do you remember how
you fell off your horse over the tail? "I'm coming off, I'm
coming off!" And a bump, and you yelling "I say, I'm off!"
sitting on the ground and holding on to your spectacles. You
were a sight . . .'

Sometimes Porter came to add his lively wit and long memory
to the discussions. There was little about him now of the young
West Pointer who had contended against Stanton himself for
permission to join Grant's staff. He had left the White House
at the end of Grant's first administration, and had been in
business since then. Ulyss was always happy to see him, and
in his presence could often recapture the very atmosphere of
the more carefree hours at the City Point camp. On one occasion, however, Porter seemed uninclined to reminisce. His talk
turned on the present, on Grant & Ward, and he asked so many
questions that Ulyss grew restless.

'I have nothing to do with that,' he said impatiently. 'Mr.
Ward looks after getting the contracts and placing them. Why
do you want to know?'

'I was just wondering,' Porter began carefully. 'As a rule,
when a firm makes so much money ———'

'Well, you can ask Ward about it.' Ulyss turned to greet his partner, who had entered rather abruptly. 'This is General Porter, Ward. He wants to know things about the firm that I can't tell him, but I know you can.'

'Certainly.' Ward's smile was bright. 'If you'll excuse me a moment, General Porter —— These have just been finished, sir, and if you'll sign them the secretary can take them as he leaves.' He laid a pile of letters on the desk, overlapping so that the spaces for signature were left open, and as soon as Grant's name was added he withdrew each one. He spoke with pleasant deference: 'Any information I can give you, General Porter, is at your disposal. Were you thinking of investing in our little enterprise?'

'No, I think not,' said Porter, watching Grant rapidly signing his name to letters he was not reading; watching Grant's warm smile as Ward picked up the last one and thanked him; remembering certain immutable, implacable elements in Grant's character. 'No, not just now,' said Porter. 'I must be getting on, anyway — another day, perhaps.' Ward opened the door for him with a flourish, and Porter bowed as he passed.

After a few months Ward proposed that they take in a special partner, the head of the Marine National Bank, which handled Grant & Ward's account. Ulyss and Buck made no objection, and James Fish was added to the firm, at a salary of three thousand dollars a week, rather than the larger, more irregular sums that the other partners received. He seemed an unusually quiet man, though he and Ward sometimes talked for a long time in Ward's office. Ulyss found him entirely unresponsive, even when sounded by a subject that would presumably be of great interest to him. 'Ward's a clever young man, isn't he?' said Ulyss. Fish made no answer, and looked stubbornly at the floor.

'There's no getting anything out of him,' Ulyss told Julia. 'He talks sometimes, so fast you can hardly make it out, but mostly he just sits and looks at you. Queer duck, but Ward says he does good work for us.'

'What kind of work, Ulyss?'

'I don't know, exactly. Something to do with the bank. Why?'

'No particular reason. It's just that it all seems so vague to me, as if the money fell right out of the sky.'

'But this is business, dear — why should you bother about it?'

'I know. I don't, much. I just think about it sometimes, it seems so wonderful.'

Long Branch in summer, with Childs and the other friends who had cottages there. New York in winter, always with some of Ulyss's children near, and now their children. It was a good life, in its rounded years. There was a sense of success and completion in it, and it was adorned with friendships like jeweled souvenirs of the years behind him: Badeau and Porter; Hamilton Fish advancing into stately age; Ward, young and enterprising to fit the country. True, there was a certain softness in the life that startled Ulyss when he thought about it. He had no need to worry about anything, nothing to fear, nothing to struggle against, and there were times when his ease seemed somewhat tasteless. But he knew that at his age he could not expect to have the quick enjoyment of youth, and he could always instill a flavor in his days with the memory of past storms.

Once the *Century*, which was discovering the possibilities of the war as magazine material, asked him to write an article on Shiloh. He refused.

'I don't want to go over all that again,' he told Badeau, who had carried the proposition. 'It's twenty years since Shiloh, and what's the use of raking it up now?'

'It has a good deal of historic interest. And five hundred dollars is a lot of money.'

'I don't need it. Let them get somebody else.' Ulyss liked to talk of the war with men who had experienced it with him, but he had no interest in writing an account of it for strangers. If people must read about Shiloh they could get Badeau's military history, or one of the other memoirs that were thick in the bookstores. The head of Grant & Ward need not trouble himself about it.

This detachment was increased when Ulyss fell on an icy pavement and ruptured a leg muscle so badly that he was kept in bed for weeks. At first he was in so much pain that it washed the reality from everything else, and then his recovery took a long time, and he was so warmly cradled in family solicitude that the affairs of the world reached him only in a lulling murmur. Ward came regularly to see him, but did not trouble him with details of the firm's affairs. Once the young man showed him the commercial rating of the firm, higher than it had ever been, and told him that their assets amounted to twenty-seven million dollars. Ulyss tried to visualize that sum, but could not. Reality was in the elegance of his house, the instant satisfaction of Julia's desires, the deference shown him by other men of affairs, not in the figures of a huge sum sprawled across a sheet of paper.

The presidential election came again that year, and Ulyss realized that it was the first in a quarter of a century in which he had no vital interest. Echoes came to him even in his sickroom early in the year, and he was aware that this time Blaine would almost certainly get the nomination he hungered and thirsted after; that apparently the Democrats would choose Grover Cleveland, and that they would probably win. None of it mattered, not to him. He disliked Blaine and was indifferent to the Democrats: his days were marked by his grandchildren, coming in to vary the monotonous hours; by Julia, so dear a nurse that he all but enjoyed being an invalid; by small, pleasant things, and quiet, and peace.

Not until mid-spring was he well enough to go forth on crutches, and to ride sedately through Central Park in his carriage. Then he did think with regret of other drives, when he had raced chance comers with some damage to his dignity but great credit to his horsemanship. He appeared regularly once more at the office, although there was little to do there. A few letters to sign, some callers, and he was free to go home again.

On the first Saturday evening in May Ward came to see Grant at his home. 'There's a little trouble, General,' he said. 'Oh, no, not about the firm. That's right as rain. But you know the Marine National is a depository for city funds, and Fish tells me that on Monday they're going to be withdrawn. He hasn't expected it, and he hasn't got quite enough liquid funds on hand to meet a withdrawal like tha

'What's it got to do with us?'

'Well, if he can't meet the demand he'll have to close up for a while, and we won't be able to get at our account. It wouldn't be any serious damage, but it would hold us up, and it'd be better if the firm gave him a loan for a week or so. He lacks only a hundred and fifty thousand in cash.'

'All right. I've no objection, and I'm sure Buck wouldn't mind.'

'But you see, we haven't got that much in cash either. All but a thousand or two is out working for us, and we couldn't get hold of it by Monday.'

'We could borrow it, couldn't we?'

'Yes, sure we can. Not from a bank, of course, they won't open soon enough — but the Commodore would let us have it. Would you go talk to him? You know him so much better than I do ...'

Early in the morning Ulyss drove through the sunny Sabbath quiet of the streets to Vanderbilt's house. The financier came at once to receive him, and listened without comment or change of expression to Grant's story of the bank and the city funds and the interests of Grant & Ward.

'I'll tell you,' he said when Ulyss finished. 'I wouldn't give a red cent to save Fish from ruin and suicide. I don't like him. Nor Ward. But you, personally, can have whatever you want. Did you say it was a hundred and fifty thousand?' Ulyss took the check and murmured his thanks, torn between pride in the implicit compliment the great man had paid him, and resentment at the slurs on his associates. Ward did not seem at all surprised that the check was made out to Grant rather than the firm, but took it quietly and assured Ulyss that the money could be returned at the end of the week.

Monday was a quiet day. There was no word of trouble at the bank, and Ulyss thought with satisfaction that probably the loan had not been necessary after all, and he could repay it at once, perhaps the next day. He would ask Ward about it, for borrowing money troubled him, even though this sum could be of little moment to Vanderbilt and could hardly be ruinous to himself. Ward was not in the office, for he frequently spent the days elsewhere, interviewing prospects, but Ulyss planned to talk to him in the morning.

On Tuesday Ulyss came down early. The clerks were not at their desks when he entered the office. They were standing in little groups around the room, and they all turned to stare at him. He did not at once notice them, and before he did Buck came toward him, his face stamped with a look that would arrest even the most unsuspicious.

'Father,' he said, 'you'd better go home. The — bank's failed.'

'The bank ——'

'We've failed. It's all gone, everything.' Buck put out his hand as if to steady his father, but Ulyss had not swayed. He moved forward, past the silent, staring clerks, past the loaded desks and spread ledgers that had a too sharp look of reality, like a stage setting designed by someone with a loving eye for detail. They were still there, but the curtain had fallen. He sat down at his own desk and stared at his hands, not hearing while Buck talked. It's all gone. All. Julia, the house. The firm, the pride, the money. The belief in himself, the structure of his life, the trust of others — don't let me see them, I am seeing them — the men who put their faith in their old commander ... It's all gone, all of it, all. He had not the respite of the instant's unbelief before the mind has really felt the blow. A buried knowledge, made up of comments and the absence of comment, of a glance and a word and an instant's perception, sealed up from his consciousness by his trust in Ward, had come to hateful life as soon as he saw his son's eyes. He knew. Not even the outline of the facts was yet clear to him, but he knew the truth of them.

Somehow that day he heard and understood the story that poured in on him, in a murky flood that tossed the twisted, broken remnants of his life. There had never been a legitimate operation of Grant & Ward. The Napoleon of Wall Street had talked of the government contracts that the General's influence procured; talked guardedly, saying that the General did not want the fact widely known, but of course he could produce telegrams in evidence. Forged telegrams. The few who grew uneasy about the firm or Ward were reassured by unequivocal letters over Grant's genuine signature. Investors were paid fat dividends out of their own funds until they cast all their resources into the proved bonanza. Fish had used the Marine National to support the bubble-tower, and had done good service for three years, but a bank is eventually accountable, and the bank's failure was one difficulty Ward could not circumvent. He had disappeared, with the money Vanderbilt had lent to Grant.

Someone found the private ledger that Ward had kept, and in it was set down the condition of the firm. The liabilities —

the sums ventured in the Grant enterprise by the Grant family, the Grants' friends, the strangers who put their faith in Grant's name — were nearly seventeen million dollars. The assets were sixty-seven thousand. The figures swirled through Grant's head, and beyond them he saw Ward's fingers lifted one by one to emphasize the simple logic of his points; beyond Ward a list of names, hundreds of names that had followed his own to ruin; beyond the list a black emptiness that would be his annihilation, the emptiness of a cannon's mouth. His throat grew dry and his eyes were hot as he listened to the disjointed tale of the enterprise he had believed in, as he heard the fragmentary admissions proving that the whole of Grant & Ward had been a fraud, and as he realized that had he known anything whatever of the business he was engaged in he could not have failed to see it. Much of the world would certainly call him dishonest, and although he could be cleared of that charge there was another verdict that he knew himself was just: he was guilty of towering stupidity.

This was the knowledge that gave him the real agony of failure. He had had a long experience of defeat and despair and humiliation, but never before had he felt that the integrity of his own spirit was touched. He had been forced out of the army in California by the conjunction of a rigid superior and his own restlessness for home. His troubles at Hardscrabble and Galena might have humiliated him in the sight of more successful citizens, but had not sullied his own inner pride. His reverses in the first years of the war had been matters of military accident and the temperament of his superiors. All the storms of his presidency had shaken and tormented him, but had never forced him to call himself culpable. Only now, sitting alone in his office while his very blood whispered ruin, ruin, ruin, in his ears, did he suffer the realization that he had done great injury to hundreds of people through his own fault. It was not only the firm of Grant & Ward that had failed that morning, but Ulysses Grant.

A small crowd was standing outside the office when he emerged. There were many reporters; some investors who had come down in fruitless fury to argue with the clerks; and some others who had come simply because an exciting event had happened, and any trace of it that they might find would give them something to think about for a while. Half a dozen of them pulled off their hats as Grant appeared and made his hobbling way to his carriage; but most of them stared and murmured with the interest of seeing a man whose name appeared in the newspapers, and the added spice of seeing him at a crisis, not just on his way to some dull meeting. Ulyss did not look at anything, but discovered that all the way home those faces were in his mind, with the eyes round and hard, the mouths a little ajar. Thus did people look at a man of fame who had been President, who had betrayed his friends, and strangers who trusted him, and himself.

Telling Julia was not easy, but it was quickly finished. She did not cry, nor insist that it could not be true and thus force a detailed recital, nor say a word of what it meant to her and to the position she had so much enjoyed, nor encourage Buck's lamentations. First she kissed her husband with warm firmness, then she spoke indignantly of Ward and trusted that he would soon be found and properly punished. Then she asked how much cash was left to them. Wallets and pocketbooks were searched, and produced some eighty dollars. The family had little money in any bank, for it had seemed wisest to invest any surplus in the firm.

'I have a hundred dollars in the house,' said Julia. 'That will help pay some of the bills — I expect they'll be coming in right away, now. And there's the trust fund.'

'That hasn't been paying,' Ulyss reminded her, 'and the guarantee doesn't apply until it's been six months in default.' He somehow disliked using the terms, the business argot that had once delighted him.

'I see. That won't help us much right now.'

'Well, there's some other property, isn't there?' asked Buck, with his first slight tinge of optimism. 'You've got some houses, and there's the farm in St. Louis ——'

'You're forgetting Vanderbilt's loan.' Ulyss's lips felt rigid, and the troublesome dryness in his throat made it difficult to speak. 'That was made to me, personally, because he wouldn't trust the firm. It must be paid.'

'Of course it will be.' Julia spoke with as much conviction as though payment would be simple, and gave both men a momentary feeling that it might be. 'Things are pretty tight just now, but they'll be all right. We've had hard times before, Victor, and they didn't hurt us any.'

Her warm smile brought an automatic response from him, but it could not reach the congealed weight in his heart. He knew, and certainly she knew, that poverty and the pity of their associates could not be the same thing at Hardscrabble in their youth and in New York when they were approaching age. He could fight. Even now he could have faced the struggle back to contentment and the respect of his fellows, but he did not respect himself. With no solid conviction of his own worth to stand on he had not the strength to rebuild that conviction in other people. Julia's smile and Julia's hand could not help him now, for the bottomless faith of one so much a part of himself only doubled his self-abasement.

At once, as Julia had foreseen, outstanding bills were hurried to the family, with requests for immediate payment varying from the suave to the verge of insult. The mail was very heavy in the first days after the collapse, not only with bills but with some notes of condolence and many of outrage. Ulyss read them all, not because there was anything he could answer to either type, but because he felt that he had no right to avoid even these pointless consequences of his failure. He was not conscious of any reaction to them, only of a dull, buried pain when he read them, as a numb limb responds to pressure.

On the fourth day he wearily sat down to his task, scrupulously reading each letter and adding it to the pile on the table before him. One thin envelope dropped out a check when he slit it open. It was made out to Ulysses Grant, for one thousand dollars. There was a slip of paper with it, requesting General Grant to accept the money as a loan 'on account of my share for services rendered ending April 9, 1865.' It was signed by one Charles Wood, of Lansingburgh, New York. Ulyss had never heard of him.

For a long time he sat looking at the slip. April 9, 1865. The strange quiet when the guns were silent and the armies no longer moved; Babcock's grave, impressive bearing; Porter suddenly seeming boyish when Lee borrowed a pencil of him; the feel of his own mud-stiffened boots; ' ... this will have a very happy effect ...' That had been a good day. There had been as much sorrow as joy in it, but it was such a day as measures the stature of a man. Ulyss had almost forgotten it, save for casual anecdote.

Odd that this stranger should remember, should feel so much significance in a day that had died in darkness nineteen years ago that he should send a thousand dollars to a man he had never seen. But maybe he had seen him. Perhaps Charles Wood's was one of the faces that turned eyes right to the reviewing stand when the triumphant armies marched down Pennsylvania Avenue. Perhaps Charles Wood had stood in the crowd in the intolerable cold of Grant's second inauguration day, and had heard Ulyss's silent cry: ' ... he shall not judge after the sight of his eyes, neither reprove after the hearing of his ears.' Perhaps Charles Wood had never left Lansingburgh, and all he had seen of Grant was in the distorting mirror of the newspapers. Yet something he had seen, and seen truly.

There was a stir in Ulyss's heart. He did not altogether want to feel it. He did not want to be dragged out of the icy quiescence of resignation to suffer the agonizing warmth of new hope, new desire. If he came out he must fight, and it would be a harder battle than he had ever undertaken, for his only ally and his chief opponent would be himself. It would be his last battle, for he was very tired and past the age for struggle, and it might be that even if he could win he would not live to know it. It would be so much easier to accept defeat, to be marked forever with the stain of failure and utter stupidity. Surely no one but himself cared what happened to his name, and he was so tired . . .

Charles Wood cared, and how many others he could not know. And even if there were no others, even if there were no Wood, the Ulysses Grant who had marked the day of April 9, 1865, had more right in the matter than the weary, half-crippled, discredited head of Grant & Ward. Ulyss smiled with some grimness and began to smoke thoughtfully, his mouth set and his eyes narrowed to bright points.

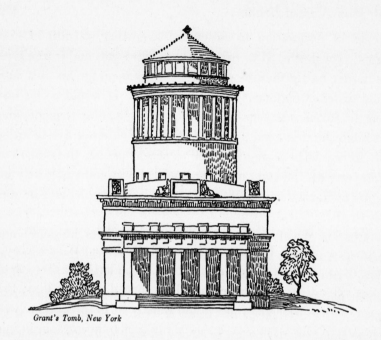

Grant's Tomb, New York

CHAPTER THIRTY

HIS weapon lay ready to his hand, as soon as he opened
his eyes to look for it. The *Century* renewed its request for
an article, and this time he accepted eagerly. Perhaps it was
absurd to assault the public opinion of him with a few thousand words on a half-forgotten subject, but he had no choice.
This was the way his battle must be fought. Not by a whining
defense of himself which could but add contempt for his lack
of spirit to contempt for his lack of wisdom. Not by another
venture into business — a general does not rely on the division
he knows to be the weakest. Not by any attempt to regain

public office. The *Century* offer was directed to the Ulysses Grant of twenty years ago in whose name he fought, and that in itself gave it weight.

The five hundred dollars he was to be paid were not his first consideration, but they were important to him. Vanderbilt's loan he settled, over the Commodore's protest, by transferring to him as security the St. Louis farm, the house in New York and all the jeweled swords and medals and other objects which commemorated his military service and his world journey. He could never repay the money his friends and old soldiers had invested in his firm: that was a weight of guilt he must carry as long as he lived. The Grants were not destitute. Wood's check was matched by another from Mexico; Vanderbilt insisted that they remain in the house they had turned over to him; the guarantee of the trust fund would shortly be in force; there was enough income from one source or another to keep them in fair comfort. But Ulyss exaggerated their straits in his reaction from the happy indifference that had been his, and he felt that he could not sit still and let his family be fed by his friends as a gesture to his former eminence. When he died they would have nothing. The *Century* money was not much, but it would be a sum that he had earned, he and that other Ulysses Grant.

Working on the article thus gave him a sense of independent action, beyond its essential importance as a return to the years which were his only unsullied pride, and which might clear his name of the equivocations which had since clustered around it. Something of himself went into each word he wrote, perhaps to be scorned, perhaps to be discovered by only a few; but there if anyone chose to search for it. The past event took on equal stature with the present, and sometimes it seemed to him that twenty years was a physical distance, that he could take up his position at either end, at will.

In June Julia insisted that they go as usual to Long Branch, though he felt that he had no right to spend money to escape the city heat.

'That's nonsense,' said Julia firmly. 'You won't do anybody any good by staying here to swelter, and you'll hurt yourself. Doctor Barker says you need rest — and you know you're not looking so well ——'

'I've never been better in my life,' he said flatly. Julia shook her head and began to speak, and he interrupted hastily, 'All right, I'll go. I guess it doesn't make much difference.'

Having won her point, she let the minor subject drop, and Ulyss was relieved when she set off in the immediate bustle that always seized her when action was decided on. He was well, certainly he must be, she had only been arguing, not observing. She could know nothing of the constant dryness in his throat, and the abominable taste that occasionally came to his mouth. There was nothing to know about it, anyway. It was just a queer sort of cold that would clear up when he got to the sea-shore. It did not clear up. It grew no better at all, and a few weeks after their arrival at Long Branch it became actual pain when he ate acid foods. He was absorbed in the *Century* article, however, and merely avoided acids, and tried to forget the dryness and the taste.

Every evening he read aloud the product of the day to his family, and was warmed by their hearty admiration. But Badeau, who came down to give him professional advice, had not such complete approval. 'Perhaps a little more incident,' he suggested gently. 'It's fine as it stands, of course, but a little elaboration ——'

'What more is there?' Ulyss demanded. He picked up the article, the few pages that held the whole story, from Albert Sidney Johnston encamped in the woods beside the unsuspecting Federals, through the dreadful hours of the first day when defeat seemed probable, to the triumphant close of the second day with the Confederates fleeing back to Corinth. 'That's all

I know about Shiloh,' said Ulyss. 'There's not much more than that in my official report, except things that wouldn't interest the readers of the *Century*.' He mentioned his prospective audience with a mixture of pride and shyness, and cleared his throat hastily.

'But there's a few things you might mention for the *Century* that you couldn't put in your official report.'

'What sort of things?' Ulyss did not like criticism, but he was touched with humility by Badeau's newspaper experience.

'Well, haven't I heard you say your sword was shot off?'

'Not my sword, the scabbard. And it wasn't shot clean off, just almost. It didn't come loose till later.'

'There were other people with you when it happened, weren't there?'

'Yes, McPherson and Hawkins. We were moving toward the river through a clearing, and didn't know the rebs were in the woods so close.' Ulyss chuckled. 'We were lucky to get out whole — I lost my scabbard, and Hawkins dropped his hat, and McPherson's horse was shot clean through. We didn't know it till we were out of range and the poor beast dropped dead.'

'Why not tell about that in the article?'

'But that's nothing to do with Shiloh. It could have happened any time — you know there were always things like that, that didn't mean anything ——'

'Just the same, this did happen at Shiloh, and people would like to hear about it as well as the movements of divisions. There's lots of things general readers want to hear about, stories like your scabbard, and what you thought of Albert Sidney Johnston — do you suppose the rebs might have won if he hadn't been killed? — and what the country looked like, all sorts of things . . .'

Thus led, Ulyss set to work again, and discovered great pleasure in setting down all the trivia that gave life to his own memory of the event, in breaking the requirements of formal detachment that had been imposed on him in all the writing he had ever done. The *Century* editors were pleased with the result. They asked for another article, on Vicksburg, and there were suggestions of still more, on Chattanooga, on the Wilderness. Ulyss had once considered the article on Shiloh finished in three or four pages, but when he wrote of Vicksburg he covered two hundred before he could stop. He began to see a shadowy possibility, frightening and entrancing: the whole story of the war as he had known and fought it. Badeau had already written his military history, in three large and authorized volumes, but however detailed, however carefully checked with Grant it had been, it was still Badeau's view, not Grant's. The fact had never troubled Ulyss, but now there was something he wanted to say for himself. There was so much he had felt, and thought about, and planned, which no one would ever know if he did not speak. The lost years started to life around him, crowding his mind, eager to be recaptured.

All that summer he wrote steadily, because he loved the work and because when he was working he could forget the strange thing in his throat. It was a quiet season. Other summers had been crowded with engagements, with people who came to see him on friendly calls, or because they wanted something of him; with invitations to appear at various functions or to make a speech in behalf of somebody's favored project. This year his friends made fewer demands on him because his time and thought were so taken up with his work; and those who had had a less disinterested connection saw little point in courting a ruined man. Ulyss believed, when he thought about it, that the general feeling of the people for him was unfriendly. There had naturally been a journalistic outcry over the failure of Grant & Ward, and it had not altogether spared him, though there had been fewer personal attacks on him than he had expected. Whether the public believed him a fool or a shyster, it must feel an aversion for him, and he had no right to resent it.

Once he was asked to make a speech to a religious convention in a nearby town, and when he came to the meeting place he found ten thousand people, who rose as one to cheer him. He could but stand still and listen, startled, touched, and humble. These people were in no way connected with him: he was not a professing member of any church; and they were not army men nor identified with his political group. They were simply people, who did not know him at all. Yet they stood and shouted as though he had come to them in triumph; shouted not in kindness, not in tact, but because in the depths of their obscure hearts they wanted to shout.

'Ladies and gentlemen,' he began when at last they were silent. 'I'm not much at making a speech ——' It was the opening he had learned to use, and he knew now how to elaborate it with graceful humor until he was safely over the discomfort of lifting up his voice on a public platform, and could proceed to what he wanted to say. The device had given him good service in the numberless speeches he had had to make abroad, to delegations of mechanics and to assemblies of ancient blood. He had used it over and over again in his own country, when he spoke in favor of some political candidate or talked to Grand Army rallies or rose in his turn in the pattern of formal dinners.

This time it failed him. 'I — I can't make a speech,' he said. 'I can only — thank you ...' Then when they cheered again he felt tears wet on his face, and did not greatly care.

'I'm getting old,' he said to Childs when he told him the story. 'I couldn't say a word, like I'd never stood on my two feet in front of an audience before.'

'I don't think anybody could have spoken after that,' Childs maintained staunchly. 'Not many people get such a demonstration.'

Reddening, Ulyss absently took a peach from the bowl at his side and made much ceremony of peeling it. He dared not trust what he had felt in those cheers; he dared not talk it over even with so good a friend as Childs, lest he be shown where his fallacy was or be given the even greater pain of easy, empty agreement. He changed the subject. He must not let himself believe, but there was no need to strip himself of even the possibility of belief.

'Is there anything wrong with the peach?' Childs asked after a few moments. 'You've scarcely touched it.'

'It's a little acid ——'

'What a shame — I'll get you another.'

'No, don't.' There was no polite deprecation in Grant's tone, but the abrupt ring of an order, and Childs stared at him. There was a moment of silence, then at last Ulyss said, 'It isn't the peach. It's me.' Childs still looked puzzled, and Ulyss elaborated, 'I couldn't swallow it, no more than I could a knife blade.'

'Oh, that's too bad, General. Do you have a sore throat?'

'No.' Ulyss's lips were hard, and each word he spoke had a weight of determination behind it. He had not meant to mention the thing at all, feeling that if he did what was now a chilly misgiving might become a terror; but it had taken a place in his thoughts unadmitted yet so great that it forced its own way to speech. Now that he had mentioned it he would not flinch. Silence had not dispelled it. Perhaps if he spoke he would find that it was mere ignorance that had kept him glancing in furtive uneasiness at something that was not there. 'That is, not like any sore throat I ever heard of. For a long time it kept getting dry, and then some things I ate made it feel queer. And now I can't eat anything like a peach at all, because it hurts too much.'

'Have you asked a doctor about it?'

'No. It didn't bother me much in New York, and I don't know enough about the man here.'

'I see.' Childs nodded and put his fingertips together. 'Now,

I've got a suggestion. Da Costa's coming up from Philadelphia next week to stay a few days with me, and he's about the best doctor in the country. He'd know what to do right off — may I bring him over?'

'Yes, bring him.' Ulyss had a sudden desperate need of word from authority, a need he could gauge by his unreasonable disappointment that Childs had given him no reassurance.

The doctor came. He was courteous, with a tinge of deference in his bearing, but to Ulyss he seemed somehow larger than a man, as though the knowledge that was in him had made him broader and taller, and more formidable, than others. Yet there was a soothing quality in the deft sureness of his movements... Ulyss discovered suddenly that the pain he had felt in trying to swallow was but a shadowy hint of the pain that dwelt in his throat and could be roused. He had never before felt any comparable sensation, and it turned him sick and aghast. It was difficult, when the probe was withdrawn and the doctor straightened up, for him to relax his clenched fists and compose his shaken lips.

He listened for Da Costa's verdict with a quiet face that belied the apprehensive eagerness in his eyes — but there was no verdict. Take this night and morning, said Da Costa, and go at once to your personal physician. The words said nothing, but by implication they said much, and Ulyss thought them over for a long time. About the best doctor in the country, Childs had said, and Ulyss knew it was true, yet this man had told him to go to his own doctor, and had said nothing himself. Ulyss thought he knew why. The thing was serious, fully as serious as he had dreaded. Had there been any possibility of recovery the doctor would have said, Such-and-such is the matter with you, and in a few weeks it will begin to clear up, or it can be cut out... He had said nothing because there was nothing to say. Whatever it was that had come into Ulyss's throat, its true name was death.

Panic seized on him, but he thrust it aside. He had not time
to be afraid. How long did people live when death had set its
mark upon them? No more than a few months, probably —
again panic, again fought down. That would not be long
enough. He needed more time than that to finish his memoirs,
or at least to set down enough so that they would be plainly
his work. But he was not really sick yet; he could still eat most
things; even the pain was trifling by comparison with what he
had discovered it could be. Perhaps he had a longer grace, he
knew little about such things. He would need a year — somehow he must get a year. He had fought against odds before,
and surely he could hold off this inner fang in his throat until
the inevitable defeat claimed only his body, not the work that
meant so much.

Death was the sentence that Ulyss heard in Da Costa's
professional silence, but after a few days he did not think of his
perception with such remorseless surety, though he never lost
sight of it altogether. He might be mistaken, and for a while
after Da Costa's examination the throat did seem better, as
though it would respond to even the threat of treatment; and
in the times when the pain was there it could be ignored. He
buried it under the pavement of paper that was his road back
to the war and the flavor of existence he had known during the
war. But the chief reason for denying his belief was that if he
did not he could not keep his knowledge from Julia. She knew
that his throat troubled him; that he had seen Da Costa about
it; that Da Costa had not said anything. She found no great
significance in these facts, for she had not felt the flaming pain
that had shown Ulyss the truth, but he knew that if he held
fast to his knowledge she would sense it in him. When she
asked, 'How's your throat this morning, dear?' he must answer,
'Better, I think.' If he added in his heart, But that means
nothing, she would hear him, and so he kept silence even to
himself.

On the whole those months at Long Branch had a savor he had not known for a long time, perhaps the sharper for his fear. 'What does Sherman say about that, Badeau?' His former secretary would find the place in Sherman's book and read aloud the nervous, vivid comment, and Ulyss could see his friend waving his arms and striding up and down, hear him shouting: Sam, I'll tell you how it is ——

'It seems to me he's wrong there. Wasn't Ord on that flank?'

'I think so, General. Ord, then McPherson ——'

'Yes, of course.' Ulyss scratched the positions on a sheet of paper, not really thinking of it, not even thinking of the similar sheet where he had first mapped his line over twenty years ago. He was seeing the long steep ridges around Vicksburg... A damn good job, Sam... 'All right, Fred, we'll go on from there.' Ulyss's son bent his head to the manuscript, and Ulyss dictated as quickly as he could, before he forgot the clear picture. His voice grew husky and he cleared his throat impatiently, jumped at the sudden stab of pain, and continued his sentence without fully noticing it.

Early in the fall the Grants went back to New York, and then Ulyss tried to work with greater speed, almost with desperation. He was no longer hopeful for Julia's sake: the optimism he showed her was all sham now. Very soon even that would be impossible. He must work quickly, crowd every day as full as possible, for he was uncertain of his own courage when he had once made the open admission. It would not be made until he could no longer avoid it, but he knew that the time was upon him.

In October it made itself. For several days he swallowed his food as he would have swallowed nettles, then he put it into his mouth but could not swallow it at all, then he sat silent and unmoving to watch the others eat. The first stage, when he could keep his secret, was over. He knew it, and when at

last Julia said, 'Go to see Barker, dear — he'll give you something to clear it up,' he nodded in silent agreement. It would
have been cruel to make any comment at all, for above her
mouth set in determined casualness her eyes were frightened,
and wide to keep back tears.

'If it were I,' said Barker, 'or a member of my family, I'd
go see Douglas.' Again the evasion, again the reluctance to
speak, as though a name would give irrevocable reality to the
pain and cold fear. Ulyss knew Douglas, had met him first at
Fort Donelson, and later when he was a famous specialist and
attended Rawlins. He would give the answer, the answer that
Ulyss was certain he already knew, that he was afraid to hear,
that he was determined to have.

There was a foolish pleasure in his heart when Douglas bowed
and asked, 'In what way can I be of service?' It was not written on his face, then; the great doctor could not glance at him
and know at once that here was a man condemned without
appeal. Ulyss mentioned briefly the dryness, the pain, the
inability to swallow. Then came the examination, and his
hand clenched at his side, involuntarily, as Douglas reached
for a probe.

'Does it hurt here?' Dully, as though the pain ground
through from the inside instead of resulting from the external
pressure. 'Here?' That pain could not be described. It
brought out a clammy sweat on Ulyss's face as he felt it now,
and also when he woke at night to remember it and to wonder
if it would be constant before it finished him. 'Here?' No
pain there, only a stiffness that sometimes tripped him when
he spoke.

Douglas turned aside to make a note, but he was not quick
enough, for Ulyss had seen his eyes. Da Costa's had been
blank, Barker's evasive. Douglas's eyes said, I can't help.
I know a great deal, but I only know the end of this, not how
to fight it.

'Is it cancer?' said Ulyss.

'It's serious,' said Douglas levelly. 'But sometimes it can be cured.' He said much more, sketching the necessary treatment, and Ulyss quietly listened. It's cancer, and Douglas can't cure it. Nobody can. He would not bait himself with any faith in the phrase, 'Sometimes it can be cured.' He knew that no man can bring himself to admit that he has utterly failed, with no chance of even a delayed or partial success, even as he cannot realize that he himself will die. Ulyss, just shouldering the weight of one impossibility, could not blame Douglas for not attempting the other.

'He says it has a cancerous tendency,' was the report Ulyss made at home. Douglas had used the phrase, and Ulyss found it convenient, since it told the truth yet did not fully convey the truth. Even that equivocation changed all their lives, as he had known it would. Only Julia stayed as she had been before. She was much concerned, and sometimes when she was alone for a while the tears ran slowly down her face, because it troubled her to see Ulyss so uncomfortable, but she was not really altered because she did not know at all that Ulyss's trouble was more than discomfort. It made her angry to realize, as she occasionally did, that the others believed it would end in death. Ulyss would not die — it was an unthinkable betrayal of him even to wonder if he might.

His sons adapted themselves to a new existence of thinking and fearing and hoping without daring to make any of their emotions articulate; and the children learned quickly that their grandfather was sick, that sometimes he disappeared and they must be very quiet, and at other times he liked to have them in his room, to talk to them in a strangely hoarse voice which they soon accepted as his natural tone. The adaptations were made swiftly, and had a permanent air, as though families normally lived in suspended, unadmitted fear, with every small detail of their lives tinged and twisted by the unspoken.

Ulyss found it hard to remember that a year ago he had been absorbed in the elaborate gestures Ward had invented to keep him occupied. It was impossible to look ahead to another year. Douglas and Barker, working together with tireless inventiveness, were consistently hopeful, but Ulyss did not believe they could contrive to get him as many as twelve more months. It was strange, as the darkness fell each evening, to count that day forever gone. Never another November, never another New Year. Never another of any of these nameless days that sped so fast, that he needed so desperately to finish his work.

His work — that was the worst of the thing. He dreaded a long illness, felt a terror he had never known before at the prospect of strangling to death by degrees, with that unspeakable pain coming more and more frequently until he would have no respite at all, but he was sure he could escape it if he surrendered, if he let the thing take him, unresisting, and did not struggle and scheme for time. Yet there was his book, unfinished. His first vision had lost its clear, beautiful excitement now that he was so ill and tired, but it had made an impression on his fundamental obstinacy, that held it fast and would not let it go.

And he could not work. As he had feared, once the admission was made, once the thing was given a name, it mastered him. He fought pain and dread and weariness for each day, and when he won his prize it slipped from him while he was hypnotized by the hasty ticking of the clock, telling him how little time there was.

Day after day he sat huddled in his chair, with the paper on which he wanted to write blank under his hand, and he stared at the blankness of the wall. Across it streamed a succession of scenes and portraits: Lee absently striking his hands together as he left the house at Appomattox; Rawlins's black, compelling eyes; Julia, clinging to him in fright when she heard that Lincoln was dead; Jesse presenting his baby fists and demanding, 'Will you fight?'; Nellie, lovely and self-possessed as she came down the White House stairs to be married; the great crowds that had come to see him take the presidential oath; Babcock's face, cheerful and beloved and impenetrable; the nameless soldier who had died by the roadside on the way to Richmond.

This was what he saw of his life, a small thing here and there, without the long sweep of direction, with no driving impulse to give it form. It was as if all that had come to him had come by accident. A colonel of an Illinois regiment had been so drunk and incompetent that his men had preferred to trust themselves to the shabby stranger who had mustered them in. Political leaders had chosen for the presidency a popular man who was not really ambitious. The people had made him a hero and a scapegoat as pleased their illogical caprice. Was this, then, all he was? Was he but a man created and destroyed by circumstance; his leadership an absurdity in itself, since always he was led blindly forward by other men, by nameless forces, by the demands of the history in which he was accidentally given place? It was all that men could say of him, and in those suspended weeks it was all that he could say of himself.

Yet there was something more. The story of his life might be the story of the plans and desires and expediencies of other men — nevertheless it was his life, not theirs. If they had used him as a tool, it was his mark that had been left on their work. Lincoln had used him, Stanton and the Radical leaders and Conkling had used him, Ward had used him. But he was not wholly in the image of any of these. He had always been Ulysses Grant, and now in the last months of his life there was none but Ulysses Grant to use him. There would be no more accidents, there was no longer any pressure of circumstance beyond the physical limitations of his illness. Now at last he had a choice, with no one but himself to dictate his answer.

He could keep up the struggle to regain some stature in his
own eyes, a struggle that would grow more desperate day by
day, with no assurance whatever of victory; or he could admit
that his life and his work were finished, and take his ease until
the death rattle added the necessary technicality to the accomplished fact.

Ulyss began to write again. For his good name, for his
family's sake, but chiefly for himself. There was a nameless
necessity in him to finish his work, and when he considered
and set aside all other incentives it remained, immovable and
unarguable, and it gave him the power to answer it. As long
as he could he dictated, and when his voice was taken from
him he wrote by hand. The pages were pushed one by one from
his table, for someone else to pick up and arrange. It did not
matter, once they were written.

Early in the new year the newspapers announced that
General Grant was very ill and would probably not recover.
Many people had known the fact, but it had not been made
public, and Ulyss was startled by the effect it had. He had
been certain that the country was apathetic toward him, if not
hostile, yet when the papers carried the story of his illness
crowds came to stand in front of his house. They seemed to
have no definite purpose there. They did not shout for him nor
shout at him, yet they came day after day, individuals standing
for a little while and then moving on, but the crowd always
there. Sometimes Ulyss could go to the window and look
at them, and each time he was puzzled. He had known popularity in the years following the war, at intervals in his presidency, and when he had first returned from his world journey,
before it crumbled at the touch of politics. But the thing that
brought these people to stand before his house was not his
popularity, but their affection, something he had never known
before. He was afraid to believe it, but their steady attendance
proved it, and gave assurance that his final battle would not

be a barren victory. It was easier to drive himself to labor when he could hear the faint, subdued sound of them outside.

Messages poured in to the house on Sixty-Sixth Street, from Jefferson Davis, Hayes, Buell; from Victoria of England and other rulers of the earth; from Lincoln's son, from Democrats and Republicans and men of no party who had founded political careers on attacking Grantism. And when Grant was well enough to receive them he had dozens of callers, men he had not seen in years, men he had thought never to see. One was Simon Buckner, whose unconditional surrender at Donelson had been the beginning of Grant's popular reputation. The former Confederate shook hands as warmly as though the fingers in his were not brittle and weak, and talked of the old days as eagerly as though he could still see the obstinate Union commander in this shawled figure of an old man.

'If we'd gone on through when we had the chance, made that sortie count, it would have been a different story ———'

'Yes, it would.' Grant's voice had entirely changed, the growth in his throat so clogging it that the tone had scarcely any resonance, but the ring of certainty in it was so clear that it made all the physical changes in him seem irrelevant. 'If you hadn't had a couple of blockheads for superiors you'd have got clear away from Donelson. If Jeff Davis hadn't thought he knew better than any of his generals, and relieved Johnston...' His voice failed him for the moment, and Buckner helped him hold a glass of water to his lips, so absorbed by the light in Grant's eyes that he did not notice the pathos of his act. '...Sherman might never have reached the sea. If Smith hadn't sat down to wait for re-enforcements he'd have marched straight into Petersburg and cut a year off the war...'

'They call it the fortune of war,' Buckner said while Ulyss sat with twisted lips, dragging a few stertorous breaths into his lungs. 'Maybe misfortune would be a better word.'

Ulyss shook his head until he was able to speak again.

'They call it luck, too, but it isn't. It's — just the way things work out. If we had the whole war to fight over again, and knew . . . how to avoid the mistakes we made, we'd make others and come out in the same place. It had to be that way, and it was.' He held up his hand when Buckner would have spoken. 'I think people know that now, and are willing to forget it. Since I've been sick a lot of old Confederates have come to see me, like you — and messages from Davis. Peace between the sections — I think it's here. It's what I wanted, more than anything else.' He had spoken with so much vehemence that he was for the moment exhausted, and leaned back in his chair with his eyes closed.

It was so quiet in the room that Buckner could hear the stirring of the silent crowd outside. Then Ulyss began to chuckle.

'D'you remember how cold it was, Buckner? And my men had thrown away their blankets so they could march faster — thought they'd just come up to Donelson and say boo ——'

Another visitor Ulyss sent for himself. He wanted to speak to Bristow, and through Bristow to a multitude of others. The former Secretary of the Treasury came at once, and Ulyss did not wait for an opening, nor cast about for a subtle phrase that would express his meaning without embarrassing either of them. His tongue was stiff with more than the creeping cancer. 'I wanted to tell you,' he said abruptly, 'that I misjudged you. I thought you were after Babcock to get me, and my administration. I was wrong, and you were right.' He scarcely listened to Bristow's answer, scarcely cared whether he had heard. The important thing was that the words had been said. Babcock was dead now, drowned in a storm off the Florida keys, a dramatic end that would have pleased his imagination. Grant would soon be dead. Bristow had not attained the presidency after all. All the personal elements had faded from the affair of the whiskey ring, remaining only as small pegs on which to fasten the threads of history, but it was important to Ulyss to make his apology, not for Bristow's sake, but for his own.

Work, work fast — but he could not do it fast enough. He had overcome the reluctant spirit that had threatened to block him, but he could not forever command his body. A few months was all he needed now, only a little time, but as winter melted into spring his strength dwindled away from him. He was unable to eat or sleep, almost unable to breathe. Sometimes he framed a sentence and forced it from his ravaged throat for Badeau to take down, but he knew that it had no meaning, like the arrangements of words that explain the universe to a dreamer, and resolve into gibberish when he wakes.

The doctors strove valiantly to draw him back. It was necessary to use drugs lest he die of sheer pain, but the sedatives sent him into a tormented drowsiness that was almost worse than the unveiled agony. All the scenes of horror he had ever known crowded back upon him with a nightmare quality more hideous even than their reality. He was cast into a world that swarmed and leered and gibbered with men torn to pieces by the guns he had sent them against, with heads torn off, limbs crushed, bowels gaping, and always with throats mangled and astir with maggots. He would cry, 'The cannon did it!' and be awakened by his own rasping whisper, 'The cannon did it.' The doctors tried other expedients, cozening him to rest as they would a child, inventing diversions and deceptions as they would for a child, and still his vitality sank with hopeless rapidity.

They thought that perhaps he would be helped when Cleveland, as one of the first acts of his administration, signed a bill restoring Grant to the army, but it had no great effect on him. True, he was eager to draw his pay, and smiled a little when he had the money in his hands and divided it between Julia and the four children. 'It's all I have,' he said, looking at the five faces. Julia composed and steadfast. Nellie, who had come from England to see him die, weeping as openly as she had when she was a young girl. The three boys with set lips, save Fred, who had bitten his until the blood came. Ulyss was proud to be able to give them something. The *Century* had given him a thousand dollars more than they had promised for his articles, but the sum had gone to Charles Wood in payment of the double debt of money and symbol. Mark Twain, who was to publish the memoirs, had spoken of the profit they would make with enthusiastic western extravagance, but no one would ever know if his predictions had been justified. 'My book,' said Ulyss, and stopped. It lay on the table a little distance from him, untouched for days, never to be touched again.

Still Julia could not accept the fact that was so heartrendingly clear to everyone else. 'He isn't going to die,' she said. 'Not yet.' There was no possible basis for her belief, save her own intention, but she held to it so firmly that she all but gave conviction to the others. And the doctors were glad that her illogic kept her calm on the night in early April when they saw that the struggle was at last at an end, and summoned Ulyss's family to say good-bye to him. He was still conscious, and quietly made his farewell to each of them, but they sensed a remoteness in him. They stood helplessly around his bed, horrified, sick with grief, and touched by a ghastly impatience.

The circle of faces was very clear to Ulyss, with the clarity verging on blankness that can be seen in any object when it is stared at too long. He looked at all of them, at the familiar eyes and mouths and chins he had watched for so many years, but with the swirling blackness behind them they seemed strange, as though they had nothing to do with him. Perhaps that always happened when someone died, and he knew that death was coming to him in a few minutes. He was frightened, but with no tinge of terror, frightened as he had been when he was a little boy and was first set on a horse, with a great proportion of curiosity and a certain pride. It was coming, in a moment, it was coming — he was a little annoyed with its slowness now that he was ready, and a little grateful for being allowed more time... He had wanted more time for something... time for... he was going now... quickly, through the blackness and the cold... wait, there was something not yet done... wait, wait....

The doctors spoke to each other, and one leaned over Ulyss's body with a hypodermic needle. Julia did not see him, though he stood in her line of vision. She was not seeing or hearing anything, not even thinking very much. She was pouring all her being into a bond drawn taut, strained to the breaking point but not broken yet.

In a few moments the doctor said quietly, 'I think he's passed the crisis — this one.'

'I know it,' said Julia. She looked at him, tried to smile, and ran from the room before her sobs of witless exhaustion might disturb her husband.

Some part of the growth that had been strangling Ulyss came away that night, filling his mouth with coppery blood, but it was not yet his life's blood. For a day or two he lay spent and inert, then came slowly back to life, a life without nearly so much pain, without the constant sense of a fist closing on his throat, without the morbid weakness that had made him as helpless as the dead while he yet suffered the agony of the living. Julia rejoiced with unalloyed triumph: no one had yet said that a cure was impossible, and would complete recovery be more miraculous than this return from death itself? But Ulyss knew that he had been given a respite, not a hope. He had returned to life, but his hold on it was precarious, and would soon be broken by the weight that dragged so heavily upon him. Nevertheless, what he had wanted most was time, and now he had a little. How much he did not know, and therefore he did not reckon how much he needed.

As soon as he could close his fingers around the pen he set to work again. He had finished the first part of his story, the brief pages summing up his life to the summer of 1861, the account of his groping progress as colonel and brigadier, the great campaign of Vicksburg and the episode of Chattanooga. Next came the Wilderness, and he had already set down much of that material in an article for the *Century*. But from there on he must drag from his weary mind the story of Spottsylvania, the crossing of the James, the siege of Petersburg, the final maneuvers from Five Forks to Appomattox. It was a frightening vista, so crowded with men and actions and plans and events that it seemed to him it would take as long to write it as it had to live it. He refused to think of it as a whole, and fixed his mind on that small section he could set down in an hour. The time he had wrested from eternity could not be squandered in uncertainty and fear.

Sometimes it seemed to him that the world to which he had returned was not the one he had left. He had gone forth from a house in New York where an old man fought with death; he had come back to another place, to a high hill by a river, where Lincoln spoke of simple things, where Babcock laughed and Rawlins saw a bright vision of America, where there were tangible weapons in his hand and the enemy he fought was named and embodied. These things were more clear to him, while he wrote of them and while he slept in exhaustion, than the gray unease that surrounded him in fact.

In June the heat of summer fastened on the city, and even such air as he could draw into his lungs was heavy and lifeless. The pain was returning, but worse than that was his consuming weariness, that added to itself day by day. It did not matter: he was nearly finished. Whatever happened now, the book was his, the preservation of his Ulysses Grant was assured. His doctors consulted on taking him away from the city, and decided to risk moving him to Mount McGregor, the Drexels' summer cottage in the Adirondacks. Ulyss did not care: he was nearly finished. That was important to him, not what place was chosen in which to end the rest of him.

The journey was made shortly after the middle of the month. Ulyss lay weakly in the train, thinking of the house he had left, knowing that he would not see it again. He was so tired. As the train approached West Point he asked to be lifted up, that he might look at the gray buildings across the river. They were beautiful, but he remembered that he had hated them. He had walked under those towering trees, pinched into his uniform, thinking hopefully that there was talk of Congress abolishing the place, and praying that it might be true. The army had meant much to him, but it was not West Point that had given it meaning. He looked at the majestic view as long as it was in sight, and then lay back, thinking of the wavering line of the 21st Illinois, drawn up for the first test of him, its new commander.

Mount McGregor was a pleasant place, set high in the hills with the summer sky arched over it, and at a point some distance from the house there was a wide view that delighted Ulyss when he was strong enough to be taken in a wheel chair to see it. Usually, however, he was not strong enough, and could go no farther than the porch. He sat there for hours, looking at the people who passed down the road, alone or in couples or in groups, but always turning to look at him. They did not speak to him, nor annoy him in any way, and he knew that the motive of their formless procession was not offensive curiosity. In a few weeks there grew up a silent, undemanding relationship between himself and them. They tipped hats or waved to him: if he were not too tired he lifted his hand in answer; and if he were too tired they understood.

By the first of July the body of the book was completed,

and then Ulyss went back over the manuscript, expanding sections that he might have skimped in fear that he could not reach the end. For three weeks he worked thus, and then at last the final word was said.

'I feel that we are on the eve of a new era, when there is to be great harmony between the Federal and Confederate. I cannot stay to be a living witness to the correctness of this prophecy; but I feel it within me that it is to be so. The universally kind feeling expressed for me at a time when it was supposed that each day would be my last, seemed to me the beginning of the answer to "Let us have peace."

'The expressions of these kindly feelings were not restricted to a section of the country, nor to a division of the people. They came from individual citizens of all nationalities; from all denominations — the Protestant, the Catholic, and the Jew. . . . Politics did not enter into the matter at all.

'I am not egotist enough to suppose all this significance should be given because I was the object of it. But the war between the States was a very bloody and a very costly war. One side or the other had to yield principles they deemed dearer than life before it could be brought to an end. I commanded the whole of the mighty host engaged on the victorious side. I was, no matter whether deservedly so or not, a representative of that side of the controversy. It is a significant and gratifying fact that the Confederates should have joined heartily in this spontaneous move. I hope the good feeling inaugurated may continue to the end.'

I cannot stay. Ulyss gave orders that all his notes and papers be removed. It was strange to see them go, and he felt no joy of accomplishment, no release, only a certain flatness. Perhaps when he had rested a little he would realize the triumph that was his. Yet he could not rest. He could sit inert, sometimes could even doze a little, but his fatigue banked higher and higher around him, as if he were caught in a drift of dust, almost intangible and of overwhelming weight.

'Sleep, dear.' Julia's hands were cool and firm on his forehead. 'Sleep . . . you'll feel so much better . . .' He slept, and she stood watching him. He had changed. His hair was almost white, and had a strawy texture; his short-fingered hands looked weak; even his mouth, that had always been so straight, had drooped and twisted in the countless times it had been set against his pain. Julia looked at her husband. There was a shadow in her eyes, cast by fear, by certainty, by the black wings of loneliness.

The day after the book was finished Ulyss asked to be taken out to the garden to see the view. He felt a return of energy, as bright and sudden as the flame that leaps from a log burned almost through, and he made haste to his vantage point. For a long time he sat and looked at the high hills, changing in form and color from minute to minute in the day, from month to month in the year, yet essentially changeless. Their massive solidity, unaltered by all the circumstances of wind and rain and the caprice of man, gave him a pleasure that he could not name, roused an emotion he had never felt. He looked at the hills, breathed deep of the limitless air, bared his head to the free wind. Then exhaustion flooded up in him, but he smiled a little as he turned from the hills to go home, for he knew that he could rest now.

THE END

INDEX